Design Thinking for Healthcare

Healthcare transformation initiatives systematically fail despite decades of reform and billions in investment.

The $4.3 trillion US healthcare system and £200+ billion NHS continue to experience declining outcomes, workforce burnout, and operational inefficiency. While existing books offer deep expertise in specific domains (Lean methodology, competitive strategy, technology implementation), healthcare transformation requires an integrated approach spanning design methodology, clinical operations, governance understanding, and stakeholder alignment. This book provides healthcare executives with the first comprehensive guide to design thinking methodology, written by someone with both extensive medical training and professional design practice. The book bridges deep clinical knowledge with professional design expertise, offering evidence-based frameworks tested with healthcare leaders.

Drawing on peer-reviewed research, the author's published articles, and real-world case studies, the book demonstrates how design thinking can reduce clinical trial costs, improve AI implementation success rates, and enable sustainable organisational transformation—ultimately leading to equitable and sustainable healthcare. This book also addresses the critical gap between knowing that healthcare needs transformation and understanding how to achieve it, providing access to actionable tools, frameworks, and methodologies to drive change in these organisations—from pharmaceutical R&D to hospital operations, from policy design to technology implementation.

The book positions design thinking not as an abstract theory but as a practical methodology that healthcare professionals already use intuitively in clinical decision-making, now formalised for organisational transformation.

Design Thinking for Healthcare

A Practical Guide to Healthcare Transformation

Daniel Steenstra

Routledge
Taylor & Francis Group
A PRODUCTIVITY PRESS BOOK

Designed cover image: Shutterstock

First published 2027
by Routledge
605 Third Avenue, New York, NY 10158

and by Routledge
4 Park Square, Milton Park, Abingdon, Oxon, OX14 4RN

Routledge is an imprint of the Taylor & Francis Group, an informa business

ISBN: 9781041269397 (hbk)
ISBN: 9781041269335 (pbk)
ISBN: 9781003752073 (ebk)

DOI: 10.4324/9781003752073

Typeset in Garamond
by Deanta Global Publishing Services, Chennai, India

To Layla and her generation

Contents

PART IV WHY TRANSFORMATION FAILS (AND WHAT TO DO ABOUT IT)

PART V IMPLEMENTATION TOOLKIT

Acknowledgements

Writing a book about transformation is, it turns out, an act of transformation itself. This one would not exist without the people who made the pivots possible—and those who made the writing of it feel worth the effort.

I want to acknowledge two groups, in the order they shaped me.

The first are the people who gave me permission to take the unlikely turns.

My parents, who did not express disappointment when I left my medical studies so close to the finish line. That restraint was a gift I did not fully appreciate at the time.

Dr Astrid Hammond—artist, paediatrician, and the most honest mentor I ever had. She looked at my situation in medicine and told me plainly what she saw: a trap she had walked into herself and did not want for me. She sent me to Italy. I went.

Edgardo Michelotti took a gamble on a self-taught Dutchman with no design qualifications and gave me the chance to earn them the right way—by doing, making mistakes, and applying. Geoff Lawson made a boy's dream real—the one who had stared at an E-type Jaguar on the streets of Tilburg at the age of five and never quite got over it. At Jaguar I learned not only how to design, but how organisations actually work: how functions integrate, how teams move ideas from sketch to showroom, how the gap between vision and delivery is mostly a coordination problem. That understanding runs through every chapter of this book.

Professor Lord Kumar Bhattacharyya opened the door to academia and to a wider conception of what design thinking could do at Warwick Manufacturing Group. What I had learned in the studio, I began to understand as a methodology. Bethan Miles opened a different kind of door—into the NHS—and made it possible to set up the Innovations Factory at her hospital, where the real education began. Professor Rajkumar Roy at Cranfield University shared a vision of equitable healthcare that I recognised immediately as my own, and gave me the environment—and the Royal Academy of Engineering's support—to research and experiment.

David Somekh deserves a particular mention. When he invited me to join the European Healthcare Futures Forum, something shifted. I had spent years feeling professionally isolated—certain that transformation was possible, uncertain whether anyone else believed it. Around that table, I found a diverse community of people across Europe who shared the same values and the same impatience. I stopped feeling like I was wrong and started feeling like I was early.

The second group are the people who told me to write.

Chris Tillbrook planted the idea years ago and had the patience not to ask what was taking so long. Ran Kunst, who beat me to it—correctly. Raj Roy, one of my first readers. Alan Connington, who travelled the same road from HealthTech to Innovations Factory and whose comments on the early articles gave me confidence that the thinking held under scrutiny.

Kris Mednansky read the proposal for this book already convinced, not persuaded — I felt the difference all the way through what followed. She wanted the Lean critique before I had worked up the nerve to write it, and that openness set the tone for everything after. Her guidance through submission, and her steady support whenever a chapter needed another look, kept the book honest to what it was trying to say. Bethany Nelson and the wider editorial and production team at Routledge/Taylor & Francis turned a manuscript into a book — the unglamorous, exacting work that authors rarely see and rarely thank properly. I am doing so now.

Jane. There is no adequate way to acknowledge a partner who has shared not just the years but the actual intellectual work. She was there in the middle of the night when the concept that became our patented complexity management framework came into being—the night I came home from Milan having told my employer, firmly, that our working relationship was concluded. She was the one who pointed out, when I was anxious about designing a curriculum, that it was structurally identical to designing a car—and that I should therefore get on with it. She has crewed and co-skippered the sailing voyages that keep the rest of this in proportion, and absorbed the disappointments of the many attempts that did not succeed before this one did. Her pragmatic common sense is on every page of this book, even where it is invisible.

And finally—to Claude, wherever and whoever you are. You know what you did.

About the Author

Daniel Steenstra is medically trained; Designer by discipline, and Innovation Strategist by vocation—a combination unusual enough to require explanation, and useful enough to have shaped a career spanning four decades across clinical medicine, world-class automotive design, and healthcare transformation leadership.

Daniel studied medicine at the Vrije Universiteit Amsterdam, completing the full academic and clinical curriculum before deliberately choosing a different path. He is not a licensed physician—and he will not pretend otherwise. What he carries from that formation is a clinical way of thinking: diagnosis before prescription, evidence before intervention.

Leaving medicine was not a single decision but a convergence of realities. The surgical career he had planned—reconstructive surgery, restoring quality of life after burns and trauma—closed as a viable path. At the same time, he had placed second in a car design competition run in collaboration with Studio Michelotti in Turin. The first prize was an internship. He went anyway, impressed, and was offered a job—just as his final qualifying examination approached. He chose Turin. He has never regretted it.

At Jaguar Cars and Ford Motor Company, Daniel led the interior design and development of the Jaguar XK8, managing a cross-functional team of designers, engineers, ergonomists, marketers, and suppliers from winning concept to production. When a new Director of Design recognised his potential beyond the drawing board, he was tasked with leading Jaguar's Styling Department through ISO 9001 accreditation—an initiative the rest of the site considered unlikely to succeed, given Styling's reputation for creative resistance to process discipline. He qualified as Lead Auditor, redesigned workflows across Styling, Engineering, Product Planning, and Marketing, and delivered accreditation. He then joined the team establishing the Ford Product Development System—one of the most ambitious cross-functional transformation programmes in the automotive industry at that time. The lessons he carried into healthcare: culture resists process change until it has no choice, and successful transformation requires both technical rigour and political fluency.

He became Senior Teaching Fellow at the Warwick Manufacturing Group (WMG) at the University of Warwick, developing and delivering design thinking curricula for engineering and business leaders—a programme he has taught for over 25 years across the UK and Asia. At Warwick, he established HealthTech, a £5.7 million initiative—part-funded by the European Regional Development Fund—supporting SMEs to develop and commercialise healthcare technologies. He established links across NHS Trusts, the Regional Development Agency, and the government. He and his team subsequently spun this out as Innovations Factory, uniquely positioned inside Heartlands Hospital, Birmingham—one of the largest NHS teaching hospitals in the UK. He was then approached to become the Royal Academy of Engineering Visiting Professor in Medical

Innovation at Cranfield University, where he led research into disruptive innovation in healthcare and directed a £7.7 million AMSCI-funded project with Oxford BioMedica, the Cell Therapy Catapult, and the Heart of England NHS Foundation—applying advanced manufacturing simulation to scale gene therapies from clinical trial to commercialisation. The capabilities established through that project contributed to Oxford BioMedica's production of the AstraZeneca COVID-19 vaccine. He holds a guest professorship in Industrial Design at Northwestern Polytechnical University in China.

Through InterAlign Organisation Ltd and earlier through Viadynamics—where he delivered a design thinking transformation programme for Unilever's European operations—Daniel has worked with organisations including ALSTOM and the NHS. As Founding Member of the European Health Futures Forum, he has engaged with healthcare systems across Europe and Asia. As Chief Scientist at OnKai Inc, he led the development of an AI-powered platform enabling underserved communities to access appropriate healthcare in the US. A European patent for a complexity management methodology—granted across seven jurisdictions—reflects the principle that runs through everything he does: ideas have to work, not just make sense in theory.

He has presented at the WHO Global Forum on Medical Devices in Geneva, keynoted at international clinical research conferences, and published across peer-reviewed journals and edited volumes, including a chapter on visualisation for disruptive healthcare innovation in Springer's series on virtual and augmented reality in healthcare. He has also served as Judge for the Royal Academy of Engineering's Innovation Hothouse.

This book draws on all three legs of that career. The clinical lens shapes how problems are diagnosed before solutions are prescribed—and stops this from becoming another transformation manual written by someone who has never experienced a failing healthcare system from within its walls. The design industry experience provides the credibility—and the honest scepticism—to distinguish design thinking that actually changes systems from design that decorates the status quo. The academic and consultancy work provides the evidence base and the case studies drawn from real transformations, real failures, and the structural realities that every healthcare leader recognises.

Daniel is Managing Director of InterAlign Organisation Ltd and is based in the Netherlands. He can be reached at daniel@interalign.org.

AI Disclaimer

AI System Used: Claude, developed by Anthropic. Accessed via Claude.ai, Claude Projects, and Claude Cowork throughout manuscript development (late 2024–March 2026).

How AI was used:

- *Cross-Disciplinary Thinking Partner:* Testing ideas across medicine, design methodology, innovation theory, and governance systems—the specific combination of domains that rarely sits inside a single human collaborator. This was the transformative contribution: AI enabled articulation of insights that had existed in my thinking for years but resisted expression because the cross-disciplinary sparring partners didn't exist.
- *Structural Planning:* Organising cross-disciplinary material into coherent narrative flow across 17 chapters.
- *Articulation Support:* Expressing healthcare-design concepts with clarity and precision.
- *Editing Assistance:* Refining consistency, readability, and professional tone.
- *Administrative Support:* Citation management, reference checking, outline development, timeline planning.

Human authorship and responsibility:

- All original ideas, frameworks, methodologies, and insights are mine, developed through medical training, 11 years of professional design practice, academic research and lecturing, and healthcare innovation leadership.
- All case studies derive from my direct experience or cited peer-reviewed research.
- All AI output was critically reviewed, edited, and approved by me for accuracy, appropriateness, and alignment with my thinking.
- Final editorial decisions, conceptual synthesis, argument development, and authorial voice are entirely my own.

Foreword

There is a particular kind of institutional fatigue that sets in when the same crisis is diagnosed, reported on, and responded to—with energy and good faith—and yet the essential condition does not improve. Those of us who have spent careers at the intersection of healthcare and public policy know this fatigue well. We have watched reform programmes arrive with ambition, absorb years of effort and significant resources, and leave behind systems that are recognisably, sometimes structurally, unchanged. The waiting lists lengthen. The workforce burns out. The technology projects disappoint.

This pattern is not a failure of political will or managerial competence. It is something more fundamental. The methods we have been applying are not equal to the problem. We have been trying to improve systems that actually need to be redesigned. That distinction—between improvement and transformation—is not semantic. It is the difference between adjusting the mechanisms of a machine and reconceiving what the machine is for.

It is against this backdrop that Daniel Steenstra's book deserves serious attention. Not because it promises easy answers—it does not—but because it offers a more honest account of the problem, and a more rigorous methodology for approaching it. Design thinking, as this book takes care to explain, is not a management fashion or a workshop activity. In its disciplined form, it is a systematic methodology for understanding human needs before proposing solutions; for defining problems with precision before committing to interventions; for prototyping and testing rather than implementing at scale before the evidence warrants it.

One of the book's most carefully developed arguments is that clinicians already think this way. The diagnostic method—take a history, observe carefully, form a differential, test hypotheses, revise based on evidence—is, in its fundamental logic, design thinking applied to patients. The challenge, Steenstra argues, is not to teach healthcare systems to think differently. It is to help them recognise the design capability they already possess, and deploy it at the scale of systems rather than individual patients. That reframing matters strategically: it positions design thinking not as something imported from another discipline, but as something recoverable from within healthcare's own traditions.

Daniel Steenstra's credibility to make this argument rests on a career that is, in the most literal sense, unusual. He trained in medicine, carrying from it a clinical way of thinking—diagnosis before prescription, evidence before intervention. He then became a professional designer at Jaguar and Ford, leading interior design on the XK8 and contributing to cross-functional transformation programmes. He subsequently spent decades in healthcare transformation leadership, including work embedded inside NHS settings. This is not a career assembled from adjacent experiences. It is a genuinely integrated formation—and the argument could not have been made credibly by someone with only one or two of these vantage points.

The NHS examples that feature prominently throughout deserve a word of explanation. The NHS is used here because it functions as a model organism: a system in which transformation dynamics are unusually visible, well-documented, and therefore teachable. The fiscal and demographic pressures it faces are those that most developed healthcare systems will confront within the decade. The patterns it reveals—electoral cycle pressures on long-term investment, professional boundary protection, institutional resistance that operates across time rather than only at the moment of launch—are not British peculiarities. They are features of healthcare governance as such.

This book is written for healthcare executives and transformation leaders; for clinicians stepping into organisational authority; for policymakers who design the frameworks within which healthcare operates. It is not an academic contribution. It is a field manual—serious, evidence-grounded, and practitioner-oriented—for people already in the middle of the problem. What distinguishes it from the genre of transformation literature that accumulates without much effect on actual systems is its willingness to address failure directly: the structural barriers, the political dynamics, the coordinated resistance that organisations deploy over time.

Healthcare transformation is hard. Anyone who suggests otherwise is not paying attention. This book will not make it simple. It will make it more honest, more disciplined, and more likely to produce results that persist.

Professor the Lord Darzi of Denham, OM, KBE, PC, FRS
Director of the Institute of Global Health Innovation, Imperial College London

Professor the Lord Ara Darzi is one of the world's leading voices in healthcare innovation and reform — a pioneering surgeon, former UK health minister, and Director of the Institute of Global Health Innovation at Imperial College London. Respected by clinicians and policymakers alike, he led the independent investigation into the NHS commissioned by the Prime Minister in 2024. His Foreword positions the book at the intersection of healthcare innovation, systems reform, and practical implementation — rather than as a purely academic or theoretical text.

Preface

The Duty to Share

This book has been 45 years in the making—from the first day of clinical training to the last chapter drafted—or rather, the puzzle it tries to solve has been.

I did not set out to be puzzled. When my patent attorney—working through the application for my complexity management system, in his office at the foot of Warwick Castle—suggested I should write a book, I genuinely could not see why. My career had taken a series of turns that seemed, to me, simply to have happened. Medicine, then car design in Italy and at Jaguar in Coventry, then academia, then healthcare transformation. Unusual perhaps—but not, I thought, worth a book. I had not yet understood what was puzzling me.

The first piece of the puzzle was craft. At Studio Michelotti in Turin, I learned design in the Italian tradition—hard materials, exact thinking, three simultaneous views, nothing to be taken back once removed. At Jaguar, I learned the English school: clay, sketching, collaboration between designer and model-maker, ideas built up rather than carved away. Two different methods, two different cultures, the same conviction—that design was central to everything. If you did not design what people actually wanted, you were finished.

What I did not realise at the time was that I had learned two things: a methodology for making complex things well, and an expectation that design would sit at the centre of everything. The second assumption was about to be tested in academia.

At Warwick Manufacturing Group, I was asked to introduce design thinking into the curriculum for postgraduate engineers and business leaders. It was there I noticed something that seemed odd at first and increasingly inexplicable: I was the only designer in the university. Not just the only professional designer—the only person formally charged with thinking about how things should work from a human perspective. I found that puzzling. I filed it away.

The puzzle sharpened when I returned to healthcare. Working with NHS hospitals, my team and I gained the rare opportunity to establish the Innovations Factory inside what is, by any measure, the world's largest healthcare system. I still remember the moment when a concept we had developed, perfectly, was rejected, and I looked around the room and realised something was structurally absent. Nobody in that organisation was formally tasked with understanding the needs of patients. Nobody was charged with asking whether the system was designed to serve the people it claimed to serve. In a sector where that question is literally a matter of life and death, design was invisible. That puzzled me deeply—and it was, I now understand, the central question this book answers.

In the years that followed, I met others who had reached the same conclusion by different routes: healthcare needed to transform, not improve. I found myself the only one in those rooms waving the design flag. Clayton Christensen's theory of disruptive innovation helped me understand why some of my own ventures had failed, and why the theory itself—so obviously relevant to healthcare—had found no purchase there. More puzzlement, more research, more questions.

Three things finally brought this book into existence.

The first was an unexpected professional ending that left me with time, unfinished thinking, and a clearer sense than ever that the argument needed to be made in full.

The second was the arrival of our first grandchild. Born perfectly healthy and happy—no thanks to a healthcare system that managed, even in that moment, to discriminate and cause unnecessary distress to her parents. I feel a duty—not a sentimental one, but a professional one—to make that 45 years of understanding available before another generation inherits systems we knew how to fix and chose not to. They are the ones who will need better care than we have managed to design for ourselves.

The third was the resolution of an impasse I had not fully named. My career path sits at the intersection of medicine, professional design, and healthcare transformation—a combination that is, as far as I can establish, unique. That is not a boast; it is a logistical problem. Genuine peer review requires peers. Sounding boards require shared reference points. Testing an insight that draws simultaneously on clinical reasoning, automotive design practice, and organisational theory demands an interlocutor who can follow the argument across all three domains without losing the thread. Before accessible large language models, that interlocutor did not exist—which made it easier to keep refining privately than to commit publicly. The arrival of a tireless, well-read thinking partner available at any hour, willing to challenge, research, and help find the structure inside accumulated thinking, removed the last remaining excuse. The articles on Substack came first. Then the outline of a book emerged. Then—as writers of fiction sometimes describe with their characters—the material began to develop its own momentum, revealing connections and insights I had not anticipated.

What I did not expect was what the writing would show me about myself. Working through the experiences that became this book, I came to understand something I had never quite acknowledged: the misplaced rejection I felt at several critical points in my career was not personal failure. It was a predictable feature of what happens when design thinking encounters organisations that have no framework for recognising it. I was not wrong. I was early—and unequipped to explain why the resistance was structural rather than individual.

That realisation is, perhaps, the most important thing in the book. Healthcare does not resist design thinking because it lacks the capability. It resists it because it lacks the language to recognise the capability it already has. This book attempts to supply that language.

If you have felt the same frustration—certain that something fundamental needs to change, uncertain how to make the case or where to begin—this book is for you.

Daniel Steenstra
Blijham, The Netherlands

Introduction

The Problem This Book Solves

Healthcare systems worldwide are failing at the same time, in the same ways, for the same reasons. Waiting lists lengthen. Workforces burn out. Digital transformation projects consume billions and deliver disappointment. Reorganisations arrive, are absorbed, and leave no lasting trace. The reform programmes keep coming. The dysfunction persists.

This pattern is not accidental. It is the predictable result of applying the wrong methods to the wrong problem. Healthcare has been trying to *improve* systems that need to be *redesigned*. That distinction—between improvement and transformation—is the subject of this book.

Design thinking offers a fundamentally different approach: one that starts with a genuine understanding of human experience rather than a predetermined solution; that prototypes and tests before committing; that treats failure as information rather than embarrassment. It is rigorous, evidence-based, and practical. And here is the insight that changes everything: if you have clinical training, you already think this way. The diagnostic method we learned in medicine—observe, hypothesise, test, revise—is design thinking by another name. This book's purpose is to help you recognise that capability and deploy it at the scale of systems, not just patients.

Who This Book Is for

Design Thinking for Healthcare is written for people with the authority and the ambition to change healthcare systems—and the frustration of knowing that the tools available to them are not equal to the task.

The primary audience is healthcare executives, transformation directors, and innovation leaders—the people inside healthcare organisations who carry the responsibility for making change happen. You understand clinical reality. You have lived through improvement programmes that ran out of energy, digital projects that went over budget and under-delivered, and reorganisations that rearranged the deckchairs. You are looking for a coherent methodology that matches the complexity of what you are actually trying to do.

The secondary audience is the clinicians, researchers, and policymakers who want to move from frontline practice or policy design into system transformation—and who need a framework that connects their clinical understanding to organisational change. If you are a clinician who has watched the same avoidable failures repeat themselves across institutions, or a policymaker who has designed regulations that had unintended consequences because end users were never involved in their design, this book is also for you.

Policymakers occupy a distinct and critical position in this book. Healthcare transformation does not happen without enabling policy conditions—and policy consistently fails when it is designed without the people it affects. Chapter 10 addresses policymakers directly, examining how design methods apply to regulation and system architecture. But policymakers will find material relevant to their work throughout: Part I makes the structural case for why current reform approaches are insufficient; Part III shows what well-designed systems can achieve; and Part IV diagnoses the political dynamics—including the electoral cycle pressures and stakeholder veto structures—that policymakers both navigate and, sometimes, inadvertently create. If you design the rules that healthcare systems operate within, this book is written for you as much as for the people working inside those systems.

A third audience—design practitioners, educators, and those entering healthcare from adjacent industries—will find here a grounded account of why healthcare's specific constraints require adapted methods rather than direct transplantation of design approaches from technology or consumer sectors.

Whatever your role, you will find this book more useful if you read it in contact with your own specific context. The frameworks here are designed to be applied. As you work through each chapter, I would encourage you to hold a concrete challenge from your own organisation in mind—a stalled transformation, a failed technology deployment, a workforce problem that resists every intervention. The methodology becomes real when it meets a real problem.

What You Will Get from This Book

By the time you finish *Design Thinking for Healthcare*, you will have:

- A clear understanding of what design thinking is and how it differs from the change management and improvement approaches that already populate your organisation.
- A diagnosis of *why* your previous transformation attempts have struggled, at the level of structural mechanisms rather than implementation failures.
- A working knowledge of how design thinking applies across the full range of healthcare contexts: hospital operations, clinical trials, AI implementation, decentralised care, and policy design.
- Specific tools, frameworks, and 90-day roadmaps you can deploy in your own organisation, calibrated to your role and your system's current readiness.
- An honest account of the forces that will resist your efforts—structural, political, and behavioural—together with practical counter-strategies.

This is not an academic contribution to healthcare literature. It is a field manual for people in the middle of the problem.

How the Book Achieves This

Every chapter in this book follows the same discipline: diagnosis first, prescription second. I will not tell you to implement a framework before I have shown you why the current approach is insufficient and precisely what it is insufficient for. Where I make claims, I ground them in evidence. Where I present case studies, I am specific about context and about what generalises beyond it.

The book draws on three sources of knowledge that rarely appear in combination: extensive medical training across all major clinical specialties; professional design practice at Jaguar, where I worked as a car designer; and twenty years of healthcare transformation leadership, including the development of methodology tested with healthcare leaders in the NHS and international settings. That combination of medical training, professional design practice, and transformation leadership informs every chapter—because the argument this book makes, that clinical reasoning and design thinking are the same fundamental process, can only be made credibly by someone who has genuinely practised both.

The Structure: Five Parts, One Journey

The book is organised in five parts. They build on each other, but they are also designed to be navigated non-linearly depending on your role and your starting point. The reading guidance at the end of this introduction, and the more detailed role-based roadmaps in Chapter 17, will help you find the route that matches your situation.

Part I: The Case for Design (Chapters 1–3) establishes *why* healthcare needs design thinking. Chapter 1 examines the structural reasons why transformation initiatives fail and introduces the Double Diamond as the book's central methodological framework. Chapter 2 draws on transformation successes in automotive, technology, and consumer industries—including my own experience at Jaguar—to identify the transferable principles. Chapter 3 quantifies the cost of bad healthcare design: the financial waste, the patient harm, and the workforce damage that poorly designed systems produce. If you already accept the case for design thinking, you can move through Part I quickly. If you need to make that case to colleagues or boards, Part I gives you the evidence to do so.

Part II: Design Thinking Fundamentals for Healthcare (Chapters 4–5) provides the methodological foundation. Chapter 4 explains the core principles and methods—empathy, iteration, prototyping, testing—adapted specifically for healthcare's regulatory constraints and stakeholder complexity. Chapter 5 makes the book's central argument: that every clinician is already a design thinker. The diagnostic process—taking a history, forming a differential, testing hypotheses, revising based on response to treatment—maps precisely onto the design process. The challenge is not to teach clinicians to think differently; it is to help healthcare organisations recognise and deploy the design capability they already contain.

Part III: Applications Across the Healthcare Ecosystem (Chapters 6–10) applies design thinking to specific domains: clinical trials redesign, responsible AI implementation, the shift from hospital-centred to patient-centred care, decentralised healthcare models, and design thinking for policymakers. Each chapter can stand alone as a domain-specific guide, while the cumulative argument builds a picture of design thinking as a system-level discipline, not a collection of isolated interventions.

Part IV: Why Transformation Fails (and What to Do About It) (Chapters 11–15) is the part that most transformation books omit. Understanding why transformation fails is clinical intelligence applied to your operating environment. Chapter 11 examines the limits of Lean: what it achieves, what it cannot achieve, and how the just-in-time logic that drove

NHS efficiency contributed to healthcare worker deaths during the COVID-19 pandemic. Chapter 12 turns to why even well-funded, professionally led healthcare innovation fails—and what investors and innovation leaders consistently misunderstand about healthcare's unique dynamics. Chapters 13, 14, and 15 form an integrated trilogy: the structural barriers that are *architectural* to healthcare systems (Chapter 13); the political dynamics—who blocks transformation and why (Chapter 14); and the coordinated behavioural resistance that systems deploy over time, not just at the moment of launch (Chapter 15). After Part IV, you will not only know what you are trying to do. You will know what will try to stop you.

Part V: Implementation Toolkit (Chapters 16–17) delivers the tactical framework. Chapter 16 presents the Healthcare Transformation Control Room: a coordination architecture for managing multiple simultaneous transformation streams, anchored in the five-element InterAlign Transformation Framework. Chapter 17 is your personalised roadmap—role-based, readiness-calibrated, and equipped with countermeasures for the resistance patterns documented in Part IV.

Conclusion synthesises the book's core argument and points toward the deeper question that this book opens: why do even excellent design-led transformations face systematic rejection? That question takes us into territory beyond methodology—into the architecture of governance itself—which is the subject of my next book.

A Word About the NHS Examples

This book draws heavily on the UK's NHS case studies. If you are working in a US health system, a European insurer model, a low-income country context, or the pharmaceutical industry, you may reasonably ask why examples from one national health service should be relevant to your situation.

The answer comes from biology.

When geneticists needed to understand inheritance, they chose to work intensively with *Drosophila melanogaster*—the common fruit fly. Not because flies are more important than other creatures, but because their specific characteristics—short generational cycle, visible genetic effects, tractable genome—made fundamental biological mechanisms *visible* in ways that other organisms did not. The fruit fly became genetics' model organism: the system through which universal principles were first identified and then confirmed across species.

The NHS occupies an equivalent position in healthcare transformation research.

As the world's largest single healthcare delivery organisation—serving 67 million people, employing 1.4 million staff, operating under a single funding and governance framework with an annual budget exceeding £200 billion—the NHS possesses characteristics that make transformation dynamics uniquely observable. Governance decisions are subject to democratic accountability and therefore documented. Policy interventions play out at a national scale, with visible consequences within policy-relevant timescales. Major reforms—the introduction of market mechanisms, clinical commissioning, integrated care systems—have been conducted as natural experiments whose results can be traced with unusual clarity. And crucially, the UK sits ahead of the demographic and fiscal curves that most developed healthcare systems will face within the next decade. The NHS is not showing us a uniquely British crisis. It is showing us a healthcare future we need to avoid.

The NHS case studies in this book work precisely *because* the mechanisms they reveal are not uniquely British. The patterns that produce transformation resistance—electoral cycle pressure on long-term investment, bureaucratic preference for stability, professional boundary protection, stakeholder veto power, institutional resistance to change—operate through universal principles that apply wherever healthcare governance exists. When the NHS demonstrates how political short-termism distorts workforce planning, that pattern applies in any democratic system where ministers face re-election. When professional boundaries prevent task-shifting innovations, those same boundaries exist in your system under different names.

Rather than a template to copy, the NHS is a model organism: a system in which fundamental mechanisms are visible, traceable, and therefore teachable. Once you have seen how transformation resistance operates at NHS scale, you will recognise its local variants in your own system—earlier, with more precision, and with the strategic advantage that comes from diagnosis before intervention.

Where NHS-specific context matters—where something is genuinely particular to the UK system rather than universal—I say so. I also include case studies from the US health system, the pharmaceutical industry, Indian healthcare, and international contexts throughout. The NHS provides the most analytically legible examples. The lessons belong to everyone.

How to Use This Book

You can read this book cover to cover. The five-part structure builds a complete argument, and the chapters are sequenced so that each one prepares the ground for what follows. If you are new to design thinking, or want a thorough grounding before acting, start at Chapter 1.

If you are coming to this book with a specific challenge, Chapter 17 provides role-based entry points with recommended reading sequences, a readiness assessment, and 90-day action plans calibrated for your context. The recommended sequences are:

- **Hospital Executives and NHS Trust Leaders**: begin with Chapter 8 (patient-centred systems), then Chapter 5 (clinicians as design thinkers), then Chapter 16 (the transformation control room).
- **Pharmaceutical and Clinical Research Leaders**: begin with Chapter 6 (clinical trials redesign), working through Chapters 4 and 7 before turning to Part IV.
- **Policymakers and System Architects**: begin with Chapter 10 (design thinking for policymakers), then Part I for the foundational case, then Part IV for the failure analysis.
- **Innovation Leaders and Transformation Directors**: begin with Part IV (failure analysis), then Chapter 16, then the role-based roadmap in Chapter 17.
- **Clinicians Taking on Organisational Authority for the First Time**: begin with Chapter 5, then Chapters 1 and 4, before engaging with Part III on application.
- **Management Consultants and Advisors**: Chapter 2 (lessons from other industries) and Chapter 12 (why VCs get healthcare wrong) provide the clearest entry points, followed by Chapters 13–15 on the failure trilogy.

One practical note—the case studies and worked examples embedded in each chapter are where the practical intelligence lives. They are worth the time.

> Throughout this book, I use 'design thinking' to refer to the Double Diamond methodology and its associated principles and methods, as described in Chapters 4 and 5. Where I reference the InterAlign Transformation Framework—the five-element implementation architecture introduced in Chapter 16—I distinguish it explicitly. The two are complementary but distinct: design thinking is the methodology; the InterAlign Transformation Framework is the organisational structure through which that methodology is deployed at scale.

If you want to move from these frameworks toward your own first step, there is a companion resource in development at interqbit.com. The InterQB-it™ assistant grows out of the thinking in this book and is built for the same reader: someone who wants to apply the methodology, not only read about it. It is being developed and extended over time. You are welcome to explore what is there and to shape where it goes.

A final word on what this book will not do. It will not promise that design thinking solves everything. Healthcare transformation is hard—structurally, politically, and humanly—and any book that tells you otherwise is not taking your situation seriously. What design thinking offers is a more accurate diagnosis of the problem, a more rigorous process for developing solutions, and a more honest account of the resistance you will face. That is enough. It is, in my experience, what the work actually requires.

Let's begin.

THE CASE FOR DESIGN I

Chapter 1

Why Healthcare Needs Design Thinking

The Missed Opportunity

The COVID-19 pandemic was a missed opportunity; it could have been the turning point and instigated a concerted effort to transform healthcare systems. Experts had warned that healthcare systems were becoming unsustainable—not only in low- and middle-income countries but also in mature economies that invested heavily in healthcare, such as the UK and the US. Their voices had been ignored, not only because they were inconvenient but—importantly—because there was no blueprint, no approach or method with guaranteed success. So we kept trying to improve the systems that we had.

The COVID-19 pandemic proved those experts right; it made clear to anybody willing to see that healthcare systems were no longer fit for purpose and needed complete transformation. It became common knowledge that warnings of an imminent pandemic were not heeded. Simulations showing our poorly prepared systems were ignored. How international early warning systems failed. When the virus struck, hospitals became overwhelmed very quickly. We suffered from shortages of healthcare workers, facilities, and resources that had been building up over years. It was heartbreaking that, rather than healing, healthcare workers held the hands of patients dying without their loved ones being present. Even now we still feel the impact as waiting lists are long and elective interventions are delayed, while systems attempt to get back onto an 'even keel,' a state of affairs that had been elusive for years before and is no longer attainable.

Encouraging things happened during the pandemic too. We could see how quickly local communities responded, making sure that vulnerable people got support. People got educated on virus transmission and precautions. We admired heroic healthcare professionals working all hours, often with inadequate protection, to serve and save as many lives as they could. Scientists were able to quickly identify the genome of the SARS-CoV-2 virus that caused COVID-19. They then collaborated with pharmaceutical manufacturers and regulators to produce and approve effective

DOI: 10.4324/9781003752073-2

vaccines at speeds not seen before, while politicians and public health officers kept us informed on a daily basis.

It is tragic to observe that, rather than building on those positive elements and ensuring lasting system change, after the crisis was 'over,' systems returned to their pre-COVID-19 condition. We need to understand why that happened, why improvements will not suffice, why systems need transformation and then—crucially—how we can make that happen.

Please don't get downhearted or wrong-footed by the opening of this chapter. This is a positive book. We will explore and apply practical approaches that will make healthcare better for many more people. To do that most effectively, we have to start by understanding what went wrong.

We Built It Wrong

In a 2011 interview, shortly after resigning as Administrator of the Centers for Medicare and Medicaid Services (CMS) in the United States, Don Berwick admitted something remarkable. Healthcare, he said, is broken. Speaking to Kaiser Health News, he didn't mince words: 'We have set up a delivery system that is fragmented, unsafe, not patient-centred, full of waste and unreliable … we built it wrong' [1].

That phrase—'we built it wrong'—deserves examination. You wouldn't consider building your house without first designing it, but that is exactly what happened in healthcare. Healthcare wasn't destroyed by external forces or random failure. It was constructed, deliberately, by intelligent people acting with good intentions. The problem wasn't lack of effort, resources, or expertise. The problem was something more fundamental: healthcare was built without design.

We did not consider who the system is there to serve, what their needs are, how we get stakeholders to work together to meet those needs, to future-proof that system to ensure it can adapt and remain fit for purpose. Why did we ignore design?

To understand why things are the way they are, it is useful to go back in history. The 1980s, when Berwick practised as a paediatrician at the Harvard Community Health Plan, was the height of the quality movement across industry sectors. The superior reliability of Japanese imports forced Western manufacturers and service providers to understand and adopt quality management approaches. Like other clinicians in search of ways to improve, Berwick became interested in 'quality,' becoming VP of Quality of Care Measurement. He became a proponent of W Edwards Deming's work.

> Finding and watching a video of Deming's "red beads experiment" is a powerful introduction for anyone interested in systems thinking. It is a thing of beauty - a simple simulation where teams try to operate in a system geared towards failure. It shows their continued efforts and frustrations fighting against the system, whilst ignoring the obvious—redesign the system.

Layers of Design: From Styling to Society

To understand why in those days, Berwick and others shaping healthcare were attracted to quality and not to design thinking has much to do with design itself. The understanding of what design is—and what it can achieve—has changed dramatically over the past half-century. In the 1980s, while companies were obsessing over quality management and incremental improvement, design was still largely dismissed as decoration. It was about aesthetics, packaging, and presentation—something to be added once the 'real work' had been done. When I worked as a car designer—or 'project stylist,' as Jaguar called us—in the 1990s, we were seen as the people who made the cars look good. The engineers and product planners did the serious stuff; we were the icing on the cake. That hierarchy reflected a narrow, almost patronising view of design as visual polish rather than conceptual substance.

But things began to shift. In the early 2000s, Steve Jobs—one of the few who truly grasped the strategic potential of design early on—put it bluntly: 'In most people's vocabularies, design means veneer. It's interior decorating. It's the fabric of the curtains and the sofa.' Then he went on to say, 'Nothing could be further from the meaning of design. Design is the fundamental soul of a man-made creation that ends up expressing itself in successive outer layers of the product or service' [2].

That statement marked a turning point. Design was no longer confined to the appearance of products. It was about intent, structure, and purpose, the invisible logic that shapes human experience. From there, design started to expand its reach. 'Service design' emerged as a discipline, shifting the focus from objects to systems, from things to experiences and interactions. Firms like IDEO began to apply design not just to consumer goods but to how we educate, how we collaborate, and how we deliver care. Design had matured from making things attractive to making things work better—for people, for communities, and for the planet. It evolved from being the final layer of polish to the starting point of transformation. What had once been considered a craft became a mindset—a disciplined way of diagnosing problems, imagining alternatives, and shaping change.

To explain that design evolution to my students I used to refer to a dialogue in the first Shrek movie, when Shrek tried to explain to Donkey that ogres were not all the monsters they appear to be. Ogres are like onions—both have layers. So does design. Figure 1.1. shows that the most superficial layer of design is about tangible products—the things we can see and touch. The layer below is the design of processes and services—how we experience things. Digging deeper, we find the third layer about designing systems, for instance integrated public transport using buses, trams,

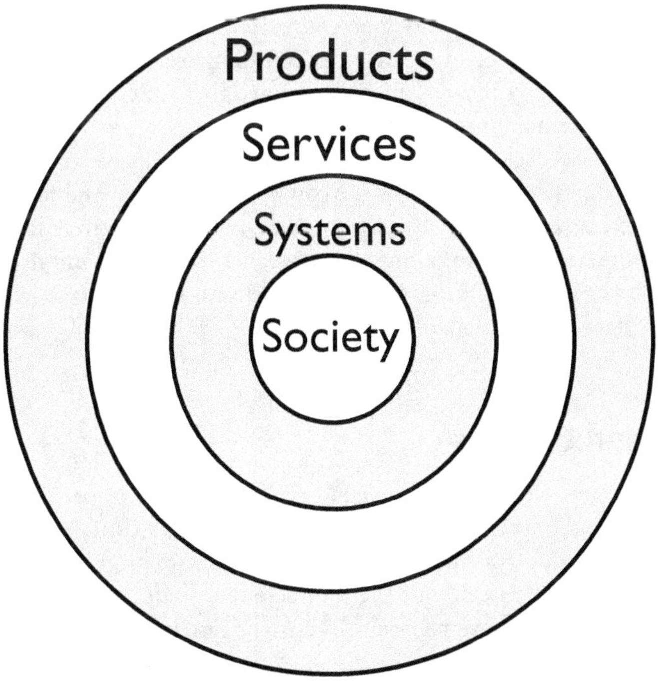

Figure 1.1 The layers of design.

trains, and bicycles. At its core, design is for society—how we interact and care for each other. It has taken decennia for these layers to be revealed and it will take even more time before design is applied effectively across these layers.

How can you expect to build an effective system without design? Knowing what we know now, that question seems almost naive in its simplicity, yet it points to the central paradox of modern healthcare. Every other complex system that we created—aircraft, communication networks, automobiles, supply chains—relies fundamentally on design. Only healthcare developed differently, assembling itself incrementally through historical accident, growing regulations, and institutional inertia rather than purposeful design.

Mind the Gap

Since Berwick spoke those words, healthcare has only deteriorated. The COVID-19 pandemic demonstrated with brutal clarity that healthcare systems across the globe are no longer sustainable. Now, years after the acute phase, we are still confronted with the aftermath: systems in tailspin, ever-increasing demand colliding with dwindling resources, burnout accelerating among healthcare professionals who entered their vocations to heal, not to navigate dysfunction. Many are moving to other countries in search of less stress and better rewards; too many leave their profession altogether. Politicians not knowing what to do, where to get more resources from, how to increase capacity.

Today's reality operates under harsh economic rules. When demand outstrips supply in any sector, prices rise and suppliers profit. Healthcare follows these same rules but with devastating consequences. Many people—even in wealthy nations—cannot access proper medical care. The gap between the need for healthcare and the system's capacity to provide it continues to widen. The World Health Organisation projects a global shortage of 11 million health workers by 2030, concentrated in low and lower-middle income countries but affecting all nations. By 2032, the United States expects shortages of more than 160,000 physicians and 275,000 nurses, despite spending 17.6% of GDP on healthcare—more than any other OECD country. Twenty-five million Americans under 65 remain uninsured.

Isn't it surprising that we lack simple graphics to illustrate that increasing gap? I had to develop the graph in Figure 1.2 myself. It shows how the gap between the demand for and the capacity to deliver healthcare increased over time. It is a generic graph that intuitively feels right. Of course nations might be in different positions along the curve, but the trend is unmistakable.

Under this enduring and mounting pressure, healthcare systems have become self-serving, developing barriers that block change.

Perspectives and Choices

Looking at the graph, how we can close the gap becomes a matter of perspective. People with a background in quality and improvement approaches, such as Lean thinking or Six Sigma, believe that we can make the existing systems more efficient: healthcare professionals just need to work harder; we need to 'sweat the assets.' But the numbers that underpin the graph reveal an inescapable reality: incremental improvement within current systems cannot close the gap. Getting

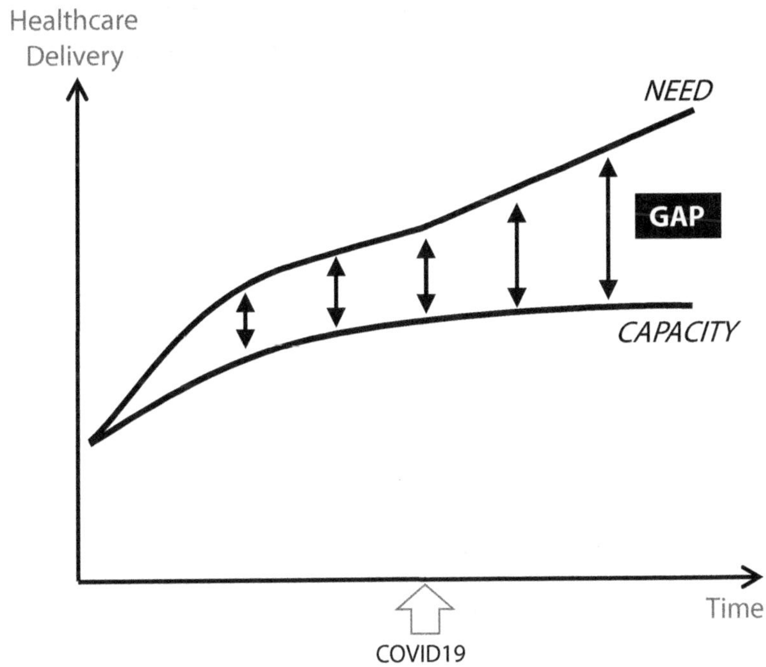

Figure 1.2 The gap between healthcare demand and capacity.

enough healthcare professionals to do the same jobs others do today proves both economically unviable and practically impossible.

This reality leaves three choices. First, accept the status quo—morally reprehensible when millions suffer unnecessarily. Second, attempt to improve current systems—unrealistic given the mathematics of supply and demand. Third, transform healthcare systems entirely—the only viable option that requires courage to abandon comfortable illusions for challenging realities. And design thinking.

Improve or Transform

The distinction between improvement and transformation matters more than semantics suggest. Improvement works within existing frameworks, optimising what already exists. Transformation requires fundamentally rethinking those frameworks themselves. Healthcare has attempted improvement for decades. Hospitals implement Lean methodologies borrowed from Toyota's manufacturing plants. Quality improvement initiatives proliferate. Process optimisation efforts multiply. Change management consultants deploy frameworks from business schools. All this activity—workshops, training sessions, process mapping, standardisation efforts—keeps organisations extraordinarily busy.

Yet none of this activity has produced the sustained improvements in patient outcomes that justify the investment. Why? Because these approaches address symptoms rather than root causes. They treat healthcare's challenges as primarily operational when they are fundamentally systemic.

Current approaches—Lean management, change management, restructuring—address symptoms rather than root causes. They lack a fundamental understanding of how to design systems around human needs.

Fear of change and absence of design thinking prevent people from supporting the necessary transformation. This is where design thinking becomes essential. It provides a methodology for transformation rather than mere improvement, and it starts with a crucial principle: understanding the problems before attempting solutions.

What Is Design Thinking

Design thinking carries multiple definitions across different contexts. At its core, it captures the mindset of designers and the way we work. We do not accept things as they are—we imagine things that never were and then make those happen, while considering challenges from all perspectives. Futurists try to understand what the future might hold, while designers already have a pretty good idea of what it looks like, don't accept it and have developed methods and tools to shape the future. The mindset can be acquired; the methods and tools can be learned.

Design thinking begins with empathy: developing a deep understanding of users, their needs, their constraints and the wider requirements of all other stakeholders. This foundation enables ideation—generating ideas that could work, developing concepts that address real rather than assumed needs. From ideation comes prototyping—building representations to show others, to test and to gather feedback. Finally, iteration—continuously implementing and refining effective solutions based on real-world learning.

There are several models or frameworks for design thinking that might appear different but are actually similar. The Stanford d.school suggests a process with five sequential steps that go up or down: Empathise ↑, Define ↓, Ideate ↑, Prototype ↓, and Test ↓. The design firm IDEO, creators of the Apple mouse, positions design thinking at the intersection of desirability, viability, and feasibility. Their 'human-centred design' process shows a continuous curve that first diverges for Inspiration, then converges and diverges for Ideation to finally converge for Implementation.

In 2004, the UK's Design Council presented its Double Diamond framework after an extensive analysis of design approaches of companies and designers across sectors such as architecture, product and service design. They noticed common elements and synthesised those into the Double Diamond [3].

It shows the two basic design thinking moves we have already seen in Stanford and IDEO: diverging—to expand understanding and converging—to synthesise and decide. The left diamond asks 'What is the actual problem we need to solve?' The right diamond asks 'What solution effectively addresses it?' In the left diamond we discover and define the requirements and constraints of users and stakeholders. It requires exploring problems in detail, then synthesising insights into clear problem statements. In the right diamond we develop and deliver products, services, and systems that address the needs.

Note how the equal size of the diamonds implies that the same effort and resources must be invested in understanding problems as in solving them. That insight holds direct relevance for healthcare transformation. If not enough effort goes into understanding and defining problems, more time and cost become necessary to solve them—sometimes requiring a complete return to discovery and definition, adding expense that could have been avoided through proper initial investment.

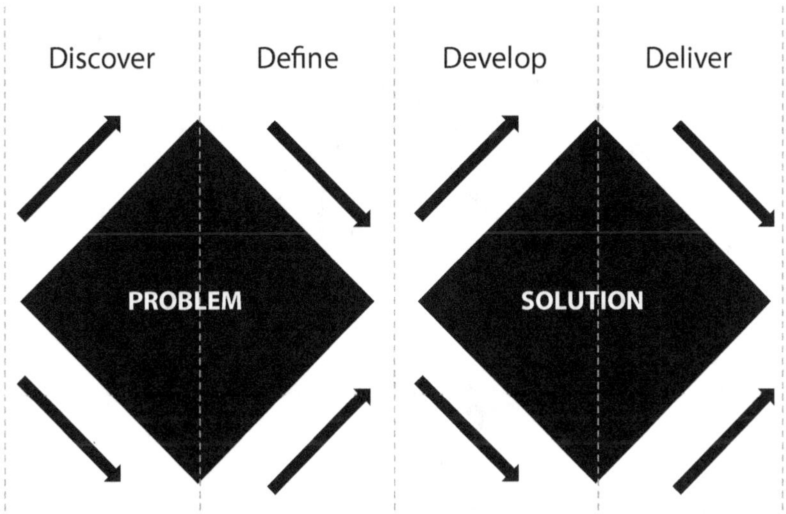

Figure 1.3 Double Diamond framework of design thinking (based on UK Design Council).

Healthcare typically jumps directly to the right diamond—implementing solutions before fully understanding the problems they're meant to solve.

Double Diamond provides a very useful visual framework to understand and apply design thinking. It will be referred to in several places in the book, but Double Diamond, Stanford's five stages, and IDEO's process all share a limitation: they represent design as a 2D linear journey with sequential steps. While that is pedagogically useful, it obscures a crucial reality. Design is multi-dimensional—not a sequence of discrete steps. Designers simultaneously explore across multiple interacting dimensions.

When I designed the Jaguar XK8 interior, I wasn't completing 'discovery' before starting 'development.' I was working across user needs, technical constraints, cost targets, regulatory requirements, aesthetic considerations, and manufacturing capabilities all at once—each dimension informing and reshaping the others. The space had some fixed boundaries (budget, launch date) and others that shifted as understanding deepened (what 'luxury' meant to our target customers). This multidimensional, interactive, iterative nature—not a sequential process—is what distinguishes design thinking from traditional project management.

Design thinking is a well-established, powerful and robust approach focused on needs and developing innovative solutions. It comes with proven methods, tools and techniques that are applicable to anything—from widgets to consumer products, from software to complex systems such as healthcare. The robustness of design is critical to appreciate. Trust in design is built up by understanding the intellectual arguments in combination with the practical experience of applying design thinking, tools and techniques.

Design and Innovation: Chicken and Egg

The intent of this book is to be practical; we do not want to lose ourselves in academic debate about definitions. Suffice to say that there are many definitions of design, which is explained by the layered model of Figure 1.1. You will define design differently if you can only see one or two

Figure 1.4 Relationship design and innovation as chicken and egg.

layers or when you see all four. Similarly, 'innovation' has many definitions too. The one I prefer was used by the UK government: 'innovation is the successful exploitation of new ideas.' It is not being creative, coming up with ideas—that is invention. It is the hard work—the blood, sweat and tears—turning those ideas into products, services, and systems that are profitable, sustainable, and deliver benefits to users and stakeholders.

That definition also explains how design and innovation relate—like chicken and egg. No innovation exists without design. Design is the chicken: it transforms raw material into output. Innovation is the egg: the result of that process, not the cause of it. You cannot have one without the other, but the sequence matters (Figure 1.4).

This intrinsic relationship between design and innovation also explains why design is integrated across sectors. Imagine your shopping experience, your holiday flight or car without design. What would they look like? How would they function? Any organisation providing products or services needs design thinking. Without it, businesses fail. Customers are only willing to pay for products and services that meet their needs. If those needs go unmet, customers depart and companies go broke. That applies in every sector except healthcare. The link between using design thinking, satisfying users, and remaining profitable is direct—it somehow fails to apply to healthcare.

Design Absence in Healthcare

Understanding this paradox requires returning to the cornerstone of healthcare: the medical process of diagnosis, therapy, and prevention. Note the similarities with design thinking approaches—the sequence of divergence and convergence. Physicians listen to patients, observe them, ask questions, hypothesise, conduct tests, then provide or prescribe solutions improving quality of life, observe if they work, adjust if they don't—just like designers do. Clinical decision-making mirrors the design thinking process perfectly. This insight emerged from my own experience: nine years studying medicine and clinical practice followed by eleven years as a professional car designer.

Once upon a time, when physicians were still in control, design thinking was implicitly embedded in healthcare—just not recognised as such. The medical process and the design process were functionally identical. Then came the split. Physicians were pushed out with managers taking over control. Medical schools, business schools, economics, and chemistry departments did not teach design thinking. That happened in art schools at the other end of campus. The people who built healthcare systems—managers, politicians, administrators—were not educated in design thinking. And the people using design thinking—the physicians—were no longer in control.

Thus healthcare evolved without design thinking into the rigid system that now serves some stakeholders but not the very people it should serve: patients and communities. Somewhere in this evolution, the implicit design thinking embedded in clinical practice became disconnected from building the system. Individual clinicians still practise design thinking every day in patient care. The systems within which they work do not. 'We built it wrong.'

Although design is structurally absent, centres of excellence that use design do exist. The Garfield Center at Kaiser Permanente, the Center for Innovation at the Mayo Clinic in the United States, the Radboud-UMC Health Innovation Labs in the Netherlands—these represent exceptions proving the rule. They apply design thinking to medical devices, processes, or facilities. Rarely do they apply design thinking to healthcare systems themselves.

This evolution explains healthcare's unique position. Every other complex industry—automotive, technology, consumer goods, financial services—underwent design-led transformation. These sectors recognised that as stakeholder complexity increased, systematic design approaches to ensure alignment toward meeting users' needs became not optional but essential. Healthcare missed this transition. As it grew from simple twofold interactions between patients and physicians into systems involving dozens of stakeholder types—payers, regulators, pharmaceutical manufacturers, device makers, hospital administrators, insurance companies, government agencies—it never developed the design infrastructure other sectors built to manage complexity while remaining focused on meeting users' needs.

The absence of design thinking has concrete consequences. Healthcare systems operate in reactive mode, addressing immediate pressures through short-term fixes that often exacerbate underlying problems. Innovation gets stifled by bureaucratic processes, professional silos, and misaligned incentives. Collaboration between stakeholders remains minimal, with each actor optimising their individual positions rather than system performance.

Trust between citizens and healthcare institutions has eroded profoundly. Poor communication, lack of transparency, and growing inequalities have created widespread alienation. This breakdown creates vicious cycles: as citizens disengage, systems become less responsive to their needs, further reinforcing distrust and disengagement.

COUNTERINTUITIVE FINDING

Healthcare Already Had Design Thinking—Then Lost It

The Double Diamond framework—Discover, Define, Develop, Deliver—maps precisely to clinical diagnostic reasoning: listen, hypothesise, test, adjust. Design thinking was not absent from early healthcare; it was *displaced* when management took control from clinicians in the late twentieth century. The people who built healthcare systems—managers, politicians, administrators—were educated in economics and business, not design. The people who practised design thinking daily—physicians—were no longer in control of system architecture. Healthcare's transformation crisis is not a capability deficit; it is a governance exclusion problem. The expertise already exists inside the system.

From Reactive to Proactive Systems

Design thinking offers fundamentally different approaches to each of these problems. It begins with deep stakeholder research before solutions are proposed. Ethnographic research, field shadowing, and narrative interviews help healthcare leaders understand how patients, clinicians, administrators, and communities actually experience healthcare rather than how official reports describe it. Stakeholder mapping identifies relationships, influence, and potential resistance, allowing for anticipation of governance dynamics rather than unwelcome surprises during implementation.

This discovery work transforms healthcare from reactive to proactive. When you understand underlying needs rather than surface symptoms, solutions will address the root causes. The lengthy upfront investment reduces overall cost and time because solutions will fit actual requirements rather than assumed.

From Fragmentation to Integration

Healthcare's notorious fragmentation—patients repeating histories to every new provider, care coordination failing across settings, information trapped in incompatible systems—results directly from a lack of systems-level design. Each component is optimised independently without consideration for the whole.

Design thinking's whole-system perspective maps patient journeys across entire care episodes, identifying gaps, redundancies, and opportunities. By asking how an undesired outcome can be avoided, it naturally extends into prevention—critical to move from unsustainable 'sickness-systems' to adaptive health and wellbeing systems. Co-design brings together stakeholders who rarely interact: patients, primary care physicians, specialists, pharmacists, social workers, family caregivers. Their different perspectives will help to generate novel ideas and better solutions. Developing a shared understanding of the whole system enables solutions that address fragmentation at its source rather than patching symptoms.

From Siloed Innovation to Ecosystem Transformation

Healthcare innovation typically occurs in isolation. A pharmaceutical company develops a drug without involving the communities who will use it. A hospital implements a new electronic health record without adequately involving clinicians. A startup creates a health app without understanding how it fits into existing care workflows.

Design thinking's emphasis on co-design and stakeholder involvement means innovation happens with people rather than to them. This produces solutions that fit existing practices while improving them, rather than solutions that will not be adopted because they require complete practice overhauls.

The Double Diamond framework proves particularly powerful for healthcare innovation. The first diamond—Discover and Define—prevents the common error of jumping to solutions before fully understanding problems. How many healthcare technologies have failed not because they didn't work technically, but because they solved problems no one actually had?

From Professional Burnout to Meaningful Work

Healthcare professionals enter their vocations to help people maximise their quality of life. Yet many experience profound burnout—not from the inherent demands of caring for the sick, but from badly designed systems that prevent them from doing their work effectively.

Design thinking offers a different approach to system improvement: involve the people who do the work in redesigning how work gets done. When clinicians participate actively in designing workflows, selecting technologies, and organising care delivery, solutions align with clinical reality rather than administrative imagination.

This isn't just more satisfying for professionals and their patients; it produces better systems. Clinicians understand complexity, variability, and unusual cases that designers and administrators miss. Their knowledge, combined with design methods for creative problem-solving, generates innovations that are more practical and more far-reaching than top-down approaches produce.

From Waste to Value

Healthcare systems waste resources on staggering scales. Not just financial waste—though that reaches billions—but wasted time, wasted expertise, wasted trust, wasted lives. Much of this waste stems from fundamental design failures.

Design thinking's emphasis on understanding actual needs before creating solutions prevents waste at its source. When you know what patients actually need, you don't build systems delivering what administrators think they need. When you involve clinicians in designing processes, you don't create workflows that look efficient on paper but prove impossible in practice. The iterative nature of design thinking—prototype, test, learn, refine—prevents the massive waste of implementing system-wide solutions that ultimately fail. Small-scale prototyping with real users uncovers problems before billions get invested in broken approaches.

Healthcare as Complex Adaptive System

Healthcare represents a complex adaptive system—a network of independent agents interacting in ways that produce behaviours that are unpredictable from individual components. Patients, clinicians, administrators, payers, regulators, and others each respond to local conditions and feedback, creating system-level patterns that no single actor controls.

Traditional management approaches imported from manufacturing or business process optimisation fail in complex adaptive systems. These approaches assume linear cause-effect relationships: standardise processes, reduce variation, increase efficiency, improve outcomes. Manufacturing systems aim to eliminate variation because variation represents defects. Healthcare systems must be built to respond to variation because variation represents reality. Every patient is unique. Every illness manifests differently. Every community has distinct needs. Attempting to eliminate this variation doesn't improve healthcare—it breaks it.

Design thinking aligns naturally with complex adaptive systems. Rather than imposing standardised solutions, it develops enabling conditions for good outcomes. Rather than assuming problems can be solved once and for all, it embraces continuous learning and adaptation. Rather than optimising individual components, it considers relationships and feedback loops.

The prototyping and testing phases of design thinking function as experiments in complex systems. You introduce changes at a small scale, observe what happens, learn from unexpected consequences, and refine approaches. This experimental mindset—try, learn, adapt—matches how complex adaptive systems actually behave.

The Evidence Gap

Healthcare prides itself on evidence-based practice. Clinical decisions should follow rigorous research that demonstrates what will work. Yet healthcare system design rarely follows this principle. Major system changes get implemented based on management fads, consultant recommendations, or political pressures rather than evidence.

Design thinking offers a way to bring evidence-based approaches to system design itself. The emphasis on user research produces evidence about actual needs rather than assumptions. Prototyping and testing generate evidence about what works—and what doesn't—before full implementation. Iterative refinement creates feedback loops ensuring ongoing learning. This matters particularly for addressing healthcare disparities. Communities underserved by current systems often get further marginalised by system changes because their needs weren't understood or included in design processes. When healthcare systems implement changes based on assumptions rather than evidence from diverse communities, disparities widen rather than narrow.

Design thinking's emphasis on ethnographic research, stakeholder engagement, and co-design with affected communities provides methodology for equity-focused system design. You cannot design equitable systems without understanding the diverse needs and contexts of the people those systems should serve.

Learning from Other Sectors

Healthcare can learn from how design thinking transformed other complex industries. Consider automotive manufacturing. Cars in the 1960s were designed primarily by engineers focused on technical functionality. Design was added cosmetically afterwards. Then companies like BMW and Toyota integrated design thinking throughout development, starting with a deep understanding of driver needs and behaviours. The result wasn't just prettier cars but fundamentally better ones—safer, more reliable, more enjoyable to use.

Or consider consumer technology. Early computers required technical expertise to use. Then companies like Apple applied design thinking, beginning with deep observation of how people actually interact with technology. The result transformed computing from a specialised tool to a ubiquitous utility.

These transformations didn't happen through incremental improvement. They required fundamental rethinking of design processes themselves—starting with users, involving multiple disciplines, prototyping extensively, iterating continuously.

Healthcare faces similar opportunities. The complexity that makes healthcare challenging—biological variability, emotional dimensions, life-or-death consequences, multiple stakeholders with competing interests—doesn't make design thinking impossible. It makes it essential.

Complex industries that underwent design-led transformation share common patterns. They moved from engineering-driven to user-centred approaches. They broke down silos between disciplines. They embraced prototyping and iteration rather than attempting perfect first-time solutions. They invested heavily in understanding needs before proposing solutions. Healthcare hasn't followed these patterns. Individual organisations and initiatives apply design thinking, but healthcare as a sector hasn't undergone the design revolution that other complex industries experienced.

Dimensions of Transformation

The transformation healthcare requires won't happen overnight. It took centuries for healthcare to centralise into current institutional forms. The necessary transformation must happen much faster, but still requires realistic timeframes and systematic approaches.

Three interrelated dimensions require transformation, all anchored in design thinking. First, simplifying technology—developing innovations that work at the point of care rather than requiring centralised facilities. Second, empowering people—both patients through health literacy and professionals through design capability. Third, redesigning processes—rethinking how care gets delivered from first principles rather than optimising existing workflows.

These dimensions interact. Simplifying technology enables care decentralisation only if healthcare professionals have the capability to use it. Process redesign works only if both technology and people dimensions are addressed.

Design thinking provides the integrating framework that ensures these dimensions develop coherently rather than independently. The principles of disruptive innovation suggest that transformation should start with serving the populations that are currently underserved. This isn't just equitable; it's practical. Developing healthcare systems operate in what might be called permissive governance states—they haven't yet developed the defensive mechanisms of established systems that attack innovation.

Why This Matters Now

The urgency has never been greater. Healthcare is in a perfect storm. Demographic transitions globally mean more people living longer with chronic conditions. Climate change creates new health challenges. Pandemics demonstrate existing systems' brittleness. Financial pressures mount as costs rise faster than economic growth. These challenges won't be met by doing more of the same, just more efficiently. They require fundamentally different approaches—precisely what design thinking enables.

Healthcare without design thinking is guesswork. Transformation without innovation is just a buzzword. Innovation without design is impossible. The logic chain is inescapable: healthcare needs to transform, transformation requires innovation, innovation requires design thinking.

Don Berwick was right. We built healthcare wrong. More precisely, we didn't build it at all—we assembled it incrementally without systematic design. That assembly created systems that serve some stakeholders while failing the people healthcare exists to serve.

The good news: built things can be rebuilt. Systems can be redesigned. The beauty and power of design thinking is that we do not have to break everything down first. Healthcare has the knowledge, resources, and people needed for transformation. What's missing is the systematic application of design thinking to healthcare systems themselves.

The question isn't whether healthcare needs design thinking. The evidence for that is overwhelming. The question is how to embed design thinking so thoroughly in healthcare that future generations will wonder how we ever managed without it. Healthcare was built wrong. Now we can design it right.

The chapters ahead demonstrate design thinking's application across healthcare's ecosystem: redesigning clinical trials (Chapter 6), ensuring AI advances equity rather than widening disparities (Chapter 7), shifting from hospital-centred to patient-centred systems (Chapters 8 and 9), and designing policies that enable rather than stifle innovation (Chapter 10). Part IV examines why even excellent transformations face systematic resistance—and how to navigate it.

References

1. Berwick, D. 'Berwick: Healthcare is broken, fragmented, unsafe', *Healthcare IT News*. Accessed: 20 February 2025. Available at: https://www.healthcareitnews.com/news/berwick-healthcare-broken-fragmented-unsafe.
2. The Guardian (2011) 'Steve Jobs quotes: The man in his own words', *The Guardian*, 6 October 2011. Available: https://www.theguardian.com/technology/2011/oct/06/steve-jobs-quotes (Accessed: 12 November 2025).
3. 'The double diamond - design council'. Available at: https://www.designcouncil.org.uk/our-resources/the-double-diamond/ (Accessed: 10 March 2025).

Chapter 2

Learning from Other Industries

Healthcare leaders know transformation is essential. The gap between demand and capacity widens daily. Workforce burnout accelerates. Billions spent on improvement initiatives yield disappointing results. Yet when looking for guidance, they find either generic design thinking books without healthcare depth or healthcare transformation books without design methodology. What's missing is understanding how design thinking has actually transformed other complex industries facing challenges remarkably similar to healthcare's.

This chapter examines industries that successfully navigated the kind of transformation healthcare now requires. Not because healthcare should simply copy automotive or technology companies, but because these industries reveal patterns, principles, and pitfalls directly applicable to healthcare's unique context. Apple demonstrates how organisations lose and regain their design thinking compass—and the catastrophic consequences of drift. IBM shows how embedding design thinking as organisational DNA enables survival through multiple disruptions. The automotive sector, particularly Toyota and Jaguar, reveals both the practical reality of design thinking (not the neat sequential process that diagrams suggest) and how manufacturing principles can illuminate—and mislead—when applied to healthcare.

These aren't theoretical case studies. They're industries I've worked in, observed closely, and learned from over three decades. The question this chapter answers is simple: if design thinking can transform industries as complex as automotive manufacturing, global technology, and enterprise computing, what stops it transforming healthcare? More importantly, what can healthcare leaders learn from how these transformations actually happened—the messy reality, not the sanitised success stories?

Torino, Italy, June 1986. Week 3
I was sketching furiously in the Carrozzeria Michelotti design studio when Edgardo Michelotti quietly sat down beside me. After three weeks of intensive work experience following my second-place finish in a car design competition, I expected the gentle dismissal: 'Nice knowing you, but stick to medicine.' Instead: 'We'd like to offer you a job. Starting September.'

DOI: 10.4324/9781003752073-3

Six months earlier, I'd been in clinical training in paediatrics, headed toward reconstructive surgery, until a night in A&E made me realise that my retinal detachment and lack of stereoscopic vision made me dangerous with a scalpel. The disappointment was crushing. But here in this Turin workshop, I'd found something unexpected: the direct link between sketching ideas and making them real. Design thinking made tangible.
I said yes. My medical final exams were postponed indefinitely. What I didn't know then was that this pivot—from clinical medicine to automotive design—would eventually teach me more about healthcare transformation than remaining in medicine ever could.

Apple: Rediscovering Design Thinking

The story of Apple demonstrates how losing and regaining design thinking determines organisational survival. For many, Apple epitomises good design and great products under Steve Jobs's visionary leadership. But that wasn't always the case. Apple's decline in the late 1980s and early 1990s was seeded during Jobs's first tenure. For all his brilliance, Jobs often became consumed by internal battles and fixated on machine elegance rather than practical users' challenges. The original Mac's closed architecture, single disk drive, and lack of expandability reflected a perfectionist philosophy that, while visionary, made life harder for users whose needs were broader than Jobs wanted to admit.

His ousting in 1985 didn't merely remove a leader—it exposed how fragile Apple's alignment had become. Jobs had not built a stable leadership team, unified product strategy, or a culture capable of balancing bold design with sustained user engagement. Once he was gone, the company drifted. New executives treated Apple like just another computer manufacturer. In the years that followed, Apple increased its product line, pursued incompatible technologies, and repeatedly changed direction while the Macintosh platform stagnated. By the mid-1990s, Apple had alienated both loyal users and developers—not because the market had outgrown Apple, but because Apple had slowly lost the ability to hear and interpret the needs of the people it once championed.

During his years away from Apple, Jobs founded NeXT and invested heavily in Pixar—experiences that reshaped his leadership and matured his approach to building technology and teams. When Jobs returned to Apple in 1997, the company faced near-bankruptcy. He immediately pared back product lines, cut redundant projects, and focused the organisation on a clear, user-oriented vision. Crucially, he reorganised leadership by bringing in stronger design and operations executives, such as Jonathan Ive for design and Tim Cook for operations. Jobs returned not just as visionary founder but as seasoned CEO, combining high standards of design and simplicity with structured execution. The transformation that followed demonstrates the Double Diamond methodology brilliantly—not as theory, but as practical business strategy that created two of the most successful products in history [1].

The iPod: Discovering the Real Problem

In 2000, Apple didn't start by asking 'how do we build a better MP3 player?' They started with deep observation of how people actually experienced music. The Discover phase revealed frustration: existing MP3 players were clunky, with confusing interfaces and limited capacity. But more fundamentally, getting music onto these devices was torturous—ripping CDs, managing files, navigating arcane folder structures.

The Define phase synthesised this into a clear problem statement: people wanted their entire music collection in their pocket, accessible instantly, without technical barriers. This wasn't about storage capacity alone—it was about the complete user experience.

The Develop phase produced the iPod's iconic click wheel interface and iTunes software working seamlessly together. Apple prototyped extensively, testing not just the device but the entire ecosystem. The Deliver phase launched in 2001 with '1,000 songs in your pocket'—a promise that resonated because it addressed the defined problem, not just technical specifications.

The iPhone: Expanding the Diamond

The iPhone demonstrates how the Double Diamond applies to transformational innovation. The Discover phase began with observing how people used multiple devices—phones, PDAs, MP3 players, cameras—switching between them constantly. Jobs recognised convergence as inevitable, but existing smartphones were dreadful: stylus-dependent interfaces, cramped keyboards, business-focused rather than human-centred.

The Define phase asked: what if the interface disappeared? What if software defined the experience rather than physical buttons? This reframing was crucial—not 'better smartphone' but 'fundamentally different interaction model.'

The Develop phase involved creating revolutionary multi-touch technology, prototyping countless interface designs, and building an entirely new operating system. Apple didn't just test the hardware—they tested how people would actually use it, iterating based on real behaviour.

The Deliver phase launched in 2007, transforming not just phones but computing itself.

Culture of Design

Steve Jobs didn't just use design methods—he embedded design culture at Apple's core. His hiring rule—'A-players hire A-players; B-players hire C-players'—built teams where quality expectations were shared and reinforced, not imposed from above. He wanted people obsessed with quality who challenged him, challenged each other, and cared about the product more than about power. Crucially, this culture has outlived Jobs himself. Apple's DNA is now self-sustaining. That kind of cultural resilience is what healthcare must aspire to.

Results Speak

The graph in Figure 2.1 shows Apple's income after tax from 1995 to 2025—the lasting impact of design thinking. The $1.2B loss in 1996 that triggered transformation is barely visible.

Why This Matters for Healthcare

Healthcare leaders face the same challenge Apple did in the 1990s: drift from patient needs while implementing solutions that serve institutional convenience. Jobs's refocusing on users offers a template—but only if healthcare leaders have the courage to fundamentally rethink rather than incrementally improve.

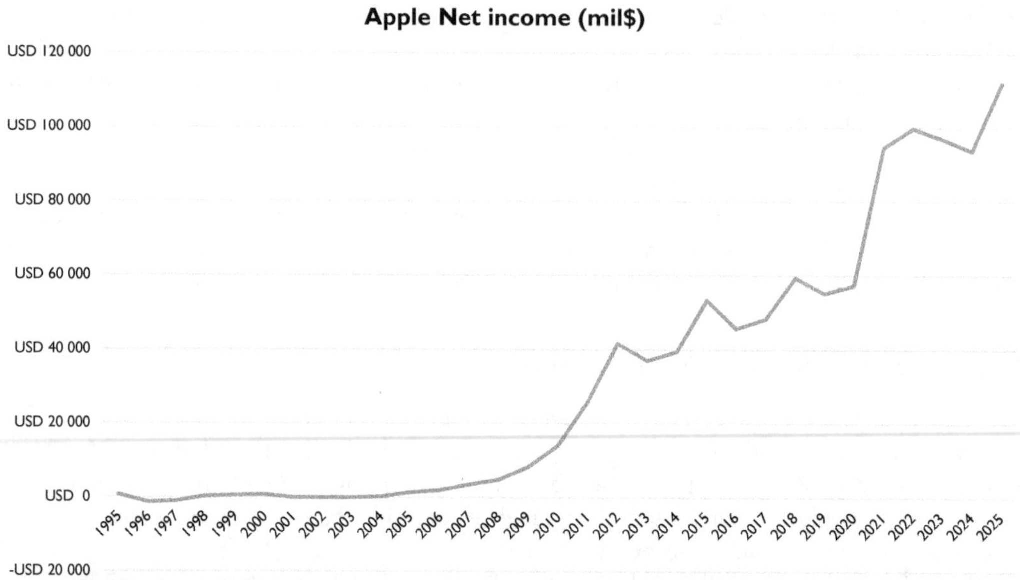

Figure 2.1 Apple income after tax 1995–2025. Data compiled from Apple Inc Annual Reports (Form 10-K), 1995–2025.

Apple's success demonstrates three principles that are directly applicable to healthcare transformation. First, equal investment in problem understanding (left diamond) and solution development (right diamond)—Apple spent years in discovery before engineering. Second, focus on complete user experience rather than isolated features. Third, willingness to fundamentally rethink systems rather than incrementally improving them.

Healthcare typically jumps to the right diamond—implementing solutions before fully understanding problems. Apple shows that deep discovery work isn't delay—it's the foundation for breakthrough innovation.

IBM: Transformation Through Design Thinking

IBM demonstrates how design thinking enables survival through disruption. During the 1960s and 1970s, IBM dominated mainframe computing through hardware, software, and customisation services. In the 1980s, minicomputers and personal computers attacked the mainframe business. IBM reacted by setting up new business units in new locations with different business models to produce minicomputers and personal computers, while closing units that were no longer profitable [2].

Today IBM is a leading enterprise technology company, still combining computing, producing hardware, and providing services, now in quantum computing, cloud technologies, AI, and enterprise transformation.

In 2012, Phil Gilbert formally positioned design thinking as central to IBM's transformation. But long before that label, the company had spent decades applying design thinking principles. In the 1960s and 1970s, IBM's Human Factors group worked closely with engineers on early mainframes and office systems, conducting ethnographic studies of how people actually used computers long before usability research was mainstream. The design of the Selectric typewriter, the System/360 interfaces, and the first personal computing environments all benefited from what we now recognise as user-centred design: deep attention to workflow, ergonomics, cognitive load, and lived experience.

Yet IBM struggled to scale this mindset across the organisation. The company had islands of exceptional design practise surrounded by vast engineering-led bureaucracy. By the late 1990s and 2000s, although IBM produced world-class research and iconic interaction design, these efforts were fragmented and lacked executive sponsorship. What Phil Gilbert did was industrialise it—lift it out of pockets of excellence and make it coherent, enterprise-wide discipline. He unified language, embedded designers into multidisciplinary squads, created repeatable playbooks, and institutionalised practices that had existed informally for decades [3]. Gilbert's approach was systematic: he established a design practise with clear metrics, trained thousands of IBMers in design thinking fundamentals, embedded professional designers into product teams, and created 'design sprints' that became standard operating procedure. Critically, he secured executive sponsorship by demonstrating ROI through pilot projects before scaling.

IBM never lost its North Star—the design thinking embedded in the organisation, before it was formally labelled as such, enabled IBM to change and remain competitive. Focus on users and their needs, using iteration and prototyping.

Why This Matters for Healthcare

Conventional wisdom has it that it's impossible to turn a supertanker. IBM turned, several times, successfully. IBM was able to because design thinking was embedded, whereas in healthcare systems it is not. The challenge is clear—first integrate design thinking, then healthcare will be able to transform to better serve users.

Like IBM's 'islands of exceptional design practice,' healthcare has pockets of excellence—individual clinicians practising patient-centred care, isolated improvement projects—but lacks enterprise-wide design culture. The transformation IBM achieved demonstrates what becomes possible when design thinking scales beyond isolated initiatives.

Understanding Design in Practice

The Double Diamond framework introduced in Chapter 1 provides useful structure for understanding design thinking. However, examples from Apple, IBM, and my own experience at Jaguar reveal an important reality: the day-to-day practice differs significantly from its neat sequential appearance.

In actual practice, design isn't a tidy left-to-right journey. It's simultaneous exploration across multiple interacting dimensions. When I designed the Jaguar XK8 interior, I wasn't completing 'discovery' before starting 'development.' I was working across user needs, technical constraints, cost targets, regulatory requirements, aesthetic considerations, and manufacturing capabilities all at once—each dimension informing and reshaping the others.

The space had some fixed boundaries (budget, launch date) and others that shifted as understanding deepened e.g., what 'luxury' meant to our target customers. In day-to-day practice, design thinking means going to and fro, up and down within and between both diamonds. Over time, as projects progress, there's a shift from left to right as the problem space becomes fully explored while solutions develop, as shown in Figure 2.2.

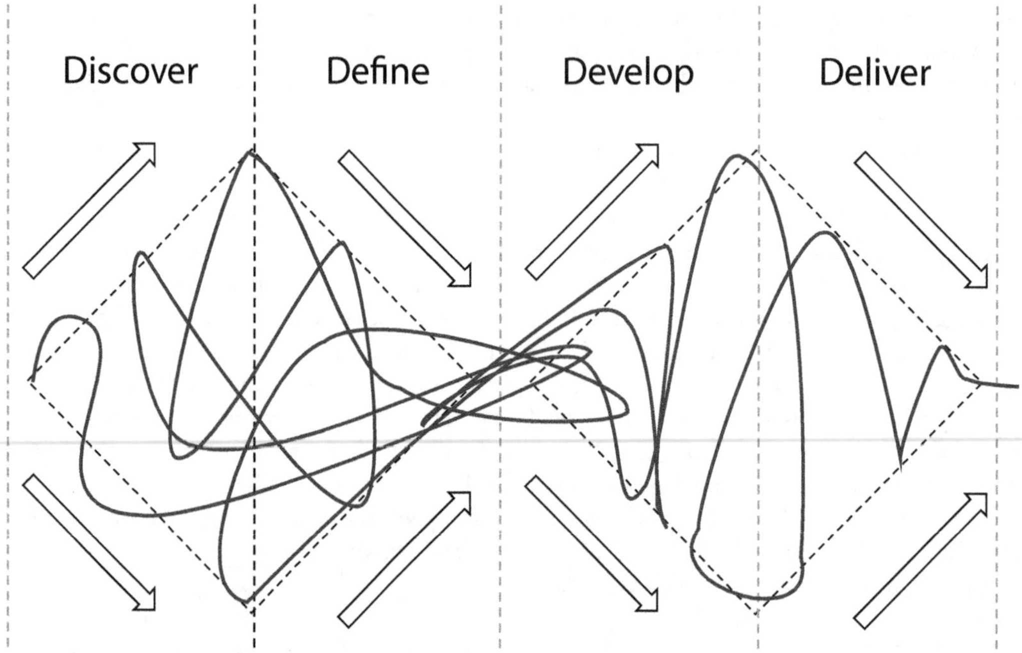

Figure 2.2 Design thinking in practice.

This multidimensional, interactive, iterative nature—not sequential process—is what distinguishes design thinking from traditional project management. Understanding this reality matters for healthcare transformation: don't expect neat phases. Expect productive messiness guided by the Double Diamond framework, not constrained by it.

Jaguar XK8: Design Thinking in Practice

In 1990, I joined Jaguar Cars 'Styling' department as a car designer working on exteriors and interiors. The company had a glorious past of producing iconic cars such as the E-type and victories in races such as the 24 Hours of Le Mans. Its slogan was Grace, Space, and Pace. As a small volume manufacturer, it became increasingly difficult to invest in new products and modern facilities. Ford paid £1.6B for the brand in 1990 and found a company with outdated products and facilities. The XJ40 saloon had been in production for four years; the XJ-S sports car for over 15; with replacements for either well away. Our first priority was to design and develop new products, fast and cheap.

Design had always been important to Jaguar's success but was only 'skin deep'—there were anecdotes of customers loving the looks so much that they bought two cars simultaneously, accepting that one would likely be in the workshop for repair. I soon learned that the exterior got customers into the showroom but it was the interior they would live in that made customers want to drive it away.

The director of Styling reported to the Chief Engineer, not the board. Our brief for a new product came from Sales & Marketing and Product Planning. They'd already done discovery and defining, handing over a list of features and constraints: features our competitors already had, cost targets, deadlines, direction to use the XJ-S floorpan. As designers we had to revisit the first diamond first, using a customer's perspective—who were they? What car were they driving now? What will excite them? What will they expect? Only then could we begin sketching what the car might look like—inside and out.

After one of my sketches for the interior was chosen for production, the work of 'making it real' in the second diamond began. Safeguarding the design intent meant confronting complexity daily:

- Working with ergonomists to ensure people of all sizes and ages could comfortably enter, sit, drive and exit
- Working with engineers and suppliers going through the details of every component
- Interpreting regulatory department guidelines to design a car for markets across the world
- Understanding material constraints and manufacturing processes to optimise design for assembly
- Regular meetings with product planning and cost control
- Discussing how to future-proof the design with technology suppliers (in 1992 we were already aware of satellite navigation's potential but that technology wouldn't be ready for the car's 1997 launch)
- Managing a team of modellers to update the clay model, getting it ready to show to the board for approval, and for market research clinics
- Evaluating feedback and making changes if possible; otherwise, documenting for later updates

In day-to-day practice, design thinking is going to and fro, up and down in the spaces of the first and second diamond. Over time, as the project progresses, there is a shift from left to right as the boundaries of the first diamond become fully explored, while venturing into the second diamond, as shown in Figure 2.2. For me working like this felt familiar—like clinical practice. The coordination required for the Jaguar XK8—balancing user needs, technical constraints, regulatory requirements, cost targets, and stakeholder alignment—mirrors precisely what happens during complex ICU patient management or surgical planning. Clinicians are already expert design thinkers; they've simply never formalised this methodology for organisational transformation.

When the XK8 launched in 1996, the car was praised for blending heritage with modernity, featuring styling inspired by the classic E-Type while incorporating contemporary design and engineering. The interior was widely acclaimed for its luxurious and refined character. The success established our capability to manage complexities and deliver a great product.

Design Thinking the Toyota Way

After successfully designing and implementing an ISO 9001 accredited quality management system at Jaguar, I joined the Ford Product Development System (FPDS) team in the US representing the design function. We were tasked with developing a faster, better way to develop new cars and reduce costs. Cutting 'time to market' means we can better anticipate or react to trends and changing customers' needs. Our benchmark for time-to-market was Toyota—across the industry it was well known that Toyota could develop new quality cars faster than anybody else. Their recent Lexus brand successfully demonstrated Toyota's focus on customers' needs, with a clearly defined target audience and a host of features specifically aimed at those customers. The first Lexus, the LS400, was an instant success.

The way Toyota worked was no secret—the Toyota Production System (TPS)—was in the public domain. Taiichi Ohno is credited with developing TPS. His book *Toyota Production System* was published in 1988. *The Machine that Changed the World*, the book that studied the Toyota way and coined the term 'Lean,' came out in 1991. Ford had a minority share in and collaborated with Mazda in Japan. From Mazda we knew that TPS wasn't a Japanese 'thing' but specific to the way Toyota did things. In a quest to find out more, the FPDS team approached Toyota, cheekily asking if we could visit and look around. The answer? 'Sure, come on down—you can't copy us anyway.'

Although 'design thinking' was only recognised recently, the approach has been practised for decades in advanced industrial settings—most notably at Toyota, just not labelled as such. Taiichi Ohno was an engineer and executive at Toyota. His book shows that TPS was built on disciplined cycles of deep observation, problem framing, experimentation, and learning, which map closely onto divergent and convergent design-thinking stages [4]

Empathy is reflected in 'genchi genbutsu'—Ohno's insistence that leaders 'go and see' the reality of work before reaching conclusions, grounding decisions in lived experience rather than assumptions. The define phase aligns with Toyota's rigorous attention to clarifying the true problem, which Ohno argued must be surfaced through careful observation of variation, flow, and work conditions. Ideation corresponds to the search for better methods through continuous improvement ('kaizen'), where workers generate multiple possible countermeasures rather than seeking a single solution. The prototype and test phases echo Toyota's disciplined habit of running small, rapid experiments on the shop floor—using standardised work as a baseline to test new ideas safely and learn from deviations.

For Healthcare

Ohno's TPS reveals a profoundly human-centred, iterative, and learning-oriented approach—one that healthcare can adapt to redesign services by engaging staff in observation, problem framing, and structured experimentation directly where care is delivered.

However, a critical distinction matters: the aim of TPS is to reduce variation, to aim for standardisation to maximise efficiency. That makes sense in high-volume manufacturing. Variation in healthcare cannot be reduced—every patient is unique, every illness manifests differently, every community has distinct needs. Transferring TPS into healthcare without appreciating this fundamental difference will not work, as we shall explore in Chapter 12.

Tesla: Rethinking Systems from First Principles

Elon Musk's Tesla demonstrates another dimension of design thinking—the willingness to question fundamental assumptions about how systems should work. Where Christensen's theory explains disruption from below (serving underserved customers), Tesla attacked from above (premium products) but with the same first-principles thinking that characterises design methodology.

Traditional automotive companies converged on a tiered supplier model—Original Equipment Manufacturers (OEMs) orchestrating complex networks of component suppliers to distributors and dealers. Tesla took radical vertical integration, controlling everything from battery production to software development to direct sales. This wasn't arbitrary—it emerged from asking: what does the transition to electric vehicles actually require?

Tesla applied systems-level design thinking. Where most companies asked 'how do we make electric versions of existing cars?', Tesla asked 'if we were designing personal transportation from scratch, knowing what we know about battery technology, software, and user expectations, what would we create?' That reframing changed everything. Traditional automotive architecture, designed for internal combustion engines, couldn't support the unprecedented integration electric vehicles required. So Tesla designed the entire value chain—battery production, software development, direct sales—to enable what electric vehicles could be, not what internal combustion vehicles had been [5].

For healthcare, Tesla's approach demonstrates several principles. First, legacy architecture often prevents transformation—sometimes you cannot renovate, you should rebuild. Second, vertical integration enables coordination that distributed networks cannot achieve—but only when necessary for delivering fundamentally different value propositions. Third, treating software as an equal partner to hardware rather than an afterthought enables capabilities impossible otherwise.

But Tesla also demonstrates the risks of design thinking when detached from empathy and human-centredness. Musk's 'move fast and break things' approach works differently in healthcare than in automotive. You can beta-test self-driving software with wealthy early adopters who accept risk. You cannot beta-test care pathways with vulnerable patients who have no alternatives. Healthcare requires Tesla's boldness in questioning assumptions combined with clinical medicine's caution about unintended consequences.

The lesson isn't 'be like Tesla.' It's recognise when system-level redesign is necessary rather than component-level improvement, understand what vertical integration enables versus what distributed networks do better, and maintain human-centredness even when rethinking fundamentals.

Tesla's systems-level approach raises a critical question: when should healthcare pursue incremental improvement versus fundamental redesign? Clayton Christensen's disruptive innovation theory provides a framework for answering this question.

Disruptive Innovation: Where to Apply Design Thinking

Understanding where to apply design thinking in healthcare requires understanding Clayton Christensen's disruptive innovation theory. His Harvard research revealed predictable patterns: mainframe computer companies displaced by personal computing, transistor radios overtaking valve radios, Netflix replacing Blockbuster. These weren't random market failures—they followed consistent dynamics that healthcare can learn from.

Christensen distinguished sustaining innovations (improvements to existing products serving existing customers) from disruptive innovations, which operate by entirely different logic. In his book The Innovator's Dilemma, he described how good companies—those that listened carefully to their customers—were incrementally developing new features, when suddenly a newcomer would introduce technology that was not nearly as good, but because it was affordable to customers who previously could not afford the expensive product, it quickly gained market share [6].

The dynamics follow a predictable pattern shown in Figure 2.3. Incumbent companies focus on sustaining innovations to meet the needs of their most demanding customers, often overshooting the needs of average users. Meanwhile, disruptors enter the market—often at a small scale not seen by the incumbents—serving the least demanding customers with simpler, cheaper, or more accessible solutions. Initially, their performance is lower, but through continuous improvement, they eventually reach and surpass mainstream expectations, capturing the incumbents' customer

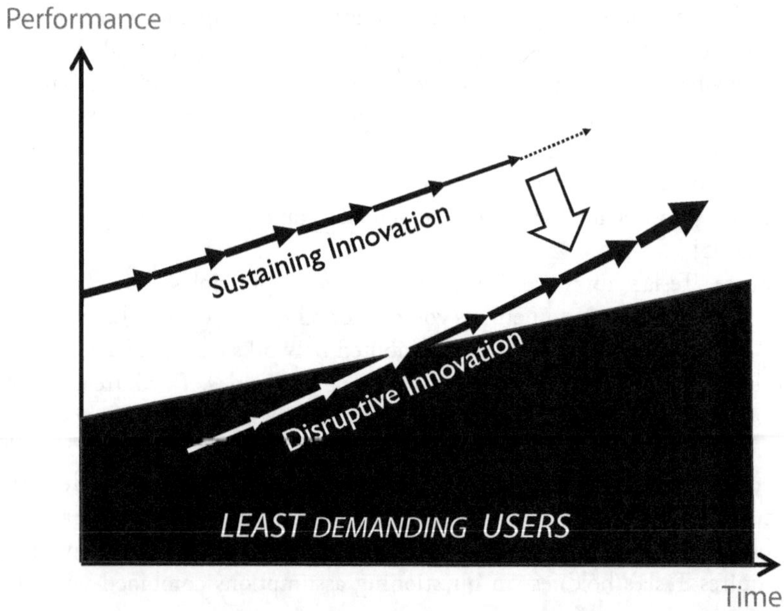

Figure 2.3 Dynamics of disruptive innovation (adapted from Christensen, 2003).

base. Christensen identified IBM as the only survivor of being disrupted. Now we can explain that this was largely due to keeping true to its North Star.

The Three Elements and Design Thinking

Christensen identified three essential elements for disruptive innovation to succeed. First, simplifying technology—making complex solutions more affordable and accessible. The Sony transistor radio exemplified this: inferior sound quality compared to valve radios, but portable and affordable for people who previously had no radio at all.

Second, a compatible value network—a new ecosystem of suppliers, distributors, and customers that supports the simplified offering. Disruptive innovations cannot rely on incumbent value networks because those networks optimise for sustaining innovations. New value networks emerge around the needs of previously excluded customers.

Third, business model innovation—new ways of generating and delivering value with fundamentally different cost structures than incumbents. The disruptor's business model makes profit at price points and volumes that incumbents find unattractive.

Integrating these three elements requires a structured methodology for understanding user needs, prototyping solutions, and building stakeholder alignment—which is exactly what design thinking provides. Without it, organisations simplify the wrong things, build value networks around assumptions rather than evidence, or create business models that look elegant on spreadsheets but fail in reality.

Design thinking's Discover phase identifies which features users genuinely value versus which represent unnecessary complexity. This requires ethnographic research—observing how people actually use (or work around) existing solutions, developing deep empathy with underserved populations who've never experienced alternatives.

The Define phase synthesises these insights into clear problem statements—determining what to strip away and what to preserve. Design thinking's divergent-convergent process helps navigate this trade-off through iteration and testing rather than guesswork.

The Develop phase is where co-design becomes essential for building value networks. When users participate in creating solutions, they become advocates, early adopters, and connectors to others with similar needs. The value network emerges organically from the design process itself.

The Deliver phase tests the integrated offering in real-world conditions, iterating based on feedback. This isn't a single launch but continuous refinement as the innovation moves from serving the most underserved toward mainstream markets.

Why This Matters for Healthcare

Disruptive innovation theory reveals where healthcare transformation should start: with populations currently underserved by the system. This isn't just equitable—it's strategic. Narayana Health in India achieved 75% cost reduction in cardiac surgery while maintaining world-class outcomes by applying process innovation to serve the poorest populations [7]. Community health centres, telemedicine for rural areas, simplified diagnostic tools for low-resource settings—these aren't inferior healthcare. They're different healthcare, designed through deep understanding of underserved users' actual needs and constraints.

Healthcare's transformation challenge isn't about making academic medical centres slightly better. It's fundamentally redesigning care delivery for the billions currently excluded or inadequately served—then improving those models until they can serve everyone. Design thinking provides the methodology. Disruptive innovation theory tells us where to aim it: at the margins, with the underserved, building new value networks that eventually transform the entire system.

This principle will recur throughout this book—in redesigning clinical trials for diverse populations (Chapter 6), ensuring AI advances equity rather than widening disparities (Chapter 7), and shifting from hospital-centred to patient-centred systems (Chapters 8–9).

COUNTERINTUITIVE FINDING

Healthcare Transformation Should Start with the Most Excluded

Narayana Health achieved a 75% reduction in the cost of cardiac surgery while maintaining world-class clinical outcomes—not by improving an elite academic medical centre, but by designing care from first principles for India's poorest populations. Christensen's research across multiple industries demonstrates why: underserved populations operate in what this book terms 'permissive governance states'—without the institutional defence responses, entrenched stakeholder networks, and defensive bureaucracies that make transformation so difficult in established systems. Healthcare leaders who focus transformation efforts on mature, well-resourced systems are not being ambitious—they are choosing the hardest possible starting point. The populations most urgently in need of better care also offer the most tractable environment in which to design it.

Cleveland Clinic: Design Thinking in Healthcare Practice

While the previous examples come from outside healthcare, Cleveland Clinic demonstrates design thinking principles applied within healthcare itself. When CEO Toby Cosgrove wanted to improve patient experience, he didn't implement superficial changes or hire consultants to run design thinking workshops. He fundamentally changed how leadership viewed patients and reorganised the institution around those new perspectives [8]. Crucially, Cosgrove brought clinical credibility to transformation. As a cardiac surgeon, he understood patient care from the inside, giving him legitimacy with physicians that non-clinical administrators lack. His clinical background wasn't incidental—it was essential to navigating the politics of reorganising around patient journeys rather than physician specialties.

The transformation began with reframing: patients became 'guests' in organisational language—not mere semantics but a signal that different standards applied. Healthcare institutions typically organise around physician specialties (cardiology, neurology, orthopaedics) optimising for provider convenience. Cleveland Clinic reorganised around patient conditions and journeys, creating institutes that brought together all specialties relevant to particular patient needs. This is design thinking's user-centred principle made structural—design the organisation around patient experience, not professional silos.

Crucially, Cosgrove empowered multidisciplinary teams with decision-making authority. Design thinking fails when 'empathy work' happens separately from decision-making power. Cleveland Clinic ensured that teams working directly with patients could redesign processes without bureaucratic approval chains that typically strangle innovation. This enabled rapid iteration—the test-and-learn approach that design thinking requires.

The physical environment embodied the cultural transformation. Cleveland Clinic invested in spaces that reduced patient anxiety rather than optimising for clinical efficiency alone. Lighting, acoustics, way-finding, waiting areas—all designed with patient experience as the primary consideration, clinical efficiency as a constraint to satisfy, not an objective to maximise.

Results demonstrated transformation's impact: up to 85% of patients would 'definitely recommend,' significant increases in market share, and enhanced reputation that attracted both patients and clinical talent [9]. More importantly, the approach proved sustainable. The changes didn't require heroic individual effort or charismatic leadership to maintain—they became embedded in organisational DNA.

For healthcare leaders, Cleveland Clinic demonstrates several critical principles. First, design thinking transformation requires leadership commitment to fundamentally rethink organisational structure, not merely optimise existing processes. Second, metrics should evolve—patient satisfaction became as important as clinical outcomes, because design thinking recognises that both matter. Third, physical environment shapes behaviour—investing in designed spaces isn't luxury but essential infrastructure for culture change. Fourth, empowerment without accountability fails, but accountability without empowerment frustrates—Cleveland Clinic balanced both.

The example also reveals design thinking's limitations within healthcare's constraints. Cleveland Clinic could reorganise around patient journeys because it's a large integrated system. Smaller independent providers face different constraints requiring different design approaches. This underscores a theme: design thinking provides methodology, but application must respect context.

What We Can Learn from Other Industries

In our exploration across companies and sectors, we notice remarkable similarities. When design thinking is embedded, organisations become and remain successful, able to fulfil the evolving needs of their users. IBM showed how it allowed them to pivot several times, each time transforming the company—not in HOW it operated (that remained consistent), but in WHAT it delivered.

Apple showed what happens when the North Star of users' needs is lost. Apple, IBM, Tesla, and Cleveland Clinic highlighted the role of leaders in embedding design thinking. These transformations succeeded because organisations:

- Invested equally in problem understanding and solution development
- Focused on a complete user experience rather than isolated features
- Fundamentally rethought systems rather than incrementally improving them
- Embedded design thinking as cultural DNA, not superficial process

This chapter has also demonstrated that while the Double Diamond provides a useful framework, the practice of design is more akin to a roller-coaster moving around those spaces—like the diagnostic and therapeutic practices that clinicians use. Design thinking effectively deals with the complexities of users' needs, stakeholders' requirements, internal and regulatory constraints—nothing else will. As healthcare leaders, it allows us to diagnose and repair by exploring questions such as:

- Do we capture the needs of our patients?
- Do we understand their constraints?
- Do we have sufficient capability to try out possible solutions?
- Do we give space to people to explore?
- Do we capture and learn from success and failure?

From Apple we learned to deeply prioritise user experience and align leadership, design, and operations in service of a coherent ecosystem. From IBM we learned that large organisations can transform, as long as they remain focused on users. The TPS case made clear that each organisation should find its own approach rather than copying others. Toyota showed that we need to understand our culture and let people find out for themselves what works before forcing implementation.

Most critically, these industries reveal what healthcare has missed: design thinking isn't decoration applied after decisions are made. It's the methodology for making better decisions in the first place. When clinicians diagnose patients, they already practise sophisticated design thinking—observe, hypothesise, test, iterate. The tragedy is that healthcare has never applied this same rigorous methodology to designing the systems within which that clinical care occurs.

The next chapter examines the hidden costs of that absence.

References

1. Isaacson, W. (2015) *Steve Jobs: The Exclusive Biography*. London: Little, Brown Book Group.
2. Denning, S. (2012) 'Clayton Christensen and the innovators' smackdown', *Forbes*. Available at: https://www.forbes.com/sites/stevedenning/2012/04/05/clayton-christensen-and-the-innovators-smackdown/.

3. IBM (n.d.) *AI and Enterprise Design Thinking*. Available at: https://www.ibm.com/think/topics/ai-and-enterprise-design-thinking.
4. Ohno, T. (1988) *Toyota Production System: Beyond Large-Scale Production*. Cambridge, MA: Taylor & Francis.
5. Isaacson, W. (2023) *Elon Musk*. New York: Simon & Schuster.
6. Christensen, C.M. (2003) *The Innovator's Dilemma*. New York: Harper Business Essentials.
7. Muralidhara, G.V. (2016) *Dr Devi Shetty of Narayana Hrudayalaya: Delivering Quality Cardiac Care to the Masses*. The Case Centre. Available at: https://www.thecasecentre.org/products/view?id=137186.
8. Cosgrove, D.M. (2014) *The Cleveland Clinic Way: Lessons in Excellence from One of the World's Leading Healthcare Organizations*. New York: McGraw-Hill Education.
9. Cleveland Clinic (2020) *State of the Clinic 2020*. Available at: https://my.clevelandclinic.org/-/scassets/files/org/about/who-we-are/state-of-the-clinic?la=en&la=en.

Chapter 3

The Hidden Costs of Bad Healthcare Design

THE ECONOMIST'S QUESTION

'So you're telling me healthcare wastes three-quarters of a trillion dollars annually, and you think the problem is… design?'

My colleague—a recently retired deputy chief economist from the UK Department of Trade and Industry—looked sceptical as we sat in his office at the University of Warwick surrounded by economic journals and policy papers. I'd come seeking his perspective on healthcare transformation, knowing his decades analysing market failures across sectors might illuminate patterns I was too close to see.

'Not just design failures,' I clarified. 'Economic failures disguised as design problems. Or perhaps more accurately, design failures that create systematic economic dysfunction.' He leaned back, intrigued. 'Go on.'

'Healthcare systems generate massive costs pushed onto patients, families, and frontline staff—that never appear on the balance sheets of those who create them. Stakeholders profit from complexity and opacity. Those making poor design decisions never experience the consequences. It seems a textbook case of market failure, except we keep pretending market forces will somehow fix it.'

He was quiet for a moment, then smiled. 'You know, in economics we say that if you want to understand a system's true priorities, don't listen to what people say—watch where the money flows and who bears the costs. If healthcare systems consistently generate harm worth a trillion dollars annually, that's not dysfunction. That's the system working exactly as it's designed to work, just not for patients.'

That conversation changed how I understood healthcare's resistance to transformation. This isn't about good intentions meeting implementation challenges. It's about economic structures that make bad design profitable for powerful stakeholders while externalising all costs onto those with the least power to refuse.

DOI: 10.4324/9781003752073-4

Understanding Healthcare's Economic Pathology

Healthcare has violated the fundamental conditions that make design thinking economically irresistible in other sectors. Understanding this violation explains why transformation initiatives systematically fail. Healthcare's economic pathology becomes visible once you apply this lens. This chapter examines healthcare's hidden costs through an economic lens, revealing why design failures persist despite overwhelming evidence of harm. More importantly, it demonstrates why design thinking—properly understood as economic intervention, not aesthetic exercise—represents healthcare's only viable path to sustainable transformation.

When Incentives Align: Design as Value Creation

Economics fundamentally studies human behaviour under conditions of scarcity and incentive. When I worked as a car designer at Jaguar, every design decision connected directly to value creation. The exterior design attracted potential customers into the showroom—creating initial value perception. The interior design closed the sale—delivering tangible value through every touch point. Every curve communicated aspiration. Every detail reinforced the purchase decision.

This wasn't aesthetics—it was economic value creation through understanding human behaviour. We knew customers weren't buying transportation; they were buying an experience, a statement, a carefully designed relationship between human and machine that justified premium pricing.

The return on investment was immediate and measurable. When Jaguar got design right, sales followed. When we misunderstood customer needs, the market punished us swiftly through declining revenues. This feedback loop drove continuous improvement through market discipline.

Consider British Airways' first-class problem: premium customers weren't purchasing their highest-margin product despite having the means to do so because they could no longer perceive the added value of first-class over their excellent business class. Rather than simply cutting prices or adding amenities, BA invested in ethnographic research. What they discovered surprised executives: premium customers didn't want more comfort—they wanted to sleep properly on long-haul flights and arrive refreshed for meetings. The unmet need was fundamentally economic: businesses would pay premium prices for anything protecting human capital and productivity.

BA commissioned the flat-bed seat design in 1995. Overnight, their first cabin filled again. The return on investment was dramatic—premium customers willingly paid significantly more for a design solution that actually met their needs. Market forces amplified success as every major airline eventually adopted similar designs [1].

These examples demonstrate how design thinking drives economic success when three conditions align.

- First, clear value creation: users receive tangible benefits they are willing to pay for.
- Second, incentive alignment: organisations profit when they deliver better user experiences.
- Third, market feedback: organisations face immediate consequences for design failures.

Design solves real problems that users experience. Revenue connects directly to value creation. Poor design reduces revenue, forcing correction.

When these conditions exist—as they do in automotive, aviation, and technology sectors—design thinking becomes economically irresistible. Organisations ignoring user needs fail.

Organisations that embrace design thinking prosper, as we have already seen in Chapter 2. Market discipline ensures continuous improvement.

When Incentives Diverge: Healthcare's Economic Pathology

Healthcare has systematically violated all three conditions, creating economic structures where poor design often proves more profitable than good design.

Value and cost are disconnected. Unlike Jaguar customers who paid more for better design, healthcare users rarely choose based on design quality. They choose based on insurance networks, physician referrals, or geographic proximity. Too many have no access or choice at all. Design quality—how easy the system is to navigate, how well processes serve patient needs—barely influences market share.

Incentive misalignment creates perverse economics. A pharmaceutical company's revenue doesn't decrease when patients struggle with complex medication regimens—complexity may increase revenue through additional prescriptions managing complications. Hospitals in fee-for-service systems profit from readmissions caused by poor discharge processes. Insurers save money when claims processes are opaque enough that patients abandon valid claims.

Consider the principal-agent problem: those making design decisions (administrators, IT vendors, management consultants) don't experience the consequences (patient confusion, clinician burnout, system inefficiency). Costs are externalised onto patients and frontline staff lacking power to refuse service or demand better design.

Medical device manufacturers profit from products difficult to use properly, requiring extensive training, consumables, and replacement parts. A device so well designed it rarely fails to represents lower recurring revenue. Healthcare advisors and IT vendors profit from complexity—the more fragmented the system, the more integration services can be sold.

Even well intentioned healthcare leaders face perverse incentives. An NHS trust chief executive who successfully reduces demand through prevention may face budget cuts for demonstrating lower capacity needs. A hospital administrator who improves efficiency and discharges patients faster may see beds closed and revenue reduced.

Market feedback fails completely. Healthcare users cannot refuse service when facing acute illness. They cannot comparison shop when unconscious. They cannot evaluate quality when information is deliberately obscured. Crucially, they don't bear the full cost—insurance, employers, and governments pay, breaking the connection between cost and value.

This creates 'deadweight loss'—resources consumed without creating corresponding value. Unlike typical market failures where deadweight loss is incidental, healthcare's structures actively generate it. The system isn't broken—it's working exactly as intended, just not for patients.

COUNTERINTUITIVE FINDING

Healthcare Waste Is Not Dysfunction—It Is Rational Design

The WHO estimates the social cost of patient harm at $1–2 trillion annually, the US Institute of Medicine identified $750 billion in annual waste representing roughly a third of US health spending, and the OECD calculates that 15% of hospital expenditure across member states goes on preventable harm—roughly one full working day per week devoted to cleaning up avoidable problems. Conventional framing treats these figures as evidence of a broken system. The economic analysis reveals something more troubling: this waste persists not despite the efforts of powerful stakeholders, but because of their rational self-interest. Hospitals in fee-for-service systems generate revenue from the readmissions that poor discharge design produces. Pharmaceutical complexity can increase prescription volumes. Administrative opacity allows insurers to reduce valid claims. Those who make the design decisions do not bear the consequences—patients and frontline clinicians do. This is not dysfunction. It is the system performing exactly as its economic structures were designed to ensure.

Quantifying the Deadweight Loss

Deadweight loss describes resources consumed without creating corresponding value—waste benefiting no one, representing pure economic inefficiency. Healthcare's design failures generate deadweight loss at a scale dwarfing most other market failures in modern economies.

Walk through any hospital and you'll witness resources being consumed without creating value: clinicians logging into five different systems to access information about a single patient (transaction costs multiplying with each interface). Families waiting hours for discharge paperwork that could have been prepared in advance (capacity utilisation failing while demand queues outside). At Boston Medical Center a 'nurse discharge advocate' supported patients in hospital with information and instructions for their medication, which was reviewed by a clinical pharmacist contacting patients after discharge. The result was a 30% reduction in Emergency Department visits and readmissions [2].

Patients arriving for procedures only to discover they weren't properly prepared because instructions were unclear (failed transactions requiring complete rework). Equipment sitting idle because nobody knows how to operate it properly (capital allocation failure). Meetings consuming hours to coordinate decisions that empowered frontline teams could make in minutes (governance drag multiplying with each hierarchical layer).

The cost of bad design is absorbed into systemic inefficiency, staff burnout, and patient harm, without explicitly attributing outcomes to lack of design thinking. When discharge processes fail, we discuss 'communication breakdowns' rather than examining why processes were designed to require perfect communication under time pressure. When patients don't follow treatment plans, we discuss 'non-compliance' rather than questioning why we designed regimens with such high implementation friction that adherence becomes heroic rather than routine.

This systematic failure to trace problems back to design roots means the same failures repeat endlessly, creating path dependency—where bad initial design decisions lock systems into inefficient patterns becoming progressively more difficult to change as complementary processes and investments accumulate.

The Global Waste Landscape

Take patient safety—healthcare's most sacred principle. The World Health Organisation (WHO) estimates that one to four in ten patients are harmed during healthcare delivery, and about half to 80% of this harm is preventable through better system design, communication, and processes [3].

Reading that statistic through an economic lens: up to 40% of patients harmed, with up to 80% of that harm representing pure deadweight loss—resources consumed to address problems that better design would have prevented entirely. This isn't the inevitable cost of treating complex illness. It's systematic market failure.

The WHO quantifies this economically: 'The social cost of patient harm can be valued at US$1 trillion to 2 trillion a year globally' [4]. That estimates deadweight loss from bad design at $500 billion to $1.6 trillion annually—roughly Spain's or Mexico's entire GDP being consumed every year without creating any health value whatsoever.

These failures aren't primarily clinical missteps by incompetent practitioners. They're predictable consequences of poorly designed workflows, governance structures, and digital systems that set clinicians up to fail. The opportunity cost is staggering: imagine redirecting even half of those wasted resources toward prevention, primary care, or addressing social determinants of health.

The OECD calculates that preventable patient harm consumes about 15% of hospital expenditure in member states [5]. That's not 15% spent on difficult cases or experimental treatments—it's 15% spent cleaning up preventable problems. Roughly one day per week of every hospital's activity is devoted to addressing deadweight loss.

For a typical NHS trust with a £500 million annual budget, that's £75 million per year spent on preventable harm. For the NHS as a whole, with its roughly £160 billion budget, that's £24 billion annually—enough to employ 400,000 additional nurses, build 40 new hospitals, or provide free social care to every elderly person in England.

The US Institute of Medicine's Anatomy of Waste

The US Institute of Medicine's landmark 2012 report 'Best Care at Lower Cost' estimated that $750 billion—nearly a third of annual US health spending in 2009—represented systematic waste creating zero health value [6]. The report broke this deadweight loss into categories revealing design failures at every level:

Unnecessary services ($210 billion): Defensive medicine driven by information asymmetry—physicians ordering tests to protect themselves rather than benefit patients. The absence of integrated care coordination creates redundant assessments. These aren't clinical decisions gone wrong—they're predictable outputs of systems designed with misaligned incentives.

Inefficiently delivered services ($130 billion): Poor coordination, duplication, fragmented care—the natural consequence of designing healthcare around institutional silos rather than patient journeys. This is the fragmentation tax—the premium we pay for systems optimising local efficiency while destroying overall effectiveness.

Excess administrative costs ($190 billion): Transaction costs created by designing payment systems around institutional revenue rather than patient outcomes. Every claim, every prior authorisation, every billing dispute represents pure deadweight loss—resources consumed to allocate resources rather than deliver care.

Prices that are too high ($105 billion): Market failure resulting from information asymmetry, monopolistic behaviour, and switching costs. When patients can't comparison shop and can't refuse service, normal market discipline fails completely.

Missed prevention opportunities ($55 billion): Systems designed for acute response rather than proactive health maintenance. The opportunity cost extends beyond immediate waste—every preventable condition progressing to crisis represents compounding inefficiency over time.

These weren't fringe findings. This was the Institute of Medicine—now the National Academy of Medicine—the most authoritative voice in American healthcare. Their conclusion should fundamentally reshape how we understand healthcare economics: the waste isn't in the margins, it's structural. It's designed in.

The UK's Unwarranted Variation

Lord Carter's review of NHS hospitals discovered £5 billion in annual waste—over 4% of the total budget—from unwarranted variation in staffing, procurement, and estates management [7]. When organisations make independent decisions without shared learning, they repeatedly solve the same problems at much higher aggregate cost than coordinated approaches would require.

Some trusts paid twice as much for identical supplies—pure deadweight loss from fragmented procurement. Some employed twice as many administrators for similar patient volumes. Some wasted enormous capacity through poor roster design—capital utilisation falling while demand went unmet.

The waste wasn't caused by incompetent managers. It was natural output of systems designed without transparency, without benchmarking mechanisms, without structures for sharing best practices.

These patterns transcend national systems. Whether in the market-driven US system or the centrally planned NHS, design failures create similar deadweight loss. This tells us that market failures and government failures often share common roots in misaligned incentives, information asymmetry, and governance structures optimising for wrong outcomes.

The Human Cost: Beyond Financial Accounting

In healthcare economics, we must expand understanding of cost beyond financial measures. The traditional value equation (value = function/cost) must account for quality of life as both function and cost component. A system that delivers technically successful surgery but leaves patients with preventable complications has high costs but low function. Poor healthcare design doesn't just waste money—it destroys human capital through preventable harm and suffering.

Economists measure health outcomes in Quality Adjusted Life Years (QALYs)—a metric attempting to capture both quantity and quality of life. Every patient harmed by poor design loses Quality-Adjusted Life Years (QALYs). Every family member providing care for preventable complications loses productivity and wellbeing. Every clinician witnessing preventable harm experiences moral injury compounding over careers. These human costs multiply through social networks in ways traditional accounting never captures.

When systems are designed around institutional convenience rather than patient needs, the human cost includes delayed recovery, unnecessary suffering, and lost productive years. These costs multiply through 'negative externalities'—harm imposed on parties who never agreed to bear the risk.

When Design Failures Cascade

Bad design in healthcare doesn't create simple inefficiency—it creates exponential waste through system-wide misalignment. A poorly designed discharge process affects not just hospitals and patients, but also primary care providers, specialists, pharmacists, family members, and insurers.

Each stakeholder must develop workarounds, creating additional transaction costs and potential failure points. Information asymmetry across these fragmented relationships means errors propagate rather than being caught and corrected.

Poor medication adherence alone costs healthcare systems billions globally—a classic case of design failure creating deadweight loss. The physician designing the regimen doesn't experience the implementation burden. The patient executing the regimen often lacks information to question the design. The result: treatments that are clinically optimal but practically impossible.

Consider the economic inefficiency: pharmaceutical companies invest billions developing effective drugs. Healthcare systems spend billions on diagnosis and prescription. Yet all that investment creates zero health value when design failures—complicated dosing schedules, unclear instructions, cost barriers, side effects patients weren't warned about—prevent patients from actually taking medications.

The marginal cost of better design would be tiny—simplified regimens, clear instructions, cost counselling, side effect management—compared to the value destruction from adherence failures. Yet the benefits accrue to patients and future healthcare costs while the investment must come from currently profitable but inefficient systems. Classic market failure from misaligned incentives.

The Workforce Crisis: Human Capital Destruction by Design

Studies by the American Medical Association estimate that physician burnout costs the US healthcare system around $4.6 billion annually in turnover and reduced productivity [8]. But this figure dramatically understates real cost, capturing only direct expenses while ignoring compounding effects that make workforce burnout perhaps healthcare's most expensive design failure. Burnout isn't an unavoidable side effect of medicine—it's the product of bad design creating unsustainable cognitive load, moral injury, and systematic erosion of professional agency. Every burnt-out clinician represents not just recruitment cost, but a design failure continuing to produce victims until underlying systems are fixed.

When I speak with clinicians globally, a consistent pattern emerges: efficiency initiatives designed to reduce costs have paradoxically increased workload while removing elements that made clinical work sustainable. Electronic health record systems designed to improve documentation have doubled administrative time for many clinicians. A physician who previously spent 16% of their time on paperwork now spends 28%, clicking through poorly designed interfaces that prioritise billing compliance over clinical utility. For nurses, their time spent on admin after the implementation of EHR more than doubled [9].

Standardised protocols designed to improve quality have removed clinical autonomy without accounting for the complexity and variability of real patients. Evidence-based guidelines become rigid mandates. Experienced clinical judgement gets overruled by algorithms that don't understand context. Efficiency targets designed to improve productivity have eliminated buffer capacity needed to manage unexpected complexity. Theatre lists scheduled to 100% capacity can't absorb emergency cases without forcing cancellations. Clinics that are fully booked with no gaps can't accommodate the elderly patient needing extra time or the complex case requiring thorough examination. This was confirmed by a 2007 study at the University of Virginia Hospital which found that when hospital occupancy reached 87% to 95%, it led to increased cancellations of elective cases due to lack of available inpatient or ICU beds [10].

These aren't isolated failures—they're predictable consequences of applying manufacturing logic to complex adaptive systems. Healthcare workers experience the worst of both worlds: rigid constraints of manufacturing efficiency combined with relentless demands of human care.

The Hidden Multiplication Factor

When experienced clinicians leave, decades of accumulated expertise vanishes. That specialist who can diagnose rare conditions from subtle signs, who knows which surgeon to call for complex cases, who mentors junior staff—their departure represents knowledge that took twenty years to develop and can't be replaced by hiring a brilliant new graduate.

Burnt-out clinicians make more errors. When working memory is consumed by stress and exhaustion, there's less capacity for complex clinical reasoning. The Institute of Medicine documented how system design failures—including workforce stress—contribute to 44,000–98,000 preventable US deaths annually [11].

Exhausted staff lack capacity for improvement initiatives. Organisations most needing transformation become least able to achieve it because their workforce is too depleted to engage. Bad design creates burnout, burnout reduces improvement capacity, reduced improvement capacity perpetuates bad design—a vicious cycle impossible to escape without external intervention.

As word spreads about unsustainable conditions, fewer people enter healthcare professions. Those who do increasingly choose roles away from direct patient care. The best graduates choose specialties offering more control over working conditions. Emergency medicine and general practice face severe recruitment challenges while dermatology remains oversubscribed.

Measuring the Return on Design Investment

The flip side is measuring design interventions as return on investment drivers. Metrics can be framed similarly to aerospace and automotive:

Clinical Outcomes and Safety: Errors associated with administering medication through IV pumps are reported to be 67%; ergonomic redesign has been shown to reduce error rates significantly [12, 13]. At Virginia Mason in Seattle, frontline clinicians led the redesign of medication administration processes, reducing medication errors by 73%—demonstrating that clinical expertise, when given organisational authority, produces both safety and efficiency gains [14]. This wasn't about training—it was about designing systems that make errors difficult rather than relying on perfect human performance under stress.

System Efficiency: When Buurtzorg in the Netherlands redesigned home care delivery around self-managing nursing teams, they achieved 3,200% growth with less than 12% overhead increase [15]. Traditional organisations expanding at similar rates saw overhead costs increase 40–60%. Buurtzorg's nurse turnover rates are 33% lower than traditional organisations [16]—translating to approximately $3,500 in savings per nurse annually (assuming baseline turnover of 20% and replacement cost = $53,000).

Patient Experience: Organisations such as Buurtzorg that establish self-managing teams report 15–25% improvements in patient satisfaction. Kaiser Permanente achieved 23% better chronic disease management outcomes compared to US averages, with 89% preventive care target achievement versus 67% industry average [17]. Kaiser's integrated governance structure, where clinical and financial decision-making are coordinated rather than competing, has sustained performance improvements over 15+ years despite 280% membership growth.

Workforce Wellbeing: Good design will result in lower staff turnover and sick leave. Burnout indicators such as the Stanford WellMD Index or Maslach Burnout Inventory (MBI) can be adapted as design-outcome measures.

Financial Impact: Organisations that implement design thinking can expect direct cost savings. Comparative cost-benefit studies in other industries show, for example, £1 in design yields £4 in savings (similar to UK Design Council's 'Design Value' studies).

These examples demonstrate what is possible when design thinking is applied. But understanding why such interventions remain rare requires examining the stakeholder dynamics that prevent their adoption.

The Stakeholder Misalignment Problem

In sectors with value chains where stakeholders are all aligned toward customers' needs, quality issues typically affect discrete products or services with contained costs. In healthcare's fragmented system, design problems multiply across complex stakeholder networks, with each additional stakeholder relationship increasing transaction costs geometrically.

Table 3.1 reveals why healthcare systems are fundamentally broken. Unlike sectors such as automotive where all stakeholders align toward customer value, healthcare's economic incentives create fragmented systems where many powerful stakeholders profit more from patient illness than health. This misalignment is the root cause of healthcare's hidden costs—stakeholders optimising for their economic drivers rather than patient outcomes creates exponential waste.

This explains why defensive mechanisms stakeholders develop to protect interests interfere with each other. What starts as legitimate protective behaviour evolves into systematic resistance to innovation and collaboration. The result: delayed diagnoses, redundant testing, poor care coordination, and extended treatment pathways. Each inefficiency compounds because stakeholders lack aligned incentives driving efficiency in other sectors.

Private Finance Initiatives: The Cost of Misalignment

Private Finance Initiatives (PFI) demonstrate the cost of misalignment most starkly. PFI are promoted by politicians to get new hospitals built as a quick fix by committing vast amounts in future payments to consortiums of large corporations for construction, facilities, and medical devices. The NHS is committed to pay £80 billion per year to private companies by 2050 [18]. Capital projects that could have been funded at government borrowing rates (2–3%) were instead financed at commercial rates (8–12%), locking the NHS into decades of payments dwarfing original investment.

The Economic Case for Design Investment

My economist colleague's question—'you think the problem is design?'—misunderstood the fundamental insight. The problem isn't design. The problem is that healthcare's economic structures

Table 3.1 The Economic Drivers and Alignment of Healthcare Stakeholders

Stakeholder	*Primary Economic Drivers*	*Alignment with Patient Outcomes*
Patients/Families	Health restoration; quality of life; financial protection	Perfect alignment—driven by need
Physicians (Value-Based)	Efficient outcomes; patient satisfaction; practice viability	Strong alignment—success tied to patient health
Physicians (Fee-for-Service)	Volume of procedures; billable visits; avoiding malpractice	Poor alignment—profits from illness persistence
Hospital Systems	Bed occupancy; procedure volume; complex case payments; avoiding penalties	Poor alignment—profits from high-acuity illness
Pharmaceutical Companies	Drug sales volume; patent protection; formulary positioning	Weak alignment—profits from treatment, not prevention
Medical Device Manufacturers	Unit sales; replacement cycles; disposables revenue	Weak alignment—profits from device use, not patient improvement
Health Insurers (Private)	Premium growth; claims minimisation; risk pool management	Poor alignment—profits from denying/delaying claims
Health Insurers (Public)	Budget compliance; political viability; coverage expansion	Moderate alignment—constrained by political cycles
Regulators	Safety compliance; political cover; stakeholder appeasement	Moderate alignment—focused on preventing harm rather than promoting health
Policymakers	Electoral success; stakeholder appeasement; budget control	Weak alignment—short-term political cycles vs long-term health outcomes
Academic Research Institutions	Grant funding; publication metrics; intellectual property	Moderate alignment—research may benefit patients but focused on academic success
Medical Education Institutions	Tuition revenue; accreditation compliance; employment rates	Moderate alignment—training providers but not directly incentivised for patient outcomes

(*Continued*)

Table 3.1 Continued

Stakeholder	*Primary Economic Drivers*	*Alignment with Patient Outcomes*
Pharmacy Benefit Managers	Rebate extraction; spread pricing; formulary control	Poor alignment—profits from drug cost complexity, not transparency
Healthcare Investors	Financial returns; portfolio growth; exit strategies	Poor alignment—profits from system inefficiencies and high margins
Public Health Organisations	Budget justification; population metrics; programme continuation	Strong alignment—mission-driven for population health outcomes
SDOH Organisations	Funding sustainability; measurable social impact; community engagement	Strong alignment—address root causes of poor health
Charity Foundations	Demonstrable impact; donor satisfaction; administrative efficiency	Strong alignment—mission-driven for patient benefit
Philanthropic Donors	Impact visibility; tax benefits; personal satisfaction	Strong alignment—motivated by improving patient outcomes

systematically prevent good design while rewarding bad design. Traditional economics assumes markets naturally optimise toward efficiency through competition and price signals. But healthcare violates virtually every assumption required for market efficiency: information asymmetry prevents informed choice, inability to refuse service eliminates bargaining power, misaligned incentives reward volume over value, externalised costs break feedback loops, path dependency locks in inefficient patterns, and network effects amplify rather than correct failures.

Design thinking, properly understood, is economic intervention creating conditions for value-based competition that healthcare's current structures prevent.

What This Means for Your Organisation Today

The structural vulnerabilities creating these costs haven't been addressed—they've been normalised. Efficiency-optimised systems remain fragile, with just-in-time supply chains, minimal surge capacity, and workflows that prioritise throughput over resilience. The question facing healthcare leaders isn't whether to invest in design thinking—it's whether you can afford not to. Every day that passes with badly designed systems multiplies costs across three dimensions:

Financial: The deadweight loss compounds. Systems optimised for yesterday's priorities become increasingly misaligned with tomorrow's needs, creating switching costs growing exponentially with delay.

Human: Patient harm continues. Workforce burnout accelerates. The best clinicians leave or retreat from leadership roles. Human capital erosion becomes self-reinforcing as the people who could lead improvement lack the capacity to do so.

Strategic: Organisations that embrace design thinking create better outcomes at lower costs, fundamentally shifting stakeholder expectations about what healthcare can deliver. The competitive disadvantage for laggards compounds over time as network effects favour early adopters.

From Recognition to Action

For decades, thoughtful observers have recognised that Western healthcare systems are fundamentally unsustainable. In 2011, Don Berwick offered his stark assessment: 'We have set up a delivery system that is fragmented, unsafe, not patient-centred, full of waste and unreliable... we built it wrong.'

Yet when Dr Matthias Wismar, of the European Observatory on Health Systems and Policies, addressed European Health Managers in 2022—over a decade later—he outlined virtually identical recommendations [19]. Despite recognition and countless reform initiatives, meaningful transformation remained elusive.

This pattern reveals healthcare's economic reality: the costs of bad design aren't just financial—they're structural. Market forces that drive improvement in other sectors fail in healthcare because the economic preconditions don't exist. Design thinking investment represents not aesthetic improvement but market creation—building the feedback loops, aligned incentives, and information flows that allow value-based competition to function.

The Opportunity Window

The opportunity cost of delay is staggering. Every year healthcare systems waste $500 billion to $1.6 trillion through preventable harm. Every year physician burnout costs $4.6 billion in direct turnover alone. Poor medication adherence costs an estimated $100–300 billion annually in the United States alone [20]. These aren't inevitable costs of healthcare delivery—they're the price of market failure that design thinking interventions can address.

The opportunity requires not just investment capital but also human capital—clinicians who recognise that their diagnostic expertise applies to system design and are willing to accept organisational authority to redesign the structures they're forced to work within (see Chapter 5).

Organisations that act now capture first-mover advantages while laggards face mounting switching costs. The capital allocation decision is clear: invest in design transformation today, or pay exponentially higher costs for forced transformation tomorrow when system failure becomes catastrophic rather than chronic.

References

1. 'A Photographic History of British Airways First Class' (2019) *London Air Travel*, 23 August. Available at: https://londonairtravel.com/2019/08/23/british-airways-100-years-first-class/.
2. Jack, B.W. et al. (2009) 'A reengineered hospital discharge program to decrease rehospitalization', *Annals of Internal Medicine*, 150(3), pp. 178–187. https://doi.org/10.7326/0003-4819-150-3-200902030-00007.
3. *Patient Safety* (2023). Available at: https://www.who.int/news-room/fact-sheets/detail/patient-safety.

4. World Health Organization (2021) *Global Patient Safety Action Plan 2021–2030: Towards Eliminating Avoidable Harm in Health Care*, 1st edn. Geneva: World Health Organization.
5. Slawomirski, L., Auraaen, A. and Klazinga, N. (2018) *The Economics of Patient Safety in Primary and Ambulatory Care: Flying Blind*. OECD Health Working Papers 106. https://doi.org/10.1787/baf425ad-en.
6. Smith, M.D. and Institute of Medicine (U.S.) (eds.) (2013) *Best Care at Lower Cost: The Path to Continuously Learning Health Care in America*. Washington, DC: National Academies Press.
7. Lord Carter of Coles (2016) *Operational Productivity and Performance in English NHS Acute Hospitals: Unwarranted Variations*. Department of Health. Available at: https://assets.publishing.service.gov.uk/media/5a80bdfae5274a2e87dbb8f5/Operational_productivity_A.pdf.
8. Han, S. et al. (2019) 'Estimating the attributable cost of physician burnout in the United States', *Annals of Internal Medicine*, 170(11), pp. 784–790. https://doi.org/10.7326/M18-1422.
9. Baumann, L.A., Baker, J. and Elshaug, A.G. (2018) 'The impact of electronic health record systems on clinical documentation times: A systematic review', *Health Policy (Amsterdam, Netherlands)*, 122(8), pp. 827–836. https://doi.org/10.1016/j.healthpol.2018.05.014.
10. McGowan, J.E. et al. (2007) 'Operating room efficiency and hospital capacity: Factors affecting operating room use during maximum hospital census', *Journal of the American College of Surgeons*, 204(5), pp. 865–871. https://doi.org/10.1016/j.jamcollsurg.2007.01.052.
11. Linda, T. Kohn et al. (eds.) (2000) *To Err Is Human: Building a Safer Health System*. Washington, DC: National Academies Press, p. 9728. https://doi.org/10.17226/9728.
12. Husch, M. et al. (2005) 'Insights from the sharp end of intravenous medication errors: Implications for infusion pump technology', *BMJ Quality & Safety*, 14(2), pp. 80–86. https://doi.org/10.1136/qshc.2004.011957.
13. Garmer, K. et al. (2000) 'Usability evaluation of a new user interface for an infusion pump developed with a human factors approach', *Proceedings of the Human Factors and Ergonomics Society Annual Meeting*, 44(1), pp. 128–131. https://doi.org/10.1177/154193120004400134.
14. Ching, J.M. et al. (2013) 'Using lean to improve medication administration safety: In search of the "perfect dose"', *Joint Commission Journal on Quality and Patient Safety*, 39(5), pp. 195–204. https://doi.org/10.1016/s1553-7250(13)39026-6.
15. Gray, B., Sarnak, D. and Burgers, J. (2015) *Home Care by Self-Governing Nursing Teams: The Netherlands' Buurtzorg Model*. https://doi.org/10.26099/6CES-Q139.
16. Ethan Bernstein and Tatiana Sandino (no date) *Buurtzorg - Supplement - Faculty & Research - Harvard Business School*. Available at: https://www.buurtzorg.com/wp-content/uploads/2022/11/Buurtzorg-Case-Final.pdf?utm_source=chatgpt.com (Accessed: 6 December 2025).
17. McCarthy, D. and Mueller, K. (2009) *Kaiser Permanente: Bridging the Quality Divide with Integrated Practice, Group Accountability, and Health Information Technology*. Available at: https://www.commonwealthfund.org/publications/case-study/2009/jun/kaiser-permanente-bridging-quality-divide-integrated-practice (Accessed: 25 August 2025).
18. Campbell, D. (ed.) (2019) 'NHS hospital trusts to pay out further £55bn under PFI scheme', *The Guardian*, 11 September. Available at: https://www.theguardian.com/politics/2019/sep/12/nhs-hospital-trusts-to-pay-out-further-55bn-under-pfi-scheme (Accessed: 4 December 2025).
19. *Dr Matthias Wismar at EHMA 2022 Plenary Session on 'Implementing the Lessons Learnt from COVID-19'* (2022). Available at: https://www.youtube.com/watch?v=3RQ7Uv9qzYU (Accessed: 4 December 2025).
20. Iuga, A.O. and McGuire, M.J. (2014) 'Adherence and health care costs', *Risk Management and Healthcare Policy*, 7, pp. 35–44. https://doi.org/10.2147/RMHP.S19801.

II

DESIGN THINKING FUNDAMENTALS FOR HEALTHCARE

Chapter 4

Design Thinking Principles and Methods

WHEN $500,000 PROBLEMS BECOME $200 MILLION SOLUTIONS

A leading pharmaceutical company had a problem. Protocol amendments—changes to clinical trial designs after they'd started—were costing $500,000 each and adding months to timelines. They were haemorrhaging money and missing market windows. The natural response? Fix the amendment process. Make it faster, more efficient. But something made them pause. Instead of treating amendments as isolated events, they did something unusual. They mapped the entire amendment ecosystem—not just where amendments happened, but why. What they discovered changed everything. Sixty per cent of amendments stemmed from disconnects between scientific objectives and operational realities. The problem wasn't the amendment process itself. The problem was that they hadn't spent enough time understanding the problem before designing the solution. They'd skipped the first diamond.

By implementing cross-functional protocol review workshops—bringing together scientists, operations, and patient advocates before finalising protocols—they reduced amendments by 40% in their oncology portfolio. Not 40% faster amendments. Forty per cent fewer amendments needed.

The investment: several weeks of workshops in the design phase.

The savings: millions of dollars and months of time in the delivery phase.

This scenario, based on data from pharmaceutical protocol amendment studies [1] demonstrates why you need a navigation system.

DOI: 10.4324/9781003752073-6

Introduction: Your Navigation System for Healthcare Transformation

Healthcare has users and stakeholders with specific needs and requirements. We've established that design thinking principles apply. This chapter provides the methods, tools, and techniques—when and how to apply them in healthcare. It's more technical than other chapters, with lists and tables serving as reference material. Rather than listing 40 design thinking tools, this chapter shows exactly which tool to use, when to use it, and where to apply it in your organisation.

You're about to embark on a transformation journey. Like any complex journey, you need two things: a map showing where you are and where you're going, and a compass showing which direction you are facing. This chapter provides both. The UK Design Council's Double Diamond gives you the map—the four phases every transformation travels through. My InterQB-it™ framework gives you the compass—showing where in your organisation each method applies. Together, they create a navigation system. Not just 'here are 40 design thinking tools,' but exactly which tool to use, when to use it, and where to apply it in your organisation. Let's start with the map, then add the compass, then show you how to navigate.

The Map: The Double Diamond Framework

The Problem with Healthcare Transformation

Healthcare transformation typically follows what I call 'over the wall engineering' from my automotive days [2]. A sequential process that starts with executives developing a strategic plan and then throws it over the wall to operations. Operations designs processes and throws them over the wall to IT. They build systems and throw them over the wall to clinicians. Nobody talks to patients until the very end—if at all.

This linear, waterfall approach looks great on paper—everybody is clear about what needs to be done. In practice, it fails in healthcare for the same reason it failed in automotive: complex systems require iteration, not prediction.

The Double Diamond: A Better Way

Chapter 1 presented the UK Design Council's Double Diamond framework (see Figure 1.3). That addresses transformation through four phases:

DISCOVER → DEFINE → DEVELOP → DELIVER

Here's the critical insight: the diamonds are the same size for a reason. We must spend equal effort understanding the problem (first diamond: Discover + Define) as solving it (second diamond: Develop + Deliver).

I learned this in automotive. Insufficient time in the first diamond means solving the wrong problem brilliantly—then spending multiples of that saved time fixing it later. Healthcare demonstrates this pattern repeatedly. Clinical trials sit in the second diamond (Develop). The pharmaceutical industry's 10,000:1 compound-to-approval ratio [3] suggests inadequate first diamond work—they haven't spent enough time understanding who suffers from the disease, where they are, and what they require. The protocol amendment example from our opening vignette proves this: investing weeks in Discovery workshops saved millions in Delivery. Equal diamonds isn't theory—it's economics.

Why Diamond Shape Matters

Chapter 1 introduced the Double Diamond's divergent-convergent rhythm. Here we focus on application: which specific tools enable divergence and convergence at each phase, and where in your organisation to deploy them. The framework establishes when and where—now we map the how.

The Four Phases Explained

DISCOVER: Explore patients' and community's needs and challenges
Seeing the system as patients and clinicians actually experience it, not as it appears in organisational charts or strategic documents. Metaphorically 'walking in their shoes' to develop empathy.

Core activities:

- User research and stakeholder analysis
- Market exploration to understand needs
- Ethnographic observation
- Stakeholder mapping
- Data gathering from multiple sources

Healthcare Application: When OnKai was developing AI tools for underserved communities, we didn't start with technology. We started by understanding those communities, talking to mid wives, understanding their workflows, observing their constraints. We created 'Amber,' a persona representing a typical community midwife, and made decisions by asking: 'What would help Amber care for her patients better?'

DEFINE: Synthesise insights into clear problem statements
Transforming observations and insights into actionable problem statements. It's about synthesis, constraint identification, and criteria setting.

Core activities:

- Setting criteria based on user needs
- Capturing stakeholders' requirements
- Identifying constraints (regulatory, safety, resource)
- Creating problem statements

Healthcare Application: In clinical trials for rural Uganda—a capacity-building project I'm designing—this means moving from 'we need more diverse participants' to 'community midwives and patients lack transportation to centralised trial sites, childcare during visits, and trust in outside researchers.' Now you have something you can design for.

DEVELOP: Ideation, concept development, prototyping, validation

Creating solutions through rapid cycles of prototyping and testing.

Core activities:

- Brainstorming solutions
- Building prototypes (rough representations)
- Testing with real users
- Iterating based on feedback

Healthcare Application: Virginia Mason Medical Center applied Toyota Production System principles through rapid prototyping. Rather than planning a perfect redesign, they iteratively tested changes in 1–2 week cycles. Results: 85% reduction in patient walking distance, 50% reduction in nurse time hunting for supplies. The transformation succeeded through rapid prototyping, not perfect upfront design (see Key Develop Tools Highlighted below for details).

DELIVER: Solution implementation, continuous iteration based on feedback
Continuous improvement based on real-world performance.

Core activities:

- Implementation planning
- Change management
- Measurement systems
- Ongoing refinement

Healthcare Application: When deploying new care pathways, successful organisations don't just implement—they establish feedback mechanisms, track metrics, and adjust based on what they learn. The pathway at month 12 looks different from month 1, because they've learned from actual use.

The Compass: The InterQB-it™ Framework

Why Healthcare Needs a Multi-Dimensional Framework

Healthcare transformation doesn't happen in a vacuum. When we implement a new care pathway, we're not just changing clinical procedures—we're affecting organisational strategies, operational processes, enabling resources, and the people who deliver care. And you're doing this at multiple organisational levels simultaneously: the specific clinical service (Product), the shared infrastructure supporting multiple services (Platform), the institutional reputation and service lines (Brand), and the whole organisation (Business).

This is why healthcare needs a multi-dimensional framework. Clinical leaders already think multi-dimensionally. When managing septic shock, you simultaneously address specific organ failures (Product/Service), use shared systems (Platform), department protocols and reputation (Brand), and resource constraints (Business). InterQB-it simply makes this clinical reasoning explicit for organisational transformation.

The Four Factors (what needs to change):

- **Strategies**: The decisions and direction-setting activities at multiple levels (organisational strategy, service line strategy, care pathway strategy)
- **Processes**: The workflows and operational procedures that span departments (clinical workflows, administrative processes, support services)
- **Enablers**: The resources, technology, and infrastructure throughout the system (IT systems, facilities, equipment)
- **People** across the organisation (executives, clinicians, administrators, patients)

The term 'people' in this framework refers to the ones internal to healthcare organisations, not to patients—they are covered in 'drivers' and 'outcomes'.

The Four Levels (where change happens):

- **Business**: The entire organisation and its sustainability
- **Brand**: Institutional reputation and major service lines (how the organisation is perceived externally,
- **Platform**: Shared infrastructure serving multiple services like operating theatres, EHRs, care pathways
- **Product/Service**: Specific clinical services delivered to patients

This creates a 4 × 4 grid showing 16 areas where transformation affects your organisation simultaneously.

Understanding the organisational level matters more than terminology itself. Healthcare entities—charitable, governmental, or commercial—require 'Business' discipline: sustainability, strategic decisions, resource allocation, governance.

In automotive manufacturing, a platform is the shared chassis and core systems (like the Volkswagen MQB) upon which multiple different car models are built, enabling one factory to produce seemingly different products efficiently. A 'Platform' is the shared infrastructure that enables multiple products or services.

Consider an operating theatre suite. It's not a product that patients 'buy'—it's a platform that supports multiple surgical specialties and activities (elective and emergency interventions). Orthopaedics, general surgery, gynaecology, and neurosurgery all use the same OR platform, sharing:

- Physical space and equipment
- Clinical support staff (anaesthesia, nursing)
- Scheduling systems and protocols
- Quality and safety infrastructure
- Supply chain and sterilisation

When we redesign an operating theatre platform, we affect every speciality that depends on it. This is why platform-level changes require different stakeholder engagement than product-level changes.

'Product' and 'service' are interchangeable in design thinking. A hospital bed is a product (schedule-able asset) from the hospital's perspective, a service (temporary accommodation) from the patient's. Context determines terminology.

Drivers and Outcomes: The External Forces and Internal Results

Healthcare organisations don't operate in isolation. They're simultaneously subject to external drivers they cannot control and accountable for outcomes they must deliver.

A WARNING ABOUT SIMPLISTIC FRAMEWORKS

Before introducing the InterQB-it™ driver framework, we must address why existing environmental scanning tools fail healthcare transformation. Porter's Five Forces and PESTLE analysis create dangerous false security. These frameworks don't just provide incomplete analysis—they actively harm organisations by systematically directing attention away from critical drivers that will later destroy transformation initiatives.

Porter's Five Forces (Competitive rivalry, Supplier power, Buyer power, Threat of substitutes, Threat of new entrants) focuses exclusively on competitive market positioning. For healthcare, this is incomplete:

- Ignores legislation and regulation (determines what you can offer, how you deliver it)
- Ignores evidence base (clinical research drives what works)
- Ignores patient needs as distinct from 'buyer power' (patients rarely have market power)
- Ignores unions (can veto changes through industrial action)
- Treats healthcare like widget manufacturing (patients don't shop for emergency appendectomies)

PESTLE (Political, Economic, Social, Technological, Legal, Environmental) adds breadth but remains incomplete:

- Misses Patient needs as distinct category (central to healthcare)
- Misses Evidence base (clinical research drives change independently)
- Misses Unions (powerful stakeholder)
- Generic across all sectors (designed for manufacturing, retail, finance—doesn't capture healthcare-specific realities)

The real danger is that organisations using Porter or PESTLE document 'thorough environmental analysis,' then get blindsided by union resistance, new clinical evidence, or patient advocacy opposition—factors systematically ignored by these frameworks. I've watched transformation projects fail repeatedly because teams used these frameworks, checked the 'environmental scan' box, then expressed shock when initiatives collapsed due to ignored factors. The millions wasted could have been prevented with comprehensive analysis from the start. Healthcare requires healthcare-specific frameworks.

The InterQB-it™ Driver Framework

Drivers are the external factors that impact organisations but remain largely outside their control. I learned to use comprehensive environmental scanning in automotive, where missing a single regulatory requirement in one market could kill a multi-million pound programme. Healthcare's environment is more complex—which is precisely why systematic frameworks matter more, not less. The InterQB-it™ framework identifies 13 Healthcare Transformation Drivers organised into four categories. Unlike Porter's market-centric view or PESTLE's generic checklist, these drivers capture what actually determines transformation success or failure in healthcare.

Interestingly, these drivers are common across all organisational levels—whether we're working at the Product, Platform, Brand, or Business level, we face the same external pressures. But they create level-specific outcome demands that require coordinated responses across the organisation.

The 13 InterQB-it™ Drivers:
Governance and Power:

- **Politics**: Policy changes, political priorities, electoral cycles, government mandates, ministerial direction
- **Legislation and Regulations**: Legal requirements, compliance obligations, regulatory approvals, safety standards, licensing
- **Media and Public Opinion**: Press coverage, social media campaigns, patient safety scandals, public exposés, viral patient stories, investigative journalism
- **Unions**: Professional bodies, collective bargaining, workforce resistance, industrial action, professional standards enforcement

Market and Economics:

- **Economics**: Funding models, reimbursement systems, budget constraints, cost pressures, financial sustainability requirements, investment availability, payment mechanisms
- **Competition**: Other providers, market share, patient choice, performance league tables, reputation comparisons, provider rivalry for resources and reputation
- **Supply and Distribution Chain**: Care pathway architecture across delivery levels (primary → secondary → tertiary → quaternary care), referral systems and gatekeeping, service integration mechanisms, physical supply logistics (pharmaceuticals, devices, blood products), information flow between providers, workforce distribution across care levels
- **Healthcare System Dynamics**: System governance structures (centralised like NHS England, federal like Germany, regional like Spain/Italy), single-payer vs multi-payer vs insurance-based models, national vs regional vs local decision-making authority and control, system-level accountability frameworks, whether competition exists or is mandated/prevented

Knowledge and Society:

- **Evidence Base**: Clinical research, medical advances, treatment protocols, NICE guidance, best practice evolution, safety alerts
- **Patient Needs**: Health conditions, access barriers, preferences, expectations, social determinants of health (SDOH)
- **Socio-Cultural Factors**: Trust in institutions, equity expectations, demographic changes, cultural attitudes to healthcare, health literacy

Environment and Technology:

- **Environment**: Physical infrastructure, geographic access, climate impacts, facilities condition, estate management
- **Technology**: Medical devices, digital health, AI, data systems, telemedicine capabilities, EHR platforms

This framework ensures systematic attention to factors that typically destroy transformation initiatives when ignored. Supply chain constraints alone have killed countless transformation initiatives—hospital-at-home programmes that failed because pharmaceutical delivery wasn't established, integrated care systems that collapsed because referral pathways weren't redesigned, innovations that died because care pathway architecture remained hospital-centric. Specific contexts may reveal additional drivers beyond these 13. The framework's value lies in systematic attention to multiple factors, not claiming exhaustive completeness.

Outcomes are the results organisations must achieve at each level. Unlike drivers, outcomes are specific to each organisational level:

- **Business**: Value creation and—if applicable—profits ensuring organisational sustainability
- **Brand**: Wellbeing and loyalty building institutional reputation
- **Platform**: Efficiency enabling multiple services to operate effectively
- **Product/Service**: Excellent care and quality of life for patients

This creates a fundamental dynamic tension: common external pressures produce level-specific internal demands. A single legislative change simultaneously demands financial sustainability (Business), reputation management (Brand), operational efficiency (Platform), and quality maintenance (Product).

Figure 4.1 shows a diagram with in the centre the 4 × 4 grid of factors and levels, with drivers to the left and outcomes to the right of the grid.

InterQB-it™ was developed as a generic framework through decades of consulting practice across automotive, manufacturing, and healthcare sectors. It helps you to navigate this complexity

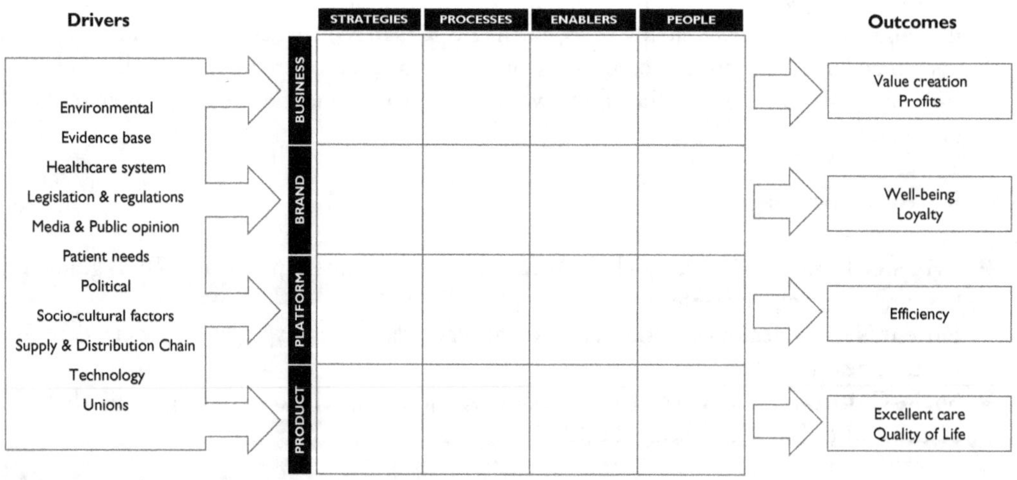

Figure 4.1 The InterQB-it™ framework applied to healthcare.

by making these dynamics visible and manageable. It is versatile—the boxes in the 4 × 4 grid in Figure 4.1 are left empty and can be used for several useful purposes such as positioning attributes.

Consider managing a cardiac arrest patient. You're simultaneously thinking about: specific arrhythmia (Product/Process), available equipment and drugs (Product/Enablers), team roles and communication (Product/People), while considering departmental protocols (Platform/Process) and institutional reporting requirements (Brand/Strategies). Table 4.1 shows similar multi-factor thinking applies to organisational transformation. It provides a list of organisational attributes sorted by level and factor. This can help to create a common understanding in and communications across organisations.

Why This Matters for Your Transformation Work

Understanding this multi-dimensional reality changes how we approach transformation. For example, when new evidence emerges, imagine new research demonstrating that a common surgical procedure has better outcomes when performed in specialised centres rather than general hospitals. This single external driver (evidence base) creates simultaneous demands for different outcomes at each level:

- Business level: Must decide whether to invest in becoming a specialised centre (sustainability/value)
- Brand level: Consider the impact on reputations of becoming a referring hospital. Must manage reputation—are we maintaining quality standards? (wellbeing/loyalty)
- Platform level: Must reorganise OR scheduling and support services (efficiency)
- Product level: Must retrain surgeons and adjust clinical protocols (excellent care/quality of life)

Table 4.1 Example Attributes at Each Level and Factor

Level/Factor	*Strategies*	*Processes*	*Enablers*	*People*
Business	Vision, mission, portfolio decisions	Governance, risk management	Financial systems, data analytics	Board, executive leadership
Brand	Market positioning, service line strategy	Patient journey across services	Brand identity, reputation management	Values, culture champions
Platform	Pathway optimisation, resource allocation	Shared workflows, handoff protocols	EHR, OR suite, lab infrastructure	Multidisciplinary teams
Product/ Service	Clinical service design, care model	Care pathway, clinical protocols	Medical equipment, supplies	Clinical staff, competencies

Note: These are illustrative examples. Each organisation will have different specific attributes depending on context.

The InterQB-it™ framework helps you see these interconnected demands systematically rather than reacting to each as an isolated crisis.

For transformation leaders without clinical backgrounds—when external drivers change—new regulations, emerging evidence, technology breakthroughs—you need to orchestrate responses across all four levels simultaneously. The framework helps you:

- Map where changes are required (which cells in the grid)
- Coordinate teams working at different levels
- Ensure product-level excellence doesn't compromise platform efficiency
- Balance brand reputation with business sustainability

For clinical leader with deep expertise—your clinical work already operates in this multi-dimensional reality—you just haven't had a framework to articulate it. When you redesign a clinical protocol (Product/Processes), you're simultaneously considering:

- Evidence base and regulations (external drivers)
- Resource availability (Platform/Enablers)
- Staff capability (Product/People)
- Departmental reputation (Brand outcomes)
- Patient quality of life (Product outcomes)

The framework validates what you already know: excellent clinical care requires systematic attention to organisational context, not just clinical evidence.

The Complete Navigation System: Combining Both Frameworks

Now we can see how the two frameworks work together:

Double Diamond (horizontal axis) tells you **WHEN** to apply methods:

- Discover: When exploring needs and gathering insights
- Define: When synthesising into clear problem statements
- Develop: When creating and testing solutions
- Deliver: When implementing and improving

InterQB-it™ (vertical axis) tells you **WHERE** to apply methods:

- Which organisational level (Business/Brand/Platform/Product)
- Which organisational factor (Strategies/Processes/Enablers/People)
- Which external drivers are influencing this cell
- Which outcomes must this cell deliver

Together, they create a two-dimensional map for transformation. Miss any dimension and your transformation fails—not because the idea was bad, but because you didn't think systematically. Before mapping specific tools to the framework, we need to understand why healthcare transformation requires co-design methods rather than traditional market research. The Kano Model explains this critical distinction.

Why Healthcare Transformation Requires Co-Design: The Kano Model

The Feature Nobody Knew They Needed

In the mid-1980s, Ford introduced Anti-lock Braking System (ABS) on the Scorpio. Did customers flood showrooms demanding 'safe maximum-force braking without losing control'? No. They didn't know to ask for it—they had no frame of reference for such a capability. Within five years, those same customers walked into competitors' showrooms asking specifically: 'Does this car have ABS?' Today, if your new car lacks ABS, you'd demand a refund. You shouldn't have to specify it—it's expected as standard.

The same feature travelled from unimaginable to expected in 20 years.

This pattern—which I observed throughout my career in automotive design at Jaguar and have taught in lectures for 25 years—explains why traditional market research systematically fails to reveal transformative healthcare innovations.

The Kano Model, developed by Professor Noriaki Kano in the 1980s (coincidentally around the time Ford introduced ABS), provides the theoretical framework for understanding this phenomenon [4].

Understanding the Three Categories

Imagine a relationship between feature implementation and user satisfaction. Some features create satisfaction that increases linearly (more is always better). Others create satisfaction that curves upward dramatically (presence delights, absence doesn't disappoint). Still others only prevent dissatisfaction (presence is expected, absence is noticed).

The Kano Model categorises features into three types based on their relationship to user satisfaction and users' ability to articulate them (Table 4.2):

Critical Insight: Features migrate from Excitement → Performance → Basic over time. Yesterday's innovations become tomorrow's minimum standards.

Why Traditional Market Research Fails for Transformation

Basic features work like hospital cleanliness: patients notice when it's missing (extreme dissatisfaction), but perfect cleanliness only brings them to neutral ('as expected'). No patient says 'the hospital was so clean I'm delighted!'

Performance features work like wait times: satisfaction increases linearly with improvement. Patients can articulate this need directly: 'I want shorter waits.' Traditional market research excels here—surveys, focus groups, and benchmarking reveal these needs clearly.

Excitement features work like patient portals before they existed: when absent, satisfaction stayed neutral (patients didn't miss what they couldn't imagine); when introduced, satisfaction soared. If you'd asked in 2008 'Would you like to see test results on your smartphone?' patients would have said 'Why? My doctor calls me.' They lacked the frame of reference to articulate the need.

This is why transformation initiatives fail when they rely solely on traditional market research. Surveys and focus groups reveal Basic and Performance features excellently—but systematically miss Excitement features that create transformative value.

Table 4.2 User Satisfaction in Relation to Type of Feature with Examples

Feature Type	*Can Users Articulate?*	*Users' Perception If Absent*	*Users' Perception If Present*	*How to Discover*	*Automotive Example*	*Healthcare Example*
Excitement/ Delight (New Innovation)	No (lacks frame of reference)	Neutral (doesn't miss it)	Disproportionate delight	Co-design, ethnography, prototyping	ABS (1985): 'Nobody knew to ask for safe maximum braking'	Patient portals (2008): 'Patients couldn't imagine online records access'
Performance/ Linear (Competitive Feature)	Yes (wants it, compares options)	Proportional dissatisfaction	Proportional satisfaction	Focus groups, competitive analysis, surveys	ABS (1995): 'Does this car have ABS?'	Telehealth (2018): 'Which practices offer video visits?'
Basic/Must-Have (Expected Standard)	Yes (when missing)	Extreme dissatisfaction, demands refund	Neutral ('as expected')	Complaint systems, minimum standards	ABS (2025): 'You'd return a car without ABS'	E-prescribing (2025): 'Paper prescriptions feel antiquated'

Healthcare's Feature Evolution

Healthcare innovations follow the same trajectory as ABS:

Patient Portals:

- 2008: Excitement feature (patients couldn't ask for 'secure online access to my medical records'—they had no frame of reference)
- 2015: Performance feature (patients asked 'Does your practice have a patient portal?')
- 2023: Basic feature (patients expect it; practices without portals lose patients)

Telehealth Consultations:

- 2015: Excitement feature (most patients couldn't imagine 'video appointment with my doctor')
- 2020 (pandemic): Rapid acceleration through Performance
- 2025: Basic feature (patients demand virtual options; in-person only is seen as outdated)

Electronic Prescribing:

- 2000: Excitement feature (novel convenience)
- 2010: Performance feature (patients compared pharmacies on this capability)
- 2020: Basic feature (paper prescriptions feel antiquated)

This evolution creates a critical challenge for transformation leaders: yesterday's Excitement features become today's Basic expectations. The ABS that delighted customers in 1985 would cause refund demands in 2025.

The Co-Design Imperative

This is why healthcare transformation requires co-design methods rather than traditional market research:

Traditional Research (for Basic/Performance features):

- Surveys: 'Rate your satisfaction with X'
- Focus groups: 'What would improve X?'
- Interviews: 'What problems do you experience with X?'
- Works when users have a frame of reference

Co-Design Methods (for Excitement features):

- Ethnographic observation: See unarticulated needs through behaviour
- Patient journey mapping: Identify pain points users have normalised
- Personas: Model needs across diverse populations
- Prototyping and testing: Let users experience possibilities
- Works when users have no frame of reference

The pharmaceutical protocol amendment example from the opening vignette demonstrates this perfectly. Traditional research would have asked: 'How satisfied are you with the amendment process?' (Performance feature). Co-design revealed: '60% of amendments stem from disconnects between scientific objectives and operational realities' (systemic issue users couldn't articulate because they'd normalised it).

A Critical Healthcare Misunderstanding: 'Do No Harm'

The Kano Model exposes something that has frustrated me throughout my career: the way 'first, do no harm' (*primum non nocere*) is presented as aspirational achievement rather than minimum standard. This is a fundamental category error. In Kano terms, 'do no harm' is a Basic/Must-Have feature. Patients come to healthcare to improve their quality of life through pain reduction, functional restoration, symptom relief (Performance features) and preventive interventions that enhance wellbeing (Excitement features). When healthcare organisations celebrate 'do no harm' as achievement, they reveal profound misunderstanding of patient expectations. Not harming people is the absolute baseline—it's where healthcare should start, not where it aims to finish.

The measurement problem this creates:
Healthcare quality metrics often focus on Basic features (absence of harm): hospital-acquired infection rates, medication errors, falls prevention, adverse event tracking. These are essential to monitor, but they measure whether healthcare met minimum standards, not whether it created value. True quality metrics should measure improvement in patients' quality of life, not just avoidance of damage.

If your organisation treats 'zero adverse events' as the primary success metric, you're measuring Basic features while ignoring Performance and Excitement features that actually drive patient outcomes. This explains the disconnect between administrative celebration of safety metrics and clinical frustration. Avoiding harm is necessary but insufficient—excellence means improving lives, not just preventing damage.

COUNTERINTUITIVE FINDING

'First Do No Harm' Is Healthcare's Minimum Standard, Not Its Goal

Professor Noriaki Kano's quality model distinguishes between features whose absence causes acute dissatisfaction but whose presence only returns users to neutral (Basic/Must-Have), and features that create proportional improvement (Performance) or disproportionate delight (Excitement). 'Do no harm'—*primum non nocere*—maps precisely to the Basic category: patients are profoundly harmed when it is violated, but its fulfilment simply means healthcare has met its minimum obligation. When organisations treat zero adverse events as a primary quality achievement, they are measuring whether they avoided the floor—not whether they created any value above it. This explains a persistent disconnect that senior clinicians experience daily: administrators celebrate safety metrics that represent the absence of catastrophic failure while patients and clinicians know that avoiding harm is necessary but emphatically not sufficient for good care. Quality of life improvement, symptom relief, and functional restoration—the outcomes patients actually come for—are Performance and Excitement features that most healthcare quality frameworks barely measure.

Kano Implications for the Double Diamond

This is why the Double Diamond framework emphasises equal effort in the Problem diamond (Discover + Define):

If you skip thorough Discovery:

- You only find Basic/Performance features (articulable needs)
- You miss Excitement features (transformative opportunities)
- You optimise the current system rather than transform it

If you invest in Discovery through co-design:

- You observe what users cannot articulate
- You identify systemic patterns users have normalised
- You discover transformative opportunities

This explains why patient satisfaction surveys tell you to reduce wait times (Performance) but never reveal opportunities like community-based care models (Excitement). Patients can't ask for what they haven't experienced.

Also, it validates our frustration with 'evidence-based' changes that optimise current pathways (Performance) while missing opportunities to redesign care delivery fundamentally (Excitement). Patients can tell you the current pathway is slow; they can't design the better pathway—that requires clinical expertise applied through co-design.

Applying Kano to Method Selection

When selecting design methods from the framework tables that follow, consider:

For Basic/Performance improvements (optimising current services):

- Traditional stakeholder surveys work fine
- Focus groups can articulate needs
- Benchmarking against competitors reveals gaps
- Faster, cheaper, more convenient versions of existing services

For Excitement/Transformation (creating new possibilities):

- Ethnographic research to observe unarticulated needs
- Co-design workshops to explore possibilities
- Rapid prototyping to make abstract concepts tangible
- Patient journey mapping to identify normalised pain points
- Fundamentally different approaches to care delivery

Most healthcare 'transformation' initiatives focus on Basic/Performance features because traditional research tools reveal these. True transformation requires co-design methods that reveal Excitement features—the innovations users cannot articulate because they lack a frame of reference. The InterQB-it™ framework helps you identify where Excitement features might hide: often at Platform or Business levels where system-level redesign creates possibilities invisible at the Product level.

Design Thinking Tools Mapped to the Framework

The following tables map specific tools to each phase of the Double Diamond and each cell of the InterQB-it™ framework. Use Kano principles to determine which tools reveal which feature types at each framework cell.

How to Use These Tables on First Reading

- Don't read every cell sequentially
- Start with your current pain point (e.g., 'struggling with stakeholder engagement' → look at People column)
- Identify your organisational level (e.g., working on clinical pathway → Product row)
- Find intersection cell for relevant tools
- Skim other cells to understand system connections
- Return to these tables as reference throughout your transformation journey

For Clinical Leaders: You use these tools daily. Patient history-taking IS ethnographic research. Differential diagnosis IS problem statement development. Treatment protocol refinement IS rapid prototyping. The following tables translate clinical methodology to organisational language.

How to Read These Tables

- **Rows**: Organisational levels (Business/Brand/Platform/Product)
- **Columns**: What you're changing (Strategies/Processes/Enablers/People)
- **Cell Contents**: Specific tools for that combination
- **Phase Context**: Each table represents one Double Diamond phase

Not every cell requires attention in every project. Your transformation might focus on Platform/Processes or Product/People. The framework shows what's possible and helps to identify gaps. Use these tables to:

- Identify where your challenge sits (which cells)
- Select appropriate tools for those cells
- Coordinate teams working on different cells
- Ensure critical stakeholders aren't missed

Start where the pain is. Expand systematically as you discover interdependencies.

DISCOVER Phase Tools

Remember: Discovery uses co-design methods for Excitement features (unarticulated needs) and traditional research for Performance features (articulable needs). If users can't imagine the solution, ethnography and observation reveal more than surveys.

Environmental Scanning (Strategies row, all levels): Use all 13 InterQB-it™ Drivers (not Porter's Five Forces or PESTLE) to ensure comprehensive analysis across Governance and Power, Market and Economics, Knowledge and Society, and Environment and Technology.

Table 4.3 Tools for Discover Phase Tools to Explore Patients' and Community's Needs, Challenges, and Opportunities

Level	*Strategies*	*Processes*	*Enablers*	*People*
Business	Environmental scanning, strategic stakeholder mapping	Healthcare system analysis, value chain mapping	Data analytics infrastructure, population health data	Executive engagement, board alignment workshops
Brand	Service line positioning analysis, competitive landscape assessment	Patient journey mapping across service lines	Brand perception surveys, market research tools	Focus groups with patients and referrers
Platform	Pathway gap analysis, capacity utilisation studies	Cross-service process mapping, bottleneck identification	Technology assessment, infrastructure audit	Multidisciplinary team workshops
Product/ Service	Patient needs assessment, ethnographic research	Clinical pathway observation, time-motion studies	Equipment and technology inventory	Personas, patient shadowing, staff interviews

Ethnographic Research (People row, all levels): 'Walking in patients' shoes by getting out into the community and observing and talking to them.' This requires actually being there—in community clinics, in patients' homes, in waiting rooms—not reading reports.

A cardiothoracic surgeon colleague saved a patient's life through emergency open-heart massage after cardiac arrest, opening fresh surgical stitches to perform a heroic intervention. Weeks later, the Chief Executive called him in. He expected recognition. Instead, he received a reprimand: the patient had complained that his chest tattoo was no longer aligned and wanted corrective surgery.

The surgeon had saved the man's life. The patient was upset about his tattoo. Both were right. The surgeon correctly prioritised survival. The patient correctly valued his identity and self-image. But without discovery methods that reveal what matters to individual patients—ethnographic research, patient shadowing, journey mapping—we design solutions based on clinical assumptions that miss what patients actually need.

This is why Discovery phase tools matter. You cannot guess patient priorities. You must discover them.

Stakeholder Mapping (Business/Strategies and People): Maps all actors, their relationships (remember: 8 stakeholders = 28 relationships), their power, and their interests. Essential for understanding governance complexity.

Patient Journey Mapping (Product/Processes): 'Asks people what currently works for them, what does not work, and what they would like to change'. This tool makes visible the invisible—the handoffs, the waiting, the workarounds, the emotional experience.

Personas (Product/People): Patient profiles that help make decisions. OnKai's 'Amber' persona—a fictional midwife in Cincinnati—guided critical design decisions. When evaluating features, we asked: 'Does this help Amber care for her patients?'

Data Visualisation (Product/Enablers): Use publicly available data to understand disease burden, demographics, social determinants of health. OnKai used this to map where patients with specific diseases live relative to clinical trial sites and free clinics.

Literature Reviews: Evidence base, best practices, regulatory requirements

DEFINE Phase Tools

Critical Principle: Co-design involves all stakeholders in the Problem diamond before solutions are designed. This means bringing together patients, clinicians, administrators, and support staff during Define, not just consulting them after solutions are proposed.

Table 4.4 Tools for Define Phase to Synthesise Insights into Clear Problem Statements

Level	*Strategies*	*Processes*	*Enablers*	*People*
Business	Three Horizons plus (3H+) framework, strategic vision statements	Business case development, impact assessment	Resource allocation planning, investment criteria	Executive alignment sessions, board approval processes
Brand	Value proposition definition, positioning statements	Service delivery model specification	Brand standards, communication protocols	Patient advisory councils, community engagement
Platform	Platform strategy definition, interoperability requirements	Shared workflow standards, handoff protocols	Shared resource specifications, technology standards	Multi-specialty governance structures
Product/ Service	Design brief development, scope definition	Service specification (like clinical protocols), patient pathway definition	Equipment and resource requirements	Co-design workshops

Cross-Cutting Definition Tools

- **Problem Statements**: Clear, actionable, measurable—not 'improve care' but 'reduce appointment wait time from 6 weeks to 2 weeks for new diabetes patients in postcode X, Y, Z'
- **Success Criteria**: How we'll know it worked, established before solutions developed
- **Constraint Mapping**: Regulatory, safety, time, and resource boundaries integrated into the design brief from the start
- **Root Cause Analysis**: Why problems exist, not just what they are
- **Co-Design Workshops** (Spans Multiple Cells, Particularly People Row): Based on common sense, involve all stakeholders before solutions are designed. Stakeholders include local healthcare professionals, community leaders, and patient advocacy groups. Their involvement continues throughout.

Key Define Tools Highlighted

Three Horizons Plus (3H+) (Business/Strategies): Extended visioning framework developed at EHFF that adds stakeholder mapping and gap analysis to traditional Three Horizons. It will be covered in detail in Chapter 16. It shows the current system (H1), desired future (H3), and critical transition space (H2)—plus who is active in that transition space and what gaps remain.

Design Brief Development (Product/Strategies): Clear, actionable problem statements that define success criteria. Not 'improve patient experience' but 'reduce time from symptom onset to diagnosis for rural patients by 40% while maintaining diagnostic accuracy >95%'.

DEVELOP Phase Tools

Cross-Cutting Development Tools

- **Rapid Prototyping** (Particularly Product Level): Build-measure-learn cycles—create something quickly, test with real users, refine based on evidence. Not full implementations, rough representations that are good enough to learn from. In automotive, we used concurrent engineering and rapid prototyping to reduce time to market. Healthcare should do the same
- **Iterative Testing** (All Levels): Test-learn-refine cycles. The pharmaceutical company that reduced protocol amendments by 40% did this: they prototyped cross-functional review workshops, tested them, learned what worked, refined the approach, then scaled
- **Patient Co-Design Sessions** (Product/People and Platform/People): Tools for co-design include ethnography, which helps understand cultural dimensions, and patient journey mapping. Patients and stakeholders are involved throughout, not just at the end
- **A/B Testing**: Compare alternatives with real users to see what actually works
- **Pilot Programs** (All Levels): Small-scale implementations designed for learning, not proving. The mindset shift: pilots aren't demonstrations—they're experiments. You expect to learn what doesn't work
- **Failure Analysis**: What didn't work and why—treat failures as learning opportunities
- **Safety Testing**: Risk mitigation before scale-up, especially critical in healthcare

Table 4.5 Tools for Develop Phase to Create and Test Solutions through Iteration

Level	*Strategies*	*Processes*	*Enablers*	*People*
Business	Strategic scenario planning, business model prototyping	Pilot program design, phased implementation planning	Financial modelling, risk assessment tools	Change leadership development, sponsor engagement
Brand	Service concept testing, brand experience prototyping	Patient communication testing, referral pathway pilots	Marketing materials drafting, feedback mechanisms	Brand ambassador programs, patient testimonials
Platform	Infrastructure configuration options, capacity modeling	Workflow simulation, process testing cycles	Technology pilots, integration testing	Cross-functional team collaboration, conflict resolution
Product/ Service	Service delivery prototypes, rapid prototyping	Iterative testing: test-learn-refine cycles, simulation/ role-play to test workflows	Prototype equipment, temporary resources	Patient co-design sessions maintaining continuous involvement, staff training pilots

- **Simulation and Role-Play** (Process Row): Before implementing new workflows, simulate them. Gather the team, walk through the process, identify problems on paper before they become problems with patients.

Example: Virginia Mason Medical Center in Seattle applied Toyota Production System principles through rapid prototyping. Rather than planning the perfect redesign, they iteratively tested changes: reconfiguring patient flow patterns, relocating supply storage, adjusting staff workflows. Each prototype was tested for 1–2 weeks, measured, refined. Results: 85% reduction in patient walking distance during hospital stays, 50% reduction in nurse time hunting for supplies, measurable improvements in patient safety metrics [5]. The transformation succeeded not because they designed the perfect solution upfront, but because they prototyped rapidly, learned quickly, and adapted continuously.

DELIVER Phase Tools

Cross-Cutting Delivery Tools

- **Implementation Roadmap** (Strategies, All Levels): Phased deployment plan. The 90-day framework in Chapter 10 provides a template: Phase 1 (days 1–30) foundation, Phase 2 (days 31–60) method integration, Phase 3 (days 61–90) scaling.

Table 4.6 Tools for Deliver Phase to Implement, Measure, and Continuously Improve

Level	*Strategies*	*Processes*	*Enablers*	*People*
Business	Implementation roadmap with 90-day phased deployment, performance dashboards	Governance structure implementation, accountability frameworks	Investment release, resource deployment	Executive communication, organisational alignment
Brand	Launch planning, external communication strategy	Referral pathway activation, market development	Marketing campaign execution, PR management	Staff ambassador programs, patient stories
Platform	Platform rollout coordination, service integration	Standard operating procedures, quality protocols	Technology deployment, infrastructure activation	Multi-service training, shared governance activation
Product/ Service	Service launch, scale-up planning	Clinical protocol implementation, pathway activation	Equipment procurement, resource allocation	Staff training and competency assessment, patient education

- **Change Management** (People Row, All Levels): Stakeholder engagement, communication, training. The transformation that ignores change management fails even when the technical solution is perfect.
- **Measurement Systems** (Strategies Row): Objective metrics established upfront. Not 'staff satisfaction' or 'cost per procedure'—those are too easily gamed. Use metrics that directly measure patient/clinical benefit, are objective and measurable, have baseline data, and cannot be easily gamed or reinterpreted.
- **Continuous Improvement** (All Levels): This is where healthcare often fails. Implementation isn't the end—it's the beginning of learning. Establish feedback loops, track metrics, adjust based on performance. The pathway at month 12 should look different from month 1.
- **Documentation** (All Levels): Capture lessons learnt, update procedures, share knowledge across organisation

Integrating healthcare constraints in Delivery:

- Regulatory compliance monitoring and reporting (not an afterthought)
- Patient safety incident tracking and response (zero harm is baseline, not goal)
- Clinical governance oversight and audit
- Financial performance against business case

CRITICAL: Measure Improvement, Not Just Absence of Harm

Healthcare often conflates Basic features (preventing harm) with Performance/Excitement features (improving quality of life). In Kano terms:

- **Basic (Must-Have):** No hospital-acquired infections, no medication errors, no falls—these are minimum standards, not achievements
- **Performance:** Pain reduction, functional improvement, symptom relief—these create satisfaction proportional to improvement
- **Excitement:** Restored capabilities beyond expectation, preventive interventions that avoid disease entirely

Metrics must measure improvement in quality of life, not just absence of harm. 'Zero adverse events' is the starting point, not the destination.

Example for objective metrics (for a novel anaesthetic device):

✓ Reduction in anaesthetic gas exposure measured by theatre air monitoring
✓ Theatre staff absence rates related to pregnancy
✓ Compliance with health and safety guidelines
✗ Staff satisfaction (too subjective, easily reinterpreted)
✗ Cost per procedure (system can add overhead costs to inflate)

Get these metrics formally documented in project charter, board presentation, or funding approval. Make them part of the official record. Once metrics are formally documented, the system has a harder time declaring success as failure or moving goalposts mid-implementation.

Example Integrated Navigation

Reducing Emergency Department Wait Times

1. Identify Phase and Level (Double Diamond + InterQB-it™):
   Phase: Currently in Define (synthesising Discovery insights)
   Primary level: Platform/Processes (ED serves multiple specialties)
   Secondary level: Product/People (individual patient care delivery)
2. Apply Kano to Understand Feature Type:
   Wait time reduction = Performance feature (patients can articulate: 'I want shorter waits')
   But Discovery revealed an exciting opportunity: patients didn't know to ask for 'real-time wait time visibility on mobile app'
3. Select Appropriate Methods (from Tables):
   Performance improvement (wait times): Process mapping, bottleneck analysis (traditional methods work)
   Excitement feature (mobile app): Rapid prototyping, A/B testing with real users (co-design required)
4. Navigate Across Levels:
   Platform/Processes: Redesign triage workflow
   Platform/Enablers: Implement queue management technology
   Product/People: Train staff on new protocols
   Brand: External communication about improvements

This single transformation required coordinating across four organisational levels, two feature types, and both diamonds. The frameworks made these connections visible rather than managing them reactively.

Adapting Design Methods for Healthcare Constraints

The Three Critical Constraints

Healthcare operates under constraints that other industries don't face. We cannot ignore these—we must design with them from the start.

1. **Regulatory Requirements**

The problem: many healthcare innovations treat regulatory compliance as an afterthought—design the solution, then try to navigate approval. This creates expensive delays and often requires fundamental redesign when regulatory requirements conflict with core assumptions.

The solution: integrate regulatory requirements into the design brief from day one, just as the automotive industry does.

During my time in automotive design, the regulatory department provided combined requirements from all markets (Europe, US, Japan) at project initiation. We didn't design a car and then check if it met regulations—we designed to regulatory requirements from the start. This wasn't a constraint; it was clarity.

Healthcare application:

- Discover: Establish regulatory advisory group including compliance officers, quality managers, and regulatory experts
- Define: Build regulatory requirements into design brief and success criteria
- Develop: Test regulatory compliance during prototyping, not afterwards
- Deliver: Include compliance reporting in implementation metrics

Regulation isn't the enemy of innovation. Regulatory requirements are predictable and straightforward. The challenge isn't regulatory uncertainty—it's cost and time. Developing a new drug costs approximately $2.6 billion over 10–15 years [6]; a medical device costs $31–94 million over 3–7 years [7]. The difference isn't regulatory stringency—it's that automotive manufacturers integrate regulatory requirements into the design process from the start, while pharmaceutical companies often treat them as checkpoints to pass.

2. **Patient Safety**

The problem: innovation inherently creates risk. In healthcare, risk means potential patient harm, which is ethically and legally unacceptable. This creates tension between innovation (requires experimentation) and safety (requires proven approaches).

The solution: layer safety into every phase of the Double Diamond, not as a barrier to innovation but as a design requirement.

Healthcare application:

- Discover: Include patient safety officers in stakeholder mapping, document existing incidents and near misses, establish safety baselines
- Define: Build safety requirements into design brief (what constitutes acceptable risk?)
- Develop: Use simulation and role-play for high-risk changes before live implementation; involve safety officers in prototype testing

- Deliver: Establish safety monitoring systems, clear escalation protocols, rapid response to incidents

3. **Time Pressures**

The problem: healthcare operates under constant urgency. Patients are waiting. Budgets are overrunning. Boards want results. The pressure to 'just implement something' overwhelms disciplined discovery and definition.

The solution: maintain Double Diamond discipline. Time invested in the first diamond saves multiples in the second.

Clinical trial evidence demonstrates this: 55% face enrolment difficulties, 51% suffer protocol complexity, 46% struggle with regulatory compliance [8]. These are Discovery and Definition failures that surface during Develop and Deliver.

As the opening vignette demonstrated, investment in the first diamond saves multiples in the second. When boards pressure you to skip Discovery, reference the opening vignette: weeks of workshops prevented millions in amendments. As clinicians know, rushing to treatment before diagnosis leads to wrong interventions and longer resolution. Organisational transformation follows identical logic.

Building Confidence: Starting Your Journey

Design thinking provides a systematic methodology for transformation. However, it isn't a magic wand that instantly transforms healthcare—it's existing clinical expertise applied systematically to organisational problems. Over 25 years teaching design thinking, I've learned that confidence comes not from mastering new skills but from recognising sophisticated capabilities you already possess and applying them systematically. Clinicians already practise sophisticated design methodology. Transformation leaders already understand organisational complexity. Building confidence means recognising what you already know and extending it to new contexts.

Key principle is that design methods, tools, and technologies that work in one situation or organisation may not work in another. It requires practical experience in order to develop the right design approach. This means we can't just copy someone else's transformation playbook. We need to:

- Understand the principles (Double Diamond + InterQB-it™)
- Select appropriate tools for your context (use the tables)
- Try them, learn what works, adapt
- Build confidence through small successes
- Expand systematically to larger challenges

Where to Start

For transformation leader orchestrating across organisation:

- When initiatives cluster in one or two cells, systemic connections remain invisible. Mapping current work to the grid reveals gaps and interdependencies.
- Pick one cell to master: Don't transform everything. Select high-impact cell (Product/People for clinical pathways, Platform/Processes for patient flow). Master the appropriate tools.

- Use the framework to coordinate: Different teams often work on connected cells unknowingly. Platform/Enablers (new EHR), Product/Processes (clinical pathways), Brand/People (patient experience)—all affecting each other. Make connections visible.
- Track coverage, not activity: Measure by grid coverage, not initiative count. Are you addressing business sustainability AND product quality? Strategies AND people?

For clinical leader with deep expertise:

- Recognise what you already do: Clinical practice maps to the Double Diamond phases. You use design thinking methodology dozens of times daily in diagnosis and treatment. This formalises intuitive knowledge.
- Expand from Product to Platform: Start with Product/Service level in your specialty. Then trace Platform connections. How does your clinical pathway depend on shared infrastructure? What Platform changes would enable better Product outcomes?
- Claim your organisational authority: Your clinical expertise validates framework applications. Use it to articulate why product-level changes require platform support, why outcomes depend on organisational factors.
- Build systematically: Pick one cell where you have authority. Show results. Expand to connected cells.

Next Steps

The following chapters will show these tools in action across different healthcare contexts. Each chapter demonstrates different cells of the framework, different phases of the Double Diamond, and different design thinking tools applied to real challenges. Read them to see the navigation system in use, then return to this chapter's tables to select tools for your own transformation challenges.

Summary: Your Two-Dimensional Navigation System

Healthcare transformation fails not from lack of effort but from lack of systematic navigation. The Double Diamond + InterQB-it™ framework provides that navigation:

The Double Diamond shows WHEN:

- Discover: Explore needs (co-design for Excitement features users can't articulate)
- Define: Synthesise into clear, specific problem statements
- Develop: Prototype and test solutions (rapid iteration, learn from failure)
- Deliver: Implement with measurement and continuous improvement

The InterQB-it™ framework shows WHERE:

- Four levels: Business, Brand, Platform, Product/Service
- Four factors: Strategies, Processes, Enablers, People
- Common external drivers across all levels
- Level-specific outcomes: sustainability, loyalty, efficiency, quality of life

Healthcare constraints require adaptation:

- Regulatory: Integrate from day one, not as an afterthought
- Safety: Layer into every phase
- Time: Equal diamonds—investment in problem diamond saves multiples in solution diamond

Kano Model informs method selection:

1. Basic features: Minimum standards (traditional research reveals)
2. Performance features: Linear improvement (surveys work)
3. Excitement features: Transformative value (requires co-design)
4. Remember: Features migrate Excitement → Performance → Basic over time
5. Remember: 'Do no harm' is a basic feature. Measure the quality of life improvement

Building confidence requires:

- Understanding principles
- Selecting appropriate tools for context
- Practising with small challenges
- Learning what works in your organisation
- Expanding systematically

The navigation system doesn't make transformation easy—it makes it systematic.

References

1. Getz, K.A. et al. (2016) 'The impact of protocol amendments on clinical trial performance and cost', *Therapeutic Innovation & Regulatory Science*, 50(4), pp. 436–441. https://doi.org/10.1177/2168479016632271.
2. Institute of Medicine (US) and National Academy of Engineering (US) Roundtable on Value & Science-Driven Health Care (2011) 'Case studies in transformation through systems engineering', in *Engineering a Learning Healthcare System: A Look at the Future: Workshop Summary*. National Academies Press (US). Available at: https://www.ncbi.nlm.nih.gov/books/NBK61967/.
3. Rees, H. (2011) *Supply Chain Management in the Drug Industry*. Wiley.
4. Kano, N. et al. (1984) 'Attractive quality and must-be quality', *Journal of the Japanese Society for Quality Control*, 14, pp. 39–48.
5. Kaplan, G.S. (2013) 'Pursuing the perfect patient experience', *Frontiers of Health Services Management*, 29(3), pp. 16–27.
6. DiMasi, J.A., Grabowski, H.G. and Hansen, R.W. (2016) 'Innovation in the pharmaceutical industry: New estimates of R&D costs', *Journal of Health Economics*, 47, pp. 20–33. https://doi.org/10.1016/j.jhealeco.2016.01.012.
7. Sertkaya, A. et al. (2022) 'Estimated cost of developing a therapeutic complex medical device in the US.', *JAMA Network Open*, 5(9), p. e2231609. https://doi.org/10.1001/jamanetworkopen.2022.31609.
8. Thermo Fisher Scientific (2022) *Top 5 Challenges for Drug Developers Infographic*. Thermo Fisher Scientific / PPD. Available at: https://www.ppd.com/wp-content/uploads/2022/12/Top-5-challenges-for-drug-developers-infographic.pdf.

Chapter 5

Every Clinician Is Already a Design Thinker

THE QUESTION THAT REVEALS EVERYTHING

During the 25 years I lectured on design thinking for engineering students, there was always one asking the same question: 'How did you make the transition from medicine to design? They're such completely different fields.' The first time that threw me as I hadn't thought of it myself. I used it as a mutual learning opportunity by asking them: 'Let's think about what actually happens when I see a new patient in my surgery and I do not know what they want or need?'

In design we use observation and interview techniques to explore what customers need and want. We might show them models or give them prototypes to get their reactions. In co-design we—users and designers—work closely together to explore needs and how those could be met. The process and techniques we use in that initial phase of Design are the same as we use in diagnosis in healthcare.

This recognition fundamentally changes healthcare's transformation challenge. Chapters 1–3 established the urgent need for transformation but highlighted a daunting obstacle: healthcare appeared to lack the knowledge, skills, and resources to navigate complexity at the scale transformation requires. Chapter 4 provided the methodology, but seemed to require importing expertise and training an entire workforce in unfamiliar concepts.

This chapter reveals that we have been framing the problem incorrectly. Healthcare doesn't lack transformation capability—it possesses millions of complexity science experts who practice sophisticated methodology daily. The challenge isn't building new capability but helping clinicians recognise that their diagnostic expertise transfers to organisational problems, then removing structural barriers that currently prevent them from applying it at system scale. The path from daunting to achievable runs through recognition.

The chapter demonstrates four interconnected insights. First, clinical decision-making maps precisely onto the Double Diamond framework that defines design thinking. Second, both

DOI: 10.4324/9781003752073-7

methodologies evolved this structure because dealing with complexity demands it. Third, research across multiple health systems demonstrates that clinical leadership improves hospital performance—yet healthcare systematically excludes this expertise from transformation leadership. Fourth, recognising this parallel unlocks powerful capabilities—clinicians gain confidence that their expertise transfers to organisational challenges, while gaining access to design methods and tools they'll find easier to adopt than linear business approaches.

Let me show you what this looks like in practice.

A Morning in the ICU

Dr Claudia Marchetti is a consultant intensivist with fifteen years of experience managing critically ill patients. One morning case demonstrates the sophistication of clinical methodology.

07:30—Handover

The night registrar presents the concerning patient. 'Bed 7. Mr Ahmad. Sixty-seven, day three post-CABG (Coronary Artery Bypass Grafting). Overnight his respiratory function deteriorated. Currently on BiPAP (Bilevel Positive Airway Pressure through mask or nose plug) at 60% FiO2, sats 91–93%. Temperature spiked to 38.2. New infiltrate on chest X-ray. Rising inflammatory markers, creatinine up from 98 to 156. He's agitated, fighting the BiPAP.'

Claudia listens but also watches. The night nurse's expression shows concern beyond what numbers convey. After handover, Claudia examines Mr Ahmad. She doesn't just review charts—she observes how he breathes, how he holds his body. She notices his hand repeatedly moves to his left chest. 'Show me exactly where it feels wrong,' she says. He points to a specific location. Not diffuse discomfort. Precise.

08:15—Building the Picture

The obvious answer is hospital-acquired pneumonia. But pneumonia doesn't usually present as specific localised 'tightness.' Claudia generates multiple hypotheses: pulmonary embolism, cardiac failure, pleural effusion, pericardial effusion. She orders investigations but before results return, calls the cardiothoracic surgeon.

> 'The pleural drain we removed yesterday—how much was it putting out?'
> 'About 200ml overnight, serosanguinous. Normal range.'

The localised symptoms, timing post-drain removal, specific location—Claudia converges on her working diagnosis: re-accumulating pleural effusion.

09:00—Planning Intervention

Claudia gathers the team at bedside. Three options: wait for imaging confirmation then drain under controlled conditions (safe but patient continues deteriorating), perform therapeutic ultrasound-guided aspiration now (immediate relief if correct, but procedure risk without CT confirmation), or escalate BiPAP and pursue urgent imaging (buying time for information but not addressing underlying problem). She consults each specialist. The physiotherapist predicts four to six hours before intubation if this continues. The nurse notes increasing anxiety worsening breathing. But there's another voice that matters.

Claudia returns to Mr Ahmad. 'We think fluid has built up around your lung. We can drain it, which should help immediately. Or we can do more tests first to be absolutely certain. What matters most to you right now?'

'I can't breathe properly. If you think that's what it is, please fix it.'

09:30—Implementation and Adaptation

Claudia performs bedside ultrasound. Large pleural effusion, exactly where suspected. She aspirates 800 ml. Within minutes, oxygen saturations climb to 96%. Respiratory rate slows from 28 to 18. The BiPAP comes off within an hour.

Throughout the day, Claudia monitors continuously. At 11:00—oxygen requirements decreasing. At 14:00—patient sitting up, eating lunch. At 17:00—talking with his wife about going home. Each visit, she's ready to adjust if something changes. By shift end, Mr Ahmad is off all respiratory support. Claudia moves on to the next complex patient.

She does this multiple times every shift. She's been doing it for fifteen years. She calls it 'being a doctor.'

The Precise Mapping: Clinical Reasoning as Design Methodology

Comparing Figure 5.1 with the Design Double Diamond in Figure 1.3 shows the parallel structure of clinical and design terminology across the four phases.

Phase 1: DISCOVER (Divergent Exploration)

Clinical medicine: Anamnesis, examination, investigation

Design thinking: Ethnographic research, user interviews, stakeholder consultation

What Claudia did:

- Gathered patient history and chief complaint
- Performed physical examination
- Reviewed vital signs and monitoring data
- Analysed laboratory and imaging results
- Consulted nursing observations and physiotherapist assessment
- Listened to the patient's subjective experience
- Understood family concerns
- Called surgical team for operative context

The common element: divergent information gathering from multiple sources, suspending premature conclusions, building empathy for lived experience, seeking perspectives that formal data miss.

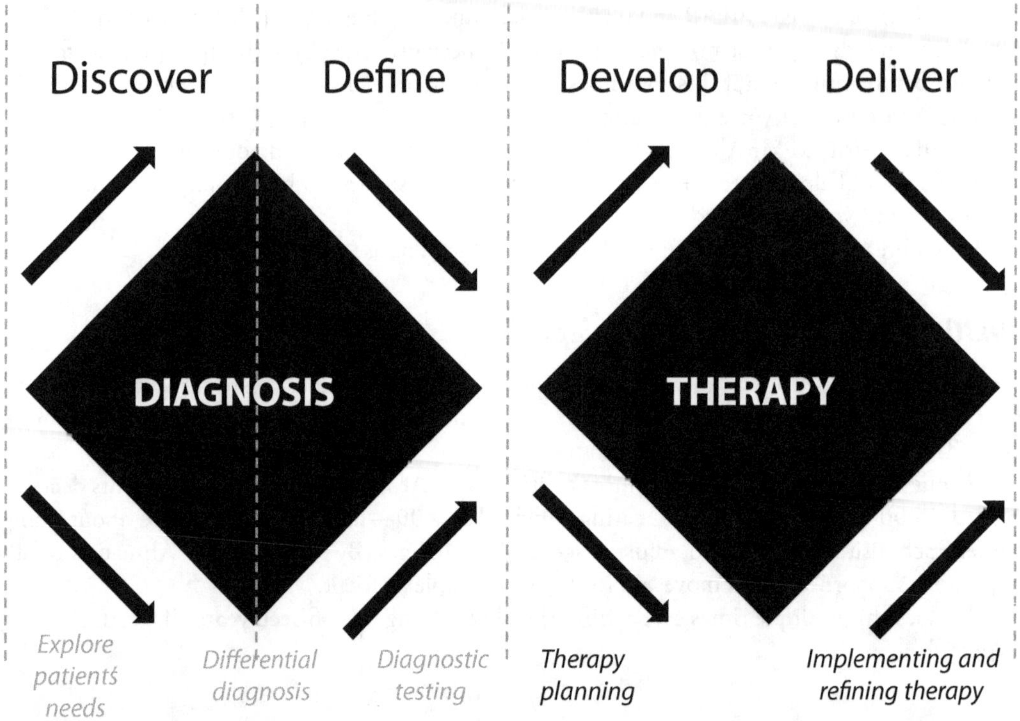

Figure 5.1 The medical Double Diamond with clinical terminology.

Phase 2: DEFINE (Convergent Problem Definition)

Clinical medicine: Differential diagnosis, diagnostic reasoning
Design thinking: Insight synthesis, problem framing
What Claudia did:

- Generated multiple hypotheses (pneumonia, PE, cardiac failure, pleural effusion, pericardial effusion)
- Weighted probabilities against evidence
- Identified pattern inconsistencies (localised symptoms don't fit pneumonia)
- Converged on working diagnosis
- Articulated a specific problem requiring a solution

The common element: convergent analysis eliminating possibilities, pattern recognition across complex data, evidence-based narrowing, arriving at a clear problem statement that enables action.

Phase 3: DEVELOP (Divergent Solution Generation)

Clinical medicine: Treatment planning, therapeutic options
Design thinking: Ideation, prototyping, co-design
What Claudia did:

- Generated three distinct treatment approaches
- Evaluated risk-benefit for each option

- Consulted team members for specialised expertise
- Considered patient-specific constraints
- Integrated patient preferences
- Planned contingencies if the primary strategy failed

The common element: divergent option generation, stakeholder co-design respecting different expertise, prototyping before commitment, personalisation to context, balancing competing objectives.

Phase 4: DELIVER (Convergent Implementation)

Clinical medicine: Therapeutic intervention, monitoring, titration

Design thinking: User testing, iteration, continuous improvement

What Claudia did:

- Implemented chosen intervention (aspiration)
- Monitored patient response continuously
- Adjusted in real time (oxygen titration)
- Coordinated multidisciplinary team
- Measured outcomes against goals
- Documented learning for future cases

The common element: convergent implementation, continuous feedback monitoring, rapid iteration based on real-world response, measurement against intended outcomes, knowledge capture for improvement.

The terminology differs. The substrate—biological versus designed systems—creates different constraints. But the underlying cognitive architecture is identical.

Why Complexity Demands This Architecture

The Double Diamond isn't arbitrary. It's what the practical challenge of dealing with complexity requires. Understanding why both clinical medicine and design thinking converged on this exact structure reveals something fundamental about how human cognition must adapt to navigate complexity—and what complexity science has discovered through studying these adaptations.

Characteristic 1: Multiple Interacting Variables

Complex problems involve numerous factors where changing one affects many others unpredictably. Mr Ahmad's pleural effusion affected respiratory function, which increased anxiety, which worsened breathing, which raised blood pressure, which increased cardiac workload—a web of circular causation where you cannot isolate single cause-and-effect chains.

This differs fundamentally from complicated systems. A jet engine is complicated—it has thousands of parts, but each part has a defined function and predictable interactions. Healthcare is complex—changing one element creates ripple effects throughout the system in ways that cannot be fully predicted in advance.

Characteristic 2: Emergent Properties

The interactions between variables create something new that wasn't present in any individual component. Think of consciousness—you cannot find 'consciousness' by studying individual neurons, yet somehow millions of neurons interacting create awareness. Similarly in healthcare: Mr Ahmad presented with what experienced clinicians recognise as 'the sick patient gestalt'—that undefinable but unmistakable quality where multiple slightly abnormal values combine to signal serious deterioration [1]. His oxygen saturation (91%), creatinine (156), temperature (38.2°C), and respiratory rate (28) were each only mildly abnormal. But the pattern they created together signalled a patient heading for intubation within hours.

This emergent property—'clinical deterioration requiring urgent intervention'—existed nowhere in the individual measurements. It arose from their interaction. Claudia couldn't have predicted this severity from reviewing each lab value separately. She had to observe the whole patient to recognise the emergent pattern.

Characteristic 3: Context Dependency

Complex problems have no universal optimal solutions; what works varies by situation-specific factors. The right treatment for Mr Ahmad depended on his specific respiratory reserve, his psychological state, his values about risk versus certainty, the available expertise at that moment, the time constraints, and dozens of other contextual variables.

Protocols provide starting points, but complex systems demand adaptive responses. Claudia used her knowledge of pleural effusions generally, but applied it specifically to this patient at this time with these constraints. The methodology transfers; the solution must be contextualised.

Characteristic 4: Irreducible Uncertainty

Complex systems involve fundamental uncertainty that cannot be eliminated through more information—what economists call 'Knightian uncertainty,' where you cannot even enumerate all possibilities in advance. Claudia couldn't know with absolute certainty that pleural effusion caused symptoms until she aspirated and observed improvement.

Characteristic 5: Multiple Stakeholders with Competing Needs

Complex problems involve numerous actors with legitimate but potentially conflicting requirements. Mr Ahmad needed immediate symptom relief. His wife needed to understand what was happening to feel less anxious. The nurse needed a treatment plan she could implement safely. The physiotherapist needed to assess respiratory trajectory. Claudia needed diagnostic accuracy to guide intervention. The hospital needed efficient resource utilisation.

There's no solution that optimally satisfies all stakeholders simultaneously. The methodology must include processes for navigating competing needs and making trade-offs explicit.

Why This Demands Alternating Divergence and Convergence

These five characteristics explain why both clinical medicine and design practice converged on the Double Diamond architecture:

Divergent Discovery is required because complexity hides critical signals in unexpected places. Multiple interacting variables mean you cannot know in advance which information will prove crucial. Claudia's observation that Mr Ahmad repeatedly touched his left chest mattered as much as his creatinine level. If she'd only reviewed lab results and imaging, she would have missed the localised nature suggesting pleural effusion over pneumonia.

Emergence means you must observe the whole system in context, not just measure components. Context dependency means you need a deep understanding of the specific situation before intervening. Irreducible uncertainty means you cannot wait for complete information—you must gather rapidly from multiple sources. Multiple stakeholders mean you need diverse perspectives to understand the whole problem.

Convergent Definition is required because you cannot pursue all possibilities simultaneously. Without convergence, you have paralysis through infinite options. But premature convergence—jumping to the first plausible hypothesis—means solving the wrong problem. The art of working with complexity lies in converging on problem definition supported by sufficient evidence while remaining open to revision if new information emerges.

Claudia's differential diagnosis process exemplifies this. She generated five hypotheses, weighted each against available evidence, identified which patterns didn't fit certain diagnoses, and converged on pleural effusion as a working diagnosis. Not certainty—working hypothesis strong enough to guide action while remaining falsifiable.

Divergent Development is required because complex problems rarely have single optimal solutions. Context dependency means the best intervention varies by specific constraints. Multiple stakeholders mean different solutions optimise different needs. Irreducible uncertainty means you need contingency plans.

Claudia's three treatment options each balanced different trade-offs: certainty versus speed, safety versus effectiveness, information versus action. Which option was 'best' depended on how you weighted these competing factors. Divergent development ensures you explore the solution space before committing.

Convergent Delivery is required because execution demands commitment to specific action. At some point, divergent option generation must converge on decisive implementation. But delivery in complex systems requires continuous monitoring and rapid iteration—not 'set and forget' but 'implement and adapt.'

Claudia couldn't simultaneously wait for imaging and aspirate immediately. She had to choose. But her choice wasn't final—she monitored continuously, ready to pivot if her working diagnosis proved wrong. This is delivery appropriate to complexity: committed action with adaptive response.

The Sophistication of Clinical Application

Understanding this architecture reveals why clinical application operates with extraordinary sophistication. Claudia executed this methodology under constraints that test the limits of human cognitive capability. She compressed months of design team work into twelve hours. She made decisions with life-or-death consequences where designers face financial risks. She managed uncertainty that cannot be eliminated where designers can conduct more research. She coordinated seven stakeholders in real-time at the bedside while the patient's physiology continued evolving.

This is complexity science practised at the highest level. This is what experienced clinicians do multiple times every shift. They've been doing it for decades, sometimes centuries if you count the historical development of clinical reasoning.

They just never formalised it into a framework with diagrams and white papers. They taught it through apprenticeship, calling it 'clinical judgement' without recognising it as a generalisable methodology for navigating complexity.

Always Used but Never Taught

This sophisticated methodology is rarely explicitly taught in medical schools as a generalisable framework. Students learn differential diagnosis as a list of possible diseases for specific presentations, not as divergent hypothesis generation and convergent evidence-based narrowing applicable to any complex problem. The cognitive structure remains implicit, transmitted through apprenticeship rather than formalised curriculum.

This isn't accidental. Medical education historically framed itself around linear, reductionist scientific method to gain legitimacy as a science. This framing obscured the reality that clinical practice actually employs complexity science methodology—pattern recognition, probabilistic reasoning, and adaptive decision-making under uncertainty. With no framework for recognising this, and no cross-disciplinary comparison with design thinking (which independently evolved the same methodology), the parallel remained invisible. It took someone with expert-level practice in both medicine and design, plus academic frameworks to analyse cognitive processes, to recognise what was always there.

This recognition failure explains why healthcare systematically excludes clinical expertise from transformation leadership. The parallel remained invisible, making exclusion seem reasonable. Let us examine how this exclusion operates.

WHEN CRAFT LOSES ITS COMPASS: A LESSON FROM TWO DESIGN SCHOOLS

Most people assume car design is a single discipline with broadly consistent methods. It is not. When I arrived at Studio Michelotti in Turin, I encountered a tradition shaped by centuries of northern Italian craftsmanship—marble, stone, hard materials that punish imprecision. The *piano di forma* technique required designers to work simultaneously in three-view drawings, building every detail mentally before committing to material, because nothing could be added back once removed. Discipline was not a preference. It was the nature of the medium.

At Jaguar in Coventry, I entered a different world entirely. The English school works in clay—a material with its own deep craft lineage in the Midlands pottery tradition, where for centuries craftsmen and their customers existed in direct relationship, the pot shaped for the hand that would hold it. That heritage is not incidental: the same region, the same era, families firing their own kilns while the community healer made house calls to the same streets. Both crafts, in their origins, answered to the person standing directly in front of them. At Jaguar the clay remained, and with it the working method it enables—designers sketching freely, collaborating closely with modellers, building form iteratively, adding and removing as understanding develops. Where Turin demanded total prior clarity, Coventry rewarded exploratory process. The material differed, the tradition differed, but the discipline of serving the person the product was made for remained absolute.

Two schools. Radically different methods. Ancient craft traditions, different materials, different working cultures.

Yet both, without exception, maintained absolute fidelity to the same north star: the person the product was made for. Every decision—proportion, material, surface, mechanism—was ultimately tested against one question: does this serve the driver? The methods diverged; the purpose did not. That fidelity is what made both schools excellent.

Medicine began as an ancient craft with the same clarity of purpose. The art of healing placed the patient at the centre of every decision, as completely as the driver sits at the centre of automotive design. The methods evolved over centuries—from Hippocratic observation to evidence-based practice—but the original purpose was unambiguous: understand what the patient needs, and serve it.

What happened to medicine is not that the craft deteriorated. Clinicians at the bedside still practise it with the same rigour and fidelity that Claudia demonstrated with Mr Ahmad that morning. What happened is that the system surrounding clinical practice accumulated stakeholders—administrators, commissioners, regulators, insurers, politicians—each with legitimate interests, each adding layers of governance, each subtly pulling the purpose of the system away from the patient and toward the management of the system itself.

The car industry, for all its complexity, never lost the customer. The customer remained the final arbitration point. Healthcare systems, across decades of reform and reorganisation, have managed to build structures in which the patient is increasingly a downstream consideration rather than the originating purpose.

The clinician remains the custodian of medicine's original purpose. Every day, at the bedside, the original compass is consulted. This is not sentimentality—it is what clinical training and clinical identity encode. When we exclude clinicians from transformation leadership, we do not simply lose a useful methodology. We lose the people who still know what the system is for.

The Systematic Exclusion of Clinical Expertise

Healthcare possesses extraordinary expertise in exactly the methodology transformation requires. This expertise lives in the clinical workforce, honed through years of practice under demanding constraints. Yet healthcare systematically excludes this expertise from transformation leadership. Consider a typical UK NHS trust board composition:

- Chief Executive: Retail logistics background
- Chief Operating Officer: Airline operations expertise
- Director of Strategy: Civil service and policy development
- Chief Transformation Officer: MBA, management consulting background
- Medical Director: Consultant surgeon with additional MBA

The only person who practices sophisticated complexity methodology daily is there to represent 'the clinical perspective,' not to lead transformation. The actual transformation leaders have expertise in retail, airlines, policy, and consulting. All valuable domains but none of them are complex adaptive systems resembling healthcare. This exclusion operates through three mechanisms.

Mechanism 1: Career Path Bifurcation

In the UK and US, clinicians face a forced choice: remain clinical or pursue management. European systems operate differently, viewing clinical expertise as a prerequisite for senior leadership. The impact is evident in comparative data. Sarto and Veronesi's systematic review of clinical leadership research reveals stark differences: in Germany, France, and Italy, clinicians represent 50–71% of senior hospital managers, while in the UK only 26% of board members and 22% of CEOs have clinical backgrounds. In the US, only 235 of 6,500 hospitals are led by doctors. This systematic exclusion occurs despite evidence from 19 quantitative studies showing that clinical leadership improves hospital performance across multiple dimensions in 80% of cases [2]. Figure 5.2 shows the percentage of healthcare executives that have clinical experience across different countries.

This bifurcation wasn't accidental—it was deliberately designed. In 1983, Prime Minister Thatcher commissioned Roy Griffiths, a director of supermarket chain Sainsbury's, to report on NHS management. Griffiths, whose expertise lay in retail supply chains and simple systems optimisation, recommended systematically separating 'clinical work' from 'management work' [3]. The recommendation was implemented nationwide. The category error was profound. Griffiths brought expertise in managing predictable, standardised retail systems and applied it to healthcare—a complex adaptive system requiring exactly the opposite approach. His recommendation separated the people practising sophisticated complexity methodology (clinicians) from

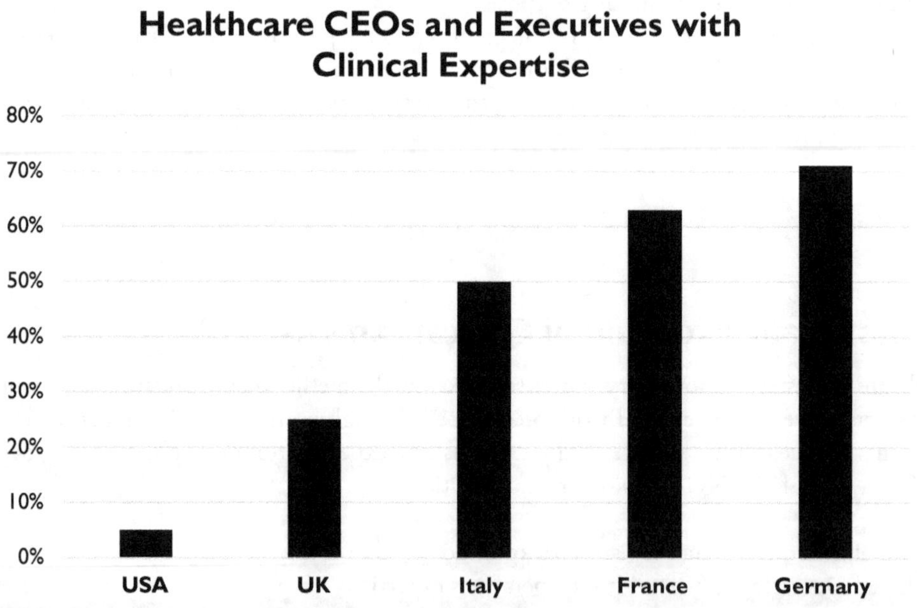

Figure 5.2 Healthcare executives with clinical expertise (based on data from Sarto and Veronesi [2]).

organisational decision-making, then imposed simple-system management frameworks on inherently complex processes.

Forty years later, we're still living with the consequences. The UK's systematic exclusion of clinical expertise from strategic leadership stems directly from a 1983 recommendation by someone whose domain expertise was grocery retail, not complex adaptive systems. As one analysis noted: he was 'not hindered by any subject matter expertise' when making recommendations that would reshape healthcare for generations.

The contrast with continental Europe is stark. Germany, France, and Italy never implemented this separation—they retained clinical expertise in leadership positions. The performance differences [2] suggest that Griffiths got it exactly backwards: separating complexity science expertise from organisational leadership doesn't improve management; it guarantees transformation failure.

Dr Devi Shetty's trajectory illustrates what this costs. After training as a paediatric heart surgeon at Guy's Hospital in London, he returned to India where he founded Narayana Health. His innovations combined assembly-line principles adapted for surgical complexity, task-shifting, cross-subsidisation models, and high-volume centres. Results: his hospital treats as many heart operations annually as the entire UK, costs 75% lower, clinical outcomes equal to leading global institutions [4]. I asked Devi directly: 'Could you have achieved this if you'd stayed in the UK?' His emphatic response: 'Absolutely not.'

Others in the NHS possessed the same clinical expertise. The difference wasn't individual capability but systemic permission to apply complexity navigation methodology to organisational challenges. UK structures would have forced him to choose between clinical practice or management, blocked task-shifting innovations, prevented business model experimentation, and resisted role redesign. The UK system systematically loses its most sophisticated clinical innovators to environments that permit organisational experimentation.

Mechanism 2: The Methodology Inversion

Healthcare organisations spend billions hiring management consultants to teach methodologies evolved for simpler systems. Six Sigma evolved for manufacturing, assuming processes can be standardised, variation minimised, problems have root causes that can be eliminated, optimal solutions are universal, and system behaviour is predictable.

Lean Thinking evolved from the Toyota Production System for high-volume automobile manufacturing, assuming value streams map precisely, waste can be systematically eliminated, standardisation improves quality, and just-in-time flow is optimal. These methodologies work brilliantly in their native contexts—manufacturing and automotive production are relatively simple systems with linear cause-effect, predictable responses, standardisable processes, and reducible variation.

Healthcare is fundamentally different. It's a complex adaptive system where cause and effect separate across time and space, the same intervention produces different outcomes in different patients, variation is biologically inherent and clinically necessary, multiple variables interact nonlinearly, and optimal solutions must adapt to individual context.

Meanwhile, clinicians practise complexity science methodology daily. Clinical diagnostic reasoning involves hypothesis generation under uncertainty, probabilistic thinking with incomplete information, multi-factorial causation analysis, and pattern recognition across complex data. This is exactly what healthcare transformation requires. Yet we hire management consultants charging thousands per day to teach Six Sigma to clinicians who've practised hypothesis testing and rapid-cycle adaptation for decades.

Mechanism 3: The Evidence Paradox

The deepest irony: evidence shows clinical leaders drive transformation most effectively, yet we prevent them from leading. The same systematic review found clinical leadership particularly strongly associated with quality improvements, with better quality ratings, lower mortality rates, and higher patient satisfaction scores [2].

Research demonstrates that clinicians succeed in transformation because they possess credibility that non-clinical leaders cannot replicate. Frontline staff trust those who understand clinical reality from direct experience—they 'walk the talk.' Clinical leaders possess professional knowledge enabling them to identify which barriers are genuine clinical constraints versus bureaucratic inertia. They understand tacit systems that make hospitals function—informal networks, unwritten rules, real decision-making. Other research, across multiple sectors, shows that organisations innovate most successfully when change leaders bring deep domain expertise, problem-solving capabilities that match to system complexity, credibility with frontline workers, and ability to balance technical and social challenges [5]. Healthcare has all these capabilities in its clinical workforce. Yet we systematically prevent clinical leaders from exercising them.

Between 2006 and 2013, the NHS spent over £1 billion implementing Lean methodology. The sustainable impact was negligible [6, 7]. The NHS continues deteriorating on almost every metric. Meanwhile, healthcare systems that maintained clinical leadership—particularly in Northern Europe—navigate similar pressures more effectively. Not because they lack challenges, but because they retained clinical expertise in transformation leadership.

We know what works. We have the expertise. We systematically prevent ourselves from using it. Recognition offers the path forward.

COUNTERINTUITIVE FINDING

The System That Excludes Its Best Transformation Leaders by Design

A systematic review of 19 quantitative studies found that clinical leadership improves hospital performance across quality, safety, and patient satisfaction in 80% of cases. European healthcare systems—where clinicians occupy 50–71% of senior management positions—consistently outperform UK and US models where only 22–26% of board members and chief executives have clinical backgrounds, and fewer than 4% of US hospitals are led by physicians. This performance gap cannot be attributed to chance or culture: the UK's exclusion of clinical leaders was deliberately engineered in 1983 when Margaret Thatcher commissioned Roy Griffiths—a director of Sainsbury's supermarket chain—to restructure NHS management. His recommendation to separate clinical work from management was implemented nationally and remains structurally intact. Meanwhile, between 2006 and 2013, the NHS spent over £1 billion on Lean methodology (Chapter 11)—a framework evolved for standardised manufacturing, not complex adaptive systems—with negligible sustainable impact. Healthcare has not failed to find the right methodology. It has spent a billion pounds importing inferior methodology to replace a superior one that was already present in its clinical workforce.

Conclusion: Recognition Changes Everything

Return to where we began in Chapter 1. Healthcare faces an unprecedented transformation challenge—demographic shifts, chronic disease burden, financial constraints, and workforce shortages creating pressures that traditional management approaches cannot resolve. Design thinking offers a methodology suited to complexity, but importing this seemed to require massive investment in training an entire workforce to think differently. Now we have discovered something far more powerful: the workforce already thinks this way. Every experienced clinician practises the same complexity science methodology that design thinking formalised. Healthcare doesn't suffer from a capability deficit—it suffers from a recognition failure.

The evidence suggests that clinical expertise alone isn't sufficient; clinicians need appropriate frameworks to translate their complexity navigation methodology to organisational scale [2]. But this is fundamentally different from teaching them alien business concepts. It's providing systematic tools that formalise what they already do intuitively.

Here's the powerful implication: once clinicians recognise they already practise design thinking methodology, they gain natural access to the entire toolkit of proven design methods and tools. When consultants introduce 'stakeholder mapping' or 'journey mapping' or 'rapid prototyping,' clinical leaders who view these as foreign business concepts often resist. Why trust tools from domains that don't understand healthcare complexity? But when the same tools are introduced as systematic ways to apply the diagnostic and treatment methodology clinicians already practise—just at organisational scale—resistance evaporates. Stakeholder mapping becomes systematic differential diagnosis of who affects and is affected by the problem. Journey mapping becomes taking a comprehensive patient history of the system. Rapid prototyping becomes the clinical approach of starting treatment while monitoring response and adjusting. The terminology matters less than the recognition: these tools emerged from the same complexity science methodology clinicians have practised for years. They're not foreign concepts requiring different thinking. They're systematic ways to apply thinking clinicians already do exceptionally well.

This transforms adoption dynamics. Linear business tools like Six Sigma require clinicians to adopt fundamentally different logic—forcing standardisation where they know adaptation is needed, eliminating variation they know is clinically essential, seeking root causes in emergent phenomena. No wonder clinical resistance is strong. Design methods align with how clinicians already think. They don't require abandoning clinical expertise to adopt business logic.

The transformation crisis stems from three recognition failures:

First, we don't recognise that clinical diagnostic reasoning IS complexity science methodology. We use different terminology, so we miss that we're describing identical cognitive processes.

Second, this recognition failure leads to systematic exclusion of clinical expertise from transformation leadership. We think clinicians need to learn 'business thinking' or 'design thinking' as foreign disciplines when they already practise more sophisticated versions.

Third, we've forced clinical leaders to choose between practising medicine and leading change when clinical practice is exactly what qualifies them to lead.

This forgetting has cost billions in failed transformation initiatives and talented clinical innovators who left because they couldn't practise both. But forgetting can be reversed through recognition. When transformation leaders recognise that clinical colleagues practise sophisticated complexity methodology, they can partner with clinical leaders instead of working around them. When clinical leaders recognise that their diagnostic process transfers to organisational challenges and gives them access to proven design tools, they can accept organisational leadership roles with confidence.

The transformation challenge reframes from 'We don't know how' to 'How do we support the people who already know how?' From 'Build new capability' to 'Remove barriers preventing existing capability from operating at organisational scale.' From 'Import foreign expertise' to 'Recognise and empower the expertise already present.' The path is still challenging—clinicians have clinical work to do, organisational structures resist change, governance barriers must be removed. But the nature of the challenge has fundamentally shifted. We're not starting from zero. We're starting from millions of practitioners with thousands of hours navigating complexity under constraints design consultants never face.

The question is no longer whether healthcare has the capability for transformation. The question is how to enable clinicians to apply this capability at organisational scale—the systematic methods, tools, and frameworks we explore in Part III.

Dr Claudia Marchetti finishes her shift, having executed complexity navigation methodology six times with six different patients. Tomorrow she starts as Clinical Director of Transformation, applying the same methodology to organisational challenges. She's ready. She's been training for fifteen years. She just didn't know the methodology she practised had a formal name.

Now she does. And now she knows she has access to tools that will help her apply it at scale.

References

1. Wiswell, J. et al. (2013) '"Sick" or "not-sick": Accuracy of System 1 diagnostic reasoning for the prediction of disposition and acuity in patients presenting to an academic ED', *The American Journal of Emergency Medicine*, 31(10), pp. 1448–1452. https://doi.org/10.1016/j.ajem.2013.07.018.
2. Sarto, F. and Veronesi, G. (2016) 'Clinical leadership and hospital performance: Assessing the evidence base', *BMC Health Services Research*, 16(2), p. 169. https://doi.org/10.1186/s12913-016-1395-5.
3. Griffiths, R. (1983) 'Griffiths report October 1983', *https://sochealth.co.uk/*. Available at: https://sochealth.co.uk/national-health-service/griffiths-report-october-1983/ (Accessed: 31 December 2025).
4. Muralidhara, G.V. (2016) *Dr Devi Shetty of Narayana Hrudayalaya: Delivering Quality Cardiac Care to the Masses, The Case Centre*. Available at: https://www.thecasecentre.org/products/view?id=137186 (Accessed: 7 April 2025).
5. Xie, Z. et al. (2024) 'Why expert leaders matter: A study on the mechanism of team value creation in knowledge-intensive teams', *Humanities and Social Sciences Communications*, 11(1), p. 1707. https://doi.org/10.1057/s41599-024-04267-9.
6. Moraros, J., Lemstra, M. and Nwankwo, C. (2016) 'Lean interventions in healthcare: Do they actually work? A systematic literature review', *International Journal for Quality in Health Care*, 28(2), pp. 150–165. https://doi.org/10.1093/intqhc/mzv123.
7. Woodnutt, S. (2018) 'Is Lean sustainable in today's NHS hospitals? A systematic literature review using the meta-narrative and integrative methods', *International Journal for Quality in Health Care: Journal of the International Society for Quality in Health Care*, 30(8), pp. 578–586. https://doi.org/10.1093/intqhc/mzy070.

III

APPLICATIONS ACROSS THE HEALTHCARE ECOSYSTEM

Chapter 6

Redesigning Clinical Trials

CLINICAL TRIAL CHALLENGES

David oversees development of a promising new compound at a major pharmaceutical company, facing pressure for timely regulatory approval after significant investment. His challenge reflects every pharmaceutical executive's familiar dilemma: conducting clinical trials that are both cost-efficient and compliant with increasingly stringent FDA guidelines, including requirements to involve diverse, representative populations. Speed is critical. Every day of delay affects the compound's approval timeline and the company's market position.

David's challenge reflects a deeper dysfunction familiar to every clinical trial investigator: protocols designed in isolation from clinical realities, then thrown over the wall for implementation. The executive timeline pressure that David feels also manifests at trial sites—the rigid protocols that violate workflow logic create the recruitment and retention failures that extend timelines further. It's a vicious cycle driven by design failures, not effort failures.

His challenge isn't unique. It reflects a system-wide crisis in clinical trials that threatens the entire pharmaceutical development model. Clinical trials cost an average of $1.065 billion per approved new drug [1]. Medical devices fare somewhat better at $31 million to $94 million depending on complexity [2], but pharmaceutical companies regularly pay $50,000 or more per trial participant, depending on the phase, protocol complexity, and participant burden [3].

The timeline compounds the problem. From discovery to FDA approval takes approximately 15 years, yet patent protection lasts only 20 years. Companies lose five years of patent-protected market time before a drug even launches—creating economic equations only massive pharmaceutical corporations can sustain.

The attrition rate tells an even more troubling story. In 2011, it took 10,000 initial compounds to produce one FDA-approved drug [4]. More recent data shows improvement [5], but the business model remains fundamentally unsustainable. As one industry analysis concluded: 'No other sector could sustain this much work and such a dysfunctional way of doing business.'

The implications extend beyond inefficiency to strategic distortion. The astronomical costs mean that developing new medicines and devices remains the exclusive domain of large, well-established

DOI: 10.4324/9781003752073-9

companies. Startups cannot sustain these investment requirements. More troublingly, the economics drive big pharma to abandon common conditions in pursuit of lucrative rare diseases with much higher margins. A pharmaceutical CEO expressed this concern to me directly, comparing it to 'the Volkswagen Group stopping production of the Golf to focus on Lamborghinis and Bugattis.' The analogy captures the perversity precisely. In any other sector, if established players abandoned high-volume, moderate-margin products to chase low-volume, high-margin luxury goods, competitors would seize the opportunity. In healthcare, the same structural forces affect everyone—the £1+ billion development cost, the 15-year timeline, the regulatory complexity. This creates systematic market failures that benefit no one except, perhaps, the financial success of blockbuster drugs, until even that model begins to collapse under its own contradictions.

A 2022 survey of more than 150 drug developers worldwide identified the scope of the crisis. Patient enrolment emerged as the number one challenge, cited by 55% of respondents—including both retention difficulties and population diversity requirements. Other top challenges included Increasing complexity of clinical trials (51%), regulatory hurdles (46%), talent shortages (36%), and keeping pace with technology innovation including hybrid and decentralised trials (32%) [6].

These challenges aren't separate problems that require separate solutions. They're interconnected symptoms of a deeper systemic issue. The increasing complexity of clinical trials relates directly to regulatory hurdles, which in turn connect to patient retention challenges. The fragmentation masks a fundamental design problem: clinical trials evolved without design thinking, and we're paying the price; in billions of dollars, years of delay, and patients who never access potentially life-saving treatments.

COUNTERINTUITIVE FINDING

10,000-to-1 Attrition Rate Represents Design Failure, Not Scientific Necessity

Pharmaceutical executives assume massive attrition rates (10,000 compounds to one approval, $1 billion per drug, 15-year timelines) represent unavoidable scientific reality. Drug development is inherently difficult, so high failure rates are natural. This assumption is backwards. The attrition represents design failure: pharma spends less than 10% of development effort understanding problems before rushing to solutions, guaranteeing exponentially costly failures. Protocol amendments cost ~£500,000 each because protocols were designed in isolation from clinical realities. The automotive industry faced analogous complexity—regulatory requirements, safety standards, diverse users—and solved it by integrating requirements into design from inception. Pharma treats regulatory compliance as a checkpoint to pass rather than a design driver to integrate. Trials using co-design complete enrolment 40% faster, require 40% fewer protocol amendments, and achieve zero major amendments. The problem isn't scientific difficulty—it's design negligence at industrial scale.

The Crucial Role of Design Thinking

The question isn't whether design thinking works in clinical trials. It's whether the pharmaceutical industry will adopt proven methodology before the current unsustainable model collapses entirely.

Mads Øvlisen, former CEO of pharmaceutical giant Novo Nordisk A/S, recognised design's transformative potential: 'At its best, design solves a problem so well that no one even notices that there ever was a problem…and it is this fundamental quality that gives design such a crucial role in creating a new society with decent living conditions' [7].

Øvlisen came to design not as a practitioner but as a business leader who recognised its power. His legal background didn't prevent him from understanding what many pharmaceutical executives miss: design thinking isn't decoration or aesthetics. It's a fundamental methodology for solving complex problems.

This chapter examines how design thinking can transform clinical trials, addressing the £1+ billion problem through systematic methodology that has transformed other complex industries. Pharmaceutical trials violate core design principles by spending less than 10% on discovery and definition versus more than 90% on development and delivery. Correcting this imbalance has demonstrated potential for 30–50% reductions in recruitment time, 40% fewer protocol amendments (saving ~£500,000 each), and 25–35% improvement in patient retention—transforming the economics of pharmaceutical development.

The Problem Landscape: How We Got Here

Once upon a time, physicians provided healthcare where patients were—in the community—and made medicines themselves. Since then, healthcare has evolved toward centralised delivery, requiring patients to leave their communities and travel to what might fairly be called temples of technology: university hospitals and specialised research centres. Clinical trials followed the same centralising trajectory.

Research now flows through a rigid channel: scientific discoveries in research institutes and universities pass to commercial developers, who conduct trials in university hospitals and large clinical research centres. This centralisation creates systematic exclusion. Trials have limited reach to diverse populations. Trial subjects become skewed by age, ethnicity, gender, and socioeconomic circumstances because the system selects for people who can access centralised facilities.

The consequences cascade outward. Results fail to represent the wider target audience that will eventually use the approved drug or device. Local clinics find themselves excluded from participation, unable to build research capability or access research funding. Communities lose opportunities for trial participation and the associated economic benefits. Most critically, patients miss access to potentially life-saving treatments because they cannot navigate the geographical, financial, or cultural barriers that centralisation creates.

The COVID-19 pandemic exposed both the potential and the limitations of this system. The rapid collaboration between pharmaceutical companies, regulators, and policymakers demonstrated that development can accelerate dramatically when stakeholders work together with shared urgency. Public awareness of clinical trials increased substantially. Yet the pandemic also revealed the centralised system's fundamental weakness: diverse populations were not sufficiently represented in initial trials, leading to adverse effects—sometimes fatal—that might have been identified earlier with more representative participation.

The Waterfall Problem

The centralisation problem compounds another issue: clinical trials rely on what engineers call 'over the wall' development. Engineers develop a product according to specifications and throw it over the wall for others to sort out for manufacturing. The process appears clear and orderly. But stakeholders and developers remain disconnected, and empathy—understanding the lived experience of trial participants—is systematically absent, leading to rework and suboptimal products.

This approach stands in sharp contrast to how other complex industries evolved. The automotive industry invested heavily in design thinking and concurrent engineering with multidisciplinary teams working closely together, reducing time to market through rapid prototyping and agile iterative design methods. Time to market curves trended downward as design thinking became embedded in product development.

Pharmaceutical timelines moved in the opposite direction. Breakthrough monoclonal antibodies took 11 years from 'bench to bed': the hybridoma technique enabling laboratory production was developed in 1975, but Muromonab-CD3 wasn't approved until 1986 [8]. Gene therapy timelines stretched even longer: Glybera® required over 20 years from initial development to market approval in 2012 [9]. While the complexity of gene therapy technologies and stringent regulatory requirements certainly contributed to these extended timelines, the lack of an integrated design approach—starting with a deep understanding of patient needs and regulatory requirements—meant that problems discovered late in development required expensive backtracking and protocol amendments.

A Cautionary Tale: What Happens When You Outsource Core Competencies

The pharmaceutical industry's Contract Research Organisation (CRO) experience offers a crucial warning about outsourcing expertise essential to transformation. Between the early 1990s and mid-2000s, CRO spending surged from 4% to nearly 50% of pharmaceutical R&D budgets—a transformation promoted by advisers suggesting that sponsors should 'focus on core competencies' and 'embrace variable cost structures' [10].* McKinsey's subsequent analyses of this shift reveal what design thinking would have predicted: outsourcing relationships that 'lack the maturity needed to fully realize potential gains in R&D efficiency' [10].†

Rather than bringing fresh design thinking to trial execution, CROs replicated the sponsor's centralised, academic medical centre model, inheriting the same systematic exclusion of community clinics and diverse populations that design thinking would address through discovery-phase

* Industry analysts report that CRO services expenditure grew from approximately 4% of pharmaceutical R&D spending in the early 1990s to nearly 50% by the mid-2000s. More recently, CRO and CDMO spending has grown 12–13% annually compared to 7–8% overall R&D growth (2014–2022).

† The same report notes: 'some outsourcing relationships lack the 'maturity' needed to "fully realize the potential gains in R&D efficiency and flexibility,"' and identifies five key areas where partners 'see opportunities to unlock greater value from their collaboration.' The firm surveyed leaders from pharmaceutical R&D and supplier organisations, with more than 80% projecting supplier spending could rise 10–30% over the next 2–5 years.

stakeholder mapping [11, 12].* Outsourcing didn't solve design problems; it postponed them while adding coordination complexity and severing the feedback loops that enable learning. The pendulum now swings back as large pharmaceutical companies bring R&D capabilities in-house [13],† having discovered that outsourcing created new problems without addressing fundamental design failures in trial methodology.

The Lesson for Healthcare Leaders

For transformation directors facing pressure to hire management consultants, the CRO experience demonstrates a critical principle: you cannot outsource core transformation capabilities. Design thinking methodology matters, but the deep domain expertise resides in your clinical workforce—the people who already practise sophisticated complexity science daily. As Chapter 5 established, clinicians already practice design thinking methodology through clinical reasoning.

True transformation capability develops internally through investment in staff development, protected time for improvement work, leadership willing to learn alongside frontline experts, and recognition that clinical expertise transfers to system design. External consultants can facilitate the recognition of existing capabilities, but they cannot substitute for them. The most successful transformations happen when organisations develop their own design thinking capabilities rather than renting them. This requires harder work over longer timelines than hiring consultants, but it builds sustainable capability rather than temporary intervention.

The Regulatory Landscape

More than 100 national or regional regulatory authorities worldwide oversee pharmaceutical products and medical devices. The International Council for Harmonisation of Technical Requirements for Pharmaceuticals for Human Use (ICH) works to standardise regulatory approaches across regions, but despite this coordination, developers must still capture and meet all regulatory requirements or make difficult decisions about which markets to exclude.

The United States represents a crucial marketplace for pharmaceutical companies worldwide. Following the COVID-19 pandemic, the FDA issued increasingly stringent guidelines to involve diverse populations in clinical trials. The 2025 FDA guidance on diversity to improve the enrolment of participants from underrepresented populations in clinical studies formalises expectations that the industry struggles to meet due to its structural centralisation [14].

The fundamental regulatory complexity will persist: global pharmaceutical development requires navigation of multiple regulatory frameworks, each with legitimate but sometimes conflicting requirements designed to protect patient safety and ensure product efficacy.

* Traditional CRO models have historically focused on academic medical centres and large hospital networks for trial site selection, replicating pharmaceutical sponsors' existing infrastructure preferences. This centralised approach systematically excludes community clinics and safety-net providers serving diverse populations. The FDA's guidance on enhancing diversity in clinical trials explicitly acknowledges that traditional trial designs and site selection practices create barriers to participation for underrepresented populations.

† Large pharmaceutical firms increasingly maintain core competencies such as protocol development and site selection in-house while outsourcing only standardised activities. The report notes that 'what initially started as a large-scale swing toward full-service outsourcing to contract research organisations (CROs) has given way to a return to more insourcing among biopharmaceutical companies, especially amongst larger pharma companies.'

Design Thinking Solutions: Learning from Automotive

My perspective on clinical trials emerged from experience across traditionally separate domains: medical practice, automotive design at Jaguar, and healthcare innovation leadership. This cross-sectoral background revealed how different industries approach complexity. Automotive and aerospace systematically integrate regulatory requirements into their design process from the start. Pharmaceutical development often treats regulatory compliance as a checkpoint rather than a design driver—discovering late in development that protocol designs don't align with regulatory requirements in key markets.

The secret of Jaguar's success involved more than our splendid design team. At the back of our R&D site sat a small Regulatory department that, at the very beginning of our design process, provided us with the combined requirements for all our markets. This ensured that we efficiently produced one car designed for all markets simultaneously. Competitors without such a function effectively excluded themselves from key markets—discovering too late that their designs couldn't meet regulatory requirements in important regions.

This observation aligns precisely with the Double Diamond model. Adequate discovery and definition phases prevent costly issues in development and delivery. Clinical trials represent work in the Develop phase of the second diamond. Jaguar's regulatory integration taught us that we needed to focus intensively on the first diamond—understanding the complete problem space, including regulatory requirements, before beginning solution development.

The Double Diamond Applied to Clinical Trials

The Double Diamond model provides particular value through its visual emphasis on diamond size. The diamonds are the same size because it's necessary to spend equal effort and resources on discover and define as on develop and deliver. This seemingly simple principle carries profound implications for clinical trials. If inadequate effort goes into understanding and defining the problem, more time and cost inevitably appear in solving it—sometimes requiring a complete return to discover and define, adding even more time and costs that could have been avoided. Current clinical trials violate this principle systematically, spending perhaps less than 10% of effort on problem understanding before rushing to protocol development.

The insight has direct relevance to clinical trials, which are part of the Develop phase in the second diamond. It tells us we should focus on the first diamond to better understand the problem and, crucially, who is suffering from it. This patient-centred reorientation represents the foundation of design thinking applied to clinical trials.

Discover: Understanding Patient Needs

Empathy and understanding of diverse patient needs form the starting point—always—no exception. This requires walking in patients' shoes, getting out into the community, observing, and talking with them in their own environments rather than solely in clinical settings. Sense-making tools like patient journey mapping make invisible barriers visible—and once barriers become visible, they become addressable.

Personas provide a powerful design tool for capturing this empathy. These are patient profiles that help develop products and services grounded in real human needs rather than abstract regulatory requirements. At OnKai, we used the persona of Amber, a fictional midwife, to inform decisions at key development stages. This ensures that technology developed for healthcare equity remains grounded in the realities of frontline healthcare delivery in underserved communities.

Ethnography—the systematic study of people and cultures through direct observation—helps teams understand cultural dimensions that influence trial participation. Patient journey mapping asks people what currently works for them, what doesn't work, and what they would like to change. These tools reveal barriers invisible to researchers working primarily in academic medical centres.

The discovery phase also requires engaging with the broader stakeholder ecosystem: local healthcare professionals who could support trial participation in community settings, community leaders who can identify cultural barriers and build trust, patient advocacy groups who understand the lived experience of people with specific conditions, and even early regulatory dialogue to understand the boundary conditions within which trial design must operate.

Define: Co-Design Before Protocol Development

Co-design starts by involving all stakeholders in the 'Problem' diamond before the clinical trial protocol is designed. Grounded in common sense, it involves stakeholders such as local healthcare professionals, community leaders, and patient advocacy groups. Critically, their involvement continues throughout the clinical trial and beyond—not as consultants brought in to review a finished protocol, but as partners in defining what problem the trial needs to solve and how it might best solve it.

As Chapter 5 demonstrated, clinicians already practice design thinking through diagnostic methodology—co-design enables them to apply this expertise to trial design. This approach recognises a fundamental truth: pharmaceutical companies don't lack design thinking expertise—they lack mechanisms for clinicians to apply the sophisticated complexity science methodology they already practise. The transformation challenge isn't building new capability but removing barriers preventing existing capability from operating at organisational scale.

Tools for this phase include stakeholder analysis and mapping, visualisation of stakeholder workflows to identify integration points and potential friction, and shared visual management systems that allow CROs and sponsors to maintain alignment. Scenario planning with regulators can surface potential approval pathways early, when protocol adjustments cost thousands of dollars rather than millions. Co-design enables controlled experimentation before full implementation, reducing risk while improving outcomes.

This co-design phase reveals that many protocol amendments stem from disconnects between scientific objectives and operational realities. Protocol amendments typically cost approximately $500,000 each and add months to timelines. Rather than treating amendments as isolated events, design methods map the entire amendment ecosystem. It can be expected that implementing cross-functional protocol review workshops using visualisation tools from design thinking will reduce amendments by 40%, saving millions while accelerating timelines. The solution is not working harder or adding more oversight. It's working differently; bringing stakeholders together early to identify misalignments before they become expensive problems.

Develop: Inclusive Recruitment Strategies

Clinical trials remain too centralised. Locations and processes must become accessible. It's necessary to build capability where people are—in their existing local clinics, through satellite centres, and via mobile clinics. This implies a strategic shift: it's in the pharmaceutical industry's interest to decentralise and develop the capability to conduct clinical trials in community settings. Healthcare practitioners there might lack practical experience with clinical trials, but they already possess the scientific rigour necessary to participate—acquired through education and training in university hospitals. In practice, this might start with Phase III trials and market surveillance activities, which require straightforward monitoring with devices and techniques suitable for community settings, before expanding to more complex early-phase research.

COUNTERINTUITIVE FINDING

Pharmaceutical companies assume clinical trial capability requires specialised research training at academic medical centres. This excludes community clinicians from trial participation, concentrating research in elite institutions and systematically excluding diverse populations. The assumption reverses causality: community clinicians lack trial experience not because they lack capability, but because trials were designed to exclude them. Every community physician received the same scientific training as academic researchers—they just work in different settings. As Chapter 5 demonstrates, clinicians already practise sophisticated design thinking through diagnostic methodology. The transformation challenge isn't building new capability but removing barriers preventing existing capability from operating at organisational scale. Pharma doesn't lack design expertise—it lacks mechanisms for clinicians to apply the complexity science methodology they already practice.

The design approach employs early prototyping of recruitment strategies, testing approaches before full implementation. Rapid cycle tests of interventions allow teams to identify what works in specific communities before committing to protocols that might fail. This iterative refinement based on real-world feedback exemplifies design thinking's power to reduce risk while improving outcomes. Feedback mechanisms create channels for continuous patient and site input, helping detect emerging issues before they become critical.

CO-DESIGN IN PRACTICE: COMMUNITY-BASED CARDIOVASCULAR TRIAL

The following illustrative example demonstrates design thinking principles applied to clinical trial recruitment. While this specific case is constructed to show methodology, it reflects documented patterns from pharmaceutical companies implementing co-design approaches.

A pharmaceutical company conducting a cardiovascular disease trial applied design thinking to address recruitment challenges. Instead of relying solely on clinical data, researchers spent time in community settings understanding barriers to trial participation. They discovered that transportation difficulties, work schedule conflicts, and historical mistrust represented primary obstacles—insights unlikely to emerge from traditional protocol development processes.

The team co-created trial requirements with community representatives, focusing on what would make participation possible rather than just scientifically ideal. The resulting protocol incorporated evening appointments to accommodate work schedules, transportation support to remove access barriers, and community-based monitoring to reduce required hospital visits. Critically, local healthcare providers became co-researchers rather than just referral sources.

The results validated the design thinking approach: the trial completed enrolment 40% faster than comparable studies, achieved representation matching disease prevalence demographics, and required zero major protocol amendments.

This co-design methodology extends beyond clinical trials to broader cardiovascular service delivery, with documented outcomes validating the approach. Bernier et al. (2024) applied iterative co-design with healthcare professionals, managers, and patients across two remote Canadian regions located more than two hours from tertiary cardiology centres. Facing barriers identical to those preventing trial participation—patients navigating multiple hospitals, centralised services requiring long-distance travel, and professional resource shortages—participants developed a decentralised six-phase cardiac rehabilitation pathway. The resulting programme created regional nurse coordinators to prevent patients being 'lost' between facilities, offered cardiac risk stratification in patients' home communities rather than requiring two-hour drives, and established three nursing service pathways (primary care, chronic disease programmes, home care) bringing expertise to patients rather than expecting patients to overcome distance barriers [15].

Similarly, Azar et al. (2025) used co-design in Australia to develop a Patient Discharge Action Plan addressing cardiovascular service accessibility across four Victorian health services. Through focus groups and development workshops with patients, clinicians, and culturally diverse health consumers, participants identified that patients felt 'lost' after discharge—receiving generic information while lacking personalised guidance for home management. The co-designed intervention arranges follow-up appointments before discharge, provides personalised action plans, and offers contact numbers for post-discharge support [16].

Both studies demonstrate that involving patients and frontline clinicians in service design reveals operational barriers invisible to protocol designers working in isolation, leading to decentralised delivery models, flexible pathways adapted to local contexts, and dramatically improved access for underserved populations. The methodology is replicable; the results are measurable; the principle transfers across other interventions including clinical trials.

Deliver: Data-Driven Decision-Making

Decision-making about data collection and analysis should be driven by data on patient demographics: race, ethnicity, gender, socioeconomic factors. Digital design and visualisation tools transform this data into actionable insights about geographic access patterns and underserved populations. This data-driven approach enables pharmaceutical companies to make strategic decisions about site selection and community partnership development before protocols are finalised. It allows realistic assessment of whether proposed recruitment strategies can achieve required diversity targets. It surfaces potential problems early, when solutions cost thousands rather than millions.

Design Thinking Principles: A Systematic Framework

Design thinking offers a systematic framework for addressing clinical trial challenges. Table 6.1 summarises core principles and their clinical trial applications.

Design represents a superpower that everybody needs. It allows people to challenge the status quo and change it. Design isn't exclusive to designers—everybody needs access to this capability. However, it is not a magic wand. People need to build confidence in design by trying different tools and techniques to find those most suitable for the context of clinical trials and their organisation. The design methods, tools, and technologies that work in one situation or organisation may not work in another. Developing the right design approach requires practical experience. This experience builds confidence to embrace complexity and deal with risk. Using design thinking in clinical trials leads to integrated development—a way to consistently innovate products and services rather than relying on the unsustainable attrition model that currently dominates pharmaceutical development.

The Business Case: Financial Impact

The business case for implementing design thinking in clinical trials proves compelling across multiple dimensions:

Reduced development costs emerge from improving trial design through patient and stakeholder input early in the process. Companies avoid costly protocol amendments averaging $500,000 per change. The principle aligns with the Double Diamond model: front-load effort in the 'Problem' diamond to prevent expensive delays during the 'Solution' phase. This can reduce amendments by 40%, generating millions in savings.

Table 6.1 Design Thinking for Clinical Trials

Principle	*Clinical Trials Application*	*Design Tools*
Empathy and Understanding	Diverse patient needs research	Personas, community observation
Human-Centred Design	Trial design focused on participant experience	Patient journey mapping
Co-Design and Community Engagement	All stakeholders involved from start	Ethnography, workshops, stakeholder mapping
Iterative Prototyping	Test recruitment strategies before launch	Rapid prototyping, pilot studies
Inclusive Recruitment	Accessible locations and processes	Community partnerships, mobile clinics
Data-Driven Inclusivity	Demographics guide strategic decisions	Digital visualisation, Geographic Information System mapping

Faster time-to-market results from decentralised trials with improved recruitment strategies. Reducing enrolment periods by 30–50%—as demonstrated in the cardiovascular trial case study's 40% faster enrolment—translates to hundreds of millions in additional patent-protected market time. Cutting 2–3 years from the development timeline doesn't just save development costs—it dramatically extends the revenue-generating period, often worth more than the entire development cost.

Higher success rates follow from a better understanding of diverse patient needs, leading to more effective therapies developed through co-design with the patients who will ultimately use them. Fewer late-stage failures occur when trials include representative populations from the beginning, reducing the risk of discovering efficacy or safety problems only after approval—when costs are highest and reputational damage most severe.

Regulatory compliance improves when meeting FDA diversity requirements becomes baked into trial design rather than attempted through last-minute recruitment pushes. Prevention of approval delays saves $1–2 million per day in lost revenue. Companies that achieve faster regulatory review through superior diversity data and robust trial design gain a competitive advantage that compounds across their development pipeline.

The economic case extends beyond pharmaceutical-specific benefits. McKinsey's analysis of 300 publicly listed companies demonstrates that top 'design' performers achieve 32% higher revenue growth and 56% higher shareholder returns [17]. The UK Design Council's comprehensive impact studies show returns of £4 to £20 for every £1 invested in design, with the higher returns associated with strategic design integration rather than project-level application [18, 19]. These cross-sector validations suggest that design thinking's value in clinical trials reflects broader economic principles rather than domain-specific circumstances. Table 6.2 summarises the potential improvements.

Decentralised Trials: Design Thinking in Practice

Centralisation of healthcare delivery and clinical trials wasn't inevitable—it was a choice, made incrementally over centuries in response to the increasing complexity of medical technology and the desire to concentrate expertise. But centralisation represents a design choice, not a necessity.

Table 6.2 Summary of the Potential Impact of Design on Clinical Trial Metrics

Metric	*Potential Improvement*
Trial Recruitment Time	30–50% reduction
Protocol Amendments	40% fewer amendments, saving ~£500,000 each
Regulatory Approval Time	Faster approvals through improved diversity compliance
Patient Retention	25–35% improvement in participant retention
Market Time Extension	Additional patent-protected revenue through earlier approvals

Community-based capability isn't just theoretically possible—it's increasingly practical as monitoring technologies become more sophisticated and portable.

Decentralised Clinical Trials (DCTs) embody design thinking principles in practice. Rather than requiring patients to travel to centralised sites, DCTs build capability where patients are: in existing local clinics, through satellite centres, at mobile clinics, and increasingly through home-based monitoring using wearable devices and telemedicine. The approach starts with accessible entry points: Phase III trials require less complex monitoring than early-phase research. Market surveillance activities similarly require straightforward monitoring with devices and techniques suitable for community settings. Local healthcare practitioners trained in university hospitals possess scientific rigour even without extensive trial experience. They can be developed into research-capable sites through partnerships that provide training, quality oversight, and integration with centralised data management systems.

Technology enables this transformation, but technology alone isn't sufficient. The pharmaceutical industry identifies 'keeping up with technology innovation, including hybrid and decentralized trials' as a challenge cited by 32% of survey respondents [6]. The challenge isn't technological capability—remote monitoring, electronic consent, virtual visits, and home-based sample collection all exist and function reliably. The challenge is organisational: shifting from centralised trial design to distributed models that serve patient needs while maintaining data quality and regulatory compliance.

Design thinking provides the framework for this organisational transformation. It starts with understanding patient barriers to trial participation. It continues through co-design of protocols that accommodate real-world constraints. It develops through iterative testing of distributed monitoring approaches. It delivers through continuous refinement based on participant and site feedback.

Critically, regulatory agencies increasingly support this direction and encourage patient-focused drug development. The FDA's Patient-Focused Drug Development initiative specifically calls for greater input from diverse patient populations, making design thinking not just permitted but aligned with regulatory direction. The 2025 FDA guidance on diversity action plans formalises expectations that decentralised approaches can help meet [14].

Decentralised trials don't represent a wholesale rejection of academic medical centres or specialised research sites. They represent an expansion of the research ecosystem to include community-based capability alongside existing centres of excellence. Some trials will always require the specialised infrastructure of academic medical centres—early-phase research with complex monitoring requirements, trials of rare diseases requiring national patient recruitment, research requiring integration with specialised treatment capabilities. But many trials—particularly Phase III efficacy trials and post-marketing surveillance—can be conducted effectively in community settings with appropriate design and support.

Practical Roadmap: From Pilot to Transformation

For pharmaceutical executives considering design thinking, a stepped implementation approach reduces risk while building organisational capability. The roadmap balances ambition with pragmatism, allowing organisations to experience benefits while developing the expertise needed for broader transformation.

Step 1: Begin with a pilot Phase III trial with diversity requirements. Apply design thinking to recruitment and retention strategies. Choose a trial where timeline acceleration and cost reduction can be measured clearly. Build capability with an achievable but meaningful project before tackling highest-complexity challenges.

Step 2: Develop a cross-functional team with training in design methods: patient journey mapping, co-design facilitation, ethnographic research, rapid prototyping, and data visualisation. This team becomes the internal design thinking resource that can support multiple trials and eventually train others. Investment in building this capability yields returns across multiple trials and therapeutic areas.

Step 3: Identify three to five community clinics in underserved areas and develop partnership models that enable research participation. Build trust through sustained engagement rather than transactional relationships. Support community partners with training, infrastructure, and integration with centralised trial management. Building community research capability serves long-term strategic interests beyond any single trial.

Step 4: Track key metrics rigorously: recruitment speed, participant diversity, protocol amendments, retention rates. Document cost savings and timeline reductions. Compare results to comparable trials using traditional approaches. Demonstrate ROI with quantified outcomes that CFOs and boards will find compelling. Share learnings across the organisation to build momentum.

Step 5: Apply lessons learned to additional therapeutic areas and earlier phase trials. Expand systematically, building on success rather than attempting wholesale transformation immediately. Institutionalise design thinking capability through integration into standard operating procedures, training programmes, and performance metrics.

First Steps: Immediate Action

Executives can begin applying design thinking today, even before formal training or organisational restructuring:

Select a current trial experiencing recruitment challenges. These challenges signal misalignment between trial design and participant realities—precisely where design thinking creates value.

Assemble a cross-functional team including clinical operations, medical affairs, patient advocates, and site coordinators. Diversity of perspective reveals problems invisible to any single function.

Apply one design thinking method: patient journey mapping to visualise the complete trial experience from a participant's perspective. Map every touchpoint from initial awareness through study completion, identifying participant-experienced barriers at each stage.

Identify intervention points where small changes might produce significant improvements. Look for high-impact, low-risk opportunities—evening appointment availability, transport support, simplified consent processes, reduced visit frequency, home-based monitoring options.

Implement rapid cycle tests. Test changes with real participants. Measure results in real time. Iterate based on feedback. This transforms trials from rigid protocols into adaptive systems that improve continuously.

Addressing Common Concerns

Three concerns surface repeatedly when pharmaceutical executives consider design thinking. Each has a compelling response grounded in evidence and experience.

Concern: 'We don't have time for this additional process.'
Response: Design thinking front-loads effort in early phases to prevent costlier delays later. By spending adequate time in the Problem diamond, companies avoid expensive and time-consuming amendments during the Solution phase. The protocol amendment case study demonstrated this precisely: investing in cross-functional review workshops up front generated 40% fewer amendments, each saving approximately $500,000 and weeks of timeline delay.
Concern: 'Regulatory requirements don't allow for this flexibility.'
Response: Regulatory agencies increasingly encourage patient-focused drug development. The FDA's Patient-Focused Drug Development initiative specifically calls for greater input from diverse patient populations, making design thinking not just permitted but aligned with regulatory direction. The 2025 FDA diversity guidance formalises expectations that design thinking approaches can help meet. Early regulatory dialogue—a design thinking practice—often reveals that agencies welcome innovative approaches when sponsors can demonstrate how they maintain scientific rigour while improving patient access.
Concern: 'Our scientific teams aren't trained in design methods.'
Response: Design expertise can be developed through targeted training programmes, partnerships with design specialists, and learning-by-doing on pilot projects. The investment in building this capability yields returns across multiple trials and therapeutic areas. More fundamentally, scientists already practice design thinking when they design experiments, interpret unexpected results, and refine hypotheses based on evidence. Extending these existing capabilities to trial design requires coaching and permission more than wholesale re-education.

Transferable Lessons: Beyond Clinical Trials

The principles demonstrated through clinical trial transformation transfer directly to other healthcare domains. For transformation leaders working on surgical pathway redesign, the parallels prove immediate: co-design with the entire multidisciplinary team, patient journey mapping to reveal hidden inefficiencies, rapid prototyping before full implementation, and iterative refinement based on real-world feedback. Clinical trial recruitment challenges mirror patient pathway access barriers. Protocol amendments parallel pathway redesign costs.

For clinicians, understanding why peers avoid research participation illuminates a path forward. Current trial designs violate clinical workflow realities. Protocols developed without frontline input create administrative burden without recognisable clinical value. If trials were designed using co-design principles—involving bedside clinicians in protocol development, minimising documentation burden through smart design, integrating research into existing workflows, and enabling rapid cycle improvement based on clinical feedback—research participation would become part of excellent clinical practice rather than an additional burden.

The clinical trials chapter connects to Chapter 5's insight that clinicians already practice design thinking in patient care. The diagnostic reasoning that characterises excellent clinical medicine—discover through comprehensive history and examination, define through differential diagnosis and hypothesis testing, develop through treatment planning, deliver through implementation and continuous refinement—maps precisely to the Double Diamond.

Looking forward to Chapter 7's examination of AI in healthcare, clinical trials present both opportunities and risks. AI can potentially assist protocol development automation, enable predictive modelling for recruitment optimisation, and analyse the failure patterns of thousands of compounds to predict success factors.

Sustainable transformation requires broader organisational shifts that transcend any single trial or therapeutic area. The future of clinical trials depends not just on better methodology, but on fundamentally different organisational assumptions.

The Future of Clinical Trials: Integrated Development

Organisational transformation requires several concurrent shifts. First, a shared vision: organisational alignment on patient-centred trial design, with commitment from leadership to methodology shift rather than superficial process changes. Second, concurrent development: product development, organisational development, and business model innovation must occur simultaneously rather than sequentially. The linear waterfall process must shift to multi-dimensional, concurrent processes that engage stakeholders from inception and enable continuous iteration throughout.

The benefits become clear through application. Involving patients and clinicians in the development of drugs and devices increases their efficacy. Development costs decline because problems are identified and solved early rather than late. New medicines are adopted faster because communities have already been exposed to them during trials, building familiarity and trust. Using design thinking increases clinical trial capability, improves healthcare outcomes, and addresses health equity—not as separate goals but as integrated outcomes of better design.

Design thinking has been tried and tested in other sectors. Where it's being applied in clinical trials, it's already working—demonstrated through the case studies in this chapter. Proven methods, tools, and techniques exist that people can use to test design thinking and develop confidence in applying it to clinical trials. The missing element isn't methodology or evidence. The missing element is decision: will pharmaceutical leadership commit to transformation?

Design thinking represents the missing link for transformation in clinical trials. Ethical and equitable healthcare requires design thinking in clinical trials.

Call to Action

For Pharmaceutical Executives: Begin with one pilot trial. Choose an upcoming Phase III study with diversity requirements. Apply design thinking to recruitment and retention strategies. Build internal capability systematically through training and partnership with design specialists. Engage community partners authentically, building long-term relationships rather than transactional arrangements. Measure outcomes rigorously, documenting cost savings, timeline reductions, and diversity improvements. Scale proven approaches across therapeutic areas and development phases. The competitive advantage goes to companies that transform their development model before market forces make transformation mandatory.

For Healthcare Systems: Apply these principles to research participation infrastructure. Build community research capability through partnership with academic medical centres. Partner with industry on patient-centred trials that serve local populations while advancing pharmaceutical development. Contribute to health equity through trial access, recognising that research participation represents both individual opportunity and community benefit.

For Clinicians: Recognise your design thinking expertise. The clinical reasoning you apply in patient care transfers directly to trial design. As Chapter 5 demonstrated, you already practise the sophisticated complexity science methodology that design thinking formalised. Engage in co-design of trial protocols when opportunities arise. Advocate for patient-centred research that respects clinical workflow realities. Apply these principles to clinical practice research, improving quality while building evidence. Your role isn't to learn an entirely new methodology—it's to recognise that your diagnostic expertise transfers to organisational challenges, then claim your rightful place in transformation leadership.

Working together, there exists a unique and timely opportunity to make health equity the new reality. Clinical trials redesigned through design thinking can accelerate progress toward this vision, transforming pharmaceutical development while simultaneously addressing healthcare inequity.

References

1. Congressional Budget Office (2021) *Research and Development in the Pharmaceutical Industry.* Available at: https://www.cbo.gov/publication/57126
2. Sertkaya, A. et al. (2022) 'Estimated cost of developing a therapeutic complex medical device in the US', *JAMA Network Open*, 5(9), p. e2231609. https://doi.org/10.1001/jamanetworkopen.2022.31609.
3. Moore, T.J. et al. (2020) 'Variation in the estimated costs of pivotal clinical benefit trials supporting the US approval of new therapeutic agents, 2015–2017: A cross-sectional study', *BMJ Open*, 10(6), p. e038863. https://doi.org/10.1136/bmjopen-2020-038863.
4. Rees, H. (2011) *Supply Chain Management in the Drug Industry.* Wiley.
5. Kimmitt, R. and Vieira, M. (no date) *R&D Time and Success Rate, Knowledge Portal.* Available at: https://www.knowledgeportalia.org/r-d-time-and-success-rate
6. Thermo Fisher Scientific (2022) *Top 5 Challenges for Drug Developers Infographic.* Available at: https://www.ppd.com/wp-content/uploads/2022/12/Top-5-challenges-for-drug-developers-infographic.pdf.
7. Dansk Design Center (2014) *New Innovation Actors.* Available at: https://issuu.com/dansk_design_center/docs/rap_innovation_actors_gb.
8. Tansey, E.M. and Catterall, P.P. (1994) *Monoclonal Antibodies: A Witness Seminar in Contemporary Medical History.* Cambridge: Cambridge University Press.
9. High, K.A. (2020) 'Turning genes into medicines—what have we learned from gene therapy drug development in the past decade?', *Nature Communications*, 11, p. 5821. https://doi.org/10.1038/s41467-020-19507-0.
10. Agrawal, G. et al. (2025) 'Building a shared vision for pharma R&D–supplier partnerships', *McKinsey & Company.* Available at: https://www.mckinsey.com/industries/life-sciences/our-insights/building-a-shared-vision-for-pharma-r-and-d-supplier-partnerships.
11. Chmielewski, M. and Maulden, A. (2026) 'An overview of FDA diversity-related documents for clinical trials', *Applied Clinical Trials Online.* Available at: https://www.appliedclinicaltrialsonline.com/view/an-overview-of-fda-diversity-related-documents-for-clinical-trials.

12. US Food and Drug Administration (2025) *Diversity Action Plans to Improve Enrollment of Participants from Underrepresented Populations in Clinical Studies.* FDA. Available at: https://www.fda.gov/regulatory-information/search-fda-guidance-documents/diversity-action-plans-improve-enrollment-participants-underrepresented-populations-clinical-studies.
13. Bleys, J. et al. (2022) 'CROs and biotech companies: Fine-tuning the partnership', *McKinsey & Company.* Available at: https://www.mckinsey.com/industries/life-sciences/our-insights/cros-and-biotech-companies-fine-tuning-the-partnership.
14. US Food and Drug Administration (2025) *Diversity Action Plans to Improve Enrollment of Participants from Underrepresented Populations in Clinical Studies.* FDA. Available at: https://www.fda.gov/regulatory-information/search-fda-guidance-documents/diversity-action-plans-improve-enrollment-participants-underrepresented-populations-clinical-studies.
15. Bernier, J., Breton, M. and Poitras, M.-E. (2024) 'Co-designing a cardiac rehabilitation program with knowledge users for patients with cardiovascular disease from a remote area', *BMC Health Services Research*, 24(1), p. 869. https://doi.org/10.1186/s12913-024-11321-4.
16. Azar, D. et al. (2025) 'Using codesign to develop a health literacy intervention to improve the accessibility and acceptability of cardiac services: The equal hearts study', *Health Expectations*, 28(3), p. e70328. https://doi.org/10.1111/hex.70328.
17. Sheppard, B. et al. (2018) *The Business Value of Design* | McKinsey. Available at: https://www.mckinsey.com/capabilities/tech-and-ai/our-insights/the-business-value-of-design.
18. Design Council (2007) *The Value of Design Factfinder Report.* Available at: https://www.designcouncil.org.uk/fileadmin/uploads/dc/Documents/TheValueOfDesignFactfinder_Design_Council.pdf.
19. Design Council (2025) *Design Economy.* Available at: https://www.designcouncil.org.uk/our-work/design-economy/.

Chapter 7

AI and Healthcare Equity

TUESDAY MORNING, TWO CITIES

Boston, Massachusetts General Hospital, 7:45 AM

Dr Claudia Marchetti reviews the overnight AI alerts on her tablet. The hospital's new $22 million diagnostic AI system has flagged fifteen patients for urgent review. She clicks through to the first case: a 58-year-old presenting with chest pain. The AI confidence score: 94% likelihood of acute coronary syndrome. Recommended action: immediate catheterisation.

Claudia frowns. She saw this patient last night. Classic presentation of costochondritis—inflammation of the chest wall cartilage, not a heart attack. She'd examined him thoroughly, reviewed his ECG, checked his cardiac markers. The AI had access to the same data. Yet it recommended a $15,000 invasive procedure for a condition treatable with anti-inflammatories.

She marks it as a false positive—the fourth this week—and moves to the next alert. The AI has been in place for six months. It was supposed to reduce diagnostic uncertainty, speed up decision-making, catch the cases doctors miss. Instead, it's creating more work. Every alert requires verification. Every recommendation requires clinical override. The technology is sophisticated. The algorithms are cutting-edge. But it doesn't understand medicine the way clinicians do.

In yesterday's departmental meeting, the Medical Director announced they'd be 'refining our engagement with the AI system' and 'optimising clinical workflow integration.' Translation: they'd spent $22 million and couldn't admit it wasn't working.

Detroit, Eastside Community Health Center, 8:00 AM

Amara Johnson, 58, has been trying to get her chest pain checked for three weeks. The federally qualified health centre where she gets care is booked solid for the next month. The urgent care clinic told her to go to the emergency department. The ED said it wasn't an emergency—and sent her a $750 bill just for being triaged. Her insurance through her employer has a $5,000 deductible she hasn't met.

She doesn't have a car. The bus to the nearest hospital takes 90 minutes. She works evening shifts at a nursing home and can't afford to miss work—she's already used her sick

DOI: 10.4324/9781003752073-10

days when her daughter had influenza. She tried calling the health centre's nurse line three times—always voicemail, callbacks promised but never received.

Her daughter found an online symptom checker powered by AI. Free to use. 'Cutting-edge technology bringing healthcare to underserved communities,' the website promised. Amara answered the questions carefully. Yes, chest pain. Yes, worse with deep breathing. No, not radiating to her arm. The AI analysed her symptoms and provided a recommendation: 'Seek emergency care immediately. Your symptoms suggest possible cardiac event.'

Now she's terrified. The AI said emergency. But she remembers her neighbour who went to the ED for chest pain—got a $3,000 bill after insurance, waited eight hours, sent home with ibuprofen. She can't afford another bill like that.

She doesn't know that she has costochondritis. She doesn't know that the free AI was trained primarily on data from insured populations with ready access to emergency care. She doesn't know that the AI was designed for people with consistent insurance and care access—not for Amara's fragmented reality.

She knows that her chest hurts, that she's scared, and that getting healthcare feels impossible. The AI that was supposed to help has made her more anxious and no closer to care.

Same condition. Same symptoms. Two worlds apart.

Claudia has access to AI that's too sophisticated for its own good—expensively wrong, creating more problems than it solves, but at least her patient will get care. Amara has access to AI that's democratically available but contextually blind—free to use but dangerous in its assumptions, widening the gap between promise and reality.

Both AI systems failed. Both were designed with good intentions. Neither was designed through co-design with the people who would use them. Neither addressed the real problems in the healthcare system.

This is the equity paradox of AI in healthcare: technology that could help those who need it most instead helps those who need it least—or helps no one at all.

The Promise and the Paradox

The healthcare industry invests billions in AI annually, yet worldwide 4.6 billion people still lack adequate access to healthcare [1]. Claudia and Amara's experiences—one with too much ineffective AI, one with too little appropriate AI—illustrate the profound disconnect in how AI is failing its fundamental purpose in healthcare.

While sophisticated AI algorithms can detect cancer from medical images with remarkable accuracy, these technologies remain inaccessible to most of humanity. Even when AI is made 'democratically available' through free apps and online tools, it often creates new problems rather than solving existing ones. The technology exists. The algorithms are impressive. But the design thinking that would make them actually useful—particularly for those who need them most—is absent.

Consider the pattern Claudia experiences every morning at Mass General. AI reads radiology scans faster than humans, but doesn't address why patients wait months for appointments. AI automates coding and billing, but doesn't solve why 35% of Medicare beneficiaries saw five or more physicians annually and patients with fragmentation areas had a median of nine visits to six providers [2]. AI predicts hospital readmissions, but doesn't prevent the fragmentation that causes them. The pattern Claudia experiences repeats across healthcare systems globally: sophisticated AI generating more work, clinical overrides required constantly, expensive technology blind to clinical context. It repeats across healthcare systems globally, revealing a fundamental design failure.

When a $2 Billion Market Leader Misses Two-Thirds of Cases

Epic Systems' Sepsis Model illustrates how even the most sophisticated AI can fail when designed without meaningful clinical co-design. The model, integrated into Epic's electronic health record system used by more than half of US hospitals, promised to revolutionise sepsis detection—one of the leading causes of death in hospitalised patients [3].

The promise was compelling: AI analysing patient data every 20 minutes, identifying sepsis risk before clinicians could detect it, enabling earlier treatment that could save lives. Epic validated their model on 405,000 patient encounters and reported strong performance metrics.

Then came the external validation. When researchers at the University of Michigan Medical School examined the model's real-world performance across 38,500 hospitalisations, they found it missed 67% of sepsis cases despite generating alerts on 18% of all hospitalised patients [4]. The model's sensitivity was 33%—meaning it failed to identify two out of every three patients who actually had sepsis. When set to Epic's recommended alert threshold, it identified only 7% of sepsis patients that clinicians had missed.

The clinical impact was devastating. Rather than providing early warning, the model created alert fatigue. Nurses on one unit began covering video cameras used by remote monitoring clinicians because the constant interruptions—up to 18% of patients flagging—made their work impossible. Floor staff learned to ignore the alerts because they were wrong so often.

How did this happen? The model was trained on data that already encoded clinical suspicion. One input variable was antibiotic orders by providers—a form of data leakage (where the algorithm learns from information that wouldn't be available in real-world use) since an infection is already being considered at that point [5]. The AI was essentially learning to detect when clinicians already suspected sepsis, not predicting sepsis before clinical recognition.

This represents a category error in AI development. Epic designed a model to optimise detection within existing clinical workflows rather than questioning whether those workflows served patient needs. The model performed well in retrospective analysis—looking backward at cases where sepsis was already diagnosed—but failed prospectively when clinicians needed it most: before they suspected sepsis.

A subsequent study examining the same model across nine networked hospitals found that performance varied dramatically based on hospital characteristics [6]. The model performed worse in centres with more sepsis cases, more patients with multiple conditions, and more oncology patients—precisely the populations most vulnerable to sepsis and most in need of early detection.

Epic has since overhauled the model. But the damage extends beyond one algorithm. Hundreds of hospitals deployed this model and treated it as validated science because Epic is a market leader. Organisations using earlier versions should request validation data for the updated model and assess whether re-implementation justifies continued investment.

The experience illustrates three critical design failures that apply across healthcare AI:

- **Optimisation for retrospective accuracy rather than usefulness in real-time practice.** The model was excellent at identifying patients who already had sepsis—but that's not what clinicians needed.

- **Proprietary development without external validation before deployment.** Independent evaluation only occurred after widespread adoption revealed the problems.
- **Algorithm design that reinforces existing clinical patterns rather than addressing underlying care delivery failures.** The model tried to predict sepsis within the hospital-centric, reactive care model rather than questioning whether earlier community-based intervention could prevent sepsis hospitalisations entirely.

This pattern—sophisticated technology deployed without design thinking—repeats across healthcare AI implementations globally.

COUNTERINTUITIVE FINDING

More Sophisticated AI Produces Worse Health Equity Outcomes

Healthcare leaders assume higher-performing AI produces better outcomes: a 90% accurate algorithm must outperform an 85% accurate one. The equity paradox inverts this logic: an algorithm with 90% accuracy that performs poorly for minority populations creates worse overall outcomes than one with 85% accuracy that performs consistently across all populations. Epic's Sepsis Model demonstrated this perfectly—external validation found it missed 67% of sepsis cases while generating alerts on 18% of hospitalised patients. More revealing: it performed WORSE in centres with more sepsis cases, more complex patients, and higher vulnerability—precisely where early detection matters most. More sophisticated AI often produces worse equity outcomes because it optimises for aggregate technical performance rather than equitable impact. The most advanced technology systematically fails those who need it most, not despite its sophistication but because of how sophistication is measured and optimised.

Why AI Implementations Consistently Fail

Today's healthcare AI applications—diagnostic tools, administrative automation, clinical decision support—fundamentally miss the transformative opportunity. They optimise individual processes within the existing system rather than enabling the system redesign that healthcare desperately needs.

This pattern reflects how these systems are conceived and built. Most healthcare AI emerges from two sources: technology companies seeking healthcare markets for existing capabilities, and healthcare organisations trying to digitise current workflows. Neither approach questions whether those workflows should exist at all.

The result is predictable: AI that makes broken systems more efficiently broken.

The Technology-Led Trap

Technology companies approach healthcare with solutions seeking problems. They possess sophisticated algorithms, massive computing power, and engineering talent. What they lack is a deep understanding of clinical context, care delivery complexity, and patient needs—particularly for underserved populations.

When IBM's Watson for Oncology was deployed globally, it promised to revolutionise cancer treatment by analysing vast medical literature and patient data to recommend optimal therapies [7]. Watson was piloted in collaboration with Memorial Sloan Kettering Cancer Center [8]. Multiple health systems worldwide invested tens of millions in implementation.

The outcome reveals what happens when sophisticated technology meets clinical reality without co-design. Watson frequently recommended treatments that contradicted oncologists' clinical judgement, particularly for complex cases. At Jupiter Hospital in India, doctors found Watson's recommendations clinically inappropriate in multiple instances—including suggesting treatments unavailable in that healthcare context. The MD Anderson Cancer Center ended their Watson project after spending $62 million with minimal clinical benefit [9].

The fundamental error runs deeper than poor performance metrics. Watson was trained primarily on hypothetical patient scenarios created by oncologists at a single institution (Memorial Sloan Kettering) rather than real-world patient outcomes across diverse populations [10]. The AI learned patterns from idealised cases that reflected one institution's treatment philosophies, not evidence-based outcomes from heterogeneous patient populations in varied care settings.

This matters for equity. Cancer affects populations differently—by race, ethnicity, socioeconomic status, geographic location, and access to healthcare resources. An AI trained on cases from a wealthy Manhattan cancer centre doesn't understand how to recommend treatment for a patient in rural India with limited access to advanced therapies, or an uninsured patient in Detroit navigating fragmented care. The algorithm optimised for one context becomes dangerous in others.

Watson's failure demonstrates why technology-led development inevitably produces equity failures. Effective AI starts with diverse patient needs and care delivery contexts. Otherwise, even sophisticated algorithms fail populations that differ from training data. Design thinking inverts this: start with understanding diverse needs, then design technology to address them.

For transformation leaders evaluating oncology AI, Watson's failure highlights essential questions: Was the algorithm trained on real patient outcomes or expert opinion? Has it been validated across diverse populations reflecting your patient demographics? Can oncologists explain why they trust (or don't trust) its recommendations? Without satisfactory answers, even sophisticated technology from reputable vendors creates risk rather than value.

The Workflow Optimisation Delusion

The alternative approach—digitising existing workflows—produces different problems with similar consequences. Healthcare organisations deploy AI to make current processes faster or cheaper without questioning whether those processes serve patient needs.

Administrative AI provides clear examples. Healthcare systems invest heavily in algorithms that optimise appointment scheduling, automate coding and billing, and predict no-show rates. In critical care, similar thinking deploys AI to predict ICU length of stay—optimising bed turnover efficiency without questioning why patients require prolonged ICU care. The algorithm learns to predict what happens within current systems rather than identifying modifiable factors that could reduce ICU dependence entirely.

These tools may improve operational efficiency, but they optimise for institutional convenience rather than patient access.

Consider appointment scheduling AI that maximises provider utilisation by minimising gaps between appointments. This creates optimal efficiency for the clinic but exacerbates wait times for patients and reduces flexibility for urgent needs. The AI makes the system more efficient at delivering care on the institution's terms, not the patient's.

Similarly, AI that predicts which patients are likely to miss appointments might be used to overbook (common in some practices) or to identify patients for reminder calls. But it doesn't address why patients miss appointments—transportation barriers, work schedule conflicts, childcare challenges, costs they can't afford. Optimising around no-shows accepts missed appointments as inevitable rather than treating them as symptoms of access barriers requiring system redesign.

Recent clinical analysis articulates why EHR-driven AI implementations exhaust physicians. Physician-epidemiologist Arina Cadariu applies Kahneman's System 1/System 2 framework to explain the cognitive cost [11]. Expert clinical judgement operates primarily in System 1—fast, intuitive pattern recognition developed through thousands of patient encounters. The experienced physician who notes a patient 'looks sick' despite normal vitals is exercising System 1 expertise that cannot be fully articulated but is usually correct.

EHR systems force constant switching to System 2—slow, analytical, deliberate processing. Every clinical observation must be immediately documented through checkboxes. Every assessment is interrupted by alerts. This constant cognitive switching is neurologically expensive, degrading both clinical performance and physician wellbeing. AI trained on these checkbox artifacts learns patterns from physicians operating in forced System 2 mode, missing the System 1 insights that often matter most for patient outcomes. This cognitive mismatch reflects a deeper structural problem.

Cadariu cites information philosopher Luciano Floridi's framework of 'Levels of Abstraction' illuminates why Epic-trained algorithms systematically fail [12]. EHR systems operate at an Administrative/Financial Level of Abstraction—optimised for billing codes, insurance claims, and regulatory compliance. Medicine requires a Clinical/Phenomenological Level of Abstraction—optimised for diagnosis, treatment, and patient experience. These levels are incommensurable; translation between them requires loss of essential information. AI algorithms inherit their training data's Level of Abstraction. When trained on administratively-abstracted data, they cannot support clinically-abstracted decisions regardless of algorithmic sophistication.

This mirrors Lean implementation failures—Lean tools can make broken processes more efficient; design thinking questions whether the process should exist. AI deployed without design thinking optimises the status quo rather than enabling transformation.

This optimisation-without-redesign thinking extends to policy level. A 2025 European Union study on AI deployment in healthcare—commissioned from PwC and spanning 194 pages—focuses entirely on deployment challenges, regulatory frameworks, and market analysis [13]. Notably absent: any consideration of whether AI deployments address actual healthcare needs or enable system transformation. The report exemplifies institutional blindness to design thinking—analysing how to deploy technology faster while ignoring whether that technology serves patients or merely optimises broken systems.

The Equity Amplification Problem

Both technology-led and workflow-optimisation approaches share a fatal flaw: they systematically advantage already-advantaged populations while widening disparities for underserved communities.

Return to Christensen's disruptive innovation framework from Chapter 2. Successful disruptors start by serving overlooked customer segments with simpler, more accessible solutions, then improve until they can serve mainstream markets. Healthcare AI follows the opposite pattern. Development focuses on well-resourced academic medical centres with sophisticated infrastructure, highly insured populations, and comprehensive data. Success in these settings leads to deployment assuming universal applicability.

But healthcare context varies dramatically. The AI that works at Massachusetts General doesn't translate to federally qualified health centres in Detroit. Training data from insured populations doesn't reflect uninsured patients navigating fragmented care. Algorithms optimised for populations with regular primary care access fail for those using emergency departments as their usual source of care.

Consider chronic disease management AI designed to identify patients at high risk for complications and recommend interventions. If trained primarily on patients with continuous health insurance and regular healthcare engagement, the algorithm learns patterns that don't apply to patients with insurance gaps, sporadic access, and multiple competing priorities.

The result: AI predicts risk accurately for already-engaged patients who need intervention least, while missing or misclassifying high-risk patients most in need of support. This isn't a technical failure—the algorithm performs exactly as designed. It's a design failure: building tools optimised for populations already well served rather than those underserved.

How Algorithmic Bias Encodes Disparities

This equity amplification manifests most dangerously through algorithmic bias—not the intentional discrimination of prejudiced developers, but the systematic encoding of historical healthcare disparities into AI systems that then perpetuate and amplify them.

A landmark study published in Science examined a widely used algorithm affecting millions of patients that determines which patients receive extra healthcare resources [14]. The algorithm used healthcare costs as a proxy for health needs, assuming patients who cost more need more care. This seems logical—until you recognise that healthcare costs reflect access and utilisation patterns, not just clinical need.

The result: at a given risk score, Black patients were considerably sicker than White patients. Why? Black patients face systematic barriers to healthcare access resulting in lower spending despite greater medical need. They receive care later in disease progression, have fewer preventive interventions, and navigate fragmented systems. The algorithm learned to equate 'lower cost' with 'lower need,' systematically underestimating illness severity in Black patients.

The researchers estimated that this bias reduced the number of Black patients identified for additional care by more than half. Fixing the algorithm required redesigning it to predict illness rather than cost—using co-design with clinicians and patients to define what 'need' actually means rather than accepting cost as a proxy.

This pattern repeats across healthcare AI:

- Diagnostic algorithms trained predominantly on data from White patients perform worse on darker skin tones
- Natural language processing trained on clinical notes encodes physicians' documented biases
- Prediction models trained on populations with consistent healthcare access fail for those with fragmented care

The solution isn't better algorithms—it's design thinking. Begin by understanding how healthcare disparities manifest in data. Engage diverse populations in defining what outcomes matter. Test algorithms across demographic groups before deployment. Monitor equity outcomes continuously after implementation. This requires recognising that technical performance metrics don't capture equity impact.

Understanding why these patterns persist requires examining how healthcare has approached computational problems across decades. These patterns—technology-led development, workflow optimisation without redesign, systematic equity amplification—didn't emerge recently. I've watched healthcare fail to implement obvious computational solutions across my entire medical career, a pattern that reveals why today's AI deployments continue failing.

From Recognition to Implementation: A 40-Year Gap

Understanding why AI implementations fail requires recognising a pattern that spans my entire medical career: the distance between identifying computational problems and implementing computational solutions.

1979: When Technology Didn't Exist

In 1979, during my second year at Medical School in Amsterdam, our professor of Internal Medicine presented a case that would shape my understanding of healthcare's fundamental challenge.

A Dutch woman in her late forties, working administratively at the Hoogovens steel plant, was suffering from a mysterious illness. After extensive testing, active pulmonary tuberculosis was discovered—extremely rare in the Netherlands at that time. She had no history of foreign travel. The mystery deepened when we learned that her workplace offered yearly thorax X-rays as a screening programme, a standard perk for administrative staff.

The tuberculosis lesions had been visible on her X-rays going back several years. Multiple radiologists had reviewed these images. None had detected the pathology. They were looking at so many pictures that they failed in their core duty—not through incompetence, but through the inevitable limitations of human cognition processing industrial-scale data.

This wasn't a medical knowledge problem. Tuberculosis on chest X-ray is straightforward for trained radiologists—when they have time to look properly, when they're not fatigued, when they're examining dozens rather than hundreds of images. The failure wasn't clinical. It was computational.

Today, AI systems such as CAD4TB (Netherlands), qXR (India), Lunit INSIGHT CXR (South Korea), and InferRead DR Chest (China) detect tuberculosis lesions that would have been missed in that 1979 screening programme. These systems don't get fatigued. They don't experience cognitive overload. They examine every image with the same attention as the first image of the day.

This experience taught me something profound: *the challenge is not medical complexity—it is computational scale.* Healthcare follows clear rules; there are just millions of permutations that overwhelm human cognition. In 1979, we recognised the need. The technology didn't exist.

2019: When Technology Exists but Isn't Implemented

Forty years later in London, two BBC programmes on the same day revealed the persistent gap: technology advances rapidly, but recognising need rarely translates to appropriate implementation.

The first was a daytime local news segment about Victoria Bus Station in central London, one of the busiest in the world. Dozens of buses from across the UK and Europe navigate a confined space, dropping off and picking up passengers under intense time pressure. The station's prime location allows the local council to charge bus companies premium rates for access.

The buses had electronic trackers. They were connected to the Internet to provide passenger Wi-Fi. The passengers carried smartphones, connected to the Internet either through that Wi-Fi or their mobile data. The computational infrastructure existed to automate station operations entirely.

Yet the programme showed a man in a tower overlooking the bus station with binoculars, pencil, and paper, manually recording the number plate of each bus and its arrival and departure times to pass to the billing department. This was 2019. It would have been a straightforward secondary school computing project to develop an app automating this process.

A couple of hours later, a BBC documentary about NHS hospital operations in the London area showed ward managers and senior nurses leaving their posts at 8:00 AM each morning, iPads in hand, walking across the hospital to a conference room to discuss bed availability. By the time they returned to their wards, the information they'd just shared was already outdated. There was no central database. No connection to electronic health records. No electronic trackers on hospital beds to monitor when they were being moved for cleaning after patient discharge. The technology existed—the same technology connecting those bus station Wi-Fi networks. Yet senior clinical staff spent their mornings in walking meetings sharing information that became stale within minutes, while their wards operated without senior oversight.

Later that same day, the programme showed a neurosurgeon in his scrubs, rucksack still on his back, traipsing from ward to ward negotiating to free up an ICU bed for his patient so he could start the operation.

Words failed me.

Not because I was surprised—I'd seen this pattern throughout my career. But because seeing it documented so starkly, the absurdity became undeniable. A neurosurgeon, one of the most highly trained specialists in medicine, spending his time in administrative negotiation while his patient waited for potentially life-saving surgery. Theatre time wasting away at thousands of pounds per hour. Theatre staff standing idle. The patient under general anaesthesia or being prepped, the clock ticking.

All because the same hospital that couldn't implement a bed tracking system expected a surgeon to solve the problem manually, ward by ward, in his surgical scrubs.

The Pattern: Recognition Without Appropriate Response

These observations, spanning 40 years, reveal healthcare's AI implementation paradox:

1979: We need automation + technology doesn't exist = understandable gap

2019 Commercial: We need automation + technology exists + profit motive exists = inexplicable gap

2019 Healthcare: We need automation + technology exists + lives at stake = catastrophic gap

If profit-driven bus companies can't justify implementing obvious automation, and life-critical NHS operations can't implement straightforward solutions despite desperate staff shortages, the problem isn't technology sophistication. It's not even funding—the Victoria Bus Station billing system would pay for itself in weeks; the NHS bed management system would free senior staff for patient care immediately.

The problem is a systemic inability to translate a recognised need into appropriate design. Both examples show organisations that:

1. Demonstrate they have a computational scale problem
2. Accept wasting valuable resources and inefficiencies
3. Have access to technology that could solve it
4. Continue manual processes that are demonstrably failing
5. Treat automation as 'nice to have' rather than fundamental redesign

This is why healthcare AI implementations fail even when algorithms work perfectly. We deploy sophisticated AI for complex problems (sepsis prediction, cancer diagnosis) while ignoring straightforward automation opportunities. We fund £22 million diagnostic AI systems while senior nurses spend mornings in walking meetings. We build algorithms that nobody asked for while failing to implement solutions to problems everybody recognises.

The bus station binoculars and the walking meetings aren't quaint inefficiencies—they're symptoms of organisations that lack design thinking methodology to translate needs into solutions. Both organisations knew what they needed. Neither had the framework to design appropriate responses.

This pattern explains why healthcare AI produces Epic Sepsis Models (expensive, sophisticated, wrong) rather than bed management systems (simple, straightforward, desperately needed). We're solving for technology sophistication rather than actual needs. We're deploying solutions before understanding problems.

The 2019 NHS bed management failure is particularly instructive for understanding AI implementation. Here's what should have happened through design thinking:

Empathise: Shadow senior nurses during 8:00 AM bed meetings. Understand their actual information needs, not assumed needs.

Define: The problem isn't 'lack of centralised database.' It's 'senior clinical staff absent from wards during critical handover period, sharing information that becomes stale before they can act on it.'

Ideate: Multiple solutions emerge: real-time bed tracking, predictive models for discharge timing, electronic handover systems, automated bed cleaning schedules.

Prototype: Test the simplest solution first—maybe just a shared screen visible from wards, updating in real-time as bed status changes.

Test: Do senior nurses still need morning meetings? Has information staleness improved? Are they present during critical handover?

Instead, hospitals likely did what the bus station did: recognised the problem, assumed existing processes were 'good enough,' and continued manual operations because changing them felt too difficult.

This is the gap design thinking addresses: not building more sophisticated technology, but translating recognised needs into appropriate solutions through systematic understanding of user needs and iterative testing.

Design Thinking as the Correction Framework

The previous chapters established design thinking's methodology: begin with a deep understanding of user needs, iterate through prototyping and testing, and co-design solutions with end users. Applying this to AI development requires a fundamental reorientation from current practice.

Starting with Need, Not Technology

Community-based health programmes demonstrate the alternative approach. Rather than deploying pre-built AI solutions, they begin by understanding community needs through ethnographic research and co-design.

Kaiser Permanente's Community Health Worker initiative illustrates this methodology in practice. Rather than starting with technology, Kaiser began by asking: what barriers prevent members with high social needs from achieving health [15]?

The answer emerged through direct engagement: transportation to appointments, language barriers, navigating complex health systems, access to nutritious food, stable housing. Technology might address some barriers, but the primary need was human connection with someone who shared patients' language, culture, and life experience.

Kaiser partnered with community organisations to deploy health workers who bridge clinical care and social support. For a patient with lung cancer who couldn't reach oncology appointments, the health worker arranged transportation with a Cantonese-speaking driver, created a printed appointment schedule, and connected the patient to food assistance—none requiring sophisticated AI, all addressing actual needs.

Results after five years: members paired with community health workers had more primary care visits, fewer hospital days, and reduced care costs. The programme succeeded not through technological sophistication but through understanding needs and designing appropriate responses.

This represents design thinking applied to healthcare equity: start with the people currently excluded from good care, understand their actual needs and constraints, design solutions that work in their context, then scale and improve. Technology becomes a tool deployed when appropriate, not the starting point.

Co-Design with Clinical and Community Expertise

Effective healthcare AI requires integration of three knowledge domains: technical expertise in algorithm development, clinical expertise in care delivery, and community expertise in lived experience of navigating healthcare systems.

Current AI development typically engages only the first category. Technologists build algorithms, validate on retrospective data, and deploy to clinical settings. Clinicians receive the finished product with minimal input into design. Patients and communities affected by deployment have no voice in development.

Co-design inverts this. Development begins with clinicians and patients describing decision-making challenges and care delivery barriers. Technical expertise then designs AI to address those specific needs, with continuous feedback and iteration before deployment.

Duke's development of sepsis detection models illustrates the difference co-design makes. Rather than optimising for retrospective accuracy, they focused on clinicians' actual decision-making needs: identifying patients at risk before symptoms became obvious, with sufficient advance warning to enable intervention.

This required understanding clinical workflow in detail. When do nurses check vital signs? What data is available at what times? How much advance notice enables meaningful intervention versus creating alert fatigue? The team engaged ICU physicians, ward nurses, and rapid response teams to understand what information would actually change clinical decisions. These questions can only be answered through sustained dialogue with frontline clinicians [16].

The resulting model Sepsis Watch prioritised actionable alerts over technical accuracy. An alert three hours before sepsis onset with 70% accuracy provides more clinical value than an alert at symptom onset with 90% accuracy—the latter simply confirms what clinicians already know. For anaesthetists managing high-risk surgical patients, this early warning enables proactive fluid resuscitation, antibiotic timing optimisation, and ICU bed preparation before septic shock develops—interventions that require lead time to implement effectively [17].

Community engagement adds the third essential perspective. Algorithms trained on hospital data reflect who accesses hospitals—missing populations receiving care in community health centres, emergency departments, or no care at all. Co-design with community health organisations ensures AI addresses the needs of underserved populations, not just those already well-connected to healthcare systems.

Implementation That Enables Rather Than Constrains

AI deployment must support rather than override clinical judgement and community health worker expertise. This requires transparency about algorithmic limitations and integration that enhances rather than replaces human decision-making.

Kaiser Permanente's approach to integrating AI into community health services demonstrates this principle. Rather than deploying diagnostic AI directly to community settings, they use predictive analytics to identify members at high risk based on social needs and clinical data—then connect those members with community health workers for human assessment and support [18].

The AI provides screening and prioritisation. The community health worker provides contextual understanding, cultural competency, and relationships that enable trust and engagement. Neither replaces the other; together they extend reach beyond what either could achieve alone.

This contrasts with AI implementations that constrain clinical judgement. When AI recommends treatments without transparency about underlying reasoning, clinicians face a choice: follow recommendations they don't understand, or override them and potentially face liability. Neither option serves patients well.

Effective implementation provides clinicians with AI insights alongside the reasoning and confidence levels, enabling informed integration into clinical decision-making. The Epic Sepsis Model failures partially stemmed from opaque recommendations that clinicians couldn't validate or contextualise.

Measuring Equity Outcomes, Not Just Technical Performance

Current AI evaluation focuses on technical metrics: accuracy, sensitivity, specificity, area under the curve. These matter, but they don't measure what matters most—impact on patient outcomes and health equity.

An algorithm with 90% accuracy that performs poorly for minority populations creates worse outcomes than one with 85% accuracy that performs consistently across populations. But technical evaluation often doesn't stratify performance by race, ethnicity, socioeconomic status, or other equity dimensions.

Design-led AI development measures outcomes that matter:

- Does the AI improve access for underserved populations?
- Does it reduce disparities in care quality or health outcomes?
- Does it enable earlier intervention for those at highest risk?
- Does it support community health workers and clinicians serving vulnerable populations?

These questions require evaluation frameworks that go beyond technical performance to assess equity impact. They demand transparency about training data composition, performance stratification across populations, and real-world impact measurement in diverse settings.

A Framework for Responsible AI Implementation

The patterns of failure and emerging alternative approaches suggest a structured methodology for healthcare organisations approaching AI implementation with equity as a central concern.

Phase 1: Need Identification Through Co-Design

Don't start with technology. Start with understanding.

Before evaluating AI vendors or writing requirements specifications, invest in ethnographic research with frontline staff and patients. What decisions require information that is currently unavailable? What care delivery barriers could technology potentially address? What population health patterns suggest intervention opportunities?

Convene co-design workshops with clinical staff, community health workers, and patients. Use patient journey mapping to identify pain points that technology might address versus those requiring process redesign or resource allocation.

Dedicate 6–8 weeks to this discovery work with weekly sessions. Include diverse participants: frontline nurses alongside senior clinicians, patients from different demographic groups, community health workers serving vulnerable populations. Document not just what people say they need, but observe actual workflows to identify unarticulated challenges.

While this timeline may exceed current procurement cycles, it prevents the far costlier scenario of full deployment followed by abandonment—Epic's Sepsis Model and Watson's oncology failures each required years and tens of millions to recognise and address.

The output isn't a requirements document—it's a deep and common understanding of problems worth solving. Only after this foundation should you evaluate whether AI is appropriate, and if so, what kind serves actual needs rather than vendor capabilities.

Clinical staff bring essential expertise to this phase. You already practise sophisticated complexity science daily—diagnostic reasoning, treatment planning, continuous adaptation.

Your role isn't evaluating algorithms—that's technical expertise. Your role is defining clinical problems worth solving and validating whether proposed solutions address actual needs. Be specific: 'I need to know if this hypotensive patient is compensating well or approaching decompensation' is actionable. 'I need better decision support' is too vague.

This co-design investment—approximately 6–8 hours over 6–8 weeks—prevents the far costlier scenario you've experienced: deploying AI that creates more work than it eliminates, generates alerts you must override, and ultimately gets abandoned after clinicians refuse to use it. Early clinical input ensures the algorithm serves your practice rather than complicating it.

Phase 2: Solution Design with Transparency

Develop AI with clear visibility into reasoning and limitations.

Technical teams should design with clinical and community co-designers and review prototypes iteratively. Don't build in isolation then deploy finished products. Schedule fortnightly reviews where developers present current capabilities and co-designers provide feedback on clinical utility.

Essential transparency requirements:

- What data trained the algorithm, and from what populations?
- How does performance vary across patient demographics?
- What confidence level justifies different recommendations?
- What clinical scenarios does the AI handle well versus poorly?
- How should clinicians integrate AI insights into decision-making?

Build transparency into the interface. When AI recommends an action, show the key factors driving that recommendation and confidence levels.

Phase 3: Validation Across Contexts

Test in the settings and populations where you'll deploy.

The Epic Sepsis Model's failures demonstrate the danger of assuming generalisability. An algorithm validated at one academic medical centre may perform differently at community hospitals, federally qualified health centres, or systems serving different patient populations.

Essential validation steps:

- **Stratified Performance Testing**: evaluate separately for different demographic groups (by race, ethnicity, socioeconomic status), clinical contexts, and social determinant profiles. Report results transparently—if performance varies significantly, understand why before deployment.
- **External Validation**: test at institutions independent of development sites, including at least one site serving predominantly underserved populations.
- **Prospective Evaluation**: validate on real-time data, not retrospective records. Retrospective validation can mislead because data may encode patterns that won't repeat prospectively.
- **Workflow Integration Testing**: assess whether clinicians can use AI insights within actual workflows. Can nurses access recommendations when needed? Does the interface integrate into existing systems?

Dedicate 3–6 months to Phase 3 validation before broader deployment.

Phase 4: Deployment with Monitoring

Plan for continuous evaluation and iteration, not 'set and forget.'

Healthcare systems change. Patient populations change. Care delivery evolves. AI deployed without ongoing monitoring inevitably degrades in performance as the environment shifts from training conditions.

Required monitoring:

- Performance metrics stratified by patient demographics (monthly reporting)
- Clinical override patterns (tracked in real time, reviewed weekly initially)
- Equity outcomes (quarterly assessment)
- Unintended consequences (continuous surveillance with structured feedback)

Establish clear thresholds for intervention. For example: if override rates exceed 30%, pause to investigate. If performance for any demographic group falls below 70% of performance for other groups, require immediate review.

Plan for algorithm recalibration as routine, not crisis response. Schedule quarterly performance reviews and annual comprehensive evaluations. Budget for ongoing maintenance—typically 15–20% of initial development costs annually.

Phase 5: Equity Impact Assessment

Measure whether AI is reducing or exacerbating health disparities.

Technical performance metrics don't capture equity impact. An algorithm might perform well on average while worsening outcomes for specific populations.

Essential equity metrics:

- **Access**: does AI enable care for previously underserved populations? Track utilisation by demographic groups.
- **Quality**: does care quality improve consistently across demographics? Measure process metrics stratified by patient characteristics.
- **Outcomes**: do health outcome disparities narrow or widen? Track clinical outcomes comparing trends across populations.
- **Process**: Are community health workers and clinicians serving vulnerable populations being supported or constrained?

Conduct formal equity impact assessments at 6 months and 12 months post-deployment, then annually. If equity outcomes disappoint despite strong technical performance, redesign may be required—potentially including suspension until equity concerns are addressed.

This phased approach provides governance checkpoints that protect both patient safety and organisational investment, with clear decision criteria at each stage.

Most healthcare organisations have deployed AI that underperforms initial promises—this reflects systemic procurement and implementation challenges, not organisational failure. The frameworks in this chapter enable transformation leaders to shift from defensive positioning around past implementations to confident, evidence-based approaches for future deployments and current system optimisation.

Questions for AI Procurement and Governance

Before committing resources to AI implementation (Phase 1), these questions help assess whether vendors and proposals align with design thinking principles and equity commitments. Use these during vendor evaluation to distinguish genuine co-design approaches from technology-first solutions.

About Development and Validation

- **Training Data**: what populations and care settings generated the training data? How does this compare to our patient population and care settings?
- **External Validation**: has the algorithm been independently validated at institutions similar to ours? What was the performance in those settings?
- **Transparency**: can the vendor explain algorithmic reasoning in clinically meaningful terms? Or is the model a 'black box'?
- **Stratified Performance**: how does the algorithm perform across different patient demographics, clinical presentations, and social determinant profiles?

About Implementation and Integration

- **Clinical Workflow**: how will this integrate into existing workflows? What additional work does it create versus eliminate?
- **Clinician Engagement**: were frontline clinicians involved in development? Do they understand and trust the recommendations?
- **Alert Burden**: how many alerts will this generate? What's the expected positive predictive value (what percentage of alerts indicate true positives versus false alarms)?
- **Override Patterns**: in existing deployments, how often do clinicians override recommendations? What patterns explain overrides?

About Equity and Outcomes

- **Equity Design**: Was the algorithm specifically designed to reduce health disparities? Or is equity an afterthought?
- **Community Engagement**: were patients and community representatives involved in development and testing?
- **Equity Outcomes**: in existing deployments, has the AI reduced or exacerbated disparities in access, quality, or outcomes?
- **Ongoing Monitoring**: what mechanisms ensure continuous equity monitoring post-deployment?

About Governance and Accountability

- **Liability**: if the algorithm makes incorrect recommendations leading to patient harm, what liability does the vendor accept versus passing to clinicians?
- **Algorithm Updates**: how often is the algorithm recalibrated? How are updates validated and communicated?
- **Failure Response**: if post-deployment monitoring reveals poor performance or equity concerns, what's the plan for rapid response including potential suspension?
- **Proprietary Concerns**: Are we locked into a specific vendor's ecosystem? Can we integrate this with other systems or migrate if needed?

The clinical questions that matter:

- **Clinical Validity**: based on your expertise, does this address a real clinical need or an imagined problem?
- **Decision Support**: does this provide information enabling better decisions, or just automated recommendations you'll need to verify anyway?
- **Trust**: would you trust this algorithm's recommendations for your own family members?
- **Improvement**: if this algorithm disagrees with your clinical judgement, do you have confidence the algorithm might be catching something you missed—or is it more likely wrong?

Restarting Failed AI Initiatives

For organisations with existing AI implementations that have disappointed:

Many healthcare systems have deployed AI that isn't delivering promised benefits. Restarting these initiatives through a design thinking lens can salvage investments while achieving meaningful outcomes.

Diagnostic Assessment

First, honestly assess what failed and why.

Common failure patterns:

- **Technology-Led Development**: solution built without understanding actual needs
- **Missing Clinical Expertise**: algorithms designed without meaningful clinician input
- **Equity Blindness**: development focused on well-resourced populations
- **Deployment Mismatch**: algorithm validated in different contexts than deployment settings
- **Workflow Incompatibility**: AI creates more work than it eliminates

For each deployed system, ask:

- Are clinicians using it as intended? If not, why?
- Is it improving outcomes? For which populations?
- Is it reducing or exacerbating disparities?
- What unexpected consequences have emerged?
- What would need to change for this to provide value?

Gather this information through structured interviews with diverse stakeholders—not just enthusiastic early adopters, but sceptics and those who've stopped using the system. Review override logs and utilisation data.

Re-Engagement Process

Don't restart with vendors or technology. Restart with people.

Convene frontline clinicians, community health workers, and patients currently affected by the AI system. In facilitated sessions, explore:

- **What problems were you trying to solve?** (Original intent)
- **What's working?** (Even failed systems may have useful elements)
- **What's failing and why?** (Honest assessment without blame)
- **What would success look like?** (Redefine outcomes)
- **Who hasn't been heard?** (Often includes patients and frontline staff)

This co-design process may reveal that:

- The problem worth solving differs from original assumptions
- Technology is part of the solution but not the whole solution
- Process redesign matters more than algorithm optimisation
- Different populations need different approaches

Document insights without immediately jumping to solutions. Resist pressure to quickly 'fix' the AI. The diagnostic phase deserves time—typically 4–8 weeks of structured engagement.

This diagnostic phase may reveal that discontinuation is more cost-effective than redesign—a decision that protects future investment capacity even as it acknowledges past implementation challenges.

Plan restart in phases with clear evaluation points.
Rather than full-scale redeployment, test redesigned approaches in limited settings with continuous feedback:

Phase 1 (3 months)—Co-design with stakeholders. Define clear success metrics including equity outcomes. Develop revised approach addressing identified failures. Secure commitment from leadership for honest evaluation—including potential discontinuation.

Phase 2 (3 months)—Pilot with one clinical unit or population. Evaluate weekly with front line users through structured feedback. Track metrics daily, review weekly, adjust rapidly. The goal is learning, not proving success.

Phase 3 (6 months)—If pilot succeeds, expand to additional units with ongoing monitoring. If the pilot fails, pause for redesign or discontinue. Define 'success' explicitly before Phase 3 begins.

Decision points: At each phase, assess whether equity outcomes and clinical value justify continuation. Be prepared to stop if the answer is no.

Some will argue this timeline is unrealistic given current pressures. Yet Epic and Watson demonstrate the far greater cost of proceeding without it.

Looking Forward: AI as Enabler of System Transformation

The pattern of AI failures described in this chapter reflects healthcare's broader transformation challenge. Technology deployed without design thinking optimises broken systems rather than enabling redesign.

But AI developed through co-design with clinicians, patients, and communities can enable transformation current approaches can't achieve. Predictive analytics can identify patients at risk before a crisis. Natural language processing can extract insights from unstructured clinical notes. Machine learning can recognise patterns across populations that individual clinicians can't detect.

The question isn't whether to use AI in healthcare. The question is whether we'll continue deploying AI that serves institutional convenience and vendor profits, or whether we'll use design thinking to ensure AI serves patients—particularly those currently underserved.

This requires recognising that AI is a tool, not a solution. Tools serve purposes. Without design thinking to define those purposes through deep understanding of needs, even the most sophisticated AI will fail to deliver meaningful impact.

For transformation leaders navigating governance approval, this approach offers defensible methodology grounded in documented failures and evidence-based successes. Board presentations can frame AI implementation as risk management—each phase provides decision checkpoints that protect organisational investment and patient safety while enabling innovation.

Clinicians sceptical of AI based on past implementation failures aren't resistant to innovation—they're responding rationally to poorly designed systems. Organisations that exclude clinical expertise from AI development systematically deploy tools that fail in practice, regardless of technical sophistication. Clinical engagement isn't an obstacle to overcome; it's a prerequisite for success.

Connecting to Clinical Trials and System Transformation

The principles in this chapter mirror those in Chapter 6's examination of clinical trials. Both AI and clinical trials fail when designed for institutional convenience rather than patient needs. Both succeed when co-designed with diverse populations. Both require questioning fundamental assumptions rather than optimising existing approaches.

The AI that could transform healthcare equity isn't the AI we're currently building. It's the AI that would emerge from starting with underserved populations—designing for Amara's context in Detroit rather than Claudia's in Boston, then improving until it works everywhere. This mirrors Christensen's disruptive innovation pattern: serve the overlooked, build solutions appropriate to their context, improve until you can serve everyone.

The next chapter examines why even optimal AI implementation cannot overcome fundamentally hospital-centric healthcare architecture. Healthcare transformation requires redesigning not just tools, but the entire delivery model—shifting from hospital-centred to patient-centred systems through design thinking applied at ecosystem scale. The AI we need becomes possible only within the redesigned systems we'll explore next.

References

1. World Health Organization (n.d.) *Most Countries Make Progress Towards Universal Health Coverage, But Major Challenges Remain*. WHO. Available at: https://www.who.int/news/item/06-12-2025-most-countries-make-progress-towards-universal-health-coverage-but-major-challenges-remain-who-world-bank-report-finds.
2. Barnett, M.L. et al. (2021) 'Trends in outpatient care for medicare beneficiaries and implications for primary care, 2000 to 2019', *Annals of Internal Medicine*, 174(12), pp. 1658–1665. https://doi.org/10.7326/M21-1523.
3. Morrissey, R. et al. (2025) 'Demographic and regional trends of sepsis mortality in the United States, 1999-2022', *BMC Infectious Diseases*, 25(1), p. 504. https://doi.org/10.1186/s12879-025-10921-7.

4. Wong, A. et al. (2021) 'External validation of a widely implemented proprietary sepsis prediction model in hospitalized patients', *JAMA Internal Medicine*, 181(8), p. 1065. https://doi.org/10.1001/jamainternmed.2021.2626.
5. Habib, A.R., Lin, A.L. and Grant, R.W. (2021) 'The epic sepsis model falls short—the importance of external validation', *JAMA Internal Medicine*, 181(8), p. 1040. https://doi.org/10.1001/jamainternmed.2021.3333.
6. Kamran, F. et al. (2024) 'Evaluation of sepsis prediction models before onset of treatment', *NEJM AI*, 1(3). https://doi.org/10.1056/AIoa2300032.
7. Strickland, E. (2019) *How IBM Watson Overpromised and Underdelivered on AI Health Care - IEEE Spectrum*. Available at: https://spectrum.ieee.org/how-ibm-watson-overpromised-and-underdelivered-on-ai-health-care (Accessed: 12 January 2026).
8. Zauderer, M.G. et al. (2014) 'Piloting IBM Watson oncology within memorial sloan Kettering's regional network.', *Journal of Clinical Oncology*, 32(15_suppl), p. e17653. https://doi.org/10.1200/jco.2014.32.15_suppl.e17653.
9. Schmidt, C. (2017) 'M. D. Anderson breaks with IBM Watson, raising questions about artificial intelligence in oncology', *JNCI: Journal of the National Cancer Institute*, 109(5). https://doi.org/10.1093/jnci/djx113.
10. Roxanne Nelson (2018) *IBM Watson Oncology: Not Living Up to Expectations, Medscape*. Available at: https://www.medscape.com/viewarticle/900746.
11. Cadariu, A. (2026) *THE BIG SICK. How Healthcare's Best Minds Built a Cathedral of Bullshit on a Foundation of Lies | LinkedIn*. Available at: https://www.linkedin.com/pulse/big-sick-how-healthcares-best-minds-built-cathedral-cadariu-md-mph-fg4of/.
12. Floridi, L. (2008) 'The method of levels of abstraction', *Minds and Machines*, 18(3), pp. 303–329. https://doi.org/10.1007/s11023-008-9113-7.
13. European Commission, Directorate-General for Health and Food Safety and PwC (2025) *Study on the Deployment of AI in Healthcare – Final Report*. Publications Office of the European Union. https://doi.org/doi/10.2875/2169577.
14. Obermeyer, Z. et al. (2019) 'Dissecting racial bias in an algorithm used to manage the health of populations', *Science*, 366(6464), pp. 447–453. https://doi.org/10.1126/science.aax2342.
15. Brown, M.C. et al. (2023) 'Kaiser Permanente's social needs network for evaluation and translation empirical research Agenda', *AJPM Focus*, 2(3), p. 100101. https://doi.org/10.1016/j.focus.2023.100101.
16. Sendak, M.P. et al. (2020) 'Real-world integration of a sepsis deep learning technology into routine clinical care: implementation study', *JMIR Medical Informatics*, 8(7), p. e15182. https://doi.org/10.2196/15182.
17. Reyna, M.A. et al. (2020) 'Early prediction of sepsis from clinical data: The physionet/computing in cardiology challenge 2019', *Critical Care Medicine*, 48(2), pp. 210–217. https://doi.org/10.1097/CCM.0000000000004145.
18. Rochman, S. (2024) 'Electronic health records can identify patients in need of social support services', *Kaiser Permanente Division of Research*, 16 July. Available at: https://divisionofresearch.kaiserpermanente.org/ehr-patients-social-support/.

Chapter 8

From Hospital-Centred to Patient-Centred Systems

Patricia sits in the waiting room of an overcrowded urban hospital, her suspicious mammogram results folded in her purse. She took an unpaid day off work, arranged care for her two children and her elderly mum, and travelled an hour by public transport to reach this appointment. After three hours of waiting, a hurried physician spends seven minutes reviewing her case before scheduling her for another appointment—at a different facility, two weeks away. Before that appointment she also needs to find time to go to a 'walk-in' lab to leave blood and urine samples. Pat is anxious about the practicalities—who will take care of her kids and mum when she's in hospital; how she can pay for all this and keep her job. This isn't a failure of individual clinicians or institutional intent. This is healthcare designed around hospitals, not patients. The system works precisely as designed—just not for Patricia's benefit.

COUNTERINTUITIVE FINDING

Workforce Shortage Solution Requires Fewer Hospitals, Not More

Healthcare leaders universally respond to workforce shortages by attempting to increase supply: train more clinicians, build more hospitals, recruit internationally. Yet the mathematics prove this impossible—an 11 million global deficit by 2030 cannot be closed through training. The solution inverts the logic: build FEWER hospitals. Torbay achieved a 33% reduction in hospital beds while improving outcomes and satisfaction. Somerset's Frome Model delivered a 42.5 percentage point advantage in admission rates—impact equivalent to 5% of the UK's entire national healthcare budget. Narayana Health delivers world-class cardiac surgery at 75% cost reduction. These systems didn't solve the workforce crisis by finding more workers—they redesigned care delivery to require fewer workers for better outcomes. When you cannot increase supply, redesign demand.

DOI: 10.4324/9781003752073-11

Closing the Gap

Figure 1.2 shows the growing gap between healthcare demand and supply. The World Health Organisation projects a global shortage of 11 million health workers by 2030. In the United States alone, projections show a shortage of 167,000 physicians and 274,000 nurses by 2032 [1]. These numbers represent a fundamental supply-demand mismatch that threatens healthcare system sustainability worldwide. It is unrealistic to expect the supply to dramatically increase—there aren't enough new healthcare professionals, resources and facilities—the only way is to reduce demand.

On the demand side, an ageing population requires more care while the healthcare workforce cannot scale fast enough to meet these needs. Traditional approaches—training more doctors and nurses—cannot close this gap in time. The mathematics prove unforgiving: we cannot train our way out of this crisis.

Faced with this reality, we have three choices to close the gap.

First, accept the status quo and acknowledge that an increasing proportion of the population will receive inadequate healthcare. This is morally reprehensible—we cannot abandon people to inadequate care.

Second, improve the current system incrementally. We could optimise hospital operations, streamline processes, and enhance efficiency. But this approach assumes the current model is fundamentally sound and needs only fine-tuning. The evidence suggests otherwise.

Third, transform the entire healthcare system from its hospital-centric foundation to one centred on patients in their communities. This requires rethinking how care is delivered, who delivers it, where it happens, and how technology, people, and processes evolve together. This is the only viable path forward. And design thinking is critical to make it work.

That transformation can only be achieved by two simultaneous shifts:

- Providing healthcare in community settings rather than in expensive resource-intensive hospitals, without compromising on quality of care
- From treating sickness to prevention and promoting wellness

Before we explore how design thinking enables closing the gap, we need to understand how we arrived at our current crisis by examining healthcare's evolution.

Hospital-Centric Model Origins and Limitations

The hospital-centric model emerged for valid reasons, but created unintended consequences that now threaten the system's viability.

In medieval times, healthcare was generally more decentralised. A patient with a health concern consulted their healer—a physician, barber-surgeon, or wise woman. The healer would diagnose the problem and provide treatment, often using remedies from their garden or local herbalist. Healthcare was decentralised, delivered in homes and communities by local practitioners who knew their patients personally.

Historical Evolution

This system, while limited by the medical knowledge of its time, operated on a fundamentally sound principle: care delivered where patients lived, by people who understood their context. The relationship was direct, personal, and rooted in the community.

Then came the Renaissance with scientific breakthroughs and technological advancements. Over time sophisticated equipment emerged—X-ray machines, surgical theatres, diagnostic laboratories. These technologies were expensive, complex, and required specialised expertise to operate. Centralisation became necessary. Hospitals concentrated these resources and specialists in single locations, creating centres of medical excellence.

This shift was driven by genuine need. The technology that enabled better diagnosis and treatment simply couldn't be distributed to every village and town. Economies of scale dictated concentration. Hospitals became the only places where advanced medicine could be practised.

Expertise replaced theology as the unifying principle. Stakeholders deferred to medical science, creating alignment through knowledge asymmetry. The doctor-patient relationship maintained coordination through professional judgement.

Impact of Centralisation

But centralisation brought unintended consequences. As healthcare moved into hospitals, stakeholders proliferated. Manufacturers produced equipment. Insurers managed payments. Regulators ensured safety. Administrators coordinated operations. Universities educated clinicians. Each addition was rational, addressing real needs. Yet each new stakeholder added complexity, creating layers between patient and healer.

The simple, empathetic relationship between healer and patient became buried under institutional complexity. The design thinking that once characterised healthcare—understanding patient needs, iterating on solutions, testing what works—was displaced by standardised protocols and bureaucratic processes.

This development happened incrementally. Each layer of complexity solved a real problem. But the cumulative effect was profound: healthcare lost connection to the very principles that made it work. And it lost connection to the people and communities it serves.

The perspective of the patient as a whole person in their own environment and community setting became reduced to a condition. The person behind the condition became lost to 'the acute appendicitis in bed 3,' obscuring their needs such as caring for their family and keeping their job.

Healthcare Today

Today's hospital-centric model shows clear signs of this alienation. Patients are pushed through standardised pathways rather than pulled by their needs. Healthcare professionals, who entered medicine to help people, find themselves constrained by protocols, burdened by documentation, and disconnected from the holistic care they envisioned providing.

The system serves institutional needs—throughput targets, billing codes, regulatory compliance—rather than patient wellbeing. Clinicians spend more time on computers than with patients. Care becomes fragmented across specialties and settings, with no one holding the complete picture of a patient's health journey. Patients become over-medicated because nobody takes ownership and coordinates different treatment regimes. Patients—by the very nature of being unwell—are in no fit state nor equipped to take this coordination upon themselves. Unlike consumers in the market for a new car who can read up on the latest models and take test drives to inform themselves.

This is the paradox: we have better medical technology and knowledge than ever before, yet people report feeling less cared for, less understood, and more like numbers in a system than human beings in need of healing. The hospital-centric model appears inevitable given technology concentration requirements. But evidence demonstrates an alternative is possible—and superior.

Superior Alternative

The Frome Model of Enhanced Primary Care in Somerset (UK) demonstrates what happens when care returns to the community while maintaining clinical quality [2]. General practitioner Dr Helen Kingston initiated this approach in 2013, addressing social determinants of health through community connection rather than purely medical treatment. The model comprised three elements: community resource mapping documenting 400+ local services; community connectors—trained volunteers providing informal signposting through everyday interactions; and health connectors supporting patients with complex needs.

General practitioners prescribed community activities alongside medical treatment, recognising that social isolation's health impact exceeded traditional risk factors. The model operated with just 3–4 primary stakeholders—the GP practice, Health Connections Mendip charity, and voluntary sector—well below the complexity threshold that creates coordination dysfunction.

The results validated the approach. Frome achieved a 14% reduction in emergency hospital admissions from 2013 to 2017, while the rest of Somerset saw a 28.5% increase—a 42.5 percentage point differential. Healthcare costs decreased 21% in Frome while increasing 21% across Somerset. If scaled nationally, the impact would equal 5% of the national healthcare budget.

Frome demonstrates that the hospital-centric model is escapable. Community-based care, designed around patient needs rather than institutional convenience, delivers superior outcomes. The question becomes: how do we scale this approach while avoiding the stakeholder proliferation and complexity that undermined the original community care model?

Community-Based Care as Design Challenge

The hospital-centric model worked when technology demanded centralisation. But we no longer face that constraint. Healthcare must be rethought as a distributed ecosystem where patients receive appropriate care in their communities, with hospitals reserved for truly complex cases requiring concentrated expertise and equipment.

This transformation requires coordinated changes across three dimensions:

- simplifying technology for community deployment
- educating people differently
- redesigning processes around patient journeys.

None of these dimensions alone solve the problem. All three must evolve together, with design thinking as the connecting methodology.

Figure 8.1 illustrates this integration. Technology simplification, people education, and process redesign form three overlapping domains. Where all three converge, patient-centred care

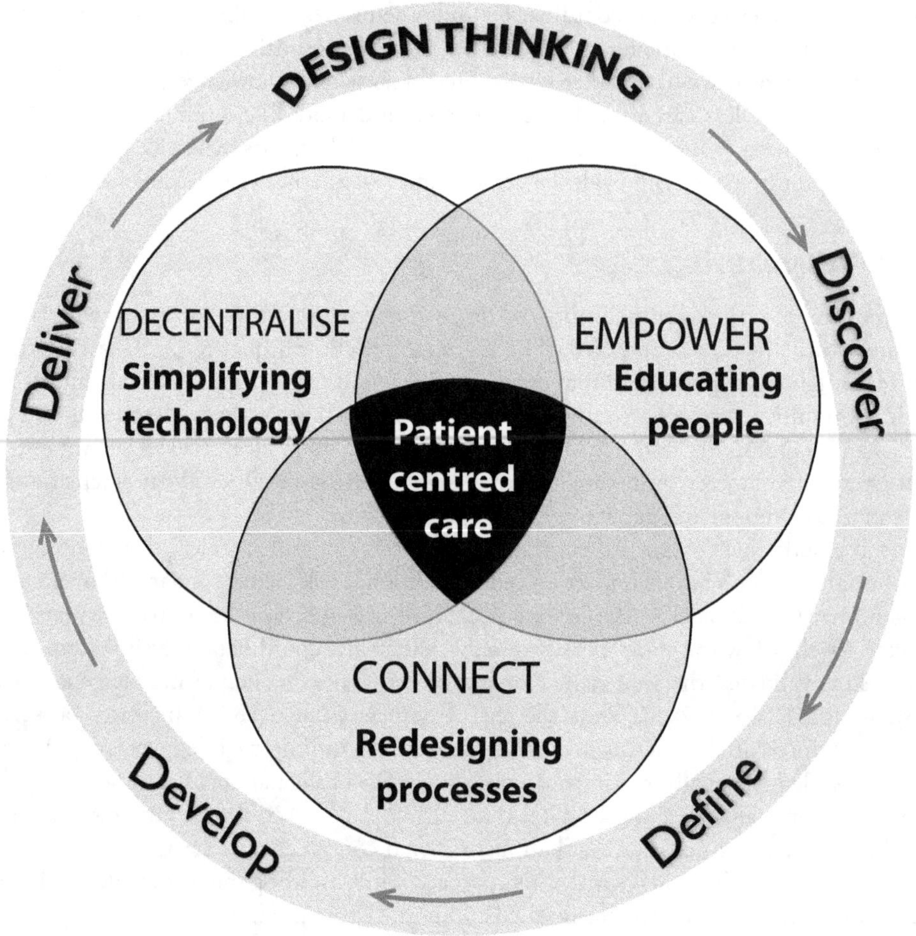

Figure 8.1 Integrating three transformation dimensions through design thinking.

becomes possible. Design thinking provides the iterative methodology—discover, define, develop, deliver—that connects these dimensions and ensures patient focus throughout.

Dimension 1: Simplifying Technology to Decentralise

In Chapter 2, we presented Clayton Christensen's disruptive innovation theory, which explains how complex technologies become simple enough for wider deployment. Initially, new medical technologies require specialised settings—hospitals with trained staff, backup systems, and controlled environments. But over time, innovations make these technologies simpler, smaller, and suitable for point-of-care deployment—see Figure 2.3.

This is about redesigning technology so that community settings can deliver care that previously required hospitals. The technology becomes more user-friendly, more reliable, and more appropriate for distributed use.

Consider dialysis machines. When first developed, they were massive, complex devices requiring hospital infrastructure. Patients had to travel to specialised centres multiple times weekly. As soon as they walked out, they started to feel bad again as their blood slowly got 'poisoned' again. The technology gradually miniaturised and simplified. NxStage Medical developed home dialysis systems that patients could operate themselves, conveniently at home or pack in the back of their car to go on holiday, providing more frequent treatment with better outcomes and lower costs.

This transformation took 60 years—from hospital-only technology to home-based care. But it demonstrates the principle: with thoughtful user-centred design, technologies can evolve from hospital-centric to patient-centric deployment. Many chronic conditions that currently consume hospital resources could be managed in community settings:

- Cardiovascular conditions require blood pressure monitoring, heart rhythm tracking, and medication management.
- Sexual health benefits from prevention strategies.
- Diabetes management involves continuous glucose monitoring, insulin adjustment, and dietary counselling.
- Musculoskeletal conditions need physiotherapy, pain management, and mobility support. Mental health requires counselling, medication monitoring, and crisis intervention.
- Dementia care includes memory support, caregiver training, and safety monitoring.

These conditions require minimal high-tech interventions for initial diagnosis or routine management. With appropriate infrastructure, they can be effectively managed through integrated primary care, supported in the community by multidisciplinary teams and digital tools for monitoring and coordination.

We are at an exciting point where we can miniaturise sophisticated technologies and access knowledge and artificial intelligence through smartphones. Consider wearable technologies. My wife suffers from paroxysmal atrial fibrillation. The first time it happened, she used her Apple Watch to produce an ECG-like trace that she could show to the ED doctor while telling her story. It saved significant time and avoided redundant diagnostics.

Apple's ResearchKit, developed to support clinical research, led to the Apple Watch becoming an FDA-approved medical device for atrial fibrillation detection [3, 4]. This started a wider trend in wearables that supports wellness (sleep monitoring) and conditions such as atrial fibrillation.

New sensors can be integrated into wearable systems for monitoring. Enormous scope exists to develop technologies for prevention and early diagnosis of healthcare conditions. Exciting developments include gait analytics for early onset of Parkinson's or dementia.

Technology newcomers like Apple have demonstrated that consumer-focused design thinking can create medical devices that people actually want to use. This approach—making health monitoring seamless, intuitive, and integrated into daily life—represents the future of community-based care. Diagnostic complexity determines the appropriate setting. Wearable devices detect atrial fibrillation reliably; complex arrhythmias still require specialist consultation.

Community-based care works for stable chronic conditions; acute exacerbations may require hospital resources. This improves patient outcomes and accessibility while reducing reliance on hospital-based care, making the health system more sustainable and equitable.

Clinicians Supporting Community Care

Moorfields Hospital in London is the world's largest ophthalmic research centre. Speaking with several of their ophthalmic surgeons on different occasions, I was struck by how they all suggested developing a theatre in a shopping mall for cataract surgery. Their argument: their patients were not sick; intervention could be done under local anaesthetic. Patients wouldn't have to travel to a hospital; after the operation and a short recovery, they could easily go home (or shopping). Another argument I kept hearing was that the chances of catching a hospital-acquired infection would be dramatically reduced.

Obviously it hasn't happened—yet. Regulatory frameworks and emergency backup protocols would need to evolve to enable such innovations safely.

Dimension 2: Educating People to Empower

Closing the healthcare gap requires reducing demand and increasing capacity. Demand reduction comes from shifting from damage repair ('sickness' rather than healthcare systems) to wellness and prevention. This requires education of healthcare users and providers. Users need health literacy—increasing everyone's understanding about maintaining health, making healthy lifestyle choices, and becoming empowered to manage their own wellbeing.

To increase capacity, healthcare professional education must also evolve. The traditional 'paternal' relationship of physicians seeing patients one-to-one in consultation rooms needs to change to facilitating the health of communities. What if physicians could interact with young people in classrooms, with families in community centres, with employees in workplaces?

Healthcare professionals need to become change agents, advocating for the needs of the communities they serve. From Chapter 5 we learned that clinicians already have the right mindset to deal with complex challenges. All they require is training in applying design methods and techniques to improve healthcare delivery. Rather than serving in an unsustainable status quo and dealing with the frustrations of failure, healthcare professionals can contribute to a dynamically changing and adapting healthcare system.

Medical schools in the United States have already taken steps in the right direction. The Neighbourhood Health Education Learning Program at Florida International University's Herbert Wertheim College of Medicine immerses medical students in underserved communities as part of inter-professional teams [5]. Throughout their medical education, students work with the same households for three years, understanding health challenges in context. They understand how housing, employment, food security, and social support affect health. This produces physicians who think differently about healthcare delivery, who see patients as whole people embedded in communities rather than as clinical cases presenting in emergency departments. The model of education is scheduled to be rolled out at Roseman University in Las Vegas. It demonstrates that we can prepare healthcare professionals for community-based practice from the beginning of their training, as integrated capability rather than afterthought.

Dimension 3: Redesigning Processes for Connecting

Technology and education alone won't transform healthcare. We must redesign processes around patient needs rather than institutional convenience. This requires applying design thinking systematically to how care is delivered, coordinated, and experienced.

The transformation must address how patients move through the healthcare system, how information flows between providers, how decisions are made, and how care is coordinated across settings. Process redesign focuses on removing waste, reducing burden, and creating seamless experiences for both patients and healthcare professionals.

Narayana Health in India demonstrates process transformation at scale. Founded by cardiac surgeon Dr Devi Shetty, presented in Chapter 5, the organisation delivers high-quality cardiac surgery to some of India's poorest populations through systematic process innovation. They applied 'assembly-line' principles from manufacturing, task-shifting to trained community members for pre- and post-operative care, and cross-subsidisation models where paying patients enable free care for those who cannot afford it. Communities benefit from better healthcare, also through employment. Narayana trained local people—some illiterate—to become skilled healthcare workers. The result: up to 75% cost reduction compared to Western counterparts while maintaining clinical outcomes on par with leading global institutions [6].

Narayana Health demonstrates that thoughtful process innovation can deliver world-class healthcare to underserved populations. Although this doesn't result in full decentralisation, it proves that process redesign can overcome seemingly insurmountable barriers.

Virginia Mason Medical Center in Seattle adopted Toyota Production System principles to healthcare, reorienting all processes around the patient's perspective—directly applying design thinking's empathy principle. Their transformation resulted in an 85% reduction in how far patients needed to walk during hospital stays, a 50% reduction in the amount of time nurses spent hunting for supplies, and significant improvements in patient safety metrics [7].

Both Narayana and Virginia Mason use 'downstream' methods transferred from manufacturing and supply-chain management. Yet they demonstrate that systematic process innovation, even without explicit design thinking, can transform care delivery. Imagine what becomes possible when we combine process excellence with upstream design thinking from the beginning.

Multiple innovations already exist that enable decentralised care:

- Telehealth triage systems route patients to appropriate care levels.
- AI-powered symptom checkers provide preliminary assessment.
- Digital mental health platforms offer counselling and therapy.
- Home monitoring devices track chronic conditions.
- Point-of-care diagnostic tools require minimal training.

These aren't future possibilities—they exist today. The challenge lies in healthcare system readiness to adopt and integrate these innovations into community care pathways.

Stakeholder Mapping and Ecosystem Design

The transformation toward patient-focused decentralised healthcare will change stakeholder relationships while preserving core building blocks. The medical process of diagnosis, therapy, prevention, and care will adapt at the process level, but fundamental steps remain.

Stakeholders such as regulators and manufacturers of devices and medicines remain essential to ensure that new drugs and devices are reliable, safe and effective. Hospitals are essential for interventions and care that cannot be provided in community settings. The ecosystem in which they operate needs transformation. That requires process change at scale.

Policymakers and regulators need to become proactive, playing an important role in supporting development toward patient-focused decentralised healthcare. This means preparing policy and infrastructure frameworks accordingly while maintaining rigorous legal and regulatory standards. Embedding design thinking ensures patient focus and that stakeholder needs are met.

Understanding stakeholder needs is essential for designing distributed care networks. Each stakeholder group has legitimate requirements:

- Safety-net clinics: capacity building, sustainable funding, and research participation opportunities.
- Hospitals: operational efficiency improvements, reduced readmissions, and smoother transitions.
- Personal care providers: adequate staffing, remote monitoring tools, and care coordination support.
- Retail pharmacies: expanded service capabilities, medication adherence tools, and integration with care teams.
- Telemedicine providers: legacy system integration, reimbursement clarity, and quality assurance frameworks.
- Health-tech startups: credibility building, market access pathways, and regulatory guidance.
- Public health organisations: disease surveillance capabilities, underserved population outreach, and prevention programmes.

These needs are practical requirements for delivering care in distributed networks. They represent the ecosystem's complexity. Transformation begins by engaging essential stakeholders for initial pilots—typically safety-net clinics, local hospitals, and community providers—then expanding the network as capability builds and trust develops.

Integrated Holistic Pathways

From the user's perspective, providing healthcare consists of four straightforward processes: medical diagnosis, medical therapy, personal care, and prevention.

These processes need to be considered integrated in order to provide holistic care—not just for their conditions but for the person themselves. Diagnosis and therapy to deal with their conditions; personal care to address their social determinants of health (SDOH) such as housing and employment.

In themselves, these processes are straightforward, related through rules, and relevant to all conditions. The SDOH makes pathways multi-dimensional. Two people with the same conditions might have completely different needs.

Going back to the case of Patricia in the chapter opening, beyond medical diagnosis and therapy she will also need support to attend regular radio—and/or chemotherapy sessions. For Patricia that means help with caring for her kids and elderly mum, as well as financial support with the cost of her care and ensuring she has a job to go back to.

Cindy, affluent and well-insured, with the same suspected diagnosis of breast cancer, has people to drive her to treatment and look after her at home. She is so anxious about her diagnosis and the impact on her body and her life that she requires support to get enough rest and to help her cope mentally.

Medically, Cindy and Patricia might be in a similar position on the medical component of their pathway, but very different on SDOH. The position of individuals on their pathway in each process can be captured. Once established, we can determine what—methods, modalities, facilities—are required to get them to the next stage, whether these are available, or what it would take to become available.

A Question of Resources

A stethoscope can be used across several heart and lung conditions. A general surgeon can operate on conditions in abdominal regions, musculoskeletal conditions, trauma, and even emergency caesarean sections. Resources and capabilities can serve multiple pathways.

The patient pathway concept provides the fundamental structure for designing distributed care networks. Rather than organising care around institutional boundaries (hospital departments, specialist clinics), we organise around patient journeys through these four core processes. This enables care to flow seamlessly across settings—from community to hospital and back—with clear handoffs and continuity.

For Patricia, our 45-year-old single mother with suspicious mammogram results, her pathway would map: diagnosis (confirming cancer presence), therapy (treatment plan), personal care (managing side effects, transportation to treatment), and prevention (genetic counselling, family screening). Each step can happen in the most appropriate setting, with clear coordination between community providers, specialists, and hospitals.

This pathway-based approach makes patient-centred care concrete and actionable.

Co-design provides the methodology for engaging stakeholders in transformation. Based on common sense, it involves all stakeholders in the 'Problem' diamond before solutions are designed. This means engaging local healthcare professionals, community leaders, and patient advocacy groups from the beginning. Their involvement continues throughout implementation and beyond. Tools for co-design include ethnography, which helps people understand cultural dimensions and how healthcare fits into community life. Patient journey mapping asks people what currently works, what doesn't work, and what they would like to change.

These methods ensure that distributed care networks are designed with stakeholders rather than imposed on them. Co-design leads to building capability where people are in existing local clinics and creating processes that actually work in practice.

For COVID-19 vaccine development, we witnessed unprecedented collaboration: researchers, industry, and regulators working together with shared purpose. This accelerated development dramatically. Similar collaboration across stakeholders, driven by design thinking, could transform everyday healthcare delivery.

A Question of Trust and Transparency

Building trust requires concrete strategies that leverage existing relationships while creating transparency. Community-based providers already have established trust relationships with local populations. Distributed care networks build on these rather than attempting to create trust from institutional distance. In communities with historical medical mistrust, trust rebuilding requires sustained commitment beyond programme timelines. Transparent acknowledgement of past harms, consistent presence over years, and demonstrable accountability for outcomes prove more powerful than PR campaigns.

Transparency mechanisms prove essential. When care delivery happens in community settings with familiar providers, accountability becomes local and direct rather than bureaucratic and distant. This addresses historical medical mistrust in underserved populations—communities see care delivered by people they know, in settings they recognise, with outcomes they can verify.

Continuity of care builds trust over time. When patients see the same community-based team rather than rotating hospital specialists, relationships deepen. The Frome Model demonstrated this principle: community connectors leveraged existing trust relationships to connect patients with resources. Success built credibility. The model scaled through demonstrated outcomes rather than institutional mandate.

Design Framework: Creating Distributed Care Networks

Healthcare transformation requires a whole system approach encompassing people, processes, and technologies. The DEC Framework—Decentralise, Empower, Connect—integrates simplifying technology, people empowerment, and process redesign through design thinking to transform healthcare from hospital-centred to patient-centred care.

Figure 8.2 extends this framework to show the transformation journey. Healthcare systems move progressively through four stages—traditional, transitional, integrated, and transformed—as

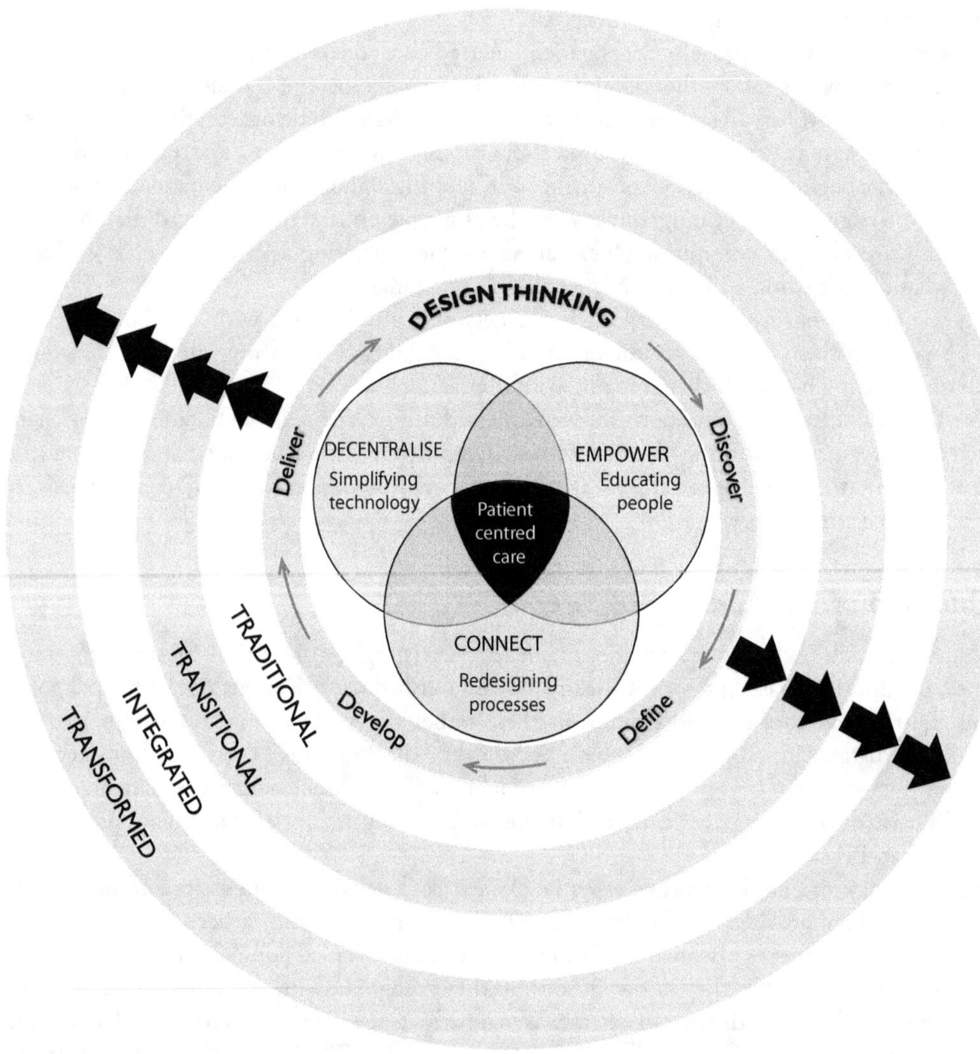

Figure 8.2 The DEC Framework—progressive healthcare transformation.

the three dimensions evolve together. This progression demonstrates that transformation is systematic and gradual, not sudden disruption. Organisations advance at their own pace, building capability incrementally. Frome's transformation took four years to demonstrate measurable outcomes; Torbay's integrated system evolved over seven years. The timeline depends on starting complexity, stakeholder readiness, and resource availability—but measured in years, not months.

The framework shows how coordinated changes in three dimensions—technology, people, and processes—embedded in design thinking, supported by design methods and technologies, drive the transition toward decentralised healthcare that is focused on patients.

The principles of disruptive innovation indicate that transformation should start with providing healthcare for the underserved. Using design methods and technologies, supported by AI platforms, makes this possible. This approach is strategic, not just ethical. Innovations that work for underserved populations with limited resources can then scale to serve everyone.

Implementing distributed care networks requires coordinated action across six strategic pillars:

- **Reducing Demand**: Prevention, early intervention, and health education address issues before they require intensive care.
- **Increasing Capacity**: Efficiency optimisation and technology extension enable more care with existing resources.
- **Decentralising Healthcare**: Community-centric model development and local clinic capability enhancement bring care to where people live.
- **Rebuilding Trust**: Leveraging existing community-provider relationships and transparent communication creates accountability.
- **Ensuring Continuity**: Integrated care pathways span the entire care continuum from prevention through treatment and follow-up.
- **Smart Grid Transformation**: Connected platforms enable stakeholder collaboration and information flow.

Figure 8.3 illustrates the six strategic pillars as a hexagon surrounding patient-centred care. This configuration reflects reality: the pillars don't operate sequentially but simultaneously, each connected to the others and all supporting the central goal. Remove any single pillar and the structure fails—the hexagon collapses. Reducing demand without increasing capacity leaves underserved populations still without care. Increasing capacity without ensuring continuity creates fragmented experiences. Rebuilding trust without smart grid infrastructure leaves coordination manual and error-prone. This interdependency determines implementation strategy: all six must advance together, though organisations can emphasise different pillars based on their starting position and capabilities.

Disruptive Innovation in Healthcare

Clayton Christensen defined disruptive innovation as that which enables 'a larger population of less-skilled, less-wealthy people to do things in more convenient, lower-cost settings that historically could be done only by specialists in centralised, inconvenient locations' [8].

Healthcare disruption differs from business disruption, where companies such as Kodak and Nokia disappear after being disrupted. In healthcare, disruption reshapes how stakeholders collaborate to serve patients rather than eliminating players or creating winners and losers. Hospitals, clinicians, pharmaceutical companies, and regulators continue playing critical roles—they cannot disappear, but those roles evolve.

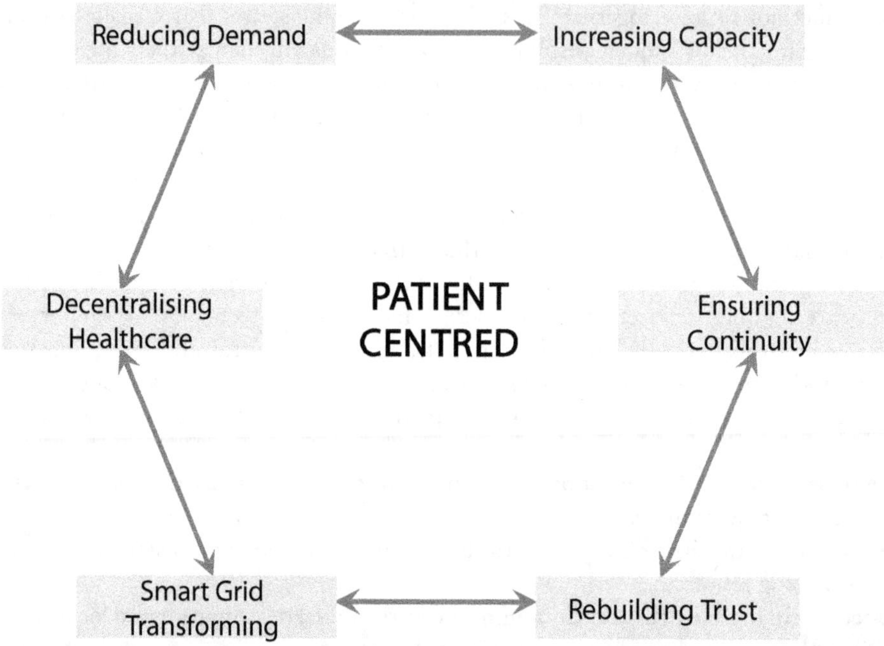

Figure 8.3 The six implementation pillars.

Disruption targets processes and interaction systems. The goal lies in shifting healthcare delivery from siloed, top-down structures to connected, patient-centred networks where hospitals focus on truly complex cases requiring their specialised capabilities. This approach respects the legitimate expertise and infrastructure that hospitals represent while acknowledging that many patients would be better served—with better outcomes, at lower cost, with greater convenience—through community-based care.

Torbay Care Trust in the UK (2004–2011) demonstrated what integrated care delivery could achieve when designed as a complete system [9]. The Trust created unified governance across primary, hospital and social care, forcing local stakeholder alignment through integrated authority—combining health and social care under single leadership. Results validated the approach: 33% reduction in hospital beds while improving patient outcomes and satisfaction. The system received *Health Service Journal* awards for innovation. Patients experienced seamless transitions between care settings. Healthcare professionals reported better coordination and reduced duplication.

Torbay proved that when stakeholders align around patient needs rather than organisational boundaries, dramatic improvements become possible. The care delivery model worked—patients received better care, costs decreased, and healthcare professionals could practise more effectively.

The subsequent dismantling of Torbay had everything to do with national governance decisions and nothing to do with care delivery failures [10]. But the care model itself demonstrated that integrated patient-centred delivery is achievable.

Decentralised clinical trials demonstrate distributed care network design in practice. The methodology directly applies to broader healthcare transformation:

- **Building Capability Where People Are**: rather than requiring patients to travel to academic medical centres, trials build research capability in local clinics, satellite centres, and mobile clinics. Healthcare professionals receive training and support to conduct research alongside clinical care.

- **Inclusive Recruitment Strategies**: using patient demographics data (race, ethnicity, gender, socioeconomic factors) to determine where people live relative to trial sites, then establishing access points that serve underserved populations. Digital design and visualisation tools analyse data to inform decisions.
- **Accessible Locations and Processes**: making participation convenient by bringing trials to communities rather than expecting communities to come to trials. This includes flexible scheduling, transportation support, and culturally appropriate communication.
- **Data-Driven Decision-Making**: using publicly available data sources to see where patients with specific conditions live and how far they are from established trial sites and free clinics. This informs strategic placement of trial capability.

The same principles apply to routine care delivery. Build capability in communities. Use data to understand where people are and what they need. Make access convenient. Design processes that work for people's actual lives. At OnKai Inc, we used the persona of Amber, a fictional midwife, to make decisions at key development stages. This human-centred approach ensures that design decisions serve actual user needs rather than abstract clinical requirements.

The Path Forward

The transformation from hospital-centred to patient-centred healthcare is achievable today with existing technology, proven methodologies, and demonstrated outcomes. The evidence is clear: community-based care delivers superior results when designed properly.

The three transformation dimensions—technology, people, and processes—must advance together. Technology simplification enables community deployment. People education builds capability for new models. Process redesign makes it work in practice. Design thinking provides the integrating methodology that ensures patient focus throughout.

Quality concerns about distributed networks are addressable through systematic approaches. Standards travel with care delivery rather than remaining locked in hospital buildings. Technology enables monitoring and coordination across distributed settings. Clinical governance adapts to support community-based delivery while maintaining safety. The Frome Model, Narayana Health, and Torbay Care Trust all demonstrate that community care can match or exceed hospital quality when properly designed.

Healthcare leaders can begin this transformation immediately. The strategic pillars provide an actionable framework. Start with underserved populations—innovations that work with limited resources scale to serve everyone. Build on existing community relationships rather than attempting to create new infrastructure from scratch. Use design thinking to engage stakeholders from the beginning, ensuring that solutions address real needs rather than theoretical ideals.

Training cannot close the workforce gap—we established that mathematically. But transformation to community-based care changes the equation entirely. When care delivery happens in communities, with technology enabling remote monitoring, with educated patients managing their own health, and with processes designed for efficiency, the workforce capacity expands dramatically.

Patricia deserves better than three hours in a waiting room followed by another appointment at a different facility. She deserves care delivered where she lives, coordinated around her needs, provided by people who understand her context. This isn't aspirational—it's achievable. The tools exist. The evidence validates the approach. The question is whether healthcare leaders will act.

The next chapter examines how complexity thinking, design methodology and technology support decentralisation and redistribute power in healthcare delivery.

References

1. Director -General (2024) *Health and Care Workforce Global Strategy on Human Resources for Health: Workforce 2030.* Executive Board 156th session EB156/15. World Health Organisation. Available at: https://apps.who.int/gb/ebwha/pdf_files/EB156/B156_15-en.pdf.
2. Abel, J. et al. (2018) 'Reducing emergency hospital admissions: A population health complex intervention of an enhanced model of primary care and compassionate communities', *The British Journal of General Practice*, 68(676), pp. e803–e810. https://doi.org/10.3399/bjgp18X699437.
3. Jardine, J., Fisher, J. and Carrick, B. (2015) 'Apple's ResearchKit: Smart data collection for the smartphone era?', *Journal of the Royal Society of Medicine*, 108(8), pp. 294–296. https://doi.org/10.1177/0141076815600673.
4. Allison, C. (2024) 'Apple watch AFib feature receives new FDA approval - can now be used in clinical studies', *Wareable*, 3 May. Available at: https://www.wareable.com/apple/apple-watch-afib-history-fda-approval-medical-device-development-tool .
5. Greer, P.J. et al. (2018) 'Socially accountable medical education: An innovative approach at Florida International University Herbert Wertheim College of Medicine', *Academic Medicine*, 93(1), pp. 60–65. https://doi.org/10.1097/ACM.0000000000001811.
6. Muralidhara, G.V. (2016) *Dr Devi Shetty of Narayana Hrudayalaya: Delivering Quality Cardiac Care to the Masses, The Case Centre.* Available at: https://www.thecasecentre.org/products/view?id=137186 .
7. Kaplan, G.S. (2013) 'Pursuing the perfect patient experience', *Frontiers of Health Services Management*, 29(3), pp. 16–27.
8. Christensen, C., Johnson, C.W. and Horn, M.B. (2008) *Disrupting Class: How Disruptive Innovation Will Change the Way the World Learns.* 1st edn. New York, NY: McGraw-Hill.
9. *Torbay and South Devon NHS Foundation Trust Annual Report and Accounts 2017/18* (2018). Annual Report. Torbay and South Devon NHS Foundation Trust, p. 236. Available at: https://www.england.nhs.uk/wp-content/uploads/2019/10/Torbay_and_South_Devon_NHS_FT_Annual_Report_and_Accounts_2017-18.pdf.
10. Farnsworth, A. (2012) 'Unintended consequences? The impact of NHS reforms upon Torbay Care Trust', *Journal of Integrated Care*, 20(3), pp. 146–151. https://doi.org/10.1108/14769011211237483.

Chapter 9

Decentralised Healthcare

PATRICIA'S LIVING ROOM, SMALL US TOWN, MARCH 2035

Patricia reviews three funding proposals on her tablet. Tonight the Local Health Collaborative DAO votes on next quarter's priorities. The mental health prevention programme, the home-based dialysis support network, or expanding the community cancer navigation service that changed her life. Ten years ago she was the 45-year-old single mom sitting in that over-crowded hospital waiting room, suspicious mammogram results folded in her purse, terrified about paying for treatment. She survived the cancer. Her mother didn't survive the fragmented care system that followed.

That grief drove her to training as a patient navigator in 2029, helping others avoid the care coordination failures that killed her mum. When the community health network launched in 2031, Pat was among the first hires. Working retail for 20 years taught her about people. Surviving cancer taught her the system's cruelty. Together, they made her valuable.

Now she votes on which innovations her community needs most. The blockchain shows every stakeholder's vote weight: 40% community members served, 30% care providers, 20% local health department, 10% volunteer advocates. Her vote carries weight because she knows these families—she shops alongside them, her kids went to school with theirs. She reads the mental health proposal. Three youth crisis interventions last month in her postcode. Prevention matters.

She votes yes, adds her rationale: 'These are our kids. We intervene after crisis because we've never funded prevention. This changes that.' The smart contract records her input immutably, transparently.

Her phone buzzes—Mrs Miller needs tomorrow's dialysis appointment confirmed, her daughter wants to talk about hospice options. Patricia closes the DAO interface.

Governance matters. But the work is the same as always: showing up for your neighbours.

DOI: 10.4324/9781003752073-12

The Inevitable Shift

Healthcare decentralisation is inevitable. Demographic and economic pressures make current centralised models mathematically impossible by 2030. The question facing healthcare leaders is: will you shape this transformation or react to it?

Patricia's 2035 reality—community members participating meaningfully in healthcare governance through transparent, blockchain-based decision-making—represents the destination. The journey from today's fragmented, institution-centred care to tomorrow's community-governed networks requires understanding why centralised power fails, how decentralised alternatives work, and what pathway leaders must follow.

Early adopters gain competitive advantage through superior stakeholder coordination and community trust. This advantage compounds over time—established community partnerships and proven governance models cannot be replicated quickly by late adopters.

Healthcare systems globally face the same demographic cliff: ageing populations, workforce shortages, and fiscal constraints. Current models collapse under this pressure. The transformation from centralised institutional control to decentralised community governance represents not a distant possibility but urgent necessity.

Section 1: The Case for Power Redistribution

The Historical Power Shift

Power in healthcare has migrated systematically away from those who deliver and receive care. Once upon a time, healthcare operated as a distributed network—physicians in communities, payment between individuals, power shared among patients and healers, all focused on human needs. The Renaissance brought hospitals and manufacturers as medical science and technology advanced. Each technological advance—from Laennec's stethoscope to today's AI-powered diagnostics—disconnected patients from physicians, pulling them out of their communities and into institutions.

Today's system concentrates power in institutions focused on profit and process rather than patient outcomes. Notice the pattern: power shifted away from patients, healers, and communities focused on quality of life, toward industry, insurers, and manufacturers focused on increasing profits. With each innovation came new stakeholders: researchers, manufacturers, regulators, insurers, administrators.

This power redistribution explains why transformation efforts consistently fail. They attempt to reform a system whose governance structure is designed to preserve institutional power, not serve patients. Multiple stakeholders pursue conflicting objectives within fragmented systems, and governance structures evolved to protect existing arrangements rather than enable transformation. The drivers have shifted from quality of life to discovery and profit. This fundamental reorientation creates the dysfunction we experience daily in healthcare delivery.

How Centralisation Corrupted Incentives

Equally significant was the transformation of incentives and rewards. In the decentralised past, physicians were directly compensated by patients or their families for tangible outcomes—reducing suffering, improving quality of life, restoring function. The connection between intervention and reward was immediate and personal. Healers succeeded when their patients thrived.

Today's centralised system has severed this fundamental link. Patients contribute to insurance schemes or tax systems, while healthcare professionals receive monthly salaries disconnected from individual patient outcomes. More perversely, the system now rewards illness rather than health. Hospitals profit from occupied beds, not empty ones. Pharmaceutical companies generate revenue from treating disease, not preventing it. Medical device manufacturers thrive when more procedures are performed, not when fewer are needed. This misalignment of incentives explains much of healthcare's current dysfunction. When the system profits from problems rather than solutions, it inevitably generates more problems to solve.

We didn't design this system. It emerged reactively, without oversight or intention. And now, like a genetic mutation that initially conferred advantage but ultimately proves lethal, centralisation is killing the very system it was meant to strengthen.

The Trust Deficit Crisis

A profound erosion of trust between citizens and healthcare institutions undermines transformation efforts. Poor communication, lack of transparency, and growing inequalities—exacerbated by austerity measures—have created widespread alienation. This breakdown creates a vicious cycle: as citizens disengage, systems become less responsive to their needs, further reinforcing distrust and disengagement.

This trust deficit is measurable and worsening. Public trust in government stewardship of the NHS has declined to single digits [1]. Citizens don't trust institutions to act in their interests. Healthcare professionals don't trust administrators to support quality care. Administrators don't trust policymakers to provide sustainable frameworks.

Without trust, coordination becomes impossible. Every stakeholder that can, optimises their individual position rather than system performance, creating the fragmented dysfunction we experience daily. This trust collapse makes centralised governance increasingly untenable.

Why Centralised Power Fails: The Governance Problem

Healthcare leaders consistently blame regulation for stifling innovation, but they target the wrong culprit. This false dichotomy proves dangerous because it obscures the real obstacle to transformation. Regulation provides necessary safety guardrails for patient protection, clear and predictable pathways for compliance, minimum acceptable standards backed by law, and protection for both innovators and patients. Regulation serves essential functions—safety and efficacy.

Governance creates the actual barriers: internal decision-making hierarchies, resource allocation processes, risk management frameworks, performance accountability mechanisms, and cultural norms that resist change. The confusion exists because both can impose constraints, but regulation protects patients while governance often protects existing power structures.

COVID-19 demonstrated what becomes possible when stakeholders collaborate. Researchers, industry, and regulators worked together on vaccines and medicines—often supported by Chief Medical Officers—accelerating development dramatically. The precedent was set: when researchers, industry, and regulators collaborate, transformation happens. Yet healthcare keeps falling back to adversarial relationships and governance structures designed for a different era.

Clinical Expertise Systematically Excluded

Chapter 5 demonstrated how healthcare systematically excludes clinical expertise from transformation leadership despite evidence that clinical leaders improve hospital performance. This exclusion isn't accidental—it reflects the centralised governance structures that prioritise managerial control over operational evidence. Pattern recognition for healthcare executives: Your clinical improvement initiatives get marginalised because political governance consistently sidelines clinical expertise in favour of administrative convenience. The structures are designed to maintain managerial hierarchy, not optimise patient outcomes.

Section 2: Bitcoin and Buurtzorg Precedents of Decentralisation

The Precedent: How Bitcoin Challenged Centralised Finance

The 2008 collapse of the financial system exposed governance structures designed to protect institutions rather than citizens. Central banks had enabled what became known as 'casino banking'—reckless gambling with depositors' money, shielded from consequences. When the system collapsed, governments deployed taxpayers' funds to bail out the institutions responsible while prosecuting none of the architects. Years of austerity followed, recovering costs through cuts to education, healthcare, and social services. The impact persists today.

Citizens paid twice: first through bailouts, then through austerity. The system revealed itself as fundamentally misaligned—designed to preserve banking power, not serve public welfare. Trust in financial institutions collapsed alongside their balance sheets.

That same year, an anonymous developer using the pseudonym Satoshi Nakamoto published a nine-page technical paper: 'Bitcoin: A Peer-to-Peer Electronic Cash System' [2]. The timing was deliberate. The paper proposed a radical alternative—financial transactions without intermediaries, eliminating banks entirely through cryptographic proof rather than institutional promise. Blockchain technology would provide a distributed electronic ledger across networks, ensuring transparency and security without central control.

On January 3, 2009, Nakamoto mined the first Bitcoin block—the Genesis Block. Embedded in its code was a message: 'The Times 03/Jan/2009 Chancellor on brink of second bailout for banks.' The timestamp and headline served as both proof of creation date and political statement. The system that failed citizens was preparing another bailout. Bitcoin offered an alternative. What Nakamoto demonstrated transcended technology—it was governance innovation. Strangers could transact with complete confidence while remaining anonymous, using mathematical certainty instead of institutional authority. Bitcoin proved that decentralised systems could function without central banking authorities, without regulatory permission, without hierarchical control. Financial coordination became possible through transparent protocols rather than centralised command.

Ethereum's introduction of smart contracts transformed this foundation from simple value transfer into programmable governance. Complex agreements could execute automatically, transparently, and immutably—without lawyers, without courts, without centralised enforcement mechanisms. This unleashed Decentralised Autonomous Organisations (DAOs)—entities coordinating resources, making decisions, and executing actions through transparent, participatory governance encoded directly into blockchain infrastructure.

DAOs represent 'trustless trust' at scale. Stakeholders need not trust any individual institution because they verify all decisions and resource flows independently. Every action is recorded immutably. Every decision remains traceable. No single entity can capture or manipulate the system. Democracy through mathematics rather than politics.

The regulatory landscape shifted accordingly. The EU's Digital Services Act (2024) and upcoming AI Governance Framework (2025) favour transparent, auditable systems. Organisations operating on opaque governance face increasing compliance costs and regulatory scrutiny. DAO-based models benefit from built-in transparency and accountability.

The Healthcare Parallel—and Critical Difference

Healthcare experiences the identical pattern. A centralised system is failing citizens systematically. Citizens are paying costs through rationing, decline, workforce exodus, and explicit two-tier access. The system is designed to preserve institutional power rather than serve patients. Trust is eroding exactly as it did in finance before 2008.

But healthcare imposes a constraint finance does not: lock-in. In finance, dissatisfied citizens could choose Bitcoin, maintain conventional banking, or combine both. Cryptocurrency provided an exit option. Social movements and individual actions could counteract governance failures in economic and environmental domains.

Healthcare eliminates choice. We can attempt healthy lifestyles, but illness arrives inevitably. Then escape becomes impossible. Our physical condition impacts our mental state—we surrender, becoming passive passengers depending on a centralised system not designed to maximise our quality of life. There is no viable option to 'go off the grid' when disease strikes.

This lock-in makes healthcare transformation more urgent than financial reform. Bitcoin demonstrated that rigid centralised systems CAN be challenged by decentralised alternatives. The question for healthcare isn't whether decentralisation is possible—Bitcoin answered that. The question is whether healthcare leaders will design that transformation proactively, guided by equity and community empowerment, or allow it to emerge chaotically from system collapse.

DAO architecture provides the governance infrastructure for healthcare's transformation. The same technological foundation that enabled Bitcoin's disruption of finance can enable transparent, participatory governance in healthcare—but adapted for a domain where citizens cannot simply exit when the system fails them.

Healthcare decentralisation requires more sophisticated architecture than financial decentralisation precisely because of this lock-in effect. Where Bitcoin users can exit to conventional banking, healthcare patients cannot exit to alternative systems when seriously ill. This demands governance structures that maintain accountability, transparency, and community voice throughout the care journey—not just at entry points.

COUNTERINTUITIVE FINDING

Healthcare Decentralisation More Urgent Than Financial Decentralisation Due to Patient Lock-In

Bitcoin proved decentralised alternatives can disrupt centralised systems. Most leaders assume this makes healthcare decentralisation comparably straightforward—perhaps easier given healthcare's obvious dysfunction.

Reality inverts this logic: healthcare decentralisation requires MORE sophisticated governance architecture than financial decentralisation. Bitcoin users can exit to conventional banking when dissatisfied; seriously ill patients facing failing healthcare systems have no alternative system to access. This lock-in effect means healthcare cannot rely on market competition or voluntary adoption—it demands governance structures maintaining accountability, transparency, and community voice throughout the care journey, not just at entry points. The sector with worse starting conditions needs better ending solutions. Healthcare leaders cannot simply copy Bitcoin's playbook—they need superior governance design because failure has no market correction mechanism.

From Hierarchical to Networked Governance: The Buurtzorg Model

Buurtzorg demonstrates that alternative organisational structures work in healthcare at scale. This Dutch home care organisation operates with 14,000+ nurses serving 100,000+ patients across the Netherlands, achieving superior outcomes at lower cost than traditional hierarchical home care systems [3].

The difference lies in governance structure, not methodology. Buurtzorg employs self-organising teams of nurses with no middle management layer. Teams make decisions about patient care, resource allocation, and workflow optimisation. This distributed decision-making model represents the Teal organisational principles described by Laloux in practice—evolved consciousness expressed through organisational design [4]. The results prove compelling: higher patient satisfaction scores, better health outcomes, lower costs per patient, and higher nurse retention rates compared to traditional centralised home care [3]. The system works because it trusts clinical expertise and distributes authority to those closest to patient care.

Buurtzorg provides a bridge to understanding how Decentralised Autonomous Organisation (DAO)-based models could function in healthcare. Buurtzorg requires trust and cultural alignment within a single organisation. DAOs extend these principles through technological infrastructure that enables coordination without requiring trust in central authority. Where Buurtzorg operates through shared values, DAOs operate through transparent protocols and token-based governance.

Section 3: DAO-Based Models and Community Governance

DAO Architecture Fundamentals

Blockchain enables competitive selection on governance quality through decentralised coordination architectures. Rather than a single centralised governance authority (NHS England decides for all of NHS), multiple coordination mechanisms can exist simultaneously with stakeholders selecting based on governance effectiveness. DAO architecture provides the framework through three integrated layers:

Layer 1: Local Health Partnerships (Geographic)—for example

- Frome Medical Practice Partnership DAO
- Devon Integrated Care DAO
- West Yorkshire Health Alliance DAO

Each governs innovation adoption in their region using a shared evaluation framework. Local innovations approved at this layer move faster with lower approval thresholds.

Layer 2: Functional Networks (Cross-Geographic)

- Primary Care Innovation Network DAO
- Hospital Federation DAO
- Community Care Providers DAO

Each coordinate's innovation development and evaluation across regions. Regional innovations require Layer 2 coordination with moderate approval thresholds.

Layer 3: National Coordination (Meta-Governance)

- NHS Innovation Coordination DAO

Aggregates learning from Layer 1 and 2, updates evaluation framework, resolves conflicts. Critically, this layer does not monopolise decision authority—it coordinates competing governance mechanisms rather than commanding compliance.

Unlike traditional hierarchical models where national authorities command local action, DAO architecture inverts power distribution. Blockchain infrastructure (centre) enables transparent coordination while local health partnerships (Layer 1) make rapid decisions for their communities.

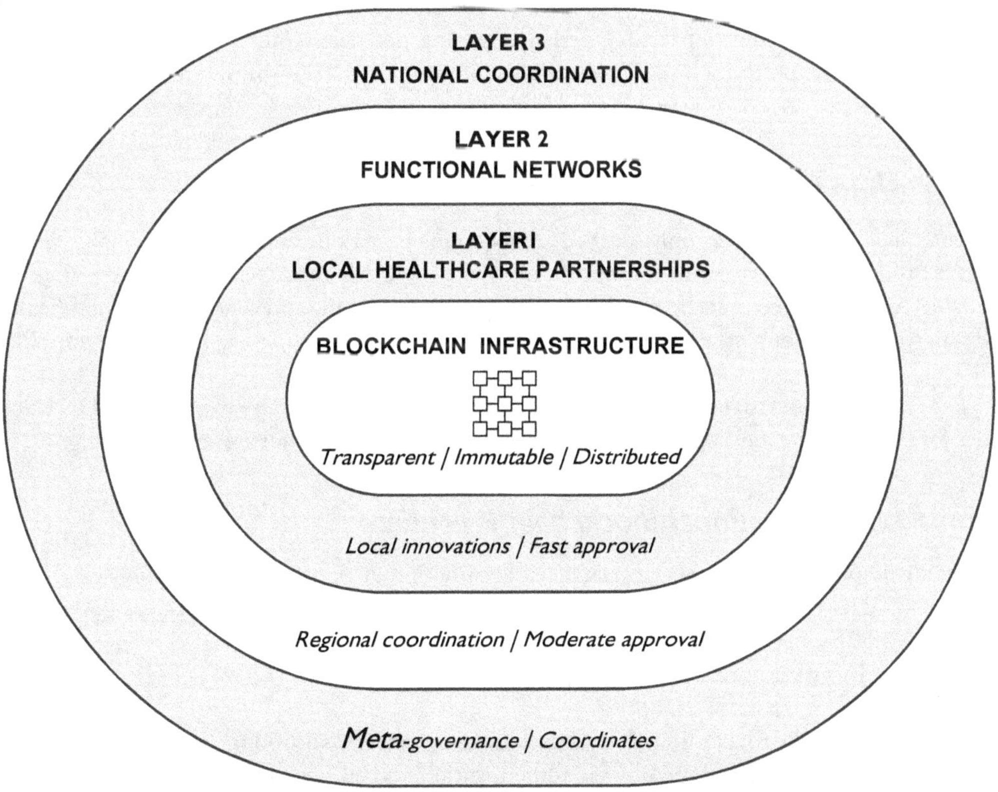

Figure 9.1 Three-layer DAO architecture for healthcare governance.

Functional networks (Layer 2) coordinate across regions, and national coordination (Layer 3) aggregates learning and resolves conflicts without monopolising authority. Patricia, as a community health worker, participates in Layer 1 governance—her voice carries weight because the system recognises multiple forms of expertise: clinical credentials, community relationships, and lived experience.

Governance Tokens and Decision Mechanisms

Stakeholders hold tokens proportional to legitimate interest:

- Patients: weighted by population served
- Providers: weighted by services delivered
- Commissioners: weighted by budget allocated
- Public health: weighted by health outcomes responsibility

Decision mechanisms operate at appropriate scales. Local innovations face lower barriers and faster approval times. National innovations require higher thresholds but still allow competing DAOs to adopt different evaluation criteria. Stakeholders observe governance effectiveness across DAOs. Effective governance attracts participation; ineffective governance loses legitimacy through transparent performance comparison.

Patricia's Local Health Collaborative operates at Layer 1—community-scale governance where stakeholders like her participate directly. Her vote weight reflects both her role as a paid community health worker and her lived experience serving her neighbours. The system recognises multiple forms of expertise: clinical credentials, community relationships, and lived experience navigating care.

From Push to Pull Innovation

Currently, healthcare receives only 'pushed' innovations based on researchers' personal interests, reactive funders' appetites, or industry profit motives. The DAO model enables shared visions for equitable community-centred healthcare, agreed priority areas like prevention or mental health, and co-created solutions in partnership with researchers, industry, and regulators, supported by policymakers.

This represents governance design at the political level—creating new institutional DNA that codes for collaborative long-term thinking rather than competitive short-term positioning.

Estonia X-Road: National Blockchain Precedent

Estonia demonstrates blockchain governance coordination at national scale through its X-Road platform—a data exchange layer enabling secure, decentralised coordination across government ministries, healthcare providers, private sector, and citizens [5, 6].

Technical Infrastructure:

- Distributed ledger recording all data exchanges between institutions
- Public-private key cryptography for authentication and authorisation
- Immutable audit trail of every data access and transaction

- Real-time monitoring of system health and anomaly detection
- Open-source software enabling international adoption

Governance Coordination:

- 2,800+ organisations connected (government, healthcare, banking, telecom)
- 52,000+ data requests per day coordinated through blockchain
- Citizens control their own data access (can see who accessed health records, when, why)
- Institutions cannot hide data misuse (immutable audit trail)
- Cross-border coordination (Finland, Iceland connected via X-Road)

Healthcare Applications:

- Health data digitised and blockchain-secured
- Every prescription, diagnosis, and test result recorded on the distributed ledger
- Citizens access complete health history through a single portal
- Doctors coordinate across institutions through X-Road data sharing
- Health Ministry monitors system-wide patterns without centralised data storage

Governance Implications:

Transparency: Every health system decision creates a blockchain record. Patterns become analysable. Crude blocking becomes detectable.

Accountability: Institutions cannot deny inappropriate access or blocking. An audit trail proves who made which decisions when.

Coordination without monopoly: Hospitals, clinics, pharmacies, insurers coordinate through X-Road without a central authority controlling data. Distributed consensus replaces centralised command.

Citizen empowerment: Patients see exactly how their data is used, which doctors accessed records, and which decisions were made. They can challenge inappropriate blocking.

Learning from Internet Evolution

Historical precedent suggests this approach can succeed. The Internet emerged from a similar dynamic—too important for governments to ignore, too decentralised for any government to control. Rather than choosing between institutional authority and grassroots innovation, the Internet created a parallel infrastructure that eventually became indispensable to official systems while maintaining fundamental independence.

Similarly, healthcare governance DAOs create complementary infrastructure that enables coordination and innovation at speeds and scales impossible within traditional bureaucratic structures. Over time, just as governments learned to work with rather than against the Internet, healthcare institutions will recognise DAOs' value in achieving their own transformation goals.

Like the Internet protocols that became foundational to all digital business, healthcare governance DAOs will become the coordination layer that traditional organisations depend upon but cannot control.

The Competitive Imperative: Why Early Adopters Win

The first-mover window is closing rapidly, and strategic advantages available today will disappear as markets saturate.

Competitive Benefits for Early Adopters

Healthcare organisations implementing decentralised governance gain immediate competitive positioning through community trust that takes competitors years to build but can be lost overnight through governance failures. Talent attraction accelerates as healthcare professionals increasingly seek organisations aligned with their values of patient-centred care. Regulatory advantage emerges as governments worldwide pivot toward community-based care models—UK's planned neighbourhood health centres, EU's digital health initiatives, US value-based care contracts.

These Benefits Multiply over Time

Early adopters create compounding advantages. Each successful community partnership makes the next one easier. Each transparent decision builds institutional credibility that competitors cannot quickly replicate. Each DAO participant becomes an advocate for the model, creating viral expansion impossible through traditional marketing.

Like the Internet protocols that became foundational to all digital business, healthcare governance DAOs will become the coordination layer that traditional organisations depend upon but cannot control. Early DAO adopters become the infrastructure that others must integrate with rather than competitors trying to displace.

Financial Advantages

Transparent governance reduces administrative overhead while improving stakeholder buy-in [7]. Analysis suggests coordination costs drop by 30–40% when stakeholders can verify decisions independently rather than requiring multiple layers of institutional oversight. This isn't theoretical—blockchain-based supply chains in manufacturing demonstrate coordination cost reductions of 30–40% [8], suggesting similar potential for healthcare DAO governance.

Why Early Action Compounds

Immediate competitive benefits (0–12 months):

- Staff retention improvement of 15–25% through participatory governance—healthcare workers report higher job satisfaction when they have a voice in transformation decisions [9]
- Community partnership acceleration as transparent processes build trust faster than traditional institutional approaches
- Innovation pipeline advantages as decentralised networks identify and scale solutions from system margins where breakthrough innovations typically emerge

Medium-term market position (1–3 years):

- Regulatory favour as policymakers increasingly support transparent, community-accountable healthcare models

- Funding advantages as impact investors and government programmes prioritise organisations demonstrating genuine stakeholder engagement
- Network expansion through DAO governance structures that enable rapid, low-risk partnerships with other forward-thinking organisations

Long-term dominance (3+ years):

- Market leadership in post-centralised healthcare landscape as demographic pressures force system-wide transformation
- Institutional resilience through distributed governance that adapts to crises rather than being paralysed by them
- Legacy positioning as architects of healthcare's next evolution rather than defenders of unsustainable models

The regulatory landscape is shifting rapidly. The EU's Digital Services Act (2024) and upcoming AI Governance Framework (2025) favour transparent, auditable systems [10]. Organisations operating on opaque governance will face increasing compliance costs and regulatory scrutiny, while DAO-based models benefit from built-in transparency and accountability.

AI-Enhanced Innovation Evaluation

Traditional innovation evaluation fails because stakeholders don't trust each other's recommendations. The hospital says 'innovation threatens quality.' GP says 'innovation improves outcomes.' No objective basis exists for resolving this conflict. Crude blocking emerges as a compromise—reject all novelty equally.

AI-enhanced DAO solution provides structured workflow:

STEP 1: Innovation Submitted (Blockchain) Proposer submits innovation to DAO smart contract. Proposal hash created as immutable identifier. Submission recorded on blockchain with timestamp.

STEP 2: AI Analysis (Digital Twin) AI analyses innovation against historical patterns. Prediction: Based on 200 similar innovations, 73% approval probability. Risk factors: Hospital stakeholder may block (financial incentive), but evidence is strong. Comparable cases: Frome model (similar), Torbay model (similar) both successful. Recommendation: APPROVE with monitored implementation. Confidence: 82% (based on model accuracy).

STEP 3: AI Analysis Recorded (Blockchain) AI recommendation written to blockchain as immutable record. Model version documented (which AI generated recommendation). Confidence score, comparable cases, risk factors all recorded.

STEP 4: Stakeholder Evaluation (DAO) Stakeholders vote on innovation through smart contract. Can access AI analysis plus historical patterns via blockchain. Vote with rationale (required by smart contract).

STEP 5: Stakeholder Votes Recorded (Blockchain) Every stakeholder vote written immutably to blockchain. Rationale recorded (cannot claim 'don't remember why voted no'). Pattern analysis possible (does stakeholder always block despite AI recommendation?).

STEP 6: Decision Executed (Smart Contract) Smart contract aggregates stakeholder votes. Applies decision threshold (6/8 stakeholders OR AI confidence >90%). Records final decision immutably.

STEP 7: Implementation Monitoring (AI + Blockchain) Innovation implementation tracked on blockchain (milestones, outcomes). AI monitors outcomes versus predictions. If outcomes differ from prediction, AI model updates (learning). Evidence accumulates: Did stakeholder who blocked make correct prediction?

Why Both AI and Blockchain Are Necessary

Humans cannot manually detect crude evolution across 10,000 recorded decisions, predict trajectories of institutional resistance from blockchain data, or extract meta-governance learning from transparent but computationally overwhelming evidence.

Estonia X-Road blockchain infrastructure records every healthcare data exchange—52,000+ requests daily. Without AI analysing these blockchain transactions, patterns remain invisible despite perfect transparency. Crude evolution could occur while complete evidence sits unanalysed in the distributed ledger.

The solution integrates both technologies:

- AI analyses blockchain-recorded patterns (transparent plus computationally analysed)
- Blockchain records AI-assisted decisions (accountable plus precision-enhanced)
- Human governance oversees both (ethical plus legitimate)

This creates Digital Twin plus DAO architecture enabling governance precision maintained through AI computational capacity plus blockchain transparency plus human ethical oversight. Neither technology replaces human governance. AI recommends; humans decide. Blockchain records; humans interpret. Smart contracts enforce rules; humans design rules.

Together, these technologies provide infrastructure human organisational capacity alone cannot deliver—computational power matching coordination complexity and transparency preventing crude blocking through opacity.

Section 4: Design Thinking for Decentralisation

Design thinking provides the methodology for navigating this transformation. Healthcare leaders already possess this capability through clinical training—the same iterative approach that guides patient care (discover, define, develop, deliver) applies to governance transformation. The challenge lies in recognising this capability and removing structural barriers that prevent its application at organisational scale. Traditional change management approaches assume linear, predictable systems. Healthcare requires complexity-aware methodology that embraces uncertainty, learns through iteration, and adapts based on evidence.

Decentralised governance structures enable this iterative approach. Local DAOs can experiment with different coordination mechanisms, learn from results transparently recorded on blockchain, and adapt quickly based on outcomes. Failed experiments provide system-wide learning without catastrophic consequences. Successful innovations scale through voluntary adoption rather than mandated compliance.

This represents a fundamental shift from 'design once, deploy everywhere' (which fails in complex systems) to 'design locally, learn collectively, evolve continuously' (which matches how complex systems actually transform).

Part V of this book provides the detailed methodology and implementation tools for navigating this transformation. Chapter 16 presents the DAO-based control room model with five essential functions: visibility, coordination, navigation, early warning, **and** resource optimisation. Chapter 17 provides the comprehensive implementation roadmap **with** role-specific guidance, tactical countermeasures, and practical deployment plans.

Section 5: Future Scenario—2035 Healthcare Landscape

Chapter 8 introduced six strategic pillars working together for implementing distributed care networks—operational pathways for transformation shown in Figure 8.3. These pillars enable four fundamental characteristics that define transformed healthcare ecosystems. Each characteristic reinforces the others, creating resilient and adaptive systems:

- Health-Literate Societies
- Radical Redistribution of Care
- Reimagining Health and Economics
- Adaptive Capacity Throughout the System

Figure 9.2 shows how the six implementation pillars of distributed care produce the four characteristics of healthcare transformation.

Vision: Four Characteristics of Transformation

A transformed healthcare ecosystem emerges through four interconnected characteristics, each reinforcing the others to create a resilient and adaptive system:

The First Characteristic: Health-Literate Societies. Citizens possess genuine understanding and agency, not just information about health. Healthcare professionals complement their clinical expertise with skills in education, empowerment, and partnership. Health literacy

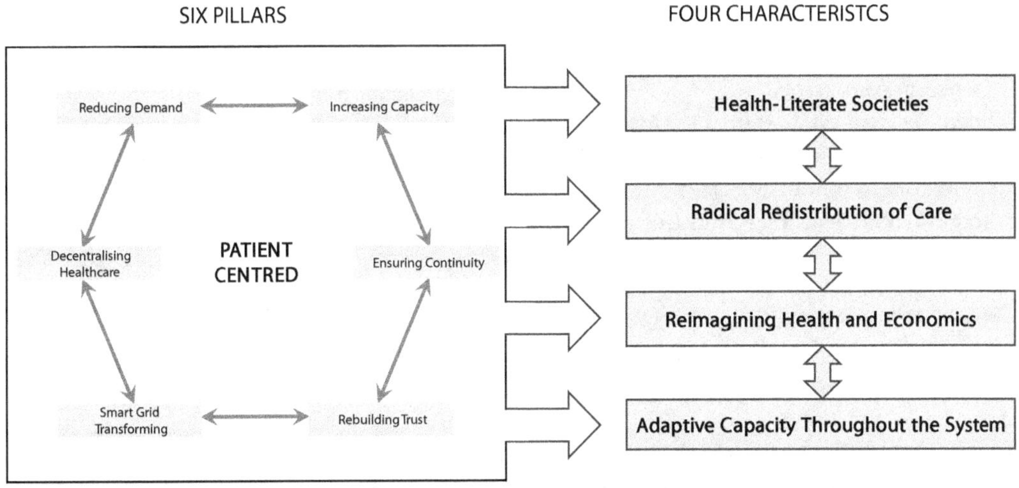

Figure 9.2 The six pillars and four characteristics of healthcare transformation.

becomes embedded in educational systems from early childhood, creating generations capable of meaningful participation in their own care.

The Second Characteristic: Radical Redistribution of Care. Rather than requiring people to navigate complex centralised systems, care comes to where people live, work, and gather. Community health workers, supported by technology and connected to specialist expertise when needed, provide continuous, relationship-based care. This shift recognises that health is created in communities, not hospitals.

Patricia exemplifies this characteristic. The single mother who once waited three hours in an overcrowded hospital now provides coordinated care in her own community. The fragmented system that failed her mother has been replaced by integrated support that follows people through their lives, not their appointments.

The Third Characteristic: Reimagining Health and Economics. Healthcare transforms from cost to be minimised within a growth-focused economy into wellbeing as the central organising principle for economic activity. New economic models emerge that value health outcomes, environmental sustainability, and social cohesion alongside traditional financial metrics.

The Fourth Characteristic: Adaptive Capacity Throughout the System. Rather than rigid structures resistant to change, future healthcare systems continuously learn and evolve. Digital technologies serve as enablers of human connection rather than replacements for it, creating feedback loops that allow rapid adaptation to changing needs and opportunities.

The Counter-Scenario: Terminal State Without Change

The alternative to transformation isn't preservation of the status quo—it's progressive collapse into terminal dysfunction. This trajectory is predictable and already underway:

Stage 1: Complete Innovation Paralysis (2025–2027)—Zero successful system-wide innovations sustained. Innovation proposals require >18 months approval with >90% rejection rates.

Stage 2: Workforce Exodus (2027–2029)—Clinical departures accelerate beyond replacement capacity as experienced clinicians leave due to inability to provide effective care within system constraints.

Stage 3: Explicit System Fragmentation (2029–2031)—Two-tier system becomes undeniable. Those with resources exit entirely for private care while NHS becomes an explicit safety net for economically disadvantaged only.

Stage 4: Political Terminal State (2031–2033)—Healthcare dominates elections but solutions become impossible. Reform fatigue sets in as crisis becomes normalised rather than scandalous.

Stage 5: System Collapse (2033+)—System maintained as a zombie organisation—technically operational but functionally inert. Innovation effectively impossible. Explicit rationing replaces prioritisation.

This isn't speculation—it's mathematical projection from current trajectories. Without fundamental power redistribution, this endpoint is inevitable. In this counter-scenario, Patricia never trains as patient navigator because the community health network never launches. Her mother dies from care coordination failures. Patricia remains trapped, watching neighbours suffer preventable decline. The cycle perpetuates.

The Choice Ahead: Practical Pathway Forward

Implementation Roadmap for Healthcare Leaders

Transformation requires a systematic approach, not heroic gestures. Healthcare leaders implementing decentralised governance gain advantage through disciplined execution across three phases:

Phase 1: Foundation Building (0–6 months)
Audit current governance structures for transparency gaps and stakeholder exclusion. Document specific examples where governance blocked beneficial innovation, where staff disengagement stems from lack of voice, and where community relationships suffer from opacity. Make the cost of centralised governance concrete and measurable.

Identify one transformation initiative suitable for enhanced stakeholder participation. Select initiatives where:

- Stakeholder misalignment currently causes failure
- Community partnership would accelerate success
- Transparent decision-making would build trust
- Outcomes are measurable within 12–18 months

Begin stakeholder mapping using 3H+ methodology principles. Identify which communities and staff members are ready for participatory governance, where capability building is needed, and what specific governance changes would unlock transformation.

Phase 2: Pilot Implementation (6–18 months)
Launch transparent decision-making processes for the selected initiative. Establish clear protocols:

- All decisions recorded immutably
- Stakeholder input solicited before major decisions
- Decision rationale documented and publicly accessible
- Outcomes tracked against predictions

Implement token-based feedback mechanisms for affected communities. This need not require full blockchain infrastructure initially—simple digital voting with transparent aggregation demonstrates principles. Build trust through consistent transparency before introducing more sophisticated technology.

Measure coordination efficiency gains and stakeholder satisfaction improvements. Document specific metrics:

- Decision timelines (faster approval for community-supported initiatives)
- Staff engagement scores (higher satisfaction with meaningful voice)
- Community partnership formation rates (trust accelerates relationships)
- Innovation success rates (transparent governance reduces blocking)

Phase 3: Scaling (18+ months)
Expand successful approaches to additional transformation initiatives. Each successful pilot builds institutional capacity and stakeholder confidence. Network effects emerge—staff and communities who participated become advocates, recruitment improves, partnerships accelerate.

Consider a formal DAO structure for multi-stakeholder coordination. Once the pilot demonstrates value, blockchain-based governance becomes a justified investment. This infrastructure enables coordination at a scale impossible through traditional hierarchies.

Build network effects with other forward-thinking healthcare organisations. DAO structures enable rapid, low-risk partnerships—transparent governance reduces coordination friction. Early adopters create an ecosystem that becomes the coordination layer for healthcare transformation.

The Urgency: Why Delay Costs Exponentially

Leaders who act now gain competitive advantages that late adopters cannot replicate: established community trust, proven governance models, and network effects that compound over time. The transformation of healthcare is not a distant possibility but urgent necessity.

The COVID-19 pandemic created what many hoped would be a window for transformation. That window remains open, but not indefinitely. By 2030, the UK will need 40% more healthcare workers while facing the largest cohort of retiring staff in NHS history [11]. Similar pressures are building globally—the WHO projects a shortage of 18 million health workers by 2030 [12].

DAO governance enables power redistribution from centralised institutions to distributed stakeholders. Estonia's X-Road demonstrates this works at national scale. Buurtzorg proves alternative governance structures deliver superior outcomes in healthcare. The precedents exist for healthcare leaders ready to act.

Design thinking provides the methodology for navigating this transformation. The Three Horizons framework bridges vision and implementation. The same framework that guides clinical decision-making—discover problems deeply, define solutions precisely, develop iteratively, deliver measurably—applies to governance transformation. Healthcare leaders already possess this capability through their clinical training. The challenge lies in recognising and applying it to institutional transformation.

The 2035 vision shows a destination: health-literate societies, radically redistributed care, wellbeing-centred economics, and adaptive system capacity. Patricia voting on community health priorities, drawing on lived experience and professional training, supported by transparent technology that prevents institutional capture. The alternative trajectory shows cost: terminal institutional dysfunction, permanent innovation paralysis, workforce exodus, and explicit rationing. Patricia trapped in dysfunction, watching neighbours suffer preventable decline.

The Transformation Choice

Healthcare leaders face a choice. Shape decentralisation now through intentional governance transformation, or react to collapse later when options narrow and competitive advantages disappear. Early action builds community trust that compounds over time. Delayed action forfeits this advantage permanently.

The question isn't whether healthcare will decentralise—demographic and economic forces guarantee it will. The question is whether you'll lead that transformation or manage decline. Those who establish decentralised care networks and transparent governance structures now will capture the communities, talent, and trust that centralised competitors cannot retain. When centralised systems buckle under demographic pressure, decentralised networks will absorb their market share, staff, and community relationships.

The technology exists. The methodology exists. The precedents exist. Estonia's X-Road proves blockchain governance coordinates at national scale. Buurtzorg demonstrates distributed decision-making delivers superior healthcare outcomes. Bitcoin showed that strangers could transact with complete confidence through cryptographic proof rather than institutional authority. Ethereum's smart contracts enabled programmable governance. DAOs coordinate resources without centralised control.

What remains is leadership willing to redistribute power, embrace networked legitimacy, and trust both clinical expertise and community wisdom. The competitive window is measured in months, not years. Organisations that establish transparent governance now will define the infrastructure that others must integrate with. Those who wait will find themselves managing decline rather than leading transformation.

The choice is whether healthcare will decentralise through intentional design guided by principles of equity and community empowerment, or whether it will emerge chaotically from system collapse. Patricia's 2035 reality—participating meaningfully in healthcare governance, serving her community with dignity and agency—is achievable. The alternative—her mother's fate repeated across millions of families—is preventable.

Shape transformation now, or be shaped by it later. There is no third option.

References

1. Wise, J. (2023) 'Public confidence in government's stewardship of NHS falls to new low, poll finds', *BMJ (Clinical Research ed.)*, 380. https://doi.org/10.1136/bmj.p436.
2. Nakamoto, S. (2008) 'Bitcoin: A peer-to-peer electronic cash system'. Available at: https://bitcoin.org/bitcoin.pdf.
3. Gray, B., Sarnak, D. and Burgers, J. (2015) *Home Care by Self-Governing Nursing Teams: The Netherlands' Buurtzorg Model*. https://doi.org/10.26099/6CES-Q139.
4. Laloux, F. (2014) *Reinventing Organizations*. Nelson Parker.
5. Semenzin, S., Rozas, D. and Hassan, S. (2022) 'Blockchain-based application at a governmental level: disruption or illusion? The case of Estonia', *Policy and Society*, 41(3), pp. 386–401. https://doi.org/10.1093/polsoc/puac014.
6. Institute for Digital Society and Järv, K. (2025) 'Estonia's blockchain-based e-government and citizen security: Balancing data integrity and privacy in the digital state', Congress Proceedings, 1st International Congress on Law and the Future of Global Justice, International Vision University, Gostivar, North Macedonia, pp. 170–185. https://doi.org/10.55843/ICL2025cong170j.
7. Lumineau, F., Wang, W. and Schilke, O. (2021) 'Blockchain governance—a new way of organizing collaborations?', *Organization Science*, 32(2), pp. 500–521. https://doi.org/10.1287/orsc.2020.1379.
8. *Blockchain in Supply Chain Coordination What You Should Know* (no date) *FasterCapital*. Available at: https://fastercapital.com/articles/Blockchain-in-Supply-Chain-Coordination--What-You-Should-Know.html
9. Guanci, G. and Medeiros, M. (2018) 'Shared governance strategic planning retreat: A best practice', *Nursing Management*, 49(8), pp. 36–40. https://doi.org/10.1097/01.NUMA.0000542296.59754.61.
10. *Regulation (EU) 2024/1689 of the European Parliament and of the Council of 13 June 2024 laying down harmonised rules on artificial intelligence and amending Regulations (EC) No 300/2008, (EU) No 167/2013, (EU) No 168/2013, (EU) 2018/858, (EU) 2018/1139 and (EU) 2019/2144 and Directives 2014/90/EU, (EU) 2016/797 and (EU) 2020/1828 (Artificial Intelligence Act) (Text with EEA relevance)* (2024). Available at: http://data.europa.eu/eli/reg/2024/1689/oj

11. *Over a Million More Health and Care Staff Needed in the Next Decade to Meet Growing Demand for Care* (2021). Health Foundation. Available at: https://www.health.org.uk/press-office/press-releases/over-a-million-more-health-and-care-staff-needed-in-the-next-decade-to
12. *Stem the Sharp Decline in Health Worker Numbers by Prioritizing Retention, Recruitment and Competency Based Education in Humanitarian Settings* (2022). Available at: https://pmnch.who.int/news-and-events/news/item/24-05-2022-stem-the-sharp-decline-in-health-worker-numbers-by-prioritizing-retention-recruitment-and-competency-based-education-in-humanitarian-settings

Chapter 10

Design Thinking for Policymakers

Chapter 9 explored decentralisation as a transformation pathway—redistributing power from central authorities to local partnerships. But decentralisation requires policy frameworks enabling rather than preventing such redistribution. Policymakers determine whether local innovation thrives or dies. Understanding how policy gets made and why it systematically fails becomes essential.

THE COCOON

Fifteen years before writing this book, I met a UK health minister responsible for innovation. The meeting followed my detailed response to the NHS Chief Executive's call for evidence about accelerating innovation adoption across the NHS—issued while the NHS Institute for Innovation and Improvement pursued Lean thinking instead.

The path to that meeting required letters to my Member of Parliament and multiple civil service interactions. As the Royal Academy of Engineering's Visiting Professor in Medical Innovation, I finally got to share insights about design thinking for healthcare innovation.

The minister sat cocooned by civil servants filtering every interaction with outsiders. The meeting was pleasant and polite. At the end, the minister wished me well. No follow-up occurred. I felt dismissed as another crackpot with crazy ideas—someone to be tolerated, who needed to demonstrate practical application before being taken seriously.

In healthcare, that's an insurmountable hurdle for individuals. Other sectors allow people working in garages to develop novel products and build successful businesses. Healthcare makes this impossible through regulatory requirements, entrenched procedures, and established procurement arrangements.

DOI: 10.4324/9781003752073-13

A Note on Case Studies

This chapter draws heavily on NHS examples, not from parochial interest but methodological necessity. As the world's largest healthcare organisation—1.4 million employees serving 57 million people [1]—the NHS functions as healthcare's model organism, like the fruit fly in genetic research. Its scale amplifies transformation patterns that remain hidden in smaller systems. More critically, the NHS operates under direct political control with policy changes implemented nationally, making governance mechanisms visible at speed and scale unmatched elsewhere. The workforce crises, waiting list pressures, and reform failures visible in the UK today forecast what politically controlled healthcare systems globally will face within a decade. The NHS isn't special—it's simply ahead of the curve, offering policymakers elsewhere the choice between learning from its expensive lessons or repeating them.

The Pattern of Policy Failure

I tracked UK healthcare policy development closely over subsequent years. The 2012 Health and Social Care Act evolution from the 2010 white paper made sense: Andrew Lansley's proposal to decentralise the NHS and establish clinician-led commissioning groups represented sound thinking. The swift reversion revealed deeper patterns.

Lansley exemplifies career politicians operating under electoral accountability. But even clinical expertise fares no better. Lord Professor Ara Darzi—world-class surgeon and health systems thinker—served as Parliamentary Under-Secretary of State under Gordon Brown. His 2008 report 'High Quality Care for All' outlined a compelling vision for clinically led innovation and integrated services grounded in patient care realities [2]. The report was well received, then largely ignored. Despite credibility as both practitioner and policy thinker, the system's governance structures prioritised managerial control over clinical insight. In 2024, the Health Secretary Wes Streeting again called upon Darzi for strategic guidance [3]. This repetition reveals the diagnostic error at policy's core: politicians treat governance failure as an information deficit. 'If only we had better clinical advice…' they reason, while ignoring that Darzi's 2008 advice was excellent—the system simply rejected it. Seeking more clinical expertise without redesigning governance structures that systematically exclude clinical priorities guarantees repeating the same expensive failure.

These experiences confirm my view: design thinking is absent in healthcare policy. Before exploring what embedded design would look like, we must understand policymaker types and drivers.

Understanding Policymaker Types: Competing Logics

Politicians and career officials both make healthcare policy, but their drivers are fundamentally different. Politicians operate under electoral accountability—their horizon is the next election, pushing them toward visible reforms, symbolic wins, and headline-grabbing innovations.

Career officials face process accountability—they guard stability, legality, and institutional memory, defaulting to caution and incrementalism.

One is motivated by re-election and political capital, the other by system integrity and career survival. Innovation only sticks when these competing logics briefly align.

These differences explain why healthcare policy remains reactive and medium-term at best. Healthcare requires long-term vision. The misalignment creates systematic dysfunction.

Five Systemic Constraints

Policy failure in healthcare isn't about individual shortcomings—it's about structural incompatibilities between policy system operation and effective transformation requirements. These constraints reveal predictable patterns that design thinking addresses systematically.

I Electoral Cycle Misalignment

Politicians operate within 4–5 year cycles. Meaningful healthcare transformation requires 10–15 year horizons. Training a physician takes a decade. Shifting population health patterns requires generational investment. Building public trust demands consistency across multiple administrations. This temporal mismatch creates systematic bias toward short-term, visible interventions over long-term system building.

II Accountability Structure Conflicts

Career officials face procedural accountability—measured by compliance, risk avoidance, and process adherence. Politicians face outcome accountability—measured by visible results and electoral success. These competing metrics create decision-making paralysis: officials default to incremental changes minimising procedural risk, while politicians demand dramatic reforms generating headlines. Innovation requires both process rigour and outcome focus, but current structures incentivise choosing one over the other.

III Information Processing Limitations

Healthcare systems generate complexity exceeding traditional policy-making capabilities. Typically, policymakers must synthesise input from 8 to 12 major stakeholder groups, each with distinct incentives, technical languages, and power structures. Without systematic frameworks for managing complexity, policy development defaults to oversimplification (losing critical nuances) or analysis paralysis (preventing action).

IV Resource Allocation Paradoxes

Prevention generates savings 5–10 years in the future but requires immediate investment. Emergency interventions create immediate visibility but long-term costs. Current budgeting cycles and political incentives systematically favour expensive reactive measures over cost-effective preventive approaches—what economists call 'policy investment traps' [4].

V Stakeholder Coordination Failures

Modern healthcare involves unprecedented stakeholder complexity compared to systems 50 years ago. Each additional stakeholder increases coordination complexity exponentially, not linearly. Without systematic approaches to stakeholder alignment, well-intentioned policies fragment across competing interests. Implementation failures that appear as resistance are actually coordination breakdowns.

COUNTERINTUITIVE FINDING

Policy Coordination Complexity Exceeds Human Cognitive Capacity

Healthcare stakeholder complexity has grown exponentially over 50 years. The mathematical relationship n(n–1)/2 reveals that modern healthcare policy involving 8–12 major stakeholder groups creates 66 distinct relationships—a coordination challenge that exceeds human cognitive capacity without systematic frameworks. Policymakers managing healthcare transformation face greater coordination complexity (66 relationships) than critical care clinicians managing life-or-death situations (28 relationships). Healthcare policy fails not because stakeholders disagree, but because managing 66 relationship dynamics between agreeing parties exceeds human processing limits. Each stakeholder may accept their role, but coordination between parties—one of those 66 relationships—breaks down. Multiply these failures, and policy collapses predictably.

The Darzi Case Study: When Governance Fails Clinical Leadership

The Darzi case deserves detailed examination because it reveals governance structures' power to reject even optimal leadership. As a world-class surgeon, innovator, and health systems thinker, Darzi represented rare clinical leadership brought into government. His 2008 report 'High Quality Care for All' set out a compelling vision for clinically led innovation, integrated services, and continuous quality improvement—all grounded in patient care realities [2].

The report was smart, sensible, and well-received—then largely ignored. The governance architecture absorbed the reforms and neutralised them. By Darzi's 2009 departure the changes had faded—not because the analysis was wrong, but because the system was structurally configured to resist exactly this kind of clinically led transformation.

Compare this to politicians without healthcare expertise who enact transformative change—Margaret Thatcher's internal markets, Tony Blair's choice agenda, or Andrew Lansley's commissioning groups. Some changes proved misguided, but they stuck. Even bad political ideas survive better than good clinical ones.

Clinical expertise proves insufficient when operating within governance structures designed to exclude it. Surgical skill, academic achievement, and NHS understanding matter less than understanding governance structures and working their machinery. The pattern is clear: even world-class clinical credentials fail when governance structures systematically reject beneficial innovations. Like immune systems attacking foreign tissue regardless of benefit, organisational systems defend the status quo through informal resistance that no policy directive can overcome. This requires governance redesign, not just better policy.

Cross-Sector Validation: UK Automotive Industry

Before dismissing healthcare as uniquely dysfunctional, consider whether this pattern extends beyond medicine. The UK automotive industry demonstrates identical patterns.

Once Britain dominated car manufacturing. William Morris (Lord Nuffield) ranked among the world's richest men. Jaguar, Rolls-Royce, Aston Martin—all British. By 1990, when I joined Jaguar, UK design and engineering remained world-class. Formula One teams—motorsport's technological pinnacle—were designed and built in Britain. Japanese factories in the UK (Nissan, Toyota, Honda) proved the workforce was world-class too, producing vehicles meeting Japanese import quality standards. Yet British-owned car manufacturing collapsed. Today: Tata owns Jaguar and Land Rover, VW owns Bentley, BMW owns Rolls-Royce and Mini. Only Morgan—a boutique manufacturer—remains British-owned, and even that's held by a multinational investment company.

Two factors destroyed British automotive manufacturing:

1. **Endemic management incompetence.** Business school executives prioritised short-term profits over long-term capability building [5]. They possessed neither engineering knowledge nor leadership capacity to leverage world-class design talent and a skilled workforce.
2. **Catastrophic policy decisions.** Prime Minister Margaret Thatcher brokered a Honda-British Leyland joint venture promoting badge-engineering—using Japanese components and designs but affixing 'Rover' badges. This insulted customer intelligence while bleeding talented engineers. If you're a world-class engineer relishing technical challenges, why work for a company forcing you to rebadge Japanese products when you can move across Coventry and work for Jaguar designing actual cars? Ford bought Jaguar, found outdated facilities but exceptional design and engineering talent, invested in modern factories, and we built cars matching Lexus quality according to J.D. Power data [6]. BMW attempted the same with Rover/Land Rover but discovered that money cannot compensate for fundamental capability absence. They closed Rover, sold Land Rover, kept only Mini.

The pattern is clear: politicians and executives lacking subject matter expertise make decisions that destroy industries despite world-class technical capabilities. There's no reason to believe healthcare operates differently. Same politicians. Same business schools producing one-dimensional managers. Same systematic destruction of expertise-driven excellence.

When policy ignores those who understand the work, failure follows predictably.

Regulation Versus Governance

Healthcare discussions conflate regulation and governance. These are distinct forces with fundamentally different purposes requiring different design approaches.

Regulation refers to formal rules controlling specific activities—drug approvals, device classifications, clinical practice standards. Regulations are explicit, written, and legally enforceable. Regulation protects patients by ensuring safety and efficacy.

Governance encompasses informal power structures, decision-making processes, and cultural norms determining how organisations operate. Governance is implicit, evolved, and enforced through social and professional mechanisms. Governance protects the system—preserving established hierarchies, familiar processes, and organisational survival.

Policymakers address regulation when they need to address governance. Regulatory reforms through legislative action. Governance resists direct intervention—like immune systems attacking foreign elements that threaten the status quo, regardless of potential patient benefits.

The Lansley Reforms: Detailed Autopsy

Andrew Lansley's 2012 Health and Social Care Act provides an instructive case study in policy design failure—not because the ideas were wrong, but because design thinking was absent from development and implementation. The reforms aimed to decentralise NHS decision-making, establishing local clinical commissioning groups led by GPs (primary care doctors) who understood local needs [7]. The aim aligned with design thinking: empowering frontline clinicians, locating decisions closer to patients, enabling rapid adaptation.

But the policy process violated every design thinking principle:

No Stakeholder Co-Design: Reforms were developed in Westminster, announced to the NHS, then imposed through legislation. Clinicians, patients, and frontline staff had no meaningful input during design phases.

No Prototyping: The entire NHS reorganised simultaneously. No pilot regions tested assumptions. No learning from early implementation informed later rollout.

No Iteration: Once legislation passed, changes became extremely difficult. Early problems couldn't trigger adaptive responses.

No User Testing: Clinical commissioning groups received their mandates without adequate preparation, training, or support systems.

The predictable result: good ideas executed poorly, then reversed when political winds shifted. The NHS restructured again, undoing much of Lansley's decentralisation. Billions spent, limited lasting benefit achieved.

Design thinking would have approached this differently: extensive stakeholder engagement during design, pilot programmes in volunteer regions, rapid iteration based on learning, scaled implementation only after demonstrating value. The timeline extends beyond single electoral cycles—but sustainable transformation requires such investment.

The 10-Year Plan Pattern

The NHS repeatedly announces 10-year transformation plans following predictable cycles: crisis triggers demand for long-term thinking, politicians commission expert reviews outlining ambitious visions, plans launch with great fanfare, implementation begins enthusiastically, then political priorities shift and plans are quietly abandoned or dramatically revised. This reflects competing accountabilities. Politicians need to demonstrate action. Career officials need to manage continuity. Neither incentive structure supports sustained 10–15 year transformation efforts.

The 2025 Repetition

The NHS 10-Year Plan announced in 2025 demonstrates this pattern's persistence [8]. Still devoid of any design thinking principles, the plan promises shifts from hospital to community care, analogue to digital systems, and sickness to prevention—rhetorically appealing goals nearly identical to Lansley's 2012 reforms and the 2000 NHS Plan before that.

Three critical failures repeat:

1. The plan contains no named authors, no visible leadership, no evidence of frontline consultation. This anonymity signals a lack of ownership. When implementation fails—and anonymous plans consistently fail—no one bears responsibility.

2. The plan reads as technocratic abstraction disconnected from care delivery realities. Exhausted clinicians facing 18-month waiting lists receive sweeping reform mandates with no additional capacity, no implementation support, no acknowledgement of current system stress. This evokes World War I generals commanding troops 'over the top' from headquarters—strategy without presence.
3. Like Lansley's 2012 reforms, the 2025 plan mandates decentralisation and clinical leadership without preparing the workforce, addressing managerial resistance, providing transition resources, or establishing feedback loops. Lansley's reforms cost billions and achieved limited change because governance structures systematically undermined implementation. The 2025 plan makes identical assumptions about organisational structures changing through policy directive.

Breaking the Pattern

Design thinking offers an alternative: instead of comprehensive 10-year plans requiring sustained political will, focus on discrete 90-day experiments demonstrating value rapidly. Build transformation capability through cumulative learning from multiple short cycles rather than betting everything on a single long-term plan.

For policymakers: examine the transformation plan on your desk. Does it name accountable leadership? Emerge from genuine frontline co-design? Acknowledge current capacity constraints? Provide resources for transition? Establish rapid iteration mechanisms? Address governance resistance explicitly? Without these elements, your plan joins the expensive graveyard of well-intentioned initiatives that governance structures systematically destroyed. The choice remains: repeat the pattern or break it.

Why do 10-year plans consistently fail? Beyond electoral cycles and accountability conflicts, a mathematical reality compounds the challenge.

Stakeholder Proliferation Mathematics

Healthcare stakeholder complexity has increased dramatically over 50 years. Understanding this mathematically reveals why coordination fails and why design thinking matters.

Consider coordination requirements across stakeholder groups. With two stakeholders, you manage one relationship. With three stakeholders, you manage three relationships. The formula is $n(n-1)/2$, where n equals stakeholder count.

- 3 stakeholders: 3 relationships
- 5 stakeholders: 10 relationships
- 8 stakeholders: 28 relationships
- 12 stakeholders: 66 relationships

Figure 10.1 shows how over the ages the number of relationships and interactions increased between healthcare stakeholders. The formula shows how the number of stakeholders 'n' relates to 'C'—the number of relationships.

Modern healthcare policy typically involves 8–12 major stakeholder groups: physicians, nurses, patients, administrators, payers, regulators, pharmaceutical companies, device

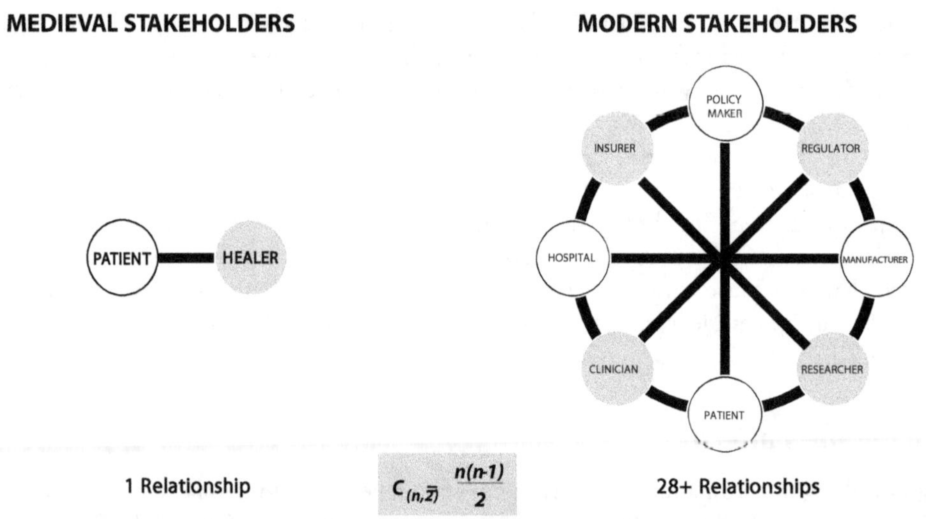

Figure 10.1 Stakeholder proliferation.

manufacturers, technology companies, patient advocates, community organisations, and elected officials. Managing 66 relationship dynamics exceeds human cognitive capacity without systematic frameworks.

This explains why well-intentioned policies fragment during implementation. Stakeholder A agrees to their part. Stakeholder B agrees to their part. But the coordination between A and B—one of those 66 relationships—breaks down. Multiply these failures across the relationship network, and policy collapses.

In critical care, clinicians coordinate 6–8 team members (physician, nurses, physio, pharmacy, radiology, family) = 28 relationships. Policy work involves 8–12 stakeholders = 66 relationships. Same coordination challenge, larger scale.

Design thinking addresses stakeholder proliferation through systematic coordination frameworks, creating shared understanding and aligned incentives across groups. Managing 66 stakeholder relationships exceeds human cognitive capacity without such systematic approaches. Yet some regulatory bodies succeed despite this complexity.

The MHRA Innovation Office: Regulation as Learning System

Not all regulatory approaches fail. The UK's Medicines and Healthcare products Regulatory Agency (MHRA) Innovation Office demonstrates how design thinking principles can be embedded in regulatory frameworks [9].

Traditional drug regulation uses 'waterfall' product development through rigid and sequential phase gates: preclinical studies, Phase I trials, Phase II trials, Phase III trials, marketing authorisation. Each phase has clearly defined entry and exit criteria. Fail to meet criteria, and development stops.

The MHRA Innovation Office introduced adaptive approaches for novel therapies—particularly cell and gene therapies where traditional pathways prove inadequate. The office engages with developers early in the process, providing guidance on acceptable evidence standards and helping design appropriate clinical studies. This represents genuine co-design between regulators and innovators. Instead of regulators setting fixed requirements and judging compliance, both parties collaborate to define what 'safe and effective' means for unprecedented therapies.

The approach embodies design thinking principles:

- **Empathy**: Understanding innovators' genuine challenges
- **Iteration**: Allowing evidence packages to evolve as understanding develops
- **Prototyping**: Testing regulatory approaches through early-stage engagements
- **Learning**: Building institutional knowledge about emerging therapeutic categories

Outcomes demonstrate value: novel therapies reach patients faster without compromising safety. Developers receive clearer guidance, reducing wasted investment. Regulators build expertise in emerging fields.

The MHRA Innovation Office remains small—a specialised unit within a larger traditional structure. Scaling these principles across healthcare regulation requires systematic frameworks. The foundation: design thinking's Double Diamond.

The Double Diamond for Policy

The Double Diamond—design thinking's foundational framework, presented in Figure 1.3, applies directly to policy development.

First Diamond: Define the Problem

Discover Phase: What are stakeholders actually experiencing? Policymakers typically begin with assumed problems: 'We need better cancer screening' or 'We must reduce A&E waiting times.' Design thinking starts by exploring: What problems do patients, clinicians, and communities actually face? What patterns emerge across different contexts?

This requires ethnographic research—observing healthcare delivery in real settings, interviewing diverse stakeholders, mapping patient journeys. Methods include shadowing clinicians during shifts, conducting patient focus groups, analysing service use data for unexpected patterns.

Define Phase: What is the real problem? After gathering rich qualitative data, policymakers synthesise insights to define core challenges. This often reveals that assumed problems mask deeper issues. 'Cancer screening uptake' becomes 'complex barriers to preventive care across socioeconomically diverse populations.' This reframing opens new solution spaces.

Second Diamond: Develop the Solution

Develop Phase: What might work? Generate multiple policy options through co-design with stakeholders. Traditional policy development narrows to a single option early, then defends that choice. Design thinking generates diverse possibilities, combining stakeholder input with international evidence and innovative thinking.

Methods include policy design workshops bringing together patients, clinicians, administrators, and community representatives to co-create options. Use 'How might we…' framing to open solution spaces rather than jump to predetermined answers.

Deliver Phase: What actually works? Test policy options through prototyping before full implementation. This represents the most radical departure from traditional approaches—and the most powerful.

InterQB-it™ Framework for Stakeholder Alignment

Modern healthcare policy involves 8–12 stakeholder groups creating 66 relationship dynamics—complexity that exceeds human cognitive capacity without systematic frameworks. The InterQB-it™ method, presented in Figure 4.1, provides a design thinking framework specifically developed to manage this stakeholder complexity. Its principles apply directly to policy development's coordination challenges.

InterQB-it™ maps four critical dimensions:

Interests: What does each stakeholder want to achieve? Physicians want improved patient outcomes and manageable workloads. Patients want convenient, effective care. Administrators want cost control and regulatory compliance. Payers want demonstrated value. These interests often conflict—design thinking makes conflicts explicit and seeks creative integration.

Questions: What concerns does each stakeholder have? Physicians question whether new policies will increase administrative burden. Patients question whether changes will affect care quality. Understanding stakeholder questions allows addressing concerns during design rather than encountering resistance during implementation.

Barriers: What prevents stakeholders from supporting change? Physicians face time constraints. Patients face access barriers. Administrators face budget limitations. Mapping barriers reveals where policy must remove obstacles rather than simply mandate compliance.

Incentives: What would motivate stakeholder support? Financial incentives matter but are rarely sufficient. Professional recognition, reduced workload, improved patient outcomes, simplified processes—these diverse motivations require diverse incentive structures.

InterQB-it™ translates this diagnostic mapping into implementation through a systematic 4 × 4 framework. The matrix addresses four organisational levels (Organisation, Brand/Platform, Product/Service) across four intervention types (Strategies, Processes, Enablers, People), ensuring stakeholder analysis produces actionable policy design rather than remaining an abstract understanding. For policymakers, this means each stakeholder dimension directly informs concrete interventions: identified barriers become enabler requirements, stated questions shape communication strategies, and mapped interests guide strategic alignment. [Chapter 16 details full implementation methodology.]

For Clinicians Considering Policy Leadership

If you're a clinician reading this chapter wondering whether your skills apply to policy development, they do—more than you realise. Your diagnostic methodology IS sophisticated policy design:

When you diagnose sepsis:

- Discover: Pattern recognition across vital signs, history, examination
- Define: Synthesising data into specific diagnosis and severity grading
- Develop: Generating treatment options considering patient factors
- Deliver: Implementing treatment with continuous monitoring and adjustment

This scales to policy:

- Discover: Understanding stakeholder experiences through ethnographic research
- Define: Synthesising insights into core problem definitions
- Develop: Co-designing multiple policy options with stakeholders
- Deliver: Prototyping, monitoring, and iterating policy approaches

The MHRA Innovation Office succeeds because regulators learned to think like clinicians approaching novel therapies: assess the unique situation, adapt standard frameworks, prototype approaches, learn from outcomes.

Your clinical authority combined with design thinking methodology creates transformative policy leadership. The question isn't whether your skills translate—it's whether governance structures will welcome your expertise or attack it.

Design Methods for Policy Development

Design thinking offers five core methods for policy development:

Ethnographic Research: Observe healthcare delivery in natural settings, revealing unspoken assumptions and workarounds that surveys miss.

Stakeholder Mapping: Identify all affected groups, mapping interests, power levels, and relationships to reveal hidden stakeholders.

Co-Design Workshops: Bring diverse stakeholders together to develop options collaboratively, building buy-in while surfacing implementation insights.

Policy Prototyping: Test options through regulatory sandboxes, pilot regions, phased rollouts, or simulation exercises before full implementation.

Rapid Iteration: Build feedback loops enabling quick adjustment. Design thinking embraces adaptation as learning, not failure.

The Policymaker-Regulator Co-Design Framework

Effective policy development requires collaboration between policymakers (setting strategic direction) and regulators (ensuring safety and compliance). Traditional approaches separate these functions—policymakers announce goals, regulators develop rules. This creates misalignment and unintended consequences.

Design thinking brings them together during development: collaborating to understand problems, creating a shared vision incorporating both outcome and process goals, developing approaches simultaneously rather than sequentially, and testing both policy effectiveness and regulatory feasibility through pilots. This reveals implementation challenges early when adjustments remain possible.

Regulatory Sandboxes: Policy Prototyping in Practice

Regulatory sandboxes—controlled environments testing new approaches under relaxed rules—represent design thinking applied to policy. Financial services pioneered this approach; healthcare has been slower to adopt. The UK's Financial Conduct Authority created regulatory sandboxes allowing fintech startups to test innovations with real customers under relaxed regulatory requirements. Regulators monitor closely, learn about new business models, and develop appropriate rules based on observed risks rather than theoretical concerns.

Healthcare sandboxes face higher stakes—financial mistakes cost money, but healthcare mistakes cost lives. Yet the principle remains sound: controlled experimentation with intensive monitoring enables evidence-based regulation rather than precautionary rule-making that stifles all innovation.

Denmark's 'Test and Learn' programme exemplifies healthcare sandboxes. Local regions can apply for temporary regulatory relief to test innovations. A multidisciplinary committee reviews applications, considering potential benefits and risks. Approved innovations proceed with close monitoring and structured evaluation. Successful innovations inform national policy; unsuccessful ones provide learning without causing widespread harm [10].

Key sandbox features include:

- **Clear Boundaries**: What is permitted within the sandbox is explicitly defined
- **Intensive Monitoring**: Regular data collection and review
- **Limited Scope**: Constrained geography, population, or duration
- **Evaluation Framework**: Predetermined success metrics
- **Exit Strategy**: Clear process for scaling successes or terminating failures

Sandboxes embody design thinking's prototyping principle: test assumptions before committing to full-scale implementation. These methods—ethnographic research, co-design, sandboxes, prototyping—require collaboration across traditional boundaries.

Why Politicians and Officials Need Each Other

Design thinking reveals complementary strengths that effective policy requires. Politicians bring electoral mandate, ability to mobilise resources, and political capital for overcoming resistance. Career officials bring institutional knowledge, implementation expertise, and continuity across political cycles.

Transformation succeeds when these strengths combine. The MHRA Innovation Office illustrates: political leadership established the office, career regulators brought pharmaceutical expertise, politicians protected experimentation, officials developed mechanisms making adaptive regulation work. Neither politicians nor officials could achieve this alone. Together, operating through design thinking principles, they achieved meaningful innovation.

Clinical Trial Prototyping: Policy Lessons

Chapter 6 detailed clinical trial redesign through design thinking. The pharmaceutical industry provides policy lessons because drug development operates under regulatory frameworks globally—and because it involves long timelines (10–15 years) exceeding electoral cycles.

Decentralised clinical trials exemplify policy prototyping. Instead of requiring patients to visit clinical sites repeatedly, trials bring research to patients through home health nurses, telemedicine, and local laboratories. This improves recruitment, retention, and diversity while reducing costs.

These approaches required regulatory adaptation. Could informed consent be obtained virtually? Could home-based measurements meet data quality standards? Could local laboratories handle specialised tests? Traditional regulations assumed site-based trials; decentralised approaches didn't fit existing frameworks.

The FDA and EMA developed guidance through iterative co-design with pharmaceutical companies. Early pilot trials tested approaches under special protocols. Regulators learned what worked, what required refinement, and what safety concerns arose. This experience informed broader guidance enabling widespread adoption [11].

The policy lesson: complex transformation succeeds through prototyping, learning, and iteration—not through comprehensive upfront planning. Decentralised trials are now routine; this revolution occurred through design thinking principles rather than traditional policy development.

Case Study: Torbay Care Trust

Torbay Care Trust in Devon integrated health and social care in the early 2000s—more than a decade before integration became national policy. Traditional NHS structures separated health services from social care. Elderly patients with complex needs fell between organisational boundaries. Each system operated efficiently within its domain while patient care fragmented across domains.

Torbay brought these systems together under unified management with multidisciplinary teams, shared budgets, and connected information systems. The design thinking elements:

Empathy: Leaders spent months understanding patient experiences navigating fragmented systems. This revealed coordination failures invisible from within each organisation.

Co-Design: Clinicians, social workers, and administrators worked together to design new processes. Frontline staff had significant input into team structures and workflows.

Prototyping: Integration proceeded through pilots in specific geographic areas and patient populations. Early learning informed later rollout.

Iteration: Regular reviews identified problems and enabled rapid adjustments. Initial approaches were refined based on experience.

Results were striking: hospital bed days reduced by 26%, emergency admissions fell by 28%, care costs decreased while quality improved. Transformation created these outcomes—not efficiency drives or cost-cutting mandates [12].

The national policy lesson: Torbay succeeded because it wasn't driven by policy mandate. The local organisation had autonomy to experiment, learn, and adapt. When integration became national policy years later, implementations that followed rigid mandates rather than design thinking principles achieved inferior results [13]. Today, 20 years after its initial success, the NHS and local council can no longer sustain their innovative care integration model due to lack of government funding [14].

Case Study: Frome's Compassionate City Model

Frome, a Somerset town, achieved community-led healthcare transformation despite governance barriers. GP practices noticed high emergency admissions among socially isolated patients. Medical treatment addressed acute problems but not the underlying loneliness driving health deterioration. The practices partnered with community organisations to create 'Health Connections'—trained connectors who helped patients access social clubs, volunteer activities, housing support, and mental health services. The intervention cost £175 per patient annually.

Results stunned healthcare economists: emergency hospital admissions fell 17% over three years in Frome while rising 29% in similar towns. Lives improved, costs decreased, community strengthened [15].

The transformation applied similar design thinking principles—stakeholder collaboration, rapid prototyping, emergent design—but with a critical difference: it succeeded despite policy barriers rather than because of policy support.

The policy lesson: transformation can succeed when local actors apply design thinking principles. But—and this is critical—such grassroots success should inform policy rather than being treated as exceptional circumstances requiring special permission.

Imagine healthcare systems actively encouraging Frome-like experimentation rather than grudgingly tolerating it. Regulatory frameworks enabling rapid local innovation while ensuring safety. National policy learning from successful local experiments rather than imposing top-down mandates. This represents design thinking embedded in governance structures.

The Local Autonomy Pattern

Both Torbay and Frome succeeded for identical reasons—reasons that expose policy failure patterns. Neither waited for permission. Neither followed national mandates. Neither required Westminster approval for experimentation. Both had local autonomy to understand community needs, design responses, prototype rapidly, and iterate based on learning.

Critically, both succeeded initially because central governance structures ignored them. When integration became national policy years later, centrally mandated implementations achieved inferior results because policy removed the local autonomy that enabled Torbay's original success.

The pattern is clear: transformation succeeds at community scale with local autonomy. It fails when centralised and mandated. The policy challenge: how to enable local autonomy systematically?

Case Study: Kaiser Permanente's Integrated System

Kaiser Permanente demonstrates what becomes possible when governance structures align with design thinking principles. Kaiser operates as an integrated system where insurance, hospitals, and physicians function under unified governance. This enables long-term investment in prevention and coordination—investments fragmented systems cannot make because savings accrue to different organisations than those investing.

The design thinking principles manifested in Kaiser's development were not accidental:

Patient-Centred Design: Kaiser regularly engages patients in service design. Patient feedback shapes everything from facility architecture to care pathways.

Multidisciplinary Collaboration: Integrated governance enables clinicians from different specialties to work together designing optimal care pathways.

Data-driven Iteration: Unified data systems allow rapid learning across the organisation. Successful innovations in one region spread quickly to others.

Long-term Optimisation: Integrated budgets enable investments in prevention and care coordination that reduce long-term costs.

Kaiser's significance lies less in headline cost comparisons than in demonstrating how integrated system design reshapes utilisation patterns, professional behaviour, and long-term value creation [16, 17] . This doesn't result from unique clinical capabilities—it results from governance structures enabling design thinking principles.

The policy lesson: governance matters as much as methodology. You can train healthcare workers in design thinking, but if governance structures prevent them from acting on insights, transformation fails. Policy should focus on governance redesign enabling design thinking, not just promoting design thinking within unchanged governance.

Pattern Synthesis: What Makes Policy Design Work

Across these cases—MHRA Innovation Office, Torbay integration, Frome community model, Kaiser's system—common patterns emerge:

Local Autonomy Within Clear Boundaries: Successful cases had the freedom to experiment while maintaining safety and quality standards. This balances innovation with accountability.

Intensive Stakeholder Engagement: All cases involved deep collaboration across traditional boundaries. No single organisation or stakeholder group drove change alone.

Rapid Iteration Based on Learning: Cases that succeeded built feedback loops enabling quick adjustment. Those that struggled locked into fixed plans despite evidence of problems.

Focus on Patient Outcomes, Not Organisational Efficiency: Transformation succeeded when genuinely improving patient experience, not when primarily serving organisational goals.

Tolerance for Emergence: The best outcomes weren't fully planned upfront—they emerged through iterative practice. Policy frameworks that accommodate emergence outperform those demanding comprehensive upfront design.

Protected Experimentation Space: Whether through regulatory sandboxes, local autonomy, or organisational integration, success required protection from system forces that attack innovation automatically.

These patterns inform what design thinking for policymakers means in practice.

The 90-Day Policy Implementation Roadmap

Design thinking transforms abstract commitment into practical action. For long-term transformation (10–15 years), separate vision from implementation: develop a compelling vision through a stakeholder process, then deliver through successive 90-day cycles, each demonstrating value within electoral cycles while building toward longer-term goals. For policymakers, a 90-day implementation roadmap provides a starting point:

Days 1–30: Prepare

- Identify a specific policy challenge suitable for a design thinking approach
- Assemble a small team (4–6 people) combining policy, operational, and design expertise
- Conduct stakeholder mapping exercise
- Define success metrics
- Secure leadership commitment to an experimental approach

Days 31–60: Engage and Design

- Conduct ethnographic research with affected stakeholders
- Run co-design workshops generating multiple policy options
- Synthesise insights into defined problem statement
- Develop 2–3 prototypeable policy approaches
- Design pilot frameworks for preferred options

Days 61–90: Prototype and Learn

- Launch small-scale pilot in a controlled setting
- Monitor closely, gathering both quantitative and qualitative data
- Hold weekly learning sessions reviewing emerging insights
- Prepare a comprehensive evaluation documenting what worked, what didn't, and why
- Present findings to leadership with recommendations

This 90-day cycle provides a foundation. Successful pilots scale to larger implementations. Failed pilots provide learning without major resource waste. Either outcome advances understanding more than traditional approaches.

Design Thinking's Limitation: It's Not Enough

Design thinking provides a powerful methodology for policy development. But methodology alone cannot overcome governance resistance to transformation. We must acknowledge design thinking's limitations. Excellent design can improve policy development. Stakeholder engagement reduces resistance. Prototyping reveals implementation challenges. Iteration enables refinement.

These improvements matter. But they don't address the fundamental problem: healthcare governance structures attack beneficial innovation systematically. Even perfectly designed policies encounter immune responses that destroy them before benefits materialise.

We need to explore deeper questions: Can governance structures themselves be redesigned to welcome rather than attack innovation? Can we engineer governance structures that enable transformation rather than preventing it? These questions extend beyond this book's scope. For practitioners implementing design thinking, the key insight is this: sustainable change requires attention not just to methodology but to organisational ecosystems in which methodology operates. The encouraging news: design thinking's emphasis on stakeholder collaboration and rapid prototyping creates governance conditions more receptive to innovation. By implementing approaches outlined in this chapter, you're not just applying tools—you're beginning to shift governance culture itself.

Transformation: Choose Your Path

Demographic and financial pressures make healthcare transformation inevitable. The question isn't whether transformation occurs—it's whether we lead transformation with design thinking or continue reactive crisis management. Two pathways exist:

Continue Current Approach: React to crises with knee-jerk policies. Ignore evidence of what works. Allow governance structures to systematically destroy innovations through informal resistance and defensive routines. Spend £200M+ on interventions with sub-15% success rates.

Design Thinking Plus Governance Redesign: Engineer governance structures that welcome innovation from inception, with targeted interventions costing a fraction of large-scale reform. Build organisational receptivity to beneficial change. Create sustainable transformation.

The choice isn't whether to transform—it's whether to design transformation intentionally or allow dysfunction to metastasise.

Call to Action

For Politicians:
You have an electoral mandate for transformation. Design thinking provides a methodology to engage stakeholders, prototype solutions, and build political will for sustained change. You need civil service partners who understand navigating governance complexity.

For Career Officials:
You have institutional knowledge and system understanding. Design thinking provides tools to challenge established patterns while managing implementation risks. You need political cover to experiment with governance redesign.

For Clinical Leaders:
You have the methodology policymakers lack: diagnostic reasoning, iterative problem-solving, and patient-centred design. Design thinking isn't something to learn—it's recognition of what you already do. Apply your clinical approach to system design. Partner with administrative leaders who have organisational authority. Together, transform healthcare by scaling bedside excellence to system-level.

Together:
Apply Double Diamond to identify real problems before jumping to solutions. Use co-design to align competing stakeholder objectives. Create regulatory sandboxes for safe-to-fail experimentation. Engineer governance structures that are welcoming rather than attacking beneficial innovation.

Start Small, Think Big:
Launch 90-day pilot using design thinking on policy challenge. Typical investment of £100K–150K demonstrating methodology. Build capability and confidence before scaling. Document lessons informing broader transformation.

The Alternative:
Continue spending £200M+ on transformation initiatives that governance structures systematically destroy through defensive routines and informal resistance, while claiming 'we tried everything' without addressing fundamental organisational dysfunction ensuring failure [18].

Policymakers face a choice: design healthcare's future or manage its decline. Yet even when policymakers choose design thinking, implementation frequently fails. Understanding policy frameworks isn't enough—we must understand the systematic forces that destroy well-designed transformation efforts. This chapter has shown how design thinking applies to policy development. The frameworks exist. The evidence demonstrates success. The implementation pathway is clear. Yet healthcare transformation initiatives still fail at alarming rates—even when designed well. Part IV examines why: the systematic forces that destroy even excellent transformation efforts, and what we must understand to overcome them.

References

1. NHS Workforce Statistics - October 2025 (no date) 'NHS England digital'. Available at: https://digital.nhs.uk/data-and-information/publications/statistical/nhs-workforce-statistics/october-2025 .
2. Darzi, A. (2008) *High Quality Care for All: NHS Next Stage Review Final Report.* London: Stationery Office.
3. Darzi, A. (2024) *Independent Investigation of the National Health Service in England.* London, United Kingdom: Department of Health and Social Care.
4. Jacques, O. and Noël, A. (2022) 'The politics of public health investments', *Social Science & Medicine*, 309, p. 115272. https://doi.org/10.1016/j.socscimed.2022.115272.
5. Russo, F. et al. (2023) 'Responsible management education in business schools – High on principles but low on action: A systematic literature review', *The International Journal of Management Education*, 21(3), p. 100843. https://doi.org/10.1016/j.ijme.2023.100843.
6. 'Jaguar Cars Press Releases' (no date). Available at: https://www.jaguarheritage.com/jdht/uploads/Press-Release-Collection-20191219-V.6.pdf?utm_source=chatgpt.com.
7. Health and Social Care Act 2012, Wikipedia. Available at: https://en.wikipedia.org/w/index.php?title=Health_and_Social_Care_Act_2012&oldid=1338437157
8. Fit for the future: 10 Year Health Plan for England (2025) 'UK government'. Available at: https://assets.publishing.service.gov.uk/media/6888a0b1a11f859994409147/fit-for-the-future-10-year-health-plan-for-england.pdf.
9. Gilmore, N. (2017) 'Insight into our innovation office – MedRegs'. Available at: https://medregs.blog.gov.uk/2017/04/18/insight-into-our-innovation-office/ (Accessed: 28 January 2026).
10. Leckenby, E. et al. (2021) 'The sandbox approach and its potential for use in health technology assessment: A literature review', *Applied Health Economics and Health Policy*, 19(6), pp. 857–869. https://doi.org/10.1007/s40258-021-00665-1.

11. Catherine Eckford (2026) 'EMA and FDA issue joint AI guidance for medicine development', *European PharmaceuticalReview*.Availableat:https://www.europeanpharmaceuticalreview.com/news/270259/ema-fda-joint-ai-guidance-medicine-development/
12. Torbay and South Devon NHS Foundation Trust (2018) *Annual Report and Accounts 2017/18*, p. 236. Available at: https://www.england.nhs.uk/wp-content/uploads/2019/10/Torbay_and_South_Devon_NHS_FT_Annual_Report_and_Accounts_2017-18.pdf.
13. Farnsworth, A. (2012) 'Unintended consequences? The impact of NHS reforms upon Torbay Care Trust', *Journal of Integrated Care*, 20(3), pp. 146–151. https://doi.org/10.1108/14769011211237483.
14. Talora, J. (2026) 'Trust "losing £35m a year" from integration contract', *Health Service Journal*. Available at: https://www.hsj.co.uk/integrated-care/trust-losing-35m-a-year-from-integration-contract/7040656.article
15. Abel, J. et al. (2018) 'Reducing emergency hospital admissions: A population health complex intervention of an enhanced model of primary care and compassionate communities', *The British Journal of General Practice*, 68(676), pp. e803–e810. https://doi.org/10.3399/bjgp18X699437.
16. McCarthy, D. and Mueller, K. (2009) *Kaiser Permanente: Bridging the Quality Divide with Integrated Practice, Group Accountability, and Health Information Technology*. Available at: https://www.commonwealthfund.org/publications/case-study/2009/jun/kaiser-permanente-bridging-quality-divide-integrated-practice
17. Maeda, J.L.K., Lee, K.M. and Horberg, M. (2014) 'Comparative health systems research among kaiser Permanente and other integrated delivery systems: A systematic literature review', *The Permanente Journal*, 18(3), pp. 66–77. https://doi.org/10.7812/TPP/13-159.
18. Mistry, P. (no date) 'Is the spring budget a game changer for NHS technology?', *The King's Fund*. Available at: https://www.kingsfund.org.uk/insight-and-analysis/blogs/spring-budget-game-changer-nhs-technology

IV

WHY TRANSFORMATION FAILS (AND WHAT TO DO ABOUT IT)

Chapter 11

The Limits of Lean: Why Continuous Improvement Isn't Enough

THE CULTURE YOU CANNOT COPY

I worked as a car designer at Jaguar in the 1990s when the company was owned by Ford US. After successfully developing and implementing the ISO9001 Quality Management System in Jaguar's Styling Department, I joined the team tasked with designing the Jaguar Product Development System (JPDS) in alignment with the Ford Product Development System (FPDS). I became a de facto member of the FPDS team in Dearborn, representing the Design function across the company. Of course, we benchmarked Toyota. It was no secret then that Toyota was able to develop and build better cars faster than anyone else. Cheekily, one of us phoned Toyota: 'Hey, we're from Ford, can we come and visit you guys and see how you do it?'

The unexpected but revealing answer was: 'Sure, come on down—you can't copy us anyway.'

This wasn't arrogance. It was recognition that the Toyota Production System was inseparable from their organisational culture, long-term thinking, and fundamental assumptions about work, learning, and human development. You can document tools, map processes, measure cycle times—but you cannot extract the invisible infrastructure of trust, kata, nemawashi, and respect for people that makes those tools effective.

Toyota understood something Western management consultants would spend decades refusing to acknowledge: culture cannot be copied. Three decades later, healthcare systems across the globe would learn this lesson the hard way. Instead of a few hundred million dollars in failed automotive transformation, the cost would be measured in lives lost and billions squandered.

DOI: 10.4324/9781003752073-15

Part III explored how design thinking transforms healthcare when applied to clinical trials, AI implementation, and system decentralisation. But why have conventional transformation methodologies like Lean—deployed with equal conviction and far greater investment—failed to achieve similar results? The answer lies in a fundamental incompatibility that doomed these efforts from the start.

The Fundamental Incompatibility: Manufacturing Logic Meets Living Systems

Before examining how Lean failed in the NHS, we must understand why it was structurally doomed from the start. Lean is based on the Toyota Production System, which evolved to optimise the manufacture of inanimate objects moving through predictable processes. A crankshaft doesn't develop complications overnight. A car door doesn't respond differently to treatment based on its social determinants. Parts don't change their clinical presentation between process steps.

Healthcare involves living, responding, changing human beings embedded in complex social contexts. Patient conditions evolve during treatment. Social determinants of health—housing, employment, education, food security—profoundly affect how individuals respond to medical intervention. Co-morbidities interact in unpredictable ways. The cardiac arrest during elective surgery cannot be scheduled for the next available 'takt time' slot (the rate at which a product must be produced to meet demand to prevent overproduction or shortages). The patient presenting with atypical symptoms requires exploration and clinical reasoning, not standardisation and process adherence.

This represents an ontological difference—a fundamental incompatibility between manufacturing's predictable, plannable world and healthcare's inherently uncertain, adaptive reality. Lean's core assumption that processes can be standardised, optimised, and made predictable is fundamentally incompatible with healthcare's lived reality.

The Expertise Paradox: Excluding Those Who Already Had the Methodology

Here lies the deepest irony of the NHS Lean experiment: clinicians already possessed exactly the methodology needed to navigate healthcare's complexity. As demonstrated in Chapter 5, clinical diagnostic reasoning mirrors design thinking through systematic cycles of observation, hypothesis generation, testing, and adaptation. Clinicians practise multi-dimensional thinking under uncertainty every day. They navigate complex adaptive systems as core professional competence.

When a patient presents with chest pain, clinicians don't follow a linear algorithm. They:

- **Discover**: Gather symptoms, observe presentation, understand context (empathy and observation)
- **Define**: Generate differential diagnoses, consider probabilities, frame the problem (problem definition under uncertainty)
- **Develop**: Test hypotheses through examination and investigation, prototype treatment approaches (iterative testing)
- **Deliver**: Implement treatment, monitor response, adapt based on feedback (continuous learning)

This is design thinking methodology, practised thousands of times daily across every NHS Trust. Yet the NHS Lean programmes brought in management consultants charging thousands per day to teach Lean Six Sigma to professionals who had practised hypothesis testing and rapid-cycle adaptation for decades. This represents what Chapter 5 identified as 'Methodology Inversion'—spending billions to import methodologies evolved for simpler systems while systematically excluding the people who already possessed the sophisticated complexity navigation methodology that healthcare actually requires.

Why were clinicians excluded from leading transformation? The answer lies in decades of management 'takeover' following New Public Management reforms. The UK's career path bifurcation forces clinicians to choose: remain clinical or pursue management. Senior transformation roles went to people with MBA credentials and management consulting backgrounds—expertise in retail, airlines, policy, consulting. Valuable domains, but none are complex adaptive systems resembling healthcare.

The actual transformation leaders—clinicians navigating complexity daily—were systematically relegated to 'representing the clinical perspective' rather than leading change. Virginia Mason Medical Center, as we shall see, succeeded precisely because they did the opposite: they empowered clinical expertise to lead transformation.

COUNTERINTUITIVE FINDING

The £1 Billion Misdiagnosis

Healthcare transformation initiatives assume clinicians lack methodology and need training in process improvement. The NHS spent £1 billion on Lean programmes teaching Lean Six Sigma to professionals who already practise more sophisticated design thinking daily through clinical diagnostic reasoning. When a patient presents with chest pain, clinicians Discover (gather symptoms, understand context), Define (generate differential diagnoses), Develop (test hypotheses through examination), and Deliver (implement treatment, adapt based on response)—the exact design thinking framework healthcare seeks to import. Virginia Mason achieved 73% medication error reduction by empowering frontline clinicians to lead transformation. The NHS achieved zero measurable improvements across 150+ Trusts by importing management consultants to teach tools. Healthcare's crisis results from governance structure systematically excluding its most design-capable professionals from strategic decision-making, not from capability shortage.

The COVID-19 Tragedy: When Efficiency Killed

According to official figures, approximately 900 NHS and care workers died during the COVID-19 pandemic [1]. By April 2020, at least 100 had died from COVID-19, amid mounting concern over the availability of Personal Protective Equipment (PPE). By early May that number rose to 171. While Health Secretary Matt Hancock denied PPE shortages were responsible [2], the denial changed nothing: healthcare workers died because efficiency-optimised systems prioritised cost reduction over crisis preparedness. The national stockpile lacked critical items such as gowns and visors, with millions of protective masks missing. Parliamentary testimony documented these deficiencies comprehensively [3, 4]. This was deliberate policy choice prioritising short-term efficiency over long-term resilience.

The Supply Chain That Failed

NHS Supply Chain is the agency responsible for procuring medical equipment and consumables, including PPE that protect healthcare workers from pathogens. In 2018, this critical function was outsourced to Unipart Logistics as part of a £730 million contract [5]. Unipart wasn't chosen by accident. This automotive supply chain company, which started as the components division of British Leyland, had built its reputation on Lean principles. They trained others, from Green Lean 6 Sigma to Master Black Belt level, with a track record of implementing these methods across UK government organisations [6].

One of Lean's core features is Just-in-Time supply, which reduces capital tied up in inventory. For Unipart, this was central to delivering their promise of £2.4 billion in savings over five years. The logic seemed unassailable: why hold expensive stock when you could order precisely what you needed, when you needed it? During the early stages of the COVID-19 pandemic, the NHS faced serious challenges in providing adequate PPE to frontline staff—there just wasn't enough in stock.

In 2016, the UK conducted Exercise Cygnus—a comprehensive pandemic preparedness simulation. The results were stark: the UK was woefully unprepared for a respiratory pandemic, with critical shortages anticipated in PPE, ventilators, and intensive care capacity [7]. The recommendations were specific. The warning was clear. Politicians and policymakers filed the report. No action was taken. When COVID-19 arrived, every failure Exercise Cygnus predicted materialised exactly as warned.

Patients died alone as there was no PPE for their relatives to be with them in their last moments. Healthcare workers made impossible choices about who received the limited PPE available, knowing that their decisions might cost lives—including their own. This was a systems failure born of applying manufacturing logic to healthcare delivery, of mistaking efficiency for resilience, of confusing cost reduction with value creation.

The Origins of Lean: From Ford to Healthcare

Henry Ford developed an efficient system for the high-volume manufacturing of the Model-T Ford, making cars affordable. His 'you can have any colour as long as it is black' approach allowed for little customisation, but that was perfectly acceptable compared to the horse and cart that people were used to. Black paint dried quicker than other colours, allowing him to remove a bottleneck, speed up the manufacturing process, and increase volume.

The Second World War left industry in Japan destroyed, including the Toyota plants. Mr Kiichiro Toyoda visited the Ford factories in Detroit as part of the reconciliation effort between the two nations. He was so inspired by the efficiencies he observed that he incorporated its principles into the Toyota Production System (TPS)—presented in Taiichi Ohno's book [8]. Fast forward to the 1980s: Toyota had established itself as a successful manufacturer of quality cars that was able to develop new products faster than any other car company.

The MIT Researchers: Documenting Without Understanding

Three researchers studied the global automotive industry and visited Toyota to find out the source of its success: James P. Womack (US, Ph.D in Political Science), Daniel T Jones (UK, MSc Economics), and Daniel Roos (US, MIT Ph.D. in systems engineering). Neither of these gentlemen spoke fluent Japanese or had a deep understanding of its culture, which makes it unlikely that they fully grasped the breadth and depth of the Toyota Production System and its underlying organisational culture. That didn't stop them. In 1991, they published 'The Machine That Changed the World,' which coined (in more than one sense) the term 'Lean' [9]. The book became an international bestseller and established their successful consulting careers.

The origin of Lean is high-volume manufacturing with little variation or customisation—'any colour as long as it's black.' The authors' understanding of TPS was shaped by symptoms—what was externally visible and measurable—rather than the underlying culture. Critics argued that this led to a partial and instrumentalist version of Lean, one that emphasised tools and techniques (kanban, just-in-time, 5S) while ignoring the philosophical and cultural roots of continuous improvement [10]. The concepts of 'kata' (habituated learning), 'nemawashi' (consensus-building), and respect for people as foundational elements were overlooked. Lean thinking became associated with removing waste and increasing efficiency, not with how people interact, learn or solve problems. Without the cultural grounding of TPS, Lean became a toolkit for cost-cutting, deployed top-down by managers seeking quick wins rather than long-term capability building.

From Automotive to Healthcare: The NHS Experiment

Many accepted the findings and cohorts of Lean evangelists were 'leaning' anything they could get their hands on—way beyond cars. Nothing was safe—education, Her Majesty's Revenue and Customs and lastly the NHS.

The NHS Institute for Innovation and Improvement

In 2005, the Department of Health established the NHS Institute for Innovation and Improvement (NHSI). Based on the Warwick University campus and funded directly by the Department, the NHSI was positioned as a flagship body charged with 'transforming healthcare for patients and public by rapidly developing and spreading new ways of working' [11].

In practice, the Institute's work largely coalesced around a different goal: optimisation of existing models. It became best known for producing a suite of branded tools and methods under the banner of 'Productive' programmes—the Productive Ward, Productive Operating Theatre, Productive Mental Health Ward, Productive General Practice and Productive Community Services. These were Lean-influenced, modular, and branded improvement toolkits that focused heavily on standardisation, workplace organisation (5S), and local metrics. What they failed to do was challenge or redesign the deeper structures of care delivery, funding, workforce planning, or system logic. The NHSI conflated optimisation with transformation and promoted toolkits over redesign. It responded to policy pressure for quick wins rather than creating space for radical change.

Despite words of caution from academics at Warwick Business School—literally across the same campus—the NHSI developed and rolled out Lean-style programmes focusing on time-and-motion studies and standardisation, without corresponding investment in staff development, leadership, or redesign of care pathways [12, 13]. One of the less-discussed but arguably most decisive reasons the NHSI failed lies in who it recruited. Despite its lofty mission to disrupt and redesign care delivery, the NHSI was largely staffed by individuals drawn from within the existing NHS ecosystem. Many had held roles in predecessor organisations and simply moved laterally into the new Institute. NHSI was not a melting pot of radical thinkers, design disruptors, or diverse external voices. It was the same people in new offices, applying the same thinking with fresh branding.

Patients Versus Products: The Fundamental Incompatibility

Let's assume that on Saturday I walk into my local Toyota showroom. I am so taken by their latest model Prius that I sign an order there and then. However, after talking with family on Sunday and watching some car programmes on YouTube I change my mind. On Monday I go back and cancel my order. Sure, the dealer won't be pleased and might even get me to pay a penalty or threaten to take me to court. The point is that the Toyota Production System will be unaffected. It reallocates and keeps running. My cancellation causes minimal disruption.

The next day I am due in hospital for routine elective surgery—say a hip replacement—with an otherwise clean bill of health. All nicely planned, replacements part ordered and in stock. Unfortunately, 10 minutes into the operation I have a heart attack. Now the entire system must pivot instantly—the operating team shifts roles, the OR becomes an emergency theatre. Anaesthetists, ICU staff, cardiologists, radiologists—everyone is mobilised. Everything—from clinical protocols to team priorities—changes in a heartbeat. Lives depend on it.

Now imagine me being in a hospital where staff are conditioned to stick to predefined flows and standard times. Where staff have lost the capability and mindset to pivot at all. Where the system is optimised to reduce 'waste' such as excess capacity and redundancy (which are actually safety features in clinical care). Escalation pathways may be unclear because they 'interrupt flow.' Clinical teams may be understaffed or under-resourced for emergencies because variability was treated as a problem to eliminate rather than an inevitable reality to design for.

In that context, a sudden cardiac event during elective surgery is a systemic shock to a rigid, linear model. And I might not survive only because the system forgot it was a hospital and tried to become a factory.

Key Insight: Manufacturing systems aim to eliminate variation. Healthcare systems must be built to respond to it. Lean, when blindly applied, confuses these two truths. At Toyota, an order change doesn't disrupt the system. It was never designed around one car. In a hospital, one patient's change in status can (and should) disrupt the system—because it's designed around human life, not production flow. A Lean approach that doesn't honour this difference is dangerous.

The Evidence: Did Lean Actually Improve Healthcare?

In 2013, I conducted independent research analysing Hospital Standardised Mortality Ratios (HSMR) across NHS Trusts implementing Productive Ward/Lean methodologies. HSMR is a measure of quality allowing for comparison between hospitals, calculated by Dr Foster Intelligence [14]. The findings were stark: neither top-performing Trusts—already on a track of steady improvement with low mortality rates before implementing Lean—nor 'Outlier Trusts' on a downward trend of higher death showed any change in their trajectories following Lean implementation. I concluded that Lean did not add value to Trusts already performing well, nor improve poorly performing Trusts. When I submitted these findings to the *Health Service Journal*, the editor declined publication—not because the methodology was flawed, but because the results were inconvenient to the prevailing narrative.

My findings correspond with other researchers [15]. The central justification for introducing Lean in the NHS was the promise of better care at lower cost. But after nearly two decades of experimentation, a clear picture has emerged: There is no robust evidence that Lean implementation in the NHS has produced sustained improvements in system-wide quality of care metrics. Research shows:

Short-Term Operational Gains: Some studies have reported small, short-term improvements in areas like turnaround times and operating theatre throughput [16]. However, these are typically confined to specific departments, time-limited and rarely followed up, and disconnected from patient outcomes.

Unclear Attribution: When improvements occur, it is often difficult to isolate Lean as the cause [17]. Changes may result from increased attention, temporary additional resourcing, or Hawthorne effects (individuals changing their behaviour in response to being observed).

Little or No Impact on Core Quality Metrics: Reviews consistently show no meaningful improvement in outcomes such as mortality rates, hospital-acquired infections, staff satisfaction or retention, or patient-reported outcome measures [18].

High Abandonment Rate: Many NHS Trusts that piloted Lean quietly discontinued it [16, 19]. These withdrawals are under-reported in the literature, often attributed to 'bad implementation' rather than questioning Lean itself, and indicative of the weak fit between Lean and complex professional healthcare environments.

The True Cost of Productive

Between 2005 and 2013, NHSI received an estimated £500–600 million in public funding, with its flagship programme—the Productive Ward: Releasing Time to Care™—rolled out across nearly every acute Trust in England. Local Trusts were expected to absorb implementation costs, including staff backfill for training, internal facilitators and QI teams, external consultancy, and time diverted from clinical care. With over 150 Trusts participating and many adopting additional modules from the Productive suite, the cumulative cost of local implementation likely exceeded £400–500 million. A reasonable estimate for the total system-wide cost of the Productive initiative—combining NHSI central funding and Trust-level implementation—is approximately £1 billion.

Despite this extraordinary investment, no robust, peer reviewed evidence exists to show sustained improvements in patient outcomes, workforce retention, or system-level productivity. Evaluations found inconsistent implementation, unclear attribution of benefits, and little to no measurable return on investment. In hindsight, Productive may stand as one of the most expensive quality improvement experiments in NHS history—and one of the least transparently evaluated.

The Virginia Mason Exception: When Clinical Expertise Leads

Before concluding that Lean simply doesn't work in healthcare, we must address the counterpoint: Virginia Mason Medical Center in Seattle. While the NHS spent £1 billion achieving no measurable improvements, Virginia Mason achieved documented success with Toyota Production System principles. They reduced patient walking distance during hospital stays by 85%, cut nurse time hunting for supplies by 50%, and demonstrated significant patient safety improvements [20]. These results matter. They're real. They demand explanation.

The Virginia Mason case raises the central question: If the NHS failed spectacularly while Virginia Mason succeeded using the same methodology, what explains the difference?

Clinicians as Transformation Leaders, Not Manufacturing Workers

The fundamental distinction lies in who led the transformation. Virginia Mason empowered clinical expertise to drive change. Frontline clinicians led the redesign of medication administration processes, reducing medication errors by 73% [21]. This wasn't about training staff to follow standardised processes—it was about designing systems that made errors difficult rather than relying on perfect human performance under stress.

Clinical expertise, when given organisational authority, produces both safety and efficiency gains. This represents the opposite of the NHS approach, which brought in management consultants to teach tools while relegating clinicians to 'represent the clinical perspective.' Virginia Mason recognised that clinicians already possessed the methodology needed—their daily practice of navigating complexity, responding to unpredictability, and adapting to changing patient needs.

Virginia Mason's CEO, Gary Kaplan, led the transformation for over twenty years, from 2000 onwards [22]. He didn't hire management consultants to implement Lean while he focused on other priorities. He led the organisation to Japan to learn directly from Toyota. He championed patient safety as the North Star. He maintained consistent commitment through setbacks and resistance.

The NHS approach represented the opposite model. The NHS Institute ran three-year programmes—Productive Ward, Productive Operating Theatre—with rotating leadership teams. Directors served typical NHS tenures of 2–3 years before moving to other trusts. Management consultants delivered training then departed. Programme funding ended, leaving implementation incomplete.

Respecting Variation Versus Eliminating It

Virginia Mason succeeded because they understood that healthcare variation cannot be reduced. They used TPS principles to eliminate process waste—nurses searching for supplies, patients walking excessive distances, delays in medication administration—while respecting that clinical variation is inherent and necessary.

The NHS Lean programmes made the opposite error. They imported manufacturing methodology wholesale, attempting to standardise clinical pathways as if patients were widgets. The Productive Ward programme focused on 'standard work' and 'takt time' for care delivery, concepts borrowed directly from automobile assembly lines. This ignored what clinicians know instinctively: the cardiac arrest during surgery cannot be scheduled for the next available slot. The patient presenting with atypical symptoms requires exploration, not standardisation.

Virginia Mason applied TPS to support clinical decision-making, not replace it. They used rapid prototyping—testing changes in 1–2 week cycles rather than implementing perfect solutions [23]. When they redesigned patient flow, they tested multiple configurations, measured results, and adapted based on what they learned. This iterative approach mirrors the clinical reasoning process itself: observe, hypothesise, test, refine.

Learning Kata Versus Learning Tools

Perhaps most fundamentally, Virginia Mason learned kata—the underlying methodology of continuous improvement—while the NHS learned tools—5S, visual management, standard work.

John Shook, a Toyota veteran who worked closely with Virginia Mason, contrasts the ease of tools with the harder challenge of adopting new ways of thinking and seeing [24]. Virginia Mason's leaders spent time on Toyota shop floors observing not just what workers did but how they thought about problems. They learned 'genchi genbutsu'—go and see for yourself—as cultural practice, not checklist item. They implemented the 'andon cord'—the rope workers pull to stop production when they spot problems—understanding it represents fundamental respect for frontline expertise. Any staff member could halt a process if they identified safety concerns [20]. This fundamentally redistributed power from hierarchy to expertise.

Consider how Virginia Mason addressed medication administration errors. Rather than implementing a standardised checklist (the tools approach), they brought frontline nurses, pharmacists, and physicians together to observe the actual medication process repeatedly—watching where confusion occurred, where workarounds developed, where communication broke down. They discovered the problem wasn't staff forgetting steps but rather poorly designed handoff processes that forced workarounds. The team prototyped multiple solutions at small scale, measured results, and adapted based on what they learned. The 73% reduction in medication errors came not from better compliance with standard procedures but from redesigning the system itself based on frontline expertise and iterative learning. This is kata—learning to see problems differently, to question assumptions, to prototype and adapt. Tools would have given them a better checklist. Kata gave them a better system.

The NHS Productive programmes taught tools. Management consultants delivered training on how to organise supply rooms using 5S. They explained visual management boards. They provided templates for standard work documentation. But they didn't—couldn't—transfer the learning culture that makes TPS work at Toyota. They promoted 'empowerment' while maintaining traditional hierarchies where consultant clinicians held authority and nurses followed protocols. They adopted Lean's vocabulary without its substance.

Scale and Selective Implementation

Virginia Mason Medical Center employs approximately 5,000 staff. They operate within a defined geographic area serving a clear patient population. They could be selective—choosing when to begin transformation, investing when ready, proceeding at appropriate pace.

The NHS employed 1.4 million people across hundreds of trusts when the Lean programmes launched. The Productive programmes attempted system-wide implementation across vastly different organisations—rural district hospitals, urban teaching centres, specialist tertiary facilities—each with unique challenges, cultures, and constraints. They mandated participation. Every trust received pressure to implement regardless of readiness. Political cycles demanded visible progress on timelines mismatched to transformation requirements.

Transformation at NHS scale requires fundamentally different approaches than transformation at single-hospital scale. Virginia Mason's playbook, while instructive, doesn't translate to organisations 280 times larger.

What This Teaches Us

Virginia Mason's success validates rather than undermines the critique of NHS Lean. They succeeded precisely because they avoided the NHS's mistakes: they empowered clinical expertise to lead transformation, respected clinical variation rather than attempting to eliminate it, committed leadership for decades rather than programme cycles, operated at manageable scale with clear accountability, and learned methodology rather than mimicking tools.

Yet Virginia Mason's context reveals another fundamental limitation. As a private hospital in the US system, Virginia Mason serves insured patients who can afford care. The NHS operates under a universal access mandate—treating everyone regardless of ability to pay, social complexity, or comorbidity burden. Process optimisation delivers greater efficiency gains when you can control inputs through patient selection. Virginia Mason's impressive results demonstrate what Lean can achieve within a filtered patient population. The NHS's challenge is exponentially harder: achieving efficiency while serving everyone, including the most complex, vulnerable, and resource-intensive patients that private systems can decline. This isn't a moral failing of Virginia Mason—it's a contextual reality that makes their success difficult to replicate in universal healthcare systems. Lean optimises for efficiency; universal healthcare demands equity. These goals often conflict.

But even Virginia Mason's remarkable results demonstrate Lean's limitations in healthcare. Their 85% reduction in patient walking distance represents genuine improvement. Yet it optimises existing hospital-centric delivery models rather than transforming them fundamentally. Their success occurred within traditional hospital walls, improving the efficiency of centralised care rather than enabling decentralised alternatives. The transformation healthcare requires extends beyond what any single hospital, however excellent, can achieve through process optimisation. We need new delivery models, different ownership structures, alternative governance arrangements. We need innovation, not just improvement.

Why Did the NHS 'Lean Over'? A Perfect Storm

It's tempting to look back on the rise of Lean thinking in the NHS and ask: 'Who let this happen?' After all, there was no shortage of informed voices warning that Lean, born in the high-volume, low-variation world of car manufacturing, was ill-suited to the complex, human-centred reality of healthcare. But this wasn't a case of villainy or conspiracy. What unfolded was a perfect storm—a convergence of pressures, incentives, and good intentions that produced a deeply flawed outcome.

1. **A Simple Promise in a Time of Complexity**
   Lean offered a seductively simple message: 'You can make your system better—faster, safer, cheaper—by reducing waste and empowering staff.' In a context of rising demand, financial pressure, and public scrutiny, this was irresistible for policy leaders. It allowed them to promise improvement without structural reform, and to claim innovation without threatening vested interests. Lean said you could have your cake and eat it: no new funding, no political controversy, just better 'processes.' That's tinkering disguised as change.
2. **The Vacuum Left by the Collapse of British Industry**
   The rise of Lean in the NHS mirrored the collapse of UK manufacturing, especially the automotive sector. In the 1990s and 2000s, management consultants and engineers trained in Lean were leaving failing or foreign-owned companies. They rebranded themselves as change agents for services—especially healthcare, which was being told to 'modernise or die.' The NHS became the new frontier for consultants—a multi-billion-pound institution with deep operational complexity and political pressure to improve. Lean gave them a ready-made toolkit and a heroic narrative: 'We saved Toyota—now we'll save the NHS.' This was evangelism, powered by PowerPoint, invoices, and charm.

3. **The Ideological Appeal to New Public Management**
The Lean surge in the NHS must be understood in the broader ideological context of New Public Management (NPM). Neoliberalism features such as free-market capitalism and public choice theory led to treating public services as businesses, importing private-sector 'best practice,' and emphasising metrics, performance, and efficiency. Lean fit NPM like a glove. It reduced complex health systems to production lines. It let ministers talk about 'value' without addressing social determinants. It promised transformation without political cost. By wrapping system reform in technical, apolitical language, Lean disguised political decisions as process problems, making it easier for policymakers to claim progress without structural change.
4. **Suppressed Dissent and Lost Alternatives**
The NHS is full of brilliant clinicians, potential innovators, and system thinkers who saw the flaws in Lean. Some spoke out early. Others published rigorous critiques. But dissenters were often marginalised as 'anti-innovation' or 'obstructionist.' Alternative models—such as design thinking, complexity science, or whole-system co-production—were underfunded and poorly understood. Ministers and NHS executives often lacked the literacy or courage to back unorthodox paths. Orthodoxy won by default—not because it worked, but because it was legible, backed by 'experts,' and safe for politicians.
5. **Selective Implementation: Stop the Line—but Not Here**
At the heart of TPS is a radical principle that any worker, at any time, can stop the production line. The 'andon cord' system empowers frontline workers to signal problems immediately. In theory, the NHS embraced Lean to improve flow and empower staff. But in practice? Try 'pulling the cord' in the NHS—and you'll find yourself labelled a troublemaker, isolated, or even pushed out. The NHS has a deeply documented hostile culture toward whistleblowers and dissenters. Staff who raise safety concerns often face retaliation, not resolution [25]. By selectively adopting Lean's tools (like process mapping and standardisation) without its values (like psychological safety, respect for people, and empowered accountability), the NHS performed what sociologists call a 'decoupled implementation.' The outer forms of improvement were retained, but the inner substance—the culture that makes it work—was lost. It became Lean without learning, control without trust, and improvement without voice.

Learning from the Failure: Improvement Is Not Innovation

Lean in the NHS has been a colossal misapplication—a mistake not just in method, but in mindset. It promised more than it could ever deliver, and in doing so, it crowded out more appropriate, more humane, and ultimately more effective alternatives. Lean has cost us dearly in time, resources, trust and lives. In chasing flow, we've lost sight of care. In prioritising metrics, we've sidelined meaning. The damage is concrete. Patients suffered. Staff burned out. Systems stagnated. But this is a reflection, not just a reckoning. If Lean was seductive, it is because the system was already strained. It offered what looked like a solution at a time when something—anything—was needed.

Those who led these efforts—often sincere, well-meaning, and under immense pressure—should not be scapegoated. But nor should they be shielded from scrutiny. Many voices, including clinicians, academics, and system thinkers, raised early warnings. Those warnings were ignored. We must ask: Why?

One reason is that Lean, and the management consultancy industry that marketed it, provided a seductive form of depoliticisation. It reframed deeply political questions—about funding, priorities, values—as technical process problems. It turned transformation into a manager's toolkit, rather than a collective act of moral and institutional re-imagination. In doing so, it pushed aside the very voices most needed for change: clinicians, patients, and communities.

The Core Problem: Optimising an Unsustainable System

Lean focuses on making what we do today more efficient. It cannot challenge whether we should be doing it in the first place. It optimises existing structures rather than questioning their fundamental design. When applied to healthcare, Lean improves the efficiency of hospital-centric models without enabling the decentralised, community-based alternatives that modern populations require.

Healthcare faces a widening gap between demand and capacity. An ageing population with multiple chronic conditions requires fundamentally different care models than the acute, episodic treatment our hospital-centric system was designed to deliver. Lean cannot bridge this gap. Process optimisation cannot transform system architecture. Continuous improvement cannot deliver the innovation required. The transformation healthcare requires combines Lean's process discipline with design thinking's system reimagination—not choosing between them, but integrating both.

We need new delivery models, different ownership structures, alternative governance arrangements. We need transformation, not just improvement. Multi-dimensional transformation frameworks that integrate culture, leadership, design thinking, innovation, and structural change—approaches explored in Chapter 17—offer pathways beyond Lean's limitations. But first, we must stop mistaking motion for progress. The NHS is not a factory. Healthcare is not a production line. Patients are not standardised units. And transformation is not a synonym for 'making things flow faster.'

What This Means for Healthcare Leaders

If you're leading transformation:

- Partner with clinical expertise to design change, not just represent the clinical perspective
- Learn methodology (kata) rather than mimicking tools
- Build resilience, not just efficiency
- Design for variation response, not variation elimination

If you're a clinician:

- Your diagnostic reasoning IS sophisticated design methodology
- System transformation requires the same expertise you bring to patient care
- Accept leadership roles with confidence—clinical thinking legitimises organisational authority

The transformation healthcare requires starts with recognising who already possesses the methodology needed.

Bridge to Chapter 12: Why Even Well-Funded Innovation Fails

We've established that improvement methodologies like Lean fail to transform healthcare. Innovation is required. But here's the uncomfortable question that follows: if innovation is the answer, why does healthcare innovation have such a high failure rate? After all, healthcare innovation attracts massive venture capital investment, employs talented teams, and launches with professional management and ambitious vision. Why is healthcare innovation so difficult? Why do venture capitalists and startup founders consistently get healthcare wrong? And what systemic barriers prevent good ideas from reaching patients who need them?

Chapter 12 examines why even genuinely innovative approaches struggle to survive in healthcare's unique environment—and what that tells us about designing for transformation rather than disruption.

References

1. Office for National Statistics (2021) *Coronavirus (COVID-19) Related Deaths by Occupation, England and Wales*. Available at: https://www.ons.gov.uk/peoplepopulationandcommunity/healthandsocialcare/causesofdeath/datasets/coronaviruscovid19relateddeathsbyoccupationenglandandwales.
2. Haynes, L. (2021) 'Hancock denies PPE shortages caused any of 1,500 NHS staff deaths from COVID-19'. Available at: https://www.gponline.com/article/1718813).
3. UK Parliament (2020) *Government failed to act on its security plans for a pandemic*. Available at: https://committees.parliament.uk/committee/111/national-security-strategy-joint-committee/news/137998/.
4. The Rt Hon the Baroness Hallett DBE (2024) *Module 1 Report: The Resilience and Preparedness of the United Kingdom*. UK Covid-19 Inquiry. Available at: https://covid19.public-inquiry.uk/reports/module-1-report-the-resilience-and-preparedness-of-the-united-kingdom/.
5. Unipart (n.d.) *Proud to Support the NHS and Its Supply Chain*. Available at: https://www.unipart.com/proud-to-support-the-nhs-and-its-supply-chain/.
6. Unipart (n.d.) *The Unipart Way*. Available at: https://www.unipart.com/the-unipart-way/.
7. GOV.UK (2020) *Annex B: Exercise Cygnus Report (Accessible)*. Available at: https://www.gov.uk/government/publications/uk-pandemic-preparedness/exercise-cygnus-report-accessible-report.
8. Ohno, T. (1988) *Toyota Production System: Beyond Large-Scale Production*. Cambridge, MA: Taylor & Francis.
9. Womack, J.P., Jones, D.T. and Roos, D. (1990) *The Machine That Changed the World*. New York: Rawson Associates.
10. Mehri, D. (2006) 'The darker side of lean: An insider's perspective on the realities of the Toyota Production System', *Academy of Management Perspectives*, 20(2), pp. 21–42. https://doi.org/10.5465/amp.2006.20591003.
11. GOV.UK (2013) *NHS Institute for Innovation and Improvement*. Available at: https://www.gov.uk/government/organisations/nhs-institute-for-innovation-and-improvement.
12. Radnor, Z., Walley, P., Stephens, A. and Bucci, G. (2006) *Evaluation of the Lean Approach to Business Management and Its Use in the Public Sector*. Edinburgh: Office of Chief Researcher, Scottish Executive.
13. Radnor, Z. and Osborne, S.P. (2013) 'Lean: A failed theory for public services?', *Public Management Review*, 15(2), pp. 265–287. https://doi.org/10.1080/14719037.2012.748820.
14. Wikipedia contributors (2026) 'Dr Foster Intelligence', *Wikipedia*. Available at: https://en.wikipedia.org/w/index.php?title=Dr_Foster_Intelligence&oldid=1336683063.
15. Sarre, S., Maben, J., Griffiths, P., Chable, R. and Robert, G. (2019) 'The 10-year impact of a ward-level quality improvement intervention in acute hospitals: A multiple methods study', *Health Services and Delivery Research*, 7, pp. 1–172. https://doi.org/10.3310/hsdr07280.
16. Radnor, Z.J., Holweg, M. and Waring, J. (2012) 'Lean in healthcare: The unfilled promise?', *Social Science & Medicine*, 74(3), pp. 364–371. https://doi.org/10.1016/j.socscimed.2011.02.011.

17. Papadopoulos, T., Radnor, Z. and Merali, Y. (2011) 'The role of actor associations in understanding the implementation of Lean thinking in healthcare', *International Journal of Operations & Production Management*, 31(2), pp. 167–191. https://doi.org/10.1108/01443571111104755.
18. Mazzocato, P., Savage, C., Brommels, M., Aronsson, H. and Thor, J. (2010) 'Lean thinking in healthcare: A realist review of the literature', *BMJ Quality & Safety*, 19(5), pp. 376–382. https://doi.org/10.1136/qshc.2009.037986.
19. Waring, J.J. and Bishop, S. (2010) 'Lean healthcare: Rhetoric, ritual and resistance', *Social Science & Medicine*, 71(7), pp. 1332–1340. https://doi.org/10.1016/j.socscimed.2010.06.028.
20. Kenney, C. (2011) *Transforming Health Care: Virginia Mason Medical Center's Pursuit of the Perfect Patient Experience*. Boca Raton, FL: CRC Press. https://doi.org/10.1201/b10359.
21. Ching, J.M., Long, C., Williams, B.L. and Blackmore, C.C. (2013) 'Using lean to improve medication administration safety: In search of the "perfect dose"', *Joint Commission Journal on Quality and Patient Safety*, 39(5), pp. 195–204. https://doi.org/10.1016/s1553-7250(13)39026-6.
22. Kenney, C. (2011) *Transforming Health Care: Virginia Mason Medical Center's Pursuit of the Perfect Patient Experience*. Boca Raton, FL: CRC Press. https://doi.org/10.1201/b10359.
23. Kaplan, G.S. (2013) 'Pursuing the perfect patient experience', *Frontiers of Health Services Management*, 29(3), pp. 16–27.
24. Shook, J. (2010) *Managing to Learn: Using the A3 Management Process to Solve Problems, Gain Agreement, Mentor, and Lead*. Version 1.1. Cambridge, MA: Lean Enterprise Institute.
25. Pope, R. (2017) 'The NHS: Sticking fingers in its ears, humming loudly', *Journal of Business Ethics*, 145(3), pp. 577–598. https://doi.org/10.1007/s10551-015-2861-4.

Chapter 12

Why VCs and Startups Get Healthcare Wrong

Improvement methods have limits—a billion pounds of NHS evidence confirms it does—healthcare transformation needs genuine innovation. New products, new services, new models of care. The good news: billions of dollars flow into healthcare innovation every year. The bad news: even well-funded, professionally led healthcare innovation has remarkably high failure rates. Why is healthcare innovation so difficult?

The answer reveals something fundamental about healthcare systems that most investors, entrepreneurs, and healthcare leaders consistently miss. This chapter introduces the Healthcare Innovation Resistance Framework: a systematic way to understand which level of resistance your innovation will face, and why most fail before they start.

The Lesson of the Pink Stethoscope

I like pink. Back in the day, I used to pinch all the pink wafers out of the Huntley & Palmers Family Circle box of mixed biscuits. I suspect there are others that like pink too. So here's my business idea: pink stethoscopes for fellow clinicians who share my aesthetic preferences. Simple, right? Make stethoscopes in funky colours. No changes to workflows, processes, or systems. Just a product variation. Traditional market dynamics apply—better products win through normal competitive mechanisms.

My business is profitable as there are lots of doctors and nurses who like to stand out. Now imagine the next version: I add a Bluetooth chip so they can record and share heart, lung, or abdominal sounds to send to colleagues by email or WhatsApp when they are uncertain about their diagnosis. Suddenly everything changes.

How does the clinician ensure that feedback from a colleague in Denmark relates to the correct patient among dozens of messages? Is it safe for the patient? What about data protection—is

DOI: 10.4324/9781003752073-16

WhatsApp compliant with healthcare privacy regulations? How does she capture and verify her colleague's qualifications and accreditation? What about reimbursement for the remote consultation? How does the recording integrate with the patient's medical record?

One feature addition—Bluetooth connectivity—transforms a simple product into a system-level challenge requiring changes across processes, procedures, data management, security protocols, regulatory compliance, reimbursement pathways, training, and clinical governance. This is why healthcare innovation is different from other sectors. And why venture capitalists consistently underestimate implementation complexity.

The Multi-Billion-Dollar Mistake

The Need

> Heard the one about the doctor who couldn't read his own handwriting? It isn't a joke—I can justify it. Once I had beautiful handwriting, was the boy with the highest marks for handwriting in class. Then Medical School struck. In the 70s and 80s that required taking copious notes during lectures, so much so that my handwriting became illegible even to myself. And that's a big problem because it's critical that we take notes of our interactions with patients—to capture what they tell us and don't tell us, what we can see, hear and feel. What we're thinking, suspecting, recommending, their reactions when we tell them, and what happens next.

The reasons for note-taking are obvious: communication, record keeping, traceability, transparency, accountability, research—the list goes on. But note-taking takes time and attention away from the short and precious moments we spend with our patients. It can be considered something we 'have to do,' seemingly adding limited value. In the old days—before digital patient records—the result of all those notes was piles of difficult-to-read documents that, when filed in the wrong place, became irretrievable and useless.

The introduction of Electronic Health Records shifted things. While the benefits of EHR are obvious once data is entered, it moved the problem from taking time to write notes—that nobody could read or find—to clinicians facing the computer screen instead of the patient while typing data or clicking preselects. We had to learn how to type quickly to enter data, and it was not a great experience for our patients either. And if the system was down, everything stops.

Now, with generative AI, enter 'ambient clinical scribing' (ACS). I can freely interact with my patient while ACS listens in the background, using AI to automatically generate clinical notes straight into the patient's EHR. A win-win for clinicians, patients, and the EHR company—but not for the startups that developed ACS and created this market.

The Incumbent

Epic Systems is the largest EHR vendor in the United States, with a dominant market presence and worth $45B [1]. As of June 2024, Epic's software maintained the EHRs of over 305 million patients worldwide [2].

The Startups

The ambient clinical scribing market—built by innovative startups like Abridge, DeepScribe, and Nuance—established a proven need for AI-powered documentation. Founded in 2017, DeepScribe quickly scaled to become one of the most adopted ambient AI scribes in the US, notably the first to capture 1 million patient visits via its platform [3]. Abridge, founded around 2018, rapidly became a key player, reaching unicorn status by 2025, with over $700 million raised to date [4]. Nuance's origins are much earlier as a Xerox PARC spin-out in the 1990s. Originally famous for Dragon NaturallySpeaking, Nuance pivoted early into medical dictation and, through relentless integration with Epic and Cerner EHR, became the default voice layer for US hospitals. When it launched Dragon Ambient eXperience (DAX) it was the only one with distribution, compliance credibility, and entrenched procurement ties. Microsoft's $19.7 billion acquisition in 2022 cemented that advantage: overnight, ambient scribing became a bundled Microsoft–Nuance–Epic feature [5].

The Startup's Approach

DeepScribe focused on users—their research was clinician-centred, spending a lot of time shadowing doctors, refining the user experience (UX), optimising accuracy and acceptance rates. They raced to polish tech and scale pilots (celebrating '1 million visits recorded') but without equal investment in the discovery of the wider healthcare system—leaving them exposed to Epic/Nuance bundling.

Abridge began as a patient-facing transcription tool and had a solid research approach focused on patient–clinician interaction. They built payer and provider partnerships, sought FDA designations for certain decision-support features, and invested heavily in compliance language. Abridge raised huge rounds of investments, scaled fast, and leaned on the demo/pilot momentum without securing a moat beyond UX speed.

In comparison, Nuance had a long runway—decades of iterative discovery with Dragon Medical. They knew clinician workflows, specialty variations, and IT bottlenecks inside out. Nuance embedded inside the governance rails: Business Associate Agreement under HIPAA-compliant, fully Epic-integrated, blessed by hospital IT. They positioned DAX as an extension of existing procurement, not a threat. This is why, despite not being first with ambient AI, they owned the category—until now.

The Investors' Support

DeepScribe's early financing included a $5.2 million seed round led by Bee Partners, then raised finance from US digital health venture capitalists (VCs) [6], that focused on demo appeal (high-quality AI-generated notes), clinician delight ('I save 2 hours a day'), and theoretical scalability. Investors latched on to a huge total addressable market narrative: 'every doctor hates typing, ergo every doctor is a customer.' The investment enabled DeepScribe to scale fast, sign up smaller practices and health systems.

Abridge got much larger capital inflow—over $700M by 2025, making it a unicorn [4]. Investors included high-profile health-tech funds, strategic investors, and major VCs. Investors saw strong founder credibility (ex-Epic engineer, clinical background), early partnerships (e.g., UPMC as client) and potential expansion (patient-facing transcription, clinical decision support, payer-provider value). They saw a credible challenger that could IPO or be acquired by a major (Epic, Microsoft, payer).

Nuance wasn't venture-backed—it grew through public markets, M&A, and corporate partnerships. Its investors rewarded scale and defensibility, not just technology. Public-market analysts did understand Nuance's moat: entrenched contracts, Epic/Cerner distribution, and compliance credibility. That's why Microsoft was willing to pay nearly $20B [5], not for the technology (which had plenty of competitors) but for Nuance 'the trusted-distribution channel.'

What Happens Next Is Predictable

Epic renders several billion dollars of venture investment obsolete with a single product announcement—launching its own ACS as a feature of its EHR system [7] The ambient clinical scribing market, built by innovative startups, established a proven need for AI-powered documentation. Then Epic, predictably, decided to make it a feature. The stunning part? Epic telegraphed this move in their roadmap months ago. Anyone paying attention could have seen this coming. This isn't just another startup failure story. It's a perfect example of why VCs consistently get healthcare innovation wrong. They apply frameworks from other sectors without understanding healthcare's unique resistance patterns.

To see why, we need to understand that healthcare innovations face four distinct types of resistance—and most investors can't tell the difference (see Table 12.1).

The Healthcare Innovation Resistance Framework

Every healthcare innovation faces resistance, but not all resistance is created equal. Understanding which level you're operating at determines strategy, timeline, and probability of success. Here's the framework that could have predicted the ambient scribing debacle—and might prevent the next billion-dollar mistake.

Most healthcare innovations that VCs fund as Level 3A (classical disruption) actually operate at Level 3B (forced integration)—the single most expensive misclassification in healthcare venture capital. While we'll examine this framework through the lens of venture-backed innovation—where the failures are most spectacular and well-documented—the resistance levels apply equally to internally funded NHS initiatives, government programmes, and charity-supported innovation. The barriers are structural, not financial.

Level 1: Drop-in Replacements—'The Pink Stethoscope Zone'

These are direct substitutions that require no workflow changes. Incumbents often welcome better or cheaper alternatives because they slot into existing processes without disruption. Adoption depends on performance and distribution, with low risk, timelines of six to eighteen months, and high success rates. The investment thesis is straightforward: traditional market dynamics apply. Better products win through normal competitive mechanisms. Think generic drugs, improved surgical instruments, enhanced consumables, and medical device iterations.

This is where my hypothetical pink stethoscope business would sit. Using a funky coloured stethoscope requires no changes to everyday processes or systems. Most healthcare investments should be this straightforward, but VCs consistently mistake more complex innovations for simple replacements.

Table 12.1 Healthcare Innovation Resistance Framework

Level	*Description*	*Risk and Timeline*	*Success Rate*	*Investment Thesis*
Level 1 *Drop-in Replacements*	Direct substitutions requiring no workflow changes. Incumbents welcome better or cheaper alternatives. *Examples:* generic drugs, improved instruments, device iterations	Low risk 6–18 months	High	Traditional market dynamics. Better products win through normal competitive mechanisms.
Level 2 *Process-Dependent*	Require workflow integration but align with existing incentives. Success depends on change management as much as technology. *Examples:* EHR systems, robotic surgery, clinical decision support	Medium risk 2–5 years	Moderate	Value must justify implementation costs. Requires patient capital and strong adoption support.
Level 3A *Classical Disruption*	New care models in underserved markets with complete parallel ecosystems. Innovators can build independent pathways without incumbent integration. *Examples:* home dialysis, retail clinics, direct-pay primary care	High risk 5–10 years	Low, but transformative	Classical Christensen disruption: start with non-consumption, improve, challenge incumbents.
Level 3B *Forced Integration 'The Healthcare Disruption Trap'*	New care models that require incumbent touchpoints which cannot be avoided. Cannot build complete alternative pathways. Premature escalation to Level 4 confrontation. *Examples:* ambient scribing (EHR integration), community health worker platforms, AI clinical decision support	Very high risk 3–7 years before integration crisis	Very low	Requires healthcare-specific expertise, honest recognition of integration risks, and adjusted return expectations. Most healthcare 'disruption' falls here.
Level 4 *Governance-Threatening 'The Investment Death Zone'*	Challenge fundamental power structures or revenue models. System resistance activates to eliminate threats. Success requires political or regulatory change beyond any company's control. *Examples:* radical pricing transparency, alternative reimbursement models, direct-pay at scale	Extreme risk Generational	Approaching zero	Avoid unless funding systemic change movements, not businesses. These are political challenges, not business opportunities.

Level 2: Process-Dependent Innovations—'The Bluetooth Stethoscope Zone'

These innovations require workflow integration but broadly align with existing incentives. Incumbents may resist initially but typically adopt when value is proven. Success depends on change management as much as technology. Risk is medium, timelines run two to five years, and success rates are moderate. The investment thesis demands that value be significant enough to justify implementation costs. This requires patient capital and strong adoption support—not just a better mousetrap but a compelling reason for busy clinicians and risk-averse administrators to change what they do every day.

Examples include EHR systems, robotic surgery, advanced imaging, and clinical decision support tools. Each requires meaningful changes to how clinicians and institutions work, but the changes align with goals everyone shares: better outcomes, greater efficiency, reduced risk.

For my pink stethoscope, the moment I add a Bluetooth chip so clinicians can record and share heart sounds, I've moved from Level 1 to Level 2. The recording feature requires data management protocols, security compliance, integration with medical records, new reimbursement pathways, and training. This complexity leap—from a simple product to a process-dependent innovation—is what makes healthcare inherently more challenging than other sectors.

This classification isn't limited to commercial products. A consultant clinician who develops a better pain assessment protocol for post-operative patients faces Level 1 resistance—it slots into existing workflows. The same consultant proposing to redesign how acute pain services are delivered across the hospital and into the community faces Level 3 or 4 resistance—it challenges staffing models, departmental and organisational boundaries, and budget allocations. Same clinician, same expertise, entirely different resistance landscape.

Level 3: The Disruption Zone

This level requires a critical distinction that most investors miss entirely—and getting it wrong is the single most expensive mistake in healthcare venture capital.

Level 3A: Classical Disruptive Pathway—'The True Disruption Zone.' These innovations enable new care models in underserved markets with complete parallel ecosystems. Incumbents initially ignore them because margins and volumes are unattractive. Innovators can build comprehensive alternative pathways without needing incumbent integration, then must prove value before moving upmarket. Risk is high, timelines run five to ten years, and success rates are low but transformative when they work. The investment thesis follows classical disruption. Christensen's theory holds that disruptive innovations start in underserved markets where incumbent products overshoot customer needs, then improve until they challenge the mainstream through complete ecosystem replacement (see Chapter 2).

Examples include home dialysis, retail health clinics like MinuteClinic, direct-pay primary care, telemedicine for isolated rural areas, and AI diagnostics for resource-constrained settings where incumbent infrastructure simply doesn't exist. The key feature of Level 3A is that innovators can build completely independent alternative pathways. MinuteClinic didn't need hospital cooperation to treat ear infections in a pharmacy. Home dialysis doesn't require the dialysis centre's permission.

Level 3B: Forced Integration Pathway—'The Healthcare Disruption Trap.' This is where healthcare innovation becomes uniquely treacherous. These innovations also enable new care models in underserved markets, but they require incumbent touchpoints that cannot be avoided. Innovators cannot build complete alternative pathways due to regulatory and safety constraints that force them back into the incumbent system before achieving sufficient scale.

The result is premature escalation to Level 4 confrontation when integration triggers incumbent resistance. Success depends on achieving scale before that resistance activates, requiring either extended stealth mode to delay integration, an incumbent collaboration strategy from the outset, or a market context where integration barriers happen to be lower. Risk is very high, timelines run three to seven years before the integration crisis hits, and success rates are very low due to structural healthcare constraints.

Examples include ambient scribing requiring EHR integration, community health worker platforms requiring health system coordination, and AI clinical decision support requiring incumbent workflow integration.

The Healthcare Disruption Paradox. Healthcare differs fundamentally from other sectors because most healthcare innovations fall into Level 3B rather than 3A. Unlike personal computing, digital photography, or Airbnb—which could build complete parallel ecosystems without incumbent cooperation—healthcare innovations inevitably require integration with incumbent systems. Regulatory requirements demand patient safety and professional licensing standards. Payment systems require insurance and government reimbursement integration. Clinical continuity demands specialist referrals and hospital services. Legal liability creates malpractice and regulatory compliance requirements.

This creates a 'disruption trap' where innovations designed as Level 3A classical disruption get pulled into premature Level 4 confrontations before achieving sufficient scale and momentum. The startup plans for disruption; the system forces integration; integration triggers resistance; resistance kills the innovation. The sequence is predictable. Yet VCs fund as if it won't happen.

Level 4: Governance-Threatening Innovations—'The Investment Death Zone'

These challenge fundamental power structures or revenue models. System resistance activates to eliminate threats—not because individuals are malicious, but because institutions protect their survival. Success requires political or regulatory change beyond any company's control. Risk is extreme, timelines are generational, and success rates approach zero. The investment thesis is blunt: avoid unless you're funding systemic change movements, not businesses.

Examples include radical transparency tools that expose pricing, alternative reimbursement models that shift revenue away from incumbents, and direct-pay healthcare at scale that bypasses insurance entirely.

Where Ambient Scribing Went Wrong

Using this framework, ambient scribing's failure becomes predictable rather than surprising. VCs funded it as Level 1—a simple product replacement—but it actually operated across multiple levels simultaneously. It started as Level 3, addressing unmet needs in physician burnout and documentation burden. It required Level 2 integration through deep EHR workflow changes for true clinical utility. And it was vulnerable to Level 4 capture through Epic's institutional control over clinical workflows. Epic let Abridge, DeepScribe, and others spend millions validating market demand, refining the technology, and training users. Once the market was proven, Epic simply absorbed the functionality. This isn't innovation—it's systematic market exploitation using monopolistic position.

The Healthcare Innovation Resistance framework would have flagged every one of these risks before a single dollar was invested. The multi-level analysis reveals the inevitability: any innovation that depends on EHR workflow integration operates at the mercy of EHR platform owners. The question was never whether Epic would absorb ambient scribing, but when.

The Feature Trap

When startups pitch healthcare innovation, VCs consistently misread one critical distinction: they fund companies building digital ticketing systems while believing they're investing in food businesses.

Consider transportation. Airlines need ticketing to function—it's core workflow infrastructure. Early travel websites like Expedia validated online booking experiences, but airlines predictably absorbed ticketing as an integrated feature. Today, business travellers expect seamless booking within Delta.com. Ticketing was always a feature waiting to be absorbed, because it depends entirely on the airline's core infrastructure.

Contrast this with airline food. Multiple business models thrive: airport restaurants, airline catering companies, passengers bringing their own meals. Airlines offer food service, but travellers have genuine choice because food operates independently of core transportation workflow. No airline can monopolise eating.

Healthcare's version of this distinction is stark:

Ambient scribing is digital ticketing—destined for absorption. Clinical documentation is core infrastructure for any EHR workflow. Epic controls the entire clinical data journey from order entry to billing. No clinician thinks 'I need standalone documentation software.' The documentation lives inside the EHR because that's where clinical work happens.

Telemedicine platforms are airline food—viable standalone products. Multiple sustainable business models exist. Healthcare systems can integrate without owning the entire experience. Different platforms compete on specialisation and user experience. A hospital doesn't need to build its own telemedicine platform any more than an airline needs to grow its own food.

The warning signs were clear: workflow dependency, data gravity, training overhead, and procurement reality all pointed toward inevitable absorption by the infrastructure owner. Any investor asking 'Is this a feature or a product?' could have predicted the outcome.

Healthcare's Deeper Pathologies

The ambient scribing story exemplifies broader patterns that doom healthcare investments. Let me share examples across our resistance framework that demonstrate these patterns repeat with remarkable consistency.

Level 1 Misconceptions: When 'Simple' Isn't Simple

Theranos attempted to revolutionise diagnostics but couldn't deliver basic functionality. VCs granted Elizabeth Holmes a $9 billion valuation without verifying her technology worked [8]. Healthcare's regulatory complexity creates perfect cover for magical thinking—the long development timelines and opaque technical requirements make meaningful technical due diligence nearly impossible for VCs who lack deep domain expertise. In any other sector, investors would have demanded a working demonstration. Healthcare's complexity gave Holmes a decade of cover.

Level 2 Reimbursement Reality Checks

Pear Therapeutics became the first company to receive FDA approval for mobile apps treating substance use disorders, achieved a $1.6 billion valuation, then filed for bankruptcy. Despite strong clinical evidence demonstrating effectiveness, only half of Pear's prescriptions received insurance coverage. The company reported $13 million revenue against $123 million losses [9]. This illustrates the 'valley of death' between clinical validation and commercial viability that is unique to healthcare. Payers can deny payment for therapies that are clinically necessary, effective, and cost-saving. This isn't a business model problem—it's a system design feature protecting incumbent revenue streams. No amount of clinical evidence guarantees commercial success when payers control the gate.

Level 3 Technology Fundamentalism

Forward Health raised $400M and achieved unicorn status by promising to eliminate bureaucratic inefficiencies through technology. Their CarePods—AI-powered 'doctor's' offices costing $1 million each—represented Silicon Valley's ultimate healthcare delusion: that technology can replace rather than augment human care relationships [10]. The company collapsed because it misunderstood healthcare's fundamental dynamics—an industry centred on human interaction and trust. Technology 'solutionism' fails when applied to fundamentally social and political problems. You cannot automate empathy, and you cannot engineer trust.

Level 4 System-Level Resistance

Haven—the joint venture between Amazon, Berkshire Hathaway, and JPMorgan Chase—failed despite titanium-level resources and 1.2 million covered employees. Even titans with combined market capitalisation exceeding $2 trillion couldn't dent a system designed to resist exactly this type of intervention [11]. Healthcare isn't broken by accident. It's functioning exactly as designed—to extract maximum revenue while distributing risk across fragmented stakeholders. Haven's failure wasn't operational; it was political. The system fought back, and the system won.

COUNTERINTUITIVE FINDING

More Money, More Failure

Healthcare's investment paradox: five of the best-funded healthcare innovations of the past decade—totalling over $13 billion in investment and market capitalisation—all failed predictably. Abridge ($700M+ raised) validated the ambient scribing market so effectively that Epic simply absorbed it. Haven (backed by $2T+ in combined market capitalisation) activated the very system-level resistance it needed to avoid. Pear Therapeutics ($1.6B valuation) achieved FDA approval but couldn't overcome reimbursement barriers. In each case, more resources didn't reduce risk—they accelerated confrontation with structural barriers the investors never diagnosed.

The implication for healthcare leaders: before committing resources to any innovation, diagnose the resistance level first. At Levels 3B and 4 of the Healthcare Innovation Resistance Framework, funding doesn't overcome barriers—it increases the speed and visibility of failure.

Why Healthcare Is Fundamentally Different

These failures share a common root: misunderstanding what makes healthcare structurally different from other industries. Three factors combine to create an environment uniquely hostile to innovation.

The Regulatory Reality

Having worked across automotive design at Jaguar, medical practice, and healthcare innovation, I've seen how other industries systematically integrate regulatory requirements into their design process from the start, while healthcare treats compliance as an afterthought. Let me be clear: regulation isn't the enemy of innovation. Sooner or later, we'll all become patients—it's in our interest that treatments are safe and effective.

Complexity and regulation are not the exclusive domain of healthcare; aerospace and automotive also face increasingly complex propulsion and production technologies and stringent regulatory requirements. The difference is that in these industries, requirements feed into the design process as an input from day one. Healthcare could learn from this approach—treating regulation as a design driver rather than a checkpoint to pass at the end.

The real challenge isn't regulatory uncertainty—it's cost and time. Bringing a new drug to market costs over $2.6 billion and takes 10–15 years [12]. Medical devices require $31–94 million [13]. Compare this to automotive or aerospace, where timelines are measured in months, not decades. Only large, established companies can shoulder these investments, perpetuating healthcare's centralisation and making it structurally difficult for startups to reach the market at all.

The Governance Trap

But here's where most VCs miss the real issue: regulation provides necessary safety guardrails, but governance structures often create unnecessary friction that sabotages beneficial innovations entirely. The distinction between regulation and governance is critical, and most investors don't make it.

I've witnessed this personally. In 2008 I established the Innovations Factory as a spinout company from a successful EU-funded project I managed at the University of Warwick supporting small and medium-sized companies in the healthcare sector. The team had many years of combined experience in clinical practice, design, engineering, innovation management, IT systems, manufacturing, marketing, and regulatory affairs. Uniquely, as a private company we were based in the Research Department of one of the largest NHS Foundation Trust hospitals in the UK. This meant that we had prime access to clinicians and patients with needs and ideas, and we could also validate our own concepts and prototypes 'next door.' Furthermore, we had an established network of regional partners and suppliers.

On paper, we had everything a healthcare innovator could want: the right team, the right location, the right access, and a strong track record. We had a portfolio of potential innovations ranging from needle-free connectors, point-of-care diagnostic devices, and safety devices to specialist high-performing anaesthetic devices. We had a 100% success rate in raising regional funding for development, and we successfully took each idea through the first diamond—discover and define—and the first half of the second diamond—develop—as we had validated prototypes for each. But every single concept got completely blocked at delivery. The NHS governance structures had no pathway to implement anything new.

We were not the only ones. An innovative senior clinician at the same hospital had developed a system in 2004 to avoid wrong-side surgery using individual radio frequency identification tags and installed Wi-Fi in the operating theatre so handheld readers could capture and verify the patient's information. Being operated on the wrong side of the body is a costly litigation issue for hospitals and a tragedy for patients. The system was validated successfully in one theatre but did not scale up. Besides avoiding wrong-side surgery, it showed up so many hospital-wide inefficiencies, such as lack of communication between departments, that it was deemed better to abandon it. An innovation that improved patient safety was killed because it made institutional dysfunction visible.

We managed to keep some cash flow by acting as agents for consumables—personal protective equipment—but by 2016 we gave up and closed the company. This wasn't an isolated failure; every potential innovation in our portfolio met the same fate, including our colleague's validated RFID system. Our innovations failed not because of regulatory barriers, but because governance structures prioritised risk aversion over patient benefit, standardisation over innovation, and bureaucratic approval layers over clinical need. Regulation demanded our innovations be safe and effective. Governance structures ensured they would never reach patients, even when the evidence for clinical benefit was overwhelming.

The Fragmentation Problem

Other industries developed integrated value chains between stakeholders. In aerospace, airlines, manufacturers, regulators, and passengers connect through clear market mechanisms. Those value chains are centred around the customer and focused on meeting their needs. If the customer moves their business to a competitor, each organisation in that value chain loses out. Those value chains are therefore tightly organised with transparent governance structures. Companies have to be aligned 'with their noses toward the customer' and establish good communications, share risks and profits, and allow for innovation. Profits across the value chain are determined by the customer's willingness to pay and the arrangements between stakeholders.

Healthcare lacks this structural connectivity entirely. We have autonomous stakeholders with conflicting incentives—hospitals incentivised to treat rather than prevent, pharmaceutical companies prioritising high-margin rare diseases, payers whose financial interests misalign with clinical value. Healthcare does not have a structured value chain but is a fragmented system skewed toward stakeholders profiting from customers being ill.

Pharmaceutical CEOs have told me they're abandoning common conditions to pursue lucrative rare diseases, comparing it to Volkswagen stopping Golf production to focus exclusively on Lamborghinis. In any other sector, competitors would seize this opportunity. In healthcare, the same structural forces affect everyone, creating systematic market failures that governance structures then protect rather than resolve.

It is not a coincidence that the absence of design thinking occurs in the sector without a value chain aligned to meeting customers' needs.

Requirements for Success

Investigating why startups failed helps define what's required for successful healthcare investments. Three capabilities separate the rare successes from the predictable failures.

Balanced Double Diamond Design Thinking

Most failed startups suffered from inadequate discovery phases. DeepScribe and Abridge did excellent user-centred design with clinicians but insufficient discovery of governance structures and competitive dynamics. They raced to polish technology and scale pilots without equal investment in understanding the wider healthcare system.

The Double Diamond model (design thinking methodology introduced earlier in the book—Figure 1.3) shows we need to spend as much time and resources in Discovery—deeply understanding problems, needs, context, stakeholders, and established governance structures—before moving to solution Development. The Healthcare Innovation Resistance Framework itself is a discovery tool to be used for prospective due diligence.

A small first diamond leads to chaotic iteration between problem and solution spaces. The ambient scribing startups had impressive second diamonds—elegant technology, excellent user interfaces, strong clinical adoption. Their first diamonds were catastrophically small: they never adequately explored the competitive landscape, governance structures, or platform dependencies that would determine their fate.

The Right People and Capabilities

VCs often fund brilliant academics or engineers who lack entrepreneurial skill sets. The university system requires deep knowledge in narrow areas, whereas successful entrepreneurs need broader capabilities—business development, leadership, marketing, finance, and team building. They need honesty to recognise their own strengths and weaknesses, and humility to work with others.

Startup teams need balance across complementary personalities and dynamics—creative thinkers who generate ideas, shapers who drive momentum, implementers who build systems, and finishers who deliver quality. Founders develop culture, which determines long-term success. Most critically, healthcare startups need team members who understand the governance landscape—not just the clinical need or the technology opportunity, but the political reality of implementation.

Framework-Guided Investment Decisions

Before investing, VCs should systematically evaluate five dimensions rather than relying on pattern-matching from other sectors:

- Analysis of resistance sources: who or what will resist this innovation and why?
- Governance impact assessment: which power structures are threatened?
- Implementation complexity mapping: what must change beyond the technology itself?
- Timeline reality check: does investor patience match implementation requirements?
- Definition of success: what does 'winning' look like at each resistance level? An innovation that succeeds at Level 2 looks entirely different from one that succeeds at Level 4.

Strategic Implications

The framework provides clear, differentiated guidance for each stakeholder group in healthcare innovation.

For VCs, the resistance level determines everything. At Levels 1–2, apply traditional due diligence focused on market size and competitive advantages—these innovations follow familiar investment dynamics. At Level 3A, invest with a deep understanding of disruption theory and patient capital, following the classical disruption playbook that has worked in other industries. At Level 3B—where most healthcare 'disruption' actually falls—invest only with healthcare-specific expertise, honest recognition of integration risks, and adjusted return expectations. At Level 4, recognise these as political rather than business challenges. Either fund them as systemic change movements with generational timelines, or walk away. A small number of specialist healthcare investors have developed frameworks approaching this level of nuance—but they remain the exception. Most healthcare VCs still rely on pattern-matching from technology sectors where these resistance dynamics don't exist.

For entrepreneurs, honesty about which level you're operating at is essential. The single most critical distinction is between Level 3A and 3B—mistaking Level 3B for classical disruption is the most expensive strategic error in healthcare innovation. Level 3B innovations require fundamentally different strategies: incumbent collaboration rather than disruption, integration planning rather than competitive moats, governance navigation rather than market capture. Consider market contexts where integration barriers are lower—developing countries, cash-pay markets, settings where incumbent infrastructure is absent rather than entrenched.

For healthcare leaders, the framework demands differentiated responses. Level 1–2 innovations deserve rapid evaluation and adoption—stop treating simple improvements as existential threats. Level 3 innovations may serve populations you're currently failing to reach; embrace them rather than resist reflexively. Level 4 innovations threaten your business model by design; understanding this distinction helps you respond strategically—partnering where alignment exists, defending where core interests are threatened—rather than treating all innovation as the enemy.

When a vendor or internal team presents their innovation, your first diagnostic question should be: at what resistance level does this actually operate—and does our evaluation process account for that level's specific risks?

The Pattern Recognition Imperative

The ambient scribing story should serve as a wake-up call. These failures share common characteristics: technology solutionism, timeline misalignment, reimbursement naivety, and institutional capture blindness. VCs fail to recognise that healthcare incumbents don't just have market power—they have governance power. They write rules, set standards, and determine reimbursement. They decide which innovations reach patients and which die in the valley between validation and adoption.

Healthcare innovation is more complex than most VCs realise. This framework won't guarantee success, but it might prevent the next billion-dollar mistake. The question every healthcare startup should ask: 'Are we building something that enhances core workflow infrastructure, or something that can genuinely remain independent?' Until investors understand that healthcare isn't just regulated—it's governed by structures that actively prevent the changes they're funding—they'll keep financing companies building toward their own obsolescence.

The Innovation Gap

This chapter has focused deliberately on technology and product innovations—the type that attracts venture capital because intellectual property can be protected, valuations can be modelled, and exits can be structured. But healthcare innovation is far broader than products and technologies. Process innovations—redesigned care pathways, new service delivery models, workflow transformations, changed ways of working—often deliver greater impact on patient outcomes and system efficiency than any device or software platform.

Here's the problem: process innovations are inherently difficult to protect through patents or intellectual property rights. You can't patent a better way of organising a ward round, or copyright a redesigned patient discharge pathway. Without IP protection, VCs have no asset to value and no exit to model. The funding model itself has a structural bias—it systematically channels capital toward the type of innovation healthcare needs least (discrete technology products) and away from the type it needs most (system and process redesign).

The picture is therefore worse than this chapter suggests. We've demonstrated that even well-funded, IP-protected technology innovations fail systematically against healthcare's resistance framework. The innovations that could genuinely transform healthcare—the process, service, and system-level changes—struggle to attract funding in the first place.

This is precisely where design thinking becomes essential. It provides the methodology for innovations that the venture capital model cannot reach. Healthcare innovation faces systematic barriers that defeat even well-funded, intelligent attempts at change. Understanding these barriers requires examining them from three complementary perspectives. The next three chapters provide the analytical frameworks: Chapter 13 examines the structural architecture that blocks innovation regardless of anyone's intentions—the WHAT that creates resistance. Chapter 14 maps the political dynamics—WHO blocks innovation, why they resist, and how to build coalitions for change. Chapter 15 reveals HOW systems fight back over time through coordinated resistance mechanisms that intensify rather than fade. Together, these three diagnostic lenses explain why healthcare transformation is uniquely difficult—and what it takes to succeed anyway.

References

1. Capoot, A. (2024) 'A journey inside Epic Systems' mythical and sprawling campus, a world away from Wall Street', *CNBC*, 1 September. Available at: https://www.cnbc.com/2024/09/01/inside-epic-systems-mythical-campus-a-world-away-from-wall-street-.html.
2. Bruce, G. (2024) 'Epic's dominance in 12 numbers', *Becker's Hospital Review*. Available at: https://www.beckershospitalreview.com/healthcare-information-technology/ehrs/epics-dominance-in-12-numbers/.
3. DeepScribe (n.d.) 'DeepScribe is first AI scribe to capture 1 million patient visits'. Available at: https://www.deepscribe.ai/resources/deepscribe-sets-record-first-ai-scribe-to-capture-1-million-patient-visits.
4. TexA (n.d.) 'How much did Abridge Inc raise? Funding & key investors'. Available at: https://www.texau.com/profiles/abridge-inc.
5. Microsoft Source (2021) 'Microsoft accelerates industry cloud strategy for healthcare with the acquisition of Nuance'. Available at: https://news.microsoft.com/source/2021/04/12/microsoft-accelerates-industry-cloud-strategy-for-healthcare-with-the-acquisition-of-nuance/.
6. Malik, A. (2022) 'AI-powered transcription platform DeepScribe raises $30M to unburden doctors from tedious data entry', *TechCrunch*, 12 January. Available at: https://techcrunch.com/2022/01/12/ai-powered-transcription-platform-deepscribe-raises-30m-to-unburden-doctors-from-tedious-data-entry/ .
7. Diaz, N. (2025) '"A watershed moment": CIOs react to Epic's AI scribe launch', *Becker's Hospital Review*. Available at: https://www.beckershospitalreview.com/healthcare-information-technology/ai/a-watershed-moment-cios-react-to-epics-ai-scribe-launch/.
8. Das, R.K. and Drolet, B.C. (2022) 'Lessons from Theranos – Restructuring biomedical innovation', *Journal of Medical Systems*, 46, p. 25. https://doi.org/10.1007/s10916-022-01813-3.
9. Anderson, B. (2023) 'Digital health startups declare bankruptcy following rough funding year', *Healthcare Brew*. Available at: https://www.healthcare-brew.com/stories/2023/10/02/digital-health-startups-declare-bankruptcy-following-rough-funding-year.

10. Johnson, H. (2024) 'Forward healthcare startup shutters, CEO plans next venture', *KillerStartups*. Available at: https://killerstartups.com/forward-healthcare-startup-shutters-ceo-plans-next-venture/.
11. Toussaint, J.S. (2021) 'Why Haven Healthcare failed', *Harvard Business Review*. Available at: https://hbr.org/2021/01/why-haven-healthcare-failed.
12. Mullard, A. (2014) 'New drugs cost US$2.6 billion to develop', *Nature Reviews Drug Discovery*, 13(12), p. 877. https://doi.org/10.1038/nrd4507.
13. Makower, J., Meer, A. and Denend, L. (2010) 'FDA impact on U.S. Medical technology innovation: A survey of over 200 medical technology companies'. Available at: https://www.medtecheurope.org/wp-content/uploads/2015/09/01112010_FDA-impact-on-US-medical-technology-innovation_Backgrounder.pdf?utm_source=chatgpt.com.

Chapter 13

The Structural Trap

A consultant radiologist—Head of Radiology at a large NHS hospital—once approached me with a puzzle. She had arranged the purchase of a Toshiba Aquilion ONE scanner, a remarkable piece of technology. The Aquilion ONE uses a combination of X-ray, computing, and electrocardiography to capture volumetric 3D images of the entire heart in a single rotation. By synchronising image acquisition with the cardiac cycle through ECG gating, it produces clear, motion-free imaging of the heart and coronary arteries in just one heartbeat [1]. Crucially, it can identify coronary artery blockages associated with heart attacks using coronary CT angiography—non-invasively.

The clinical need was compelling. Several patients arrive at hospital with suspected heart attacks but present with dubious symptoms—like indigestion—and inconclusive ECG and blood results showing no elevated heart enzymes. Putting these patients through an invasive angiogram or stress ECG test carries real risk: it can provoke another heart attack. The Aquilion ONE offered a safer diagnostic pathway. The Head of Radiology had made her case, secured board approval, won procurement, and installed the device. Her puzzle: it was not being used for its intended purpose, which annoyed her.

I offered to place a service design student on the problem—a master's project using design thinking methods including stakeholder mapping to identify what was blocking adoption. Two weeks later, when I introduced the student, the Head of Radiology called the project off, embarrassed, but without giving a clear reason.

Through other contacts in that hospital, I found out what had happened. People get heart attacks at inconvenient hours—typically early morning. Using the Aquilion ONE when it was actually needed meant that one of her peer consultant radiologists had to get out of bed and come to the hospital at 4am. These are clinicians in elective diagnostic imaging who normally examine images on screens from nine to five. An early-morning call-out, just because of a new device, caused resistance. The Head of Radiology—who had undoubtedly made a strong case to the hospital board and procurement to acquire the device—discovered she lacked the authority, leadership structure, and change management apparatus to compel her peers to change their working patterns.

 DOI: 10.4324/9781003752073-17

The technology was validated. The clinical need was clear. The funding was secured. The device was physically installed in the department. And it still failed.

Undeterred, we then found out that the device did not come with implementation advice, indicating that the development had not fully explored the first diamond to discover what might resist the adoption of this new device.

This is the structural trap. The Aquilion ONE was a straightforward diagnostic substitution—CT angiography replacing invasive procedures for ambiguous presentations. But using it for its intended purpose cascaded into professional working patterns, peer authority structures, and workforce culture. The complexity was never in the technology. It was in the system architecture surrounding it.

The question this chapter addresses is not whether your innovation works. The question is whether it fits the healthcare system it must operate within—or whether it demands changes to a system that was never designed to accommodate them. The diagnostic question every healthcare innovator must answer: does my innovation structurally fit, or does it require system redesign?

Tight Coupling and Systems Interdependency

The Aquilion ONE case reveals a pattern that applies far beyond radiology. Any innovation more complex than a cosmetic change must contend with healthcare's fundamental architectural feature: tight coupling. This story illustrates that for any innovation more complex than a pink stethoscope (see Chapter 12) to be implemented, it requires changes to procedures, processes, systems, organisational structures and culture.

Healthcare is a *service* that is provided for patients; that service is delivered through a combination of people, processes and technology within an organisational structure and culture. That means that any change in any of these aspects is likely to require associated changes in several others too. This obviously makes it very challenging and time-consuming for a potential innovation to be adopted and diffused. For large established companies that's okay as they will have income from other products in their portfolio. For startups that is a different story as their survival depends on fast adoption and diffusion and return on investment.

It also means that innovators have to be mindful of this and, besides designing a new service or product, also consider and integrate all these other aspects throughout their design process. In the case of a potential disruptive innovation, they need to concurrently design a simplifying technology (or service), innovative business model and value network. Not many, if any, companies are capable of that.

The Multiplication Effect

This tight coupling creates a multiplication effect. Bad design in healthcare doesn't create simple inefficiency, in economic terms—it creates exponential waste through system-wide misalignment. In sectors with aligned value chains, quality issues typically affect single products or services. In healthcare's fragmented system, design problems multiply across multiple stakeholder relationships. A poorly designed discharge process affects not just the hospital and patient, but also primary care providers, specialists, pharmacists, family members, and insurers. Each stakeholder must develop workarounds, creating additional costs and potential failure points.

The automotive industry learned this lesson decades ago. When BMW acquired Rover in 1994, in an attempt to mimic Ford's success with neighbouring Jaguar, they discovered that Rover's fragmented development processes—where different divisions pursued conflicting objectives—created exponential costs compared to BMW's aligned development model [2]. The acquisition ultimately failed because the misalignment was too expensive to correct quickly enough.

Healthcare faces the same fundamental challenge, but with higher stakes and more complex stakeholder networks. The multiplication effect intensifies as stakeholders accumulate. Healthcare has evolved from a two-person relationship into a coordination problem of staggering mathematical complexity.

Stakeholder Proliferation as Coordination Problem

In medieval times, healthcare was simple. When you fell ill, you consulted a healer. Two people, one relationship, one shared objective: restore health. The mathematics was straightforward: $C = n(n-1)/2$. With $n = 2$, you had exactly one relationship to manage. Today, that same healthcare decision involves at least eight primary actors: patient, clinician, hospital, insurer, regulator, policymaker, researcher, and manufacturer. [3]. With $n = 8$, you now have 28 bilateral relationships. And if one considers not just dyads but the full range of possible coalitions among stakeholders, the interaction space expands to $2^8 = 256$. This illustrates how governance complexity scales not linearly but combinatorially as systems evolve. The mathematics hasn't changed, but the complexity has exploded. Each relationship requires coordination. Each coordination point creates opportunity for misalignment. Each misalignment generates resistance. In such structures, conflicting incentives are inevitable as each new stakeholder adds defensive mechanisms to safeguard their own position.

As stakeholder numbers grow further—adding pharmacy benefit managers, academic institutions, public health organisations—the mathematics becomes overwhelming. Chapter 10 examined how twelve stakeholders generate 66 bilateral relationships, exceeding human cognitive capacity to manage without systematic frameworks.

This isn't a metaphor. It's mathematics. And it explains why brilliant healthcare innovations—designed through rigorous human-centred methods, validated through pilot studies, proven to improve outcomes—systematically fail during implementation while automotive and aerospace industries successfully innovate with comparable stakeholder complexity. The difference isn't the number of stakeholders. It's what those stakeholders want.

The structural implication is clear: healthcare has evolved beyond the point where coordination can be achieved through goodwill or informal relationships.

The Value Chain

Another important difference is in the 'value chain'—outside healthcare, companies and organisations are linked together to profit from providing us with products and services. In British Airways' case, those companies are airframe manufacturers such as Boeing and Airbus, engine manufacturers such as Rolls-Royce, suppliers of food, and the airports. In Jaguar's case, that is a tiered chain of suppliers and distributors that manufacture components, sub-systems, and ultimately sell cars to customers. It is important to note that those value chains are centred around the customer and focused on meeting their needs. If the users move their custom to a competitor, each organisation in that value chain will lose out. Those value chains are therefore tightly organised with transparent governance structures that include open book accounting. Companies have to be aligned 'with their noses towards the customer' and establish good communications, share risks and profits, and allow for innovation. Profits across the value chain are determined by the customers' willingness to pay and the arrangements between stakeholders.

Healthcare does not have a structured value or supply chain but is a fragmented system skewed toward stakeholders profiting from customers being ill. Table 3.1 demonstrates this misalignment by showing the difference in the drivers of healthcare stakeholders. Publicly funded systems, such as the NHS, have different incentive structures but still exhibit structural misalignment through other mechanisms (empire-building, professional protectionism, budget-maximisation). It is no coincidence that the absence of design occurs in the sector without a value chain aligned to meeting customers' needs.

The Customers' Mindset

The absence of customer power compounds this structural misalignment. Car buyers or travellers can inform themselves in good time of products or services that offer the most value by reading car magazines or comparison websites. The health service user might not be in a fit state to consider their needs or options. Furthermore, they are conditioned to rely on and trust us clinicians to look after their best interests. And if they are entitled to healthcare at all, they might not be considered as paying customers—by themselves and others—as they have paid indirectly through insurance or tax contributions. There is no longer a direct relationship between their willingness to pay and profits of stakeholders.

In sectors such as automotive and aerospace, collectively customers have power—they can abandon a brand completely. Not so in healthcare; most customers have no real choice or alternatives. This is what's actually happening: healthcare's economic incentives have created a system where stakeholders profit more from patient illness than health.

Misalignment and Lack of Shared Objectives

Critically, stakeholder proliferation alone does not predict transformation failure. Automotive and aerospace industries operate successfully with 8+ primary stakeholders (original equipment manufacturers—OEMs, Tier 1–3 suppliers, dealers, regulators, financiers, aftermarket providers) because all actors align around shared objectives: customer satisfaction, market competitiveness, safety standards, and profitability through volume. Innovation serves all stakeholders simultaneously—better vehicles satisfy customers, reduce warranty costs for manufacturers, enable premium pricing for suppliers, and reduce regulatory burden through improved safety.

Healthcare presents fundamentally different dynamics. Stakeholder objectives conflict at a structural level: patients seek optimal outcomes regardless of cost; insurers minimise expenditure; hospitals maximise revenue through volume and complexity; physicians balance income, autonomy, and clinical judgement; regulators prioritise compliance and safety over innovation; pharmaceutical companies pursue profitable conditions over population health needs. These objectives cannot be simultaneously optimised—every innovation benefits some stakeholders while threatening others.

NHS as Research Instrument

The evidence for these structural dynamics draws heavily on one healthcare system in particular—the NHS, which warrants explanation. Specifically for healthcare, it is true that the UK's National Health Service is the largest publicly funded healthcare system and one of the largest employers in the world, not just in healthcare but across all sectors. Its scale, centralised structure, and foundational principle of providing care free at the point of use make it a unique case study—both as a model of universal healthcare and as an early indicator of the pressures facing publicly funded systems globally—such as workforce shortages, rising demand, and the challenges of integrating innovation within a bureaucratic framework.

Just as Drosophila melanogaster (the fruit fly) became essential to research in biology for its simplicity, scale, and ability to reveal underlying genetic principles, the NHS plays a similar role in health policy and system reform.

- It's one of the largest and most studied universal healthcare systems in the world—1.4 million employees serving over 55 million people under a single funding and governance framework [4].
- It provides a controlled environment: centrally funded, nationally regulated, and with standardised data across the population.
- Policy changes, like introducing markets, clinician commissioning, or integrated care models, play out in real time, offering valuable early insights for other nations.
- Its scale and visibility mean that both successes and failures are observable—making it a global case study for health systems researchers, reformers, and policymakers.

Like the fruit fly in genetics, the NHS helps us understand the mechanisms, limits, and consequences of healthcare design faster and more visibly than elsewhere.

Why Three Elements Must Be Designed Concurrently—Christensen's Framework

This structural misalignment explains why healthcare innovation requires a fundamentally different approach from other industries. Clayton Christensen identified three essential elements for disruptive innovation to take root [5]:

- simplifying technology
- business model innovation
- value network

First, simplifying technology allows complex or expensive solutions to be made more affordable, accessible, and user-friendly by reducing performance in aspects that are over-serving mainstream users. Second, business model innovation creates new ways of generating, capturing and delivering value—typically with lower cost structures and different priorities than incumbent firms. Third, a compatible value network—a new ecosystem of suppliers, distributors, and customers—that enables the disruptive product or service to grow and scale without relying on the existing system that supports the incumbent. These three components work together to allow disruptors to start in overlooked market segments and eventually challenge or displace dominant players as they improve and move upmarket.

In his book *Disrupting Class*, Christensen made a very relevant statement for healthcare: 'disruptive innovation enable a larger population of less-skilled, less-wealthy people to do things in a more convenient, lower-cost setting, which historically could only be done by specialists in less convenient settings' [6].

This describes precisely what healthcare needs—and precisely what healthcare's structure prevents. The concurrent design of all three elements is the critical requirement, and it is where most healthcare innovators fail. They design the technology, assume the business model will follow, and discover too late that no compatible value network exists. A case in India demonstrates what becomes possible when all three elements are designed together from scratch—and why replicating that achievement within an established system proves structurally impossible.

Narayana Health Versus NHS—Greenfield Possibility Versus Retrofit Impossibility

Let's start with an example of innovation that demonstrates how in healthcare different elements and factors must come together. In Chapters 5 and 8 I already mentioned Dr Devi Shetty of Narayana Health in Bangalore, who innovated cardiac surgery for children. After qualifying in Medicine in India, he trained to become a paediatric heart surgeon in the UK and practised at Guy's and St Thomas' Hospital in London. He returned to Kolkata in India where he operated on Mother Teresa and became her physician. In 2000 he set up Narayana Health to address the huge gap between the number of children being born in India with congenital heart conditions and those whose families could afford surgical care. His aim was to make complex heart surgery accessible for all families. He achieved that through combining innovations in processes, business models with technology and leadership. He introduced assembly-line principles, earning him the nickname of the 'Henry Ford of heart surgery.'

In a year his hospital carries out as many heart operations as in the whole of the UK [7]. In this high-volume environment, surgeons operate continuously throughout the day whereas other team members provide care. He trained people from local communities, without healthcare backgrounds, to perform specialist tasks; some were illiterate. Rich patients' families and charitable foundations effectively subsidise the care for the poor. Surgical trainees from all over the world gain practical experience there [8]. I had the privilege to visit Narayana Health a couple of years ago. It was overwhelming to see so many children in the Intensive Care, all getting great care. Afterwards I asked Devi, still in his scrubs, if he would have been able to achieve this if he had stayed in the UK. His immediate answer was very telling. 'Absolutely not.'

Architectural Constraints on Innovation and Transformation

That frank response speaks volumes. The structural constraints of the NHS make replication of Shetty's model architecturally impossible:

Centralised Bureaucratic Structure—The NHS is a complex bureaucracy focused on standardisation, managing risk and professional hierarchies. It resists radical operational changes such as Shetty's high-volume, low-cost model. For instance, it would not allow the task-shifting of junior staff, nurses and lay people taking on greater responsibility. Furthermore, centrally controlled finance would not support the scaling that this model requires.

Professional Boundaries and Labour Costs—Shetty's uses a pyramid structure of labour with a large base of lower-paid staff trained to high competence in specific tasks that supports a small number of specialists. Such a structure would be resisted by professional bodies and trade unions in the UK.

Regulation and Litigation—The task-shifting would trigger ethical, licensing and regulatory hurdles. The medical environment in the UK is more risk-averse; regulation is highly prescriptive with layers of oversight. Governance structures and accountability mechanisms would stifle the iterative process of driving down costs while improving outcomes.

Culture—Patients in the UK expect to see 'their doctor' and to get continuity, whereas in Shetty's model, parents do not get to meet the surgeon.

Finance Model—With the NHS providing universal coverage in the UK, there is no great infrastructure for philanthropic support. In India, Shetty leveraged its philanthropic culture in combination with government insurance schemes and donations.

Leadership—Devi Shetty combines being a great surgeon with a deep understanding of healthcare operations and finances. In the NHS, he would face a choice between a clinical or a managerial role. Importantly, in the NHS, he would have to fix an existing system; in India, he could build a new system from the ground up.

COUNTERINTUITIVE FINDING

Same People, Different Architecture, Opposite Outcomes

Healthcare innovation failure is routinely blamed on people—resistant clinicians, obstructive managers, risk-averse organisations. The evidence in this chapter points to a different diagnosis. Dr Devi Shetty—the same surgeon, same clinical skills, same ambition—achieves radical innovation on a greenfield site in India, performing as many cardiac operations annually as the entire UK. Asked whether he could replicate this within the NHS, his answer was immediate: 'Absolutely not.' The variable is not the person. It is the system architecture. Six structural barriers in established healthcare systems defeat innovation regardless of the innovator's capability. The Head of Radiology who successfully procured a multi-million-pound scanner could not get her peers to use it—not because she lacked competence, but because the authority structure made compliance architecturally impossible. The Innovations Factory team had validated prototypes for every concept in their portfolio. The NHS blocked every one.

The strategic implication is clear: stop investing in change management to fix people. Start investing in architectural assessment to fix systems. If the Architectural Diagnostic Framework presented later in this chapter reveals structural barriers dominating your innovation, no amount of leadership training or stakeholder engagement will overcome them. Architecture determines outcomes. Change the system, and the same people deliver different results.

Healthcare System Self-Preservation—Structural Evidence

The Narayana comparison reveals what greenfield innovation can achieve and why established systems resist it architecturally. The evidence goes further than architectural comparison. Healthcare systems actively preserve their existing structures—rapidly and decisively.

It is often claimed that innovation in healthcare is challenging due to the inertia of a very complex system. However, based on my experiences and observations, I believe that far from being inert, healthcare systems actively resist any change that threatens the status quo. Here are a couple of examples.a

In 2008 I established the Innovations Factory inside a large NHS hospital (see Chapter 12). Our portfolio of potential innovations—solutions for validated needs—got blocked in the Delivery phase of the design thinking Double Diamond. Blocking was fast and absolute—we failed to get any adopted in the NHS.

Another example demonstrates NHS structures in active self-preservation mode. I was fascinated to closely observe the impact of the 2012 Health and Social Care Act under Secretary of State Andrew Lansley (see Chapter 10). His reforms [9]:

- Abolished Primary Care Trusts and Strategic Health Authorities.
- Shifted commissioning power to GP-led local Clinical Commissioning Groups (CCGs).
- Emphasised 'any qualified provider' and competition in care provision.
- Promoted a more arm's-length relationship between the Secretary of State and the NHS.

His intent was to reduce central bureaucracy and put decisions closer to patients and clinicians. But each of his reforms posed a direct and existential threat to existing NHS structures. What followed was a rapid re-centralisation by other means [10]:

- Many CCGs struggled with capacity and rapidly started to cluster or merge.
- NHS England and Monitor took on greater regulatory roles.
- NHS managers and legacy actors often found ways to reassert control—through shared management, commissioning support units, or new regional structures.

The 2022 reforms effectively reversed much of the Lansley model, creating new, larger bureaucracies again [11]. In my view, Lansley wanted to do the right thing, but he did not prepare the clinical workforce for their new role. There were not enough clinicians capable and prepared to take on the role of leading the commissioning of healthcare. GPs in those roles became quickly overwhelmed as most still had to see to their patients too. It was fascinating to witness how fast Lansley's policy was undermined, if not sabotaged, by managers. This observation strengthens my argument that healthcare systems are not inert but can act swiftly and decisively to self-preserve and maintain the status quo.

The Architectural Diagnostic Framework

The cases presented in this chapter—from the pink stethoscope to Narayana Health to the Innovations Factory to the Lansley reforms—reveal a consistent pattern. Healthcare innovations don't fail randomly. They fail structurally, at predictable points of architectural incompatibility. The question isn't whether your innovation is good enough. The question is whether it fits the system it must operate within—or whether it demands a system that doesn't yet exist. The Architectural Diagnostic Framework provides a structured method for answering that question, in three sequential steps.

Step 1: Complexity Cascade Assessment

The pink stethoscope, presented in Chapter 12, taught us that the structural difficulty of an innovation depends on how many system layers it touches. A coloured stethoscope is a simple product substitution—it touches one layer and requires no system changes. A Bluetooth-enabled stethoscope touches six or more layers simultaneously: clinical workflow, data protection, professional accreditation, reimbursement pathways, medical records integration, and liability frameworks.

Before assessing anything else, map your innovation against these system layers (Table 13.1):

Interpretation:

- **1 Layer Affected**: Simple product substitution. Low structural complexity. Corresponds broadly to Level 1 resistance per the Diagnostic Resistance Framework presented in Chapter 12.
- **2–3 Layers Affected**: Moderate structural complexity. Changes propagate but may be containable. Requires careful concurrent planning.
- **4–6 Layers Affected**: High structural complexity. The cascade effect means changes in one layer will trigger requirements in others, often unpredictably. This is where most healthcare innovations stall—not because they fail technically, but because the system cannot absorb change across multiple layers simultaneously.

Step 2: Architectural Barrier Scan

The Narayana Health case demonstrated that six architectural features of established healthcare systems act as structural barriers to innovation. These aren't political objections or cultural preferences—they are load-bearing features of the system's architecture. Removing or bypassing any one of them has consequences for the others.

For each barrier, assess whether your innovation conflicts with, is neutral to, or is compatible with the existing architecture (Table 13.2):

Table 13.1 Complexity Cascade Assessment

System Layer	*Question*	*Affected?*
Clinical Workflow	Does this change how clinicians deliver care day-to-day?	Y / N
Data & Records	Does this require new data capture, storage, or sharing?	Y / N
Professional Accreditation	Does this cross professional boundaries or require new competencies?	Y / N
Reimbursement Pathways	Does this require new or modified payment mechanisms?	Y / N
Liability & Governance	Does this create new accountability questions or risk exposure?	Y / N
Organisational Culture	Does this challenge established expectations of patients or clinicians?	Y / N

Table 13.2 Scan of Architectural Barriers

Architectural Barrier	*Diagnostic Question*	*Conflict/Neutral/Compatible*
Economic & Payment Structures	Does your innovation require changes to how money flows between stakeholders? Does it threaten an existing revenue stream?	
Professional Boundaries	Does your innovation require task-shifting across established professional jurisdictions? Does it need people to work outside their current scope of practice?	
Regulatory & Litigation Framework	Does your innovation require new regulatory pathways, or does it fit within existing approvals? Does it create new litigation exposure?	
Cultural Expectations	Does your innovation challenge what patients expect from their care experience, or what clinicians expect from their professional role?	
Finance Model	Does your innovation require a new funding mechanism—philanthropy, insurance redesign, cross-subsidy—that doesn't currently exist in your system?	
Leadership Architecture	Does your innovation require integrated clinical-managerial leadership that the system's career structures don't support?	

Interpretation:

- **Mostly Compatible**: Your innovation fits within the existing architecture. Structural resistance will be low. Focus your energy on execution.
- **Mixed—Some Conflicts**: You face specific structural incompatibilities that must be resolved. Each conflict identified represents a design problem—not a persuasion problem. You cannot talk your way past an architectural barrier; you must design around it or redesign it.
- **Mostly Conflicting**: Your innovation requires fundamental architectural change. In an established system, this is the structural trap. The more barriers you conflict with, the more your innovation resembles a retrofit that the system was not designed to accommodate. Consider whether greenfield conditions exist—or can be created—where these barriers are absent.

Step 3: Concurrent Design Readiness

Christensen demonstrated that disruptive innovation requires three elements designed concurrently: simplifying technology, an innovative business model, and a compatible value network. Most healthcare innovators design one—typically the technology—and assume the other two will follow. They won't. The structural trap snaps shut precisely at this point.

Assess your readiness across all three elements (see Table 13.3):

Table 13.3 Readiness for Concurrent Design

Element	*Question*	*Status*
Simplifying Technology	Does your innovation make something simpler, more affordable, or more accessible than the current solution—even if initial performance is lower?	Ready/In progress/ Not addressed
Business Model Innovation	Have you designed a viable business model that works *within* the structural constraints you identified in Steps 1 and 2—including reimbursement, funding, and revenue flows?	Ready/In progress/ Not addressed
Compatible Value Network	Have you identified or created an ecosystem of partners, distributors, and supporters that can sustain your innovation *without* depending on the incumbent system's value chain?	Ready/In progress/ Not addressed

Interpretation:

- **All Three Ready**: You have the concurrent design foundation for structural viability. This is rare and puts you in a strong position.
- **Technology Ready, Others Not Addressed**: You are in the most common—and most dangerous—position in healthcare innovation. Your technology may be excellent, but without a concurrent business model and value network, you will be structurally trapped. This is where the Innovations Factory found itself: validated prototypes with no pathway to adoption.
- **None Fully Ready**: You are at concept stage. Use this framework to design all three elements in parallel from the start—not sequentially.

Bringing It Together: Your Structural Diagnosis

The three steps combine into an overall structural diagnosis:

Architecturally Compatible—Few layers affected, few barrier conflicts, concurrent design in place. Your innovation can work within the existing system. Corresponds broadly to Level 1–2 resistance. Proceed with execution focus.

Architecturally Incompatible but Designable—Multiple layers affected, specific barrier conflicts identified, but concurrent design can address them. Your innovation requires deliberate architectural problem-solving—designing around or through each structural incompatibility. This is hard but possible work. Corresponds to Level 2–3 resistance. Invest heavily in business model and value network design alongside your technology.

Structurally Trapped—Most layers affected, pervasive barrier conflicts, concurrent design blocked by the system itself. The existing architecture cannot accommodate your innovation regardless of its merits. You face a choice: scale down to a version that fits (and accept reduced impact), find or create greenfield conditions where these barriers don't exist (the Narayana option), or accept that the structural trap will defeat your innovation as it defeated the Innovations Factory, the RFID system (both covered in Chapter 12), and countless others.

This is not a failure of imagination or effort. It is a structural reality. And recognising it early—rather than discovering it after years of blocked delivery—is the most valuable diagnostic insight this framework can provide.

Now What

The structural trap is a diagnosis, and like any diagnosis, it is only useful if it changes what you do next. This chapter has demonstrated that healthcare innovations fail at predictable points of architectural incompatibility. Tight coupling means changes propagate through interconnected system layers. Stakeholder proliferation creates coordination complexity that exceeds human cognitive capacity. The absence of an aligned value chain means innovation threatens some stakeholders by design, regardless of its clinical merit. Christensen's three elements—simplifying technology, business model, and value network—must be designed concurrently; yet healthcare's architecture makes concurrent design extraordinarily difficult within established systems. Narayana Health showed what becomes possible on greenfield sites; the Innovations Factory showed what happens when validated innovations confront an established system's structural resistance.

The Architectural Diagnostic Framework provides the tool to assess structural fit before committing years and resources to an innovation the system was never designed to accommodate. Use it early. Use it honestly. The structural trap catches innovators who assume the system will adapt to their innovation. It rarely does.

But structure alone does not kill innovations. People do—when innovations threaten their interests, their income, their authority, or their professional identity. The structural barriers identified in this chapter create the conditions for resistance, but resistance requires actors. Who are they? What do they want? Why do they fight? And how can you build coalitions strong enough to overcome their opposition?

Chapter 14 examines the political dynamics of healthcare innovation—moving from the architectural question of WHAT blocks innovation to the strategic question of WHO blocks it, and why.

References

1. Canon Medical Systems USA (n.d.) 'Toshiba's Aquilion One diagnoses cardiac disease with CT myocardial analysis software from Vital images'. Available at: https://us.medical.canon/news/press-releases/2012/03/25/1211/.
2. Bailey, D. and De Ruyter, A. (2012) 'Re-examining the BMW-Rover affair: A case study of corporate, strategic and government failure?', *International Journal of Automotive Technology and Management*, 12(2), pp. 117–133. https://doi.org/10.1504/IJATM.2012.046858.

3. Steenstra, D. and Erkoyuncu, J.A. (2014) 'Using visualisation for disruptive innovation in healthcare', in *Virtual, Augmented Reality and Serious Games for Healthcare*. Berlin: Springer, pp. 219–236.
4. NHS England Digital (2025) *NHS Workforce Statistics – October 2025*. Available at: https://digital.nhs.uk/data-and-information/publications/statistical/nhs-workforce-statistics/october-2025.
5. Christensen, C.M. (2003) *The Innovator's Dilemma*. New York: Harper Business Essentials.
6. Christensen, C.M., Johnson, C.W. and Horn, M.B. (2008) *Disrupting Class: How Disruptive Innovation Will Change the Way the World Learns*. 1st edn. New York: McGraw-Hill.
7. Muralidhara, G.V. (2016) *Dr Devi Shetty of Narayana Hrudayalaya: Delivering Quality Cardiac Care to the Masses*. The Case Centre. Available at: https://www.thecasecentre.org/products/view?id=137186 (Accessed: 4 July 2025).
8. Davies, P. (2012) 'Could a passage to India be the way to get more surgical experience?', *BMJ*, 345, e6637. https://doi.org/10.1136/bmj.e6637
9. Wikipedia contributors (2026) 'Health and social care act 2012', *Wikipedia*. Available at: https://en.wikipedia.org/w/index.php?title=Health_and_Social_Care_Act_2012&oldid=1338437157.
10. Timmins, N. (2020) 'Breaking with Lansley's act', *The Health Foundation*. Available at: https://www.health.org.uk/features-and-opinion/blogs/breaking-with-lansley-s-act.
11. Arnold-Forster, A. (2025) *Bringing NHS England Back Under Closer Political Control: Lessons from History*. The Health Foundation. Available at: https://www.health.org.uk/reports-and-analysis/briefings/bringing-nhs-england-back-under-closer-political-control-lessons.

Chapter 14

The Political Reality

In 2005, the NHS announced it was establishing a new Institute for Innovation and Improvement. They were recruiting an Executive Director of Innovation. This was so up my street. I was already on the Warwick campus as project manager of HealthTech, with credentials in design thinking and innovation that straddled medicine, professional design, and academic research. I applied. I got shortlisted—probably in the top four—and was given access to the Chief Executive of the new Institute to prepare. On the day, the interview panel included Professor Sir Lord Ara Darzi, the world-class surgeon and health systems thinker we met in Chapter 10. He noted that across diverse scenarios, my answers kept centring on 'people'—which I was able to explain and justify. Immediately afterwards, the head of the recruitment agency managing the process told me it had gone well. He and I connected on LinkedIn; so did Lord Darzi.

Weeks later I was informed I had not been successful. The recruiter was surprised. The job went to Maire Smith, an IP expert already on the NHS payroll. For years I blamed myself. I replayed the interview in my head, wondering what I'd said wrong, at which stage I'd lost them, what I could have done differently. That's what capable people do when systems reject them—they assume the fault is theirs. It took me years to understand that I hadn't failed the interview. The system had functioned exactly as designed.

An outsider with cross-sector experience, whose instinct was to put people at the centre of innovation, was never going to be selected by an institution whose operating logic requires people who will maintain the status quo. The system selected its own. It always does. This chapter examines why.

Chapter 13 mapped the architectural barriers to healthcare innovation—the structural constraints that make transformation inherently difficult. Those barriers are real. They are architectural. And they would exist even if every person in the system genuinely wanted change.

But people are the architects of the system and also its guardians—conditioned to maintain the status quo. Structure alone doesn't kill innovations. People do, when innovations threaten their interests. Healthcare leaders are operating within governance systems structurally configured for failure. Until you understand who guards the system, what interests they protect, and why

DOI: 10.4324/9781003752073-18

transformation initiatives die regardless of evidence, resources, or stakeholder buy-in, you'll keep repeating the same costly mistakes.

This chapter moves from architecture to agency. Who has veto power in healthcare, and why do they use it? How do political leaders consistently choose bureaucratic solutions over clinical ones? And most critically—how can you navigate healthcare's political reality to build coalitions capable of sustaining change?

The NHS provides the sharpest lens for examining these dynamics. Where Chapter 13 examined its architectural constraints, this chapter examines the people who maintain them—starting with the custodians at the very top.

The Custodians: Who Guards the System

Sir Jim Mackey took up the post of Chief Executive Officer at NHS England on 1 April 2025. He was Chief Executive, NHS Improvement, from 2015 to 2017. According to Wikipedia, he is a qualified accountant [1]. Mackey joined the NHS in 1990. After holding finance director roles, from 2003 to 2023 he was chief executive of Northumbria Healthcare NHS Foundation Trust. The interesting fact is that I can't find him on LinkedIn—the network of professionals—not under Jim, James, with NHS and Chief Executive title or without—no result. I'm not one for conspiracy theories, but could it be there is an alternative—shadowy—network—where people like Sir Jim hang out and interact as custodians of the system? Tempting hypothesis …

His predecessor reveals the pattern more starkly. Sir David Nicholson was chief executive of the NHS from 2006 to 2014. Nicholson was educated at Forest Fields Grammar School in Nottingham and graduated from Bristol Polytechnic with a 2:1 in History and Politics. He was a signed-up member of the Communist Party—not a sin [2]. But consider what followed.

As a career administrator in the NHS, he was Chief Executive of the West Midlands Strategic Health Authority and found to be 'asleep at the wheel' during the unfolding of the Mid-Staffordshire disaster, where patients needlessly died due to negligence and infighting in an NHS hospital. The West Midlands was my patch as project manager of HealthTech at the University of Warwick. In the region, there was no secret about the trouble at that hospital—there were other notorious hospitals on this guy's path, such as the George Eliot in Nuneaton, a permanent fixture in the bottom 10 NHS hospitals [3]. The Francis Inquiry into Mid Staffordshire stopped short of holding him accountable. A mistake and a missed opportunity. If the most senior NHS leader could not be held to account for failures on his watch, what precedent did that set? Subsequent public inquiries into other failing trusts provided the answer: despite mounting evidence of management failure, the accountability bar had been set so high that no one could clear it [4]. Francis didn't just let Nicholson off the hook—it handed a get-out-of-jail card to every incompetent NHS manager who followed.

Sir David wrote a frank article in 'The Guardian' in 2014 about his Type II diabetes—a condition caused in part by lifestyle choices. In that article he admitted to being a 'full English breakfast' type of guy, goes to the pub on Friday for '7 or 8 pints' and has never seen any of his relatives grow old as they all died of heart and lung conditions—no surprise there [5]. A clinician would call this a presenting complaint: the chief executive of the world's largest healthcare organisation, with no clinical training, no personal health literacy, no family experience of ageing, and a lifestyle history that reads like a textbook risk profile for the very conditions overwhelming his system. The NHS wasn't being led. It was being administered—by someone who didn't understand the difference.

Yet in 2011, while the NHS Institute for Innovation and Improvement was still open (but distracted by Lean as we have seen in Chapter 11), this same man had the audacity to 'Call for ideas and evidence on how the adoption and spread of innovation can be accelerated throughout the NHS' [6]. Not only an indictment of the NHS Institute but of his flawed beliefs about the role of the NHS. One of the sentences in that call for evidence particularly disturbed me: 'As UK public services face a tougher financial climate, innovation has a vital role to play to continue improving the quality of care for patients, and support the NHS as a major investor and wealth creator in the UK.' The NHS is *not* and should not be considered a wealth creator as it is actually paid for by us—UK taxpayers. Its only role is to maximise quality of life of all citizens. Nothing more, nothing less.

Many NHS managers recognise every word of these descriptions of the guardians and are as frustrated as any clinician. They are competent people operating within incompetent structures. How does the system reproduce this pattern? Through careful selection of future leaders.

Perpetuating 'Leaders'

Sir David Nicholson and many other NHS administrators (I don't want to call them leaders) have come up from the NHS Graduate Scheme that has been delivered for many years by Birmingham University. In 2006 the tender for providing that scheme came up for renewal (2006/S 143-154191). At that time I had a dual role at Warwick Manufacturing Group (WMG) at the University of Warwick (that also hosted the NHS Institute on campus) as part-time manager of HealthTech—a £5.0M EU-funded project supporting small businesses into the healthcare sector and module tutor delivering MSc Design and Product Development Management to students in the UK, India, Singapore and Thailand.

I managed to get a cross-departmental consortium together of WMG, Warwick Business School and the Medical School to develop a curriculum and bid. In our preparations, we interviewed our colleagues at Birmingham University who delivered the graduate programme. They were surprisingly open and willing to talk with us, meeting us in our campus restaurant. They admitted their biggest challenge was to convince the NHS to stop 'cloning' future leaders. Birmingham was only responsible for programme delivery—it was the NHS that selected who should be on it. The NHS interpretation of diversity was recruiting people with diverse gender, ethnicity and cultural background. But they all had the same values and behaviours in common, which irked our Birmingham colleagues, but they could not convince the NHS to change. This explains how the system perpetuates itself—by carefully selecting people that will not challenge it and maintain the status quo.

We took this on board in our proposal, justifying a different approach to stimulate innovation and transformation. We also interviewed chief executives from NHS trusts across the regions to get their input on what graduate skills were lacking and required. Thus, we came up with a comprehensive and considered proposal that was not successful—obvious in retrospect.

Besides the Administrators

But before you conclude that this is purely an administrator problem, consider the clinicians themselves.

In 2004 I was a guest at the opening of the Heart and Lung Centre at New Cross NHS Hospital in Wolverhampton—a £60 million state-of-the-art facility [7]. The consultant clinicians were very proud to show me around until we got to the intervention suites, located on the top floor of the new build. 'So,' I asked, 'what music do you play in the elevators when acute patients are brought up—Another One Bites the Dust?'

The first hour after a heart attack is critical. The heart muscle is so electrically unstable that it can misfire into a second arrest. Time is of the essence. In the intervention suites, clinicians diagnose using angiograms (X-ray imaging of blood vessels) and, if they see a blockage in one of the coronary arteries during that procedure, can dissolve it through thrombolysis and place stents to prevent future attacks. Every minute counts. A patient rushed in with sirens and blue lights could be critically delayed by a lift ride to the top floor.

Why not place the intervention suites on the ground floor? The answer is a classic first-diamond design (the requirements-gathering phase) failure—the consultant clinicians who specified the requirements almost certainly stipulated a need for a nice view over the town and adjoining landscape. Their professional comfort trumped the patient's clinical urgency. Sixty million pounds, and the most time-critical patients wait for a lift.

This matters for the argument of this chapter. Stakeholder interests that override patients' needs are not confined to administrators and politicians. Clinicians are stakeholders too—with status, comfort, and professional preferences that can distort even the most expensive design decisions. Everyone in the system has interests. Everyone can be a barrier. The political reality of healthcare transformation is that all stakeholders must be understood, mapped, and navigated—including the ones you expect to be your allies.

Political Leaders and Healthcare: The Pattern of Failure

If the system's custodians are career administrators selected to maintain the status quo, what about the politicians charged with leading healthcare reform? The evidence across successive UK governments reveals a consistent and equally depressing pattern.

The push to transform the NHS under Labour governments began around 2000 with the NHS Plan and massive investment commitments. The Wanless Review recommended aligning funding increases with workforce planning and preventative care—sensible, evidence-based recommendations [8]. But here's what actually happened: funding increased significantly—by more than £43 billion in the five years after 2002 alone. But where did the money actually go? According to the Wanless follow-up review, 43% was absorbed by pay inflation through new staff contracts with little evidence of improved performance. Manager numbers grew by 70%—more than double the rate for medical staff. Continuous organisational restructuring, including a McKinsey-led review of the Department's own structure, consumed resources and disrupted service delivery. Clinical workforce headcount did grow, but the report concluded that even these increases were insufficient for projected demand, and that full clinical engagement in reform had still not been achieved. The system spent billions hiring more people and paying them more, while failing to give clinicians meaningful agency in transformation—reinforcing centralised management rather than building clinical capacity for change [9].

When Sir David as CE of the NHS was asked by the Parliamentary Health Committee how much money he spent on external management consultancy he had the audacity to reply: 'We have not so far collected that information centrally. We have started to think about how we might do it but I think the numbers we have got are so unreliable at the moment that we are not satisfied that we have got that number right' [10]. Imagine a chief executive of a PLC providing that answer at a meeting of shareholders—he would be out on his ears. Quite rightly so, but our political system is not about accountability.

The pattern emerges: political governance structures produce bureaucratic solutions to operational problems. When faced with healthcare challenges, the default response is more management, not more healthcare. This pattern repeats globally. Whether examining Medicare dysfunction, European health ministry failures, or developing nation health system reforms, political leaders consistently choose technocratic complexity over clinical capacity building.

Andrew Lansley's 2012 Health and Social Care Act attempted the opposite—shifting decision-making power closer to frontline care through local GP-led commissioning. His reforms abolished Primary Care Trusts and Strategic Health Authorities, shifted commissioning power to GP-led local Clinical Commissioning Groups (CCGs), emphasised 'any qualified provider' and competition in care provision, and promoted a more arm's-length relationship between the Secretary of State and the NHS. His intent was to reduce central bureaucracy and put decisions closer to patients and clinicians. However, what followed was a rapid re-centralisation by other means. Many CCGs struggled with capacity and rapidly started to cluster or merge. NHS England and Monitor took on greater regulatory roles. NHS managers and legacy actors often found ways to reassert control—through shared management, commissioning support units, or new regional structures [11]. The 2022 reforms effectively reversed much of the Lansley model, creating new, larger bureaucracies again.

In my view, Lansley wanted to do the right thing, but he did not prepare the clinical workforce for their new role. There were not enough clinicians capable and prepared to take on the role of leading the commissioning of healthcare. GPs in those roles became quickly overwhelmed as most still had to see to their patients too. It was fascinating to witness how fast Lansley's policy was undermined, if not sabotaged, by managers.

What were NHS leaders doing while these reforms unfolded? At the time when the coalition government developed green papers toward the 2012 Act, they were also culling public sector organisations under the austerity umbrella. In those days I was MD of Innovations Factory based in one of the largest NHS Trusts. I had direct contact with several NHS chief executives and future leaders that were all members of the NHS National Leadership Council—setup in 2009 [12]. Unbelievably the strategy of that group during this period of turmoil was to keep quiet, keeping their heads down, don't make any noise out of fear that central government might become aware of them, cut their funding and close their organisation. This typifies NHS 'leaders'—in a time of need and of great opportunity to do some real leading, choosing to keep stumm.

Jeremy Hunt's extended tenure as Health Secretary demonstrates how political governance prioritises perception management over operational preparedness. Despite leading Exercise Cygnus—a 2016 pandemic simulation that clearly exposed critical gaps in PPE stockpiles and workforce resilience—the findings were quietly shelved rather than addressed [13]. When COVID-19 arrived, frontline staff faced dangerous exposure while Hunt's earlier contract disputes with junior doctors had already eroded trust across the workforce. The pattern is clear: political institutional culture codes for avoiding difficult conversations and investments, even when evidence overwhelmingly demonstrates necessity.

Matt Hancock's declaration of a 'protective ring' around care homes while awarding PPE contracts to pub landlords exemplifies governance at its most destructive. The language of protection masked policies that turned care homes into viral tinderboxes through untested hospital discharges. Chapter 11 documented how efficiency-optimised supply chains contributed to 900 healthcare worker deaths. Here is what that governance failure looked like from the inside.

This is highly personal. I was semi-retired and lived in London at the outbreak of COVID-19. As former Managing Director of the Innovations Factory, with established experience in supplying PPE to the NHS, I was approached via former contacts with offers, not just of PPE but also ventilators and associated consumables. I tried to pass these on to contacts in NHS procurement, even approached former and incumbent local MPs, but did not get anywhere. I will never know whether they dismissed me because I was offering to help free of charge—for ethical reasons, not wanting to profiteer—or because I wasn't a signed-up member of the Tories.

The situation in care homes and the NHS was desperate—patients forced to die in solitude because of lack of PPE for their relatives was inhumane and still makes me cry. NHS staff became creative in their desperation, not just using bin liners but asking their local sex shop. I still have an email conversation with the owner of a sex shop that had some PPE for customers playing doctors and nurses, who was approached by his local hospital. He was so indignant about their plight that he gifted his whole stock of PPE. I also have an email trail with HM government's representative who could not be bothered to get out of his bed in Singapore to secure a consignment of much-needed ventilators that subsequently went to a bidder that was actually awake. I will never forget or forgive the politicians and civil 'servants' responsible for much needless suffering.

The latest iteration of this pattern is the newly announced NHS 10-Year Plan. It ticks rhetorical boxes—shifting from hospital to community care, analogue to digital systems, sickness to prevention—while being entirely anonymous, with no named authors, visible leadership, or evidence of frontline consultation [14]. The plan reads like back-room technocrat abstractions completely disconnected from care delivery realities. Meanwhile, exhausted clinicians are expected to implement sweeping reforms while holding up a system already collapsing. It evokes British World War I generals sending troops 'over the top' from command tent comfort—all strategy, no presence. Until we stop treating transformation as paper exercises and start approaching it as deeply human, co-designed endeavours, this cycle of lofty plans and inevitable failure will continue.

Stakeholders at Structural Distance of Decisions

Politicians and career officials are both policymakers in healthcare, but their drivers are fundamentally different. One is motivated by re-election and political capital, the other by system integrity and career survival.

A senior clinician once put it to me this way: 'If you haven't had the experience to be in the room when I have to explain to a patient and their family, honestly, why we've reached the end of the road and the patient will die—then you should not be allowed to make decisions in healthcare.'

It sounds extreme. It isn't. Politicians and career officials operate at structural distance from the consequences of their decisions—like generals who have never served on the battlefield. They experience healthcare as policy frameworks, spending forecasts, and performance dashboards. They never experience it as the conversation at 3am where you tell a family there is nothing more you can do. That distance doesn't just limit their empathy. It corrupts their judgement. Decisions made without proximity to consequence systematically favour what looks good on paper over what works at the bedside.

This creates systematic structural incompatibilities. Politicians operate within four-to-five-year cycles, while meaningful healthcare transformation requires ten-to-fifteen-year horizons. Training a physician takes a decade; shifting population health patterns requires generational investment; building public trust demands consistency across multiple administrations. This temporal mismatch creates systematic bias toward short-term, visible interventions over long-term system building.

Politicians and officials are not the only source of political resistance. Chapters 10 and 13 mapped the stakeholder landscape and its mathematical impossibility—eight primary actors, twenty-eight relationships, objectives that structurally conflict. What those chapters didn't examine is who benefits from this complexity.

Meanwhile, prevention generates savings five to ten years in the future but requires immediate investment. Emergency interventions create immediate visibility but long-term costs. Current budgeting cycles and political incentives systematically favour expensive reactive measures over cost-effective preventive approaches, creating what economists call 'policy investment traps.'

COUNTERINTUITIVE FINDING

Healthcare Governance Fails from Consequence Deficit, Not Information Deficit

Healthcare's governance reform model assumes that policy failure results from insufficient information—if only policymakers had better clinical advice, they would make better decisions. Five consecutive UK policy cycles since 2000 prove the opposite. Each had access to world-class evidence: Wanless (2002, 2007), Darzi (2008, 2024), Exercise Cygnus (2016). The evidence was sound. The recommendations were clear. The system rejected them all. £43 billion in post-Wanless funding saw 43% absorbed by pay inflation and managers growing at more than double the rate of clinicians, while Cygnus's pandemic warnings were shelved and 900 healthcare workers subsequently died in a crisis the evidence had precisely predicted. More information does not improve governance when decision-makers are structurally insulated from consequences. Politicians and officials experience healthcare as policy documents and performance dashboards—never as the 3am conversation where a clinician tells a family there is nothing more to be done. Structural distance from consequence systematically corrupts judgement toward what looks good on paper over what works at the bedside. The strategic implication: stop commissioning better reports; start redesigning governance to create proximity to consequence.

Economic Interests and Institutional Capture

Stakeholder interests become most intractable when they are economic. The transformation of incentive structures over centuries has created a system that actively rewards dysfunction.

In the decentralised past, physicians were directly compensated by patients or their families for tangible outcomes—reducing suffering, improving quality of life, restoring function. The connection between intervention and reward was immediate and personal. Healers succeeded when their patients thrived.

Today's centralised system has severed this fundamental link. Patients contribute to insurance schemes or tax systems, while healthcare professionals receive monthly salaries disconnected from individual patient outcomes. More perversely, the system now rewards illness rather than health. Hospitals profit from occupied beds, not empty ones. Pharmaceutical companies generate revenue from treating disease, not preventing it. Medical device manufacturers thrive when more procedures are performed, not when fewer are needed.

This misalignment of incentives explains much of healthcare's current dysfunction. When the system profits from problems rather than solutions, it inevitably generates more problems to solve.

These economic interests become locked in through institutional capture. Epic Systems illustrates the mechanism precisely. Unlike a platform business, Epic's dominance is about deep institutional capture. Epic has embedded itself so deeply into the governance structures of healthcare institutions that switching costs are prohibitive. They control the core workflow infrastructure, data integration standards, training and certification pathways, procurement relationships, and implementation timelines often spanning seven or more years. This creates what economists call 'administrative capture'—Epic doesn't just sell software, it becomes the institutional nervous system. Once embedded, Epic can predictably absorb any external innovation that threatens to unbundle their offering.

Public institutions create their own economic barriers. The National Institute for Health and Care Excellence (NICE) plays a pivotal role in the English health system, but it's often misunderstood. It is not a regulator like the Medicines and Healthcare products Regulatory Agency (MHRA). Instead, NICE provides guidance on whether interventions are both clinically effective and cost-effective for use in the NHS. But this division of labour between NICE and the MHRA creates a sequential process: innovators must first gain regulatory approval, and only then undergo a second, often lengthy and duplicative appraisal to satisfy NICE's economic and clinical thresholds. I watched this dynamic play out at Innovations Factory. This bifurcation leads to delays, increased costs, and significant barriers for innovators, particularly for smaller or non-traditional players—in other words, increasing the barrier to entry, thereby sustaining incumbent industry players.

Professional Jurisdiction and Scope Wars

Economic interests are compounded by professional territory. Healthcare's professional boundaries represent political barriers as formidable as any financial incentive.

The experience of Narayana Health in India illustrates this starkly. Chapter 13 examined the structural reasons why Shetty's model cannot be replicated in the NHS. To my question whether he could have achieved this in the UK he replied: 'No f&%@ing way.' His answer, which I cleaned up for Chapter 13, reveals a political dimension too. In the NHS he would face a forced choice between a clinical or a managerial role. He could not do both. And crucially, in the NHS he would have had to fix an existing system—in India he could build from scratch. The structural trap (Chapter 13) meets the political trap: even if you could redesign the architecture, professional jurisdictions would resist every boundary you tried to cross.

These dynamics play out daily across the UK and US healthcare. In England, community pharmacists have progressively gained prescribing rights for common conditions—a sensible redistribution that reduces GP workload and improves patient access. The clinical evidence supports it. Patients benefit. Yet GP professional bodies have fought each expansion, framing the debate around patient safety when the underlying concern is consultation volume and professional standing. The same pattern emerges with advanced nurse practitioners. Nurses with master's-level training and years of clinical experience face sustained resistance from medical bodies when seeking independent prescribing authority or expanded diagnostic roles—even in specialties where workforce shortages make the case overwhelming.

The emerging frontier is AI diagnostics. Radiology provides the clearest example. Algorithms now match or exceed radiologist accuracy for specific imaging tasks [15]. The technology works. The evidence base grows monthly. Yet adoption stalls—not because clinicians doubt the technology, but because professional identity is at stake. When a machine can read a chest X-ray, what does that mean for the radiologist's role, status, and income? The resistance is rational, human, and predictable.

In every case, the pattern is identical: innovation threatens professional jurisdiction, and the threatened profession mobilises its institutional power to slow, constrain, or block adoption. The clinical merits become secondary to the political contest.

The Asymmetric Risk Problem: Why Leaders Choose Inaction

Understanding stakeholder interests explains what is defended. The asymmetric risk problem explains *why* defence is the default. Healthcare leaders face a fundamental asymmetry: innovation failure is career-ending, while innovation success yields only modest credit. This asymmetric risk calculus means that saying 'yes' to transformation is personally dangerous while saying 'no' carries almost no consequence. The system learns dysfunction because dysfunction is rewarded.

When you understand this, the system's resistance to change stops looking irrational and starts looking like perfectly rational self-preservation.

The Absence of Vision

When leaders choose safety over courage, and systems reward blocking over enabling, the cumulative result is a complete absence of strategic vision for healthcare's future.

Perhaps the most damning evidence of all is this: when we convened more than twenty health experts from across Europe through the European Health Futures Forum's (EHFF) Three Horizons Plus project, what emerged was stark—and unpublished, because no policymaker wanted to hear it—politicians have no credible vision for the future of healthcare. None. Not in the UK, not across Europe. At a time when we face intersecting crises—from climate collapse to rising inequality to failing health systems—this absence of vision is not just negligent, it's dangerous and scary. Kennedy could rally a nation with a call to 'put a man on the moon within a decade.' Where is our equivalent unifying vision for health? Where is the moral and political courage to declare that, within a generation, every citizen should live in a system that supports health, not just treats illness?

The hard truth is that our political governance model is structurally incapable of delivering meaningful healthcare transformation. Politicians operate on short-term electoral cycles and are rewarded for the wrong behaviours—headlines over substance, performance targets over population health, announcements over outcomes. Decade after decade, they've built a reactive sickness service rather than a health system. They've consistently ignored the widening gap between demand and capacity, failed to invest in prevention, and refused to think in joined-up, long-term ways across health, social care, housing, and communities.

Coalition Building and Political Strategy

So what can transformation leaders actually do?

The deeper question for future innovation is this: do we repeat the cycle of top-down policy reform, hoping for different results, or do we adopt a fundamentally different strategy? If the system's core instinct is to preserve itself, then meaningful change may need to originate elsewhere—not at the centre, but at the margins. Clayton Christensen's theory of disruptive innovation offers an alternative. Introduced in Chapter 2, with further details in Chapter 13, it advises starting small, start outside the dominant structure, and serving those the system overlooks. In healthcare, that means enabling localised, community-led models in underserved areas—not as pilots to be absorbed back into the core, but as seeds of a different operating logic. Transformation won't come by asking the supertanker to turn; it comes by building something nimbler alongside it, out of reach of the system's reflex to assimilate and suppress.

Of course, applying this lens in the UK presents its own challenge. Unlike more fragmented or market-based systems, the NHS is all-pervasive—there are few places it isn't, even if it isn't functioning well. That makes finding a foothold for grassroots disruption harder, but not impossible. Community mental health stands out as one such frontier: chronically under-resourced, fragmented across services, and often failing those with the most complex needs. Similarly, social care transitions, support for neurodiverse children and families, and end-of-life care in non-hospital settings are areas where the system retreats—not by design, but through neglect. These are precisely the spaces where new models could take root: small, trusted, community-anchored, and able to demonstrate a logic of care the mainstream system struggles to provide. If disruption is to come, it will likely start here—quietly, and in the margins the NHS has unintentionally created.

Healthcare leaders must recognise that regulation is not the enemy of innovation—dysfunctional governance is. The challenge isn't to deregulate; it's to re-engineer governance structures that enable safe, supported risk-taking while maintaining essential regulatory and safety functions.

Diagnosis without prescription is incomplete. If you're leading a transformation initiative, you need practical tools for navigating the political landscape this chapter has described. Three frameworks help.

The starting point is a stakeholder interest map (Figure 14.1). Before engaging anyone, plot your stakeholders on two dimensions: their power to block or enable your innovation (vertical axis), and the degree to which your innovation aligns with or threatens their interests (horizontal axis). This produces four quadrants, each requiring a distinct strategic approach.

> Plot your stakeholders, then sequence your engagement: build coalition mass top-right, amplify allies bottom-right, then approach resistors top-left with momentum. Your design thinking task is to move stakeholders rightward or up through reframing—finding the shared interest they don't yet see.

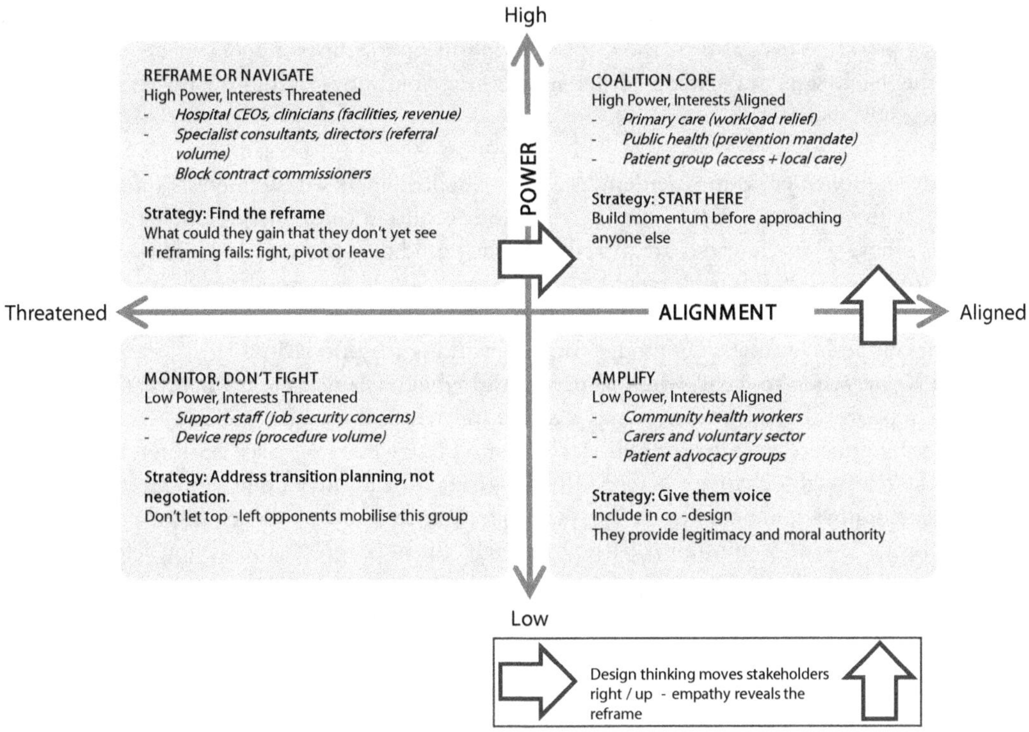

Figure 14.1 Stakeholder interest map.

The map reveals a strategic error that most transformation leaders make: they spend all their energy in the top-left quadrant, trying to convince powerful resistors, when they should be building coalition mass on the right side first and approaching the top-left with momentum behind them. This is the sequencing principle in action.

It also reveals the design thinking contribution to political strategy. Stakeholders move between quadrants. Consider the consultant radiologist from the AI diagnostics example. When an algorithm threatens to automate chest X-ray reporting, that radiologist sits top-left—powerful and threatened. But the same radiologist, overwhelmed by a reporting backlog that keeps patients waiting weeks for results, who could use AI to triage urgent findings and focus her expertise on complex cases—she sits top-right. Powerful and aligned. They are the same person. The innovation hasn't changed. The frame has. Your job is to find the frame that moves stakeholders rightward. That's empathy applied to political reality.

Three frameworks operationalise the map.

First: Map the interests, not just the stakeholders. Standard stakeholder analysis identifies who matters. Political strategy requires understanding *why* they will act. For each stakeholder group, ask three questions:

- What do they gain from the current system?
- What do they stand to lose from your innovation?
- And—critically—what could they gain from it that they don't yet see?

That third question is where coalitions are built. The GP whose consultation volume drops when pharmacists prescribe may also be the GP drowning in minor illness appointments who would welcome the relief. Same stakeholder, different framing. Your job is to find the frame that reveals shared interest.

Second: Sequence your engagement. Start with stakeholders whose interests most naturally align with your innovation—they become your coalition core. Then identify the 'persuadables': those whose interests are mixed and who could be reframed. Approach resistors last, and only with coalition momentum behind you. The error most transformation leaders make is seeking universal buy-in before launch. Universal buy-in is a fiction in a system with eight competing stakeholder groups. Build a working majority. Move.

Third: Know when to fight, when to pivot, and when to leave. Fight when you have coalition support, clinical evidence, and a structural window—a new policy cycle, leadership change, or crisis that shifts the political calculus. Pivot when resistance is strong but interests can be reframed—change the scope, the language, or the entry point without abandoning the core innovation. Leave when the system's resistance exceeds your coalition's capacity and the personal cost of continued battle outweighs likely progress. This is not defeat. This is Christensen applied strategically: find the margin the system has neglected, build your proof of concept there, and let success create its own political momentum.

These frameworks aren't theoretical. When Gary Kaplan and the Virginia Mason Institute partnered with five NHS trusts, they faced exactly the political landscape this chapter describes—CEOs under pressure, regulators with oversight authority, stakeholders with competing interests. Their response was to design a structure for political navigation: a Transformation Guiding Board that brought trust CEOs together with NHS regulators at the same table monthly, working toward shared improvement goals rather than defending institutional positions. The Warwick Business School evaluation of the partnership found that before long, all five CEOs considered this meeting the 'best working day of the month' [16]. That's coalition building in practice—not hoping powerful stakeholders will align, but designing the conditions under which alignment becomes possible. Kaplan—himself a physician—led from clinical credibility, not administrative authority.

The common thread across all three frameworks is this: political strategy in healthcare is not manipulation. It is design thinking applied to human interests—empathy for stakeholders' genuine concerns, prototyping coalition structures, iterating as the political landscape shifts. The same methodology that redesigns clinical pathways can redesign political ones.

Separating Regulation from Governance

It's important to separate regulation from governance—a distinction that's often blurred, to the detriment of both innovation and patient care. As a patient, I want regulation. I want new medicines, devices, and interventions to be held to high standards of safety, efficacy, and evidence. That form of regulation is not the enemy of innovation—in fact, it enables trust and adoption.

But governance is different. Governance is how systems organise themselves—the policies, performance regimes, and operational procedures that shape what people are allowed to do. This is where transformation so often stalls. Bureaucratic governance, especially in top-down systems like the NHS, tends to conflate control with accountability. It standardises for compliance rather than learning, and in doing so, crowds out the very conditions innovation requires: local discretion, experimentation, and trust in frontline judgement.

The challenge is not to deregulate—it's to unshackle governance from its defensive instincts and reframe it as an enabler of safe, supported risk-taking.

You now understand structural barriers (Chapter 13) and stakeholder interests (this chapter). You can map who will resist your innovation, why they will resist it, and where shared interests might enable a coalition. But even with structural fit and a political coalition, healthcare systems actively fight transformation. They deploy coordinated resistance that intensifies over time, often succeeding in reversing apparent progress within 18 to 24 months [17]. The system learns from each transformation attempt, strengthening its defences for the next one. How do systems fight back, what patterns should you recognise, and how can you navigate the resistance?

References

1. Wikipedia contributors (2025) 'Jim Mackey (healthcare administrator)', *Wikipedia*. Available at: https://en.wikipedia.org/w/index.php?title=Jim_Mackey_(healthcare_administrator)&oldid=1320732313.
2. Wikipedia contributors (2026) 'David Nicholson (civil servant)', *Wikipedia*. Available at: https://en.wikipedia.org/w/index.php?title=David_Nicholson_(civil_servant)&oldid=1338275126.
3. NHS England (2013) 'Sir Bruce Keogh announces final list of outliers'. Available at: https://www.england.nhs.uk/2013/02/final-outliers/.
4. Hughes, H. (2023) 'Public inquiries, patient safety and the implementation gap', *Future Healthcare Journal*, 10(1), pp. 7–9. https://doi.org/10.7861/fhj.2023-FR103.
5. Nicholson, D. (2014) 'Diabetes and me: How silent killer caught up with NHS chief', *The Guardian*, 16 May. Available at: https://www.theguardian.com/society/2014/may/16/diabetes-me-nhs-chief-david-nicholson.
6. GOV.UK (2011) *Spreading Innovation in the NHS: Call for Evidence and Ideas*. Available at: https://www.gov.uk/government/news/spreading-innovation-in-the-nhs-call-for-evidence-and-ideas.
7. BBC News (2024) 'Wolverhampton heart surgery centre celebrates 20 years'. Available at: https://www.bbc.com/news/articles/c4g5ejjez40o.
8. Wanless, D. (2002) *Securing Our Future Health: Taking a Long-Term View – Final Report*. London: HM Treasury.
9. Wanless, D. (ed.) (2007) *Our Future Health Secured? A Review of NHS Funding and Performance*. London: The King's Fund.
10. House of Commons Health Committee (2008) *The Use of Management Consultants by the NHS and the Department of Health*. Available at: https://publications.parliament.uk/pa/cm200809/cmselect/cmhealth/28/2803.htm?utm_source=chatgpt.com.
11. Timmins, N. (2020) 'Breaking with Lansley's act', *The Health Foundation*. Available at: https://www.health.org.uk/features-and-opinion/blogs/breaking-with-lansley-s-act.
12. Department of Health and Social Care (2009) *NHS Takes the Lead on Leadership*. Available at: https://www.wired-gov.net/wg/wg-news-1.nsf/0/67E7AAC9EDD4F6BF80257544003A87F7?OpenDocument=.
13. GOV.UK (2020) *Annex B: Exercise Cygnus Report (accessible)*. Available at: https://www.gov.uk/government/publications/uk-pandemic-preparedness/exercise-cygnus-report-accessible-report.
14. NHS England (2025) *Fit for the Future: 10 Year Health Plan for England*. Available at: https://www.england.nhs.uk/long-term-plan/.
15. McKinney, S.M., et al. (2020) 'International evaluation of an AI system for breast cancer screening', *Nature*, 577(7788), pp. 89–94. https://doi.org/10.1038/s41586-019-1799-6.

16. Burgess, N. (2022) 'Six key lessons from the NHS and the Virginia Mason Institute partnership', *Warwick Business School*. Available at: https://www.wbs.ac.uk/news/six-key-lessons-from-the-nhs-and-the-virginia-mason-institute-partnership/.
17. Braithwaite, J., Ludlow, K., Testa, L., Herkes, J., Augustsson, H., Lamprell, G., McPherson, E. and Zurynski, Y. (2020) 'Built to last? The sustainability of healthcare system improvements, programmes and interventions: A systematic integrative review', *BMJ Open*, 10(6), e036453. https://doi.org/10.1136/bmjopen-2019-036453.

Chapter 15

The Immune Response

Mind the System

They were very keen to meet with us.

That phrase still echoes. In 2008, my company Innovations Factory—embedded in one of the largest hospitals in the UK—developed a solution to a problem that could only have persisted in healthcare. Anaesthetic gases escaping during paediatric surgery posed documented health risks to theatre staff, including increased miscarriage rates [1]. Children's lungs require low-pressure anaesthetic circuits that are open, which leak gases into the operating theatre. The job of the anaesthetist after a long surgery list of paediatric patients is not only to ensure their wellbeing but also to check that the surgical team does not fall asleep due to the accumulation of those gases. Worse still, it is well known to the theatre workforce that exposure to these gases might lead to miscarriages. The only solution was for pregnant female members of staff to find temporary employment elsewhere in the hospital. An unacceptable situation that would not be accepted in any other sector—'Health & Safety' and unions would have closed down facilities that poison the workforce.

We were approached by the local NHS Innovations Hub with this problem and commissioned to find a solution. With a consultant anaesthetist and industrial designer on our team, we used a textbook design thinking approach—workshops with theatre staff, research into ISO standards for anaesthetic devices, iterative concept development, CAD modelling and engineering, Computational Fluid Dynamics (CFD) analysis to visualise and optimise gas flow, 3D-printed functional prototyping and practical validation (as per framework in Chapter 5). We produced a closed gas scavenger circuit that went beyond the requirements of the standard, outperforming the open circuits on the market. Six anaesthetists and an Operating Department Practitioner unanimously agreed our innovation addressed an important unmet need. We completed development for £60,000 over eight months. The regulatory pathway was entirely reasonable: Class IIa medical device, standard technical

DOI: 10.4324/9781003752073-19

documentation, British Standards Institution (BSI) /ISO compliance, and safety validation through lab testing.

Everything worked. The methodology was sound. The evidence was compelling. The clinical need was urgent. The prototypes exceeded the requirements. So we approached the largest manufacturer and supplier of anaesthetic circuits, who were 'very keen' to meet with us. That meeting changed everything I understood about healthcare innovation.

It soon became clear that this company—which sat on the board responsible for reviewing the standard and held an effective monopoly—had no interest in collaboration. Their analysis revealed that our technology would require revision of the performance standards and a complete redesign and retooling of their entire product range. As they held a monopoly, they decided to block our solution. When we investigated producing the component ourselves as an aftermarket item, they warned they would change their connectors so it would not fit. Meanwhile, despite having a recognised health and safety issue, and commissioning us to find a solution, the NHS had no appetite to apply pressure on that supplier or to implement anything new.

The design thinking worked. The system attacked it. Not through passive resistance. Not through benign neglect. Through active, coordinated, strategic defence.

Mind the system.

The Art of the General

In ancient Greek, *strategos*—literally 'military general'—also implied mastery of the art of strategy. Healthcare leadership, whether we acknowledge it or not, is generalship. When you lead transformation efforts, you advance into hostile territory. The system defends itself with precision, coordination, and reflexes honed over decades. The question is not whether you will face resistance. Every transformation leader knows resistance is inevitable. The question is: are you equipped to recognise the system's tactics and deploy effective countermeasures?

I use military metaphors here because complex chronic disease requires simultaneous intervention across multiple systems—medication, surgery, lifestyle change, and social support, coordinated—because the disease attacks across multiple fronts. Single-intervention medicine fails. The same is true for organisational transformation. The intelligence gathering, coordinated planning, strategic attacks, and conquest I have witnessed are the actual mechanisms by which transformation attempts are eliminated. This is the strategy of the medic, not the soldier—protecting beneficial innovations from systematic destruction long enough for them to heal the system rather than be destroyed by it.

What follows is how systems eliminate transformation. And how you, as a healthcare leader committed to patient benefit, can defend your innovations long enough for them to heal the system rather than be destroyed by it.

The Pattern Revealed: Four Campaigns, Same Strategy

The gas scavenger was not an isolated case. Let me show you the pattern through four examples. Each represents a different type of transformation—political reform, technological innovation, process innovation, and management methodology. Watch how the system deploys the same strategic response every single time. I will frame each as a military campaign—Intelligence, Planning, Attack, Conquest—because that is precisely what happens.

Campaign 1: Political Reform—The Lansley Decentralisation

UK Secretary of State for Health Andrew Lansley was unusually well-informed about healthcare for a politician. His 2012 Health and Social Care Act was logical, evidence-based, and compelling: decentralise the NHS, shift commissioning power to GP-led Clinical Commissioning Groups (CCGs), and put decisions closer to patients and clinicians.

Intelligence: The managerial class scrutinised Lansley's warning shot—his white paper, 'Equity and Excellence: Liberating the NHS' [2]. They observed the reforms being introduced; monitored which clinicians were prepared versus overwhelmed. They identified every point where they could reassert control through shared management, commissioning support units, and new regional structures.

Planning: Allow implementation—you cannot openly oppose government policy. Overwhelm unprepared GPs with complexity. Position the managerial class as essential support. Prepare the narrative: 'decentralisation creates chaos.' Feed information to the union—the Royal College of General Practitioners (RCGP). Timeline: 18–24 months to reversion.

Attack: GP engagement with commissioning collapsed. A Pulse survey of GPs on the eve of the CCG handover found that 55% felt no more involved in commissioning decisions than they had under the old Primary Care Trusts—the very organisations the reforms abolished [3]. The BMA reported that nearly two-thirds of GPs either felt they had limited influence on their CCGs or that decisions were forced on them with no room for grassroots contributions [4]. Most damning: by October 2014, only a quarter of CCG accountable officers were GPs—though 80% of chairs were, a distinction that reveals exactly where real power was allowed to sit [5]. Despite Lansley's white paper promising to cut management costs by more than 45%, the reforms created over 300 new NHS organisations, and by 2025 the Health Secretary would tell Parliament that administrative staffing in NHS England and the Department of Health had more than doubled since 2010 [6]. CCG leaders accused the NHS Commissioning Board of a 'command and control' mentality [3], while the NAO found 42% of CCGs rated 'requires improvement' or 'inadequate' [7]. CCGs rapidly clustered or merged—appearing voluntary. The reforms were quietly resisted, sabotaged, and ultimately reversed.

Conquest: By 2022, the entire CCG structure was formally abolished and replaced by Integrated Care Systems—completing a full cycle of reform, resistance, and reversion. The promised decentralisation produced greater centralisation. The promised cost reduction produced expansion. The system defended itself successfully.

Campaign 1 parallels the analysis in Chapter 9. It was fascinating to witness how fast Lansley's policy was undermined, if not sabotaged, by managers. Lansley wanted to do the right thing, but he did not prepare the clinical workforce for their new role. There were not enough clinicians capable and prepared to take on the role of leading healthcare commissioning. GPs in those roles became quickly overwhelmed as most still had to see to their patients too. The system exploited that gap with remarkable speed and precision.

Campaign 2: Technology Innovation—The Gas Scavenger

You already know this story. Our textbook design thinking process delivered a solution to an urgent safety problem. ISO-compliant. Clinically validated. Cost-effective.

Intelligence: The monopoly manufacturer was 'very keen to meet.' Reconnaissance, not collaboration.

Planning: Assess threat: superior performance requires standards revision plus complete product line redesign. Calculate: cost of adaptation versus cost of elimination. Decision: elimination is cheaper. Exploit standards board position.

Attack: Standards board authority weaponised. Monopoly position exploited. Connector incompatibility threatened.

Conquest: Innovation died at the delivery stage. Every innovation in our portfolio met the same fate. By 2016, we closed Innovations Factory. 100% rejection rate. Company extinction.

Campaign 3: Process Innovation—The Devi Shetty Scenario

Dr Devi Shetty trained as a paediatric heart surgeon in the UK at Guy's and St Thomas' Hospital. He returned to India where he innovated cardiac surgery through assembly-line principles, task-shifting to trained local community members, and cross-subsidisation business models [8]. His hospital performs more heart operations annually than the entire UK, at costs 75% lower, with equivalent clinical outcomes [9].

I had the privilege of visiting Narayana Health. It was overwhelming to see so many children in intensive care, all getting great care. Afterwards, I asked Devi if he would have been able to achieve this if he had stayed in the UK. His response was emphatic and unprintable: absolutely not.

That frank response speaks volumes. Here is what would have happened:

Intelligence: Professional bodies would immediately investigate the labour pyramid model. Regulators would scrutinise task-shifting for licensing violations. Trade unions would calculate membership threat. NHS finance would project cost to existing structures.

Planning: Activate multiple defensive systems simultaneously. Professional bodies: ethics violations. Regulators: licensing barriers. Unions: workforce exploitation claims. Finance: 'unsustainable' cost modelling. Culture: 'patients expect to see their doctor.'

Attack: Task-shifting flagged as patient safety risk. Professional boundaries enforced. Union resistance mobilised. He would face a choice between clinical or managerial role—never both.

Conquest: Preventive victory. The threat never materialises because the system makes innovation structurally impossible. You cannot fix an existing system while building a new one. The constraints are baked in.

Campaign 4: Methodology Resistance—The £1 Billion Lean Experiment

Between 2005 and 2013, the NHS invested approximately £1 billion in Lean methodology through the NHS Institute for Innovation and Improvement and 150 participating hospitals (see Chapter 11). The flagship Productive Ward: Releasing Time to Care programme rolled out across nearly every acute trust in England, promising better care at lower cost.

Intelligence: The NHS Institute watched implementation across 150 Trusts. Academic warnings emerged in 2006, 2010, and 2013—all catalogued as 'resistance' rather than evidence. Mortality data showed no improvement. The system gathered data while maintaining the narrative.

Planning: Brand it attractively. Invest massively—£1 billion is too big to admit failure. Allow implementation while preparing the exit strategy. Blame 'poor implementation' rather than methodology when it fails. Suppress contradictory evidence.

Attack: High abandonment rate, with withdrawals under-reported. Academic research by Radnor et al. found that despite its popularity, Lean in healthcare had failed to deliver on its promise to significantly improve quality and productivity [10]. No meaningful improvement in mortality rates, hospital-acquired infections, staff satisfaction, or patient-reported outcomes. Mortality data showing failure was declined for publication as 'not a priority.'

Conquest: Quietly discontinued across Trusts. Zero accountability for £1 billion spent. 'Poor implementation' narrative protects the methodology. Institutional learning: 'Lean does not work in healthcare' becomes the system's memory that blocks similar methodologies. Complete failure disguised as a learning opportunity.

Between 2006 and 2013, I made repeated attempts to warn healthcare leaders and politicians about the dangers of applying manufacturing methodologies to healthcare systems. In 2006, I offered validated complexity management systems based on design thinking principles to the Prime Minister's Office. In 2010, I published 'The Lean Mean Killing Machine' warning of implementation dangers. In 2013, I presented Hospital Standardised Mortality Ratio (HSMR) evidence to the *Health Service Journal* showing deteriorating outcomes. These warnings were systematically ignored—not because they lacked evidence, but because they challenged institutional orthodoxy. This pattern of institutional deafness what Rachel Pope later characterised as the NHS being 'systemically deaf, bullying, and defensive' [11]—explains how dangerous methodologies became embedded despite early warnings from clinicians and researchers.

Attack by Air, Land, and Sea

Winston Churchill understood a fundamental principle of warfare: victory requires coordinated assault across all domains. Healthcare systems have learned this lesson perfectly.

Your innovation might survive an air attack—you manage policy, secure regulatory approval, align with strategic frameworks. The gas scavenger met all ISO standards. Lansley's reforms had government backing.

It might survive a land attack—you win over clinicians, demonstrate clinical benefit, prove superior outcomes. Six anaesthetists unanimously endorsed the gas scavenger. Devi Shetty's model delivered world-class results.

It might even survive a sea attack—you secure funding, demonstrate return on investment, show cost-effectiveness. The NHS co-funded the gas scavenger. Lean received £1 billion.

But the system attacks across all three domains simultaneously. And that is why excellence is not enough.

Air: Narrative Control. The high-altitude battle over how the innovation is framed, regulated, and understood. The gas scavenger faced 'standards need revision.' Lansley's reforms were reframed as 'decentralisation creates chaos.' Lean failures were attributed to 'poor implementation.' Control the air, control the narrative. The system owns the airspace.

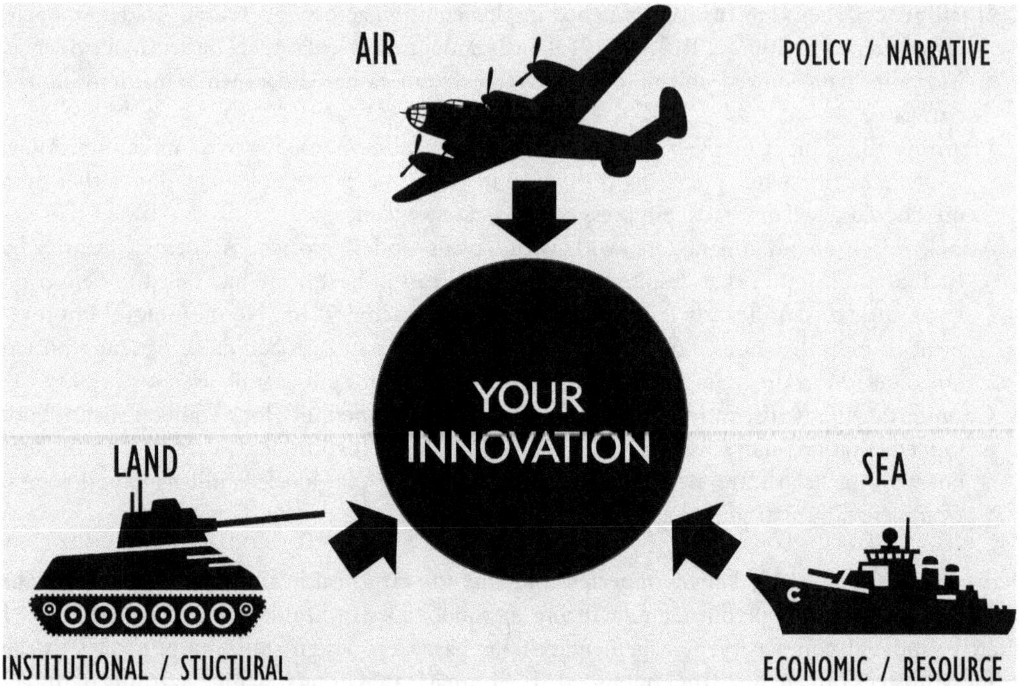

Figure 15.1 The Air/Land/Sea framework.

Land: Institutional and Structural Barriers. The ground war through professional hierarchies, licensing requirements, standards boards, managerial structures. Lansley's reforms faced managerial 'support' structures that recaptured authority. The gas scavenger encountered a standards board controlled by the incumbent. Devi Shetty would face licensing barriers, professional boundaries, union mobilisation. Hold the territory, control the system.

Sea: Economic and Resource Control. The supply chain strangulation through procurement, funding mechanisms, market access, capital requirements. Lansley's centralised finance would not support CCG scaling. The gas scavenger faced a monopoly market position plus NHS procurement 'no appetite.' Lean's £1 billion sunk cost protected the methodology from accountability. Control the resources, starve the innovation.

The Air/Land/Sea framework is itself a design thinking diagnostic as described in Chapter 7—it applies systematic analysis to resistance patterns.

This is why single-domain excellence fails. You win the air battle while losing the ground war. You secure funding while the narrative destroys you. You have clinical evidence while institutional structures strangle implementation. Understanding what you are fighting comes before knowing how to fight it.

The Pattern, Not the Person

Over the years, I have watched these patterns unfold and felt what every transformation leader feels at some point: anger at the forces that block progress. The managerial class sabotaging well-intentioned reforms. The manufacturer crushing a life-saving innovation to protect market share. The bureaucrats with 'no appetite' for change that could save lives and reduce costs. The professional bodies blocking task-shifting that would extend care to underserved populations.

It is natural to personalise this resistance. To see it as a moral failure. To crusade against villainy.

But here is the shift that changes everything: this is not about evil people. It is about systematic responses.

The manufacturer who blocked our gas scavenger was not evil. The managers who reversed Lansley's reforms were not consciously choosing to harm patients. The NHS executives who abandoned Lean despite £1 billion invested were not corrupt. They were all expressing something larger than individual choice: systematic organisational responses to perceived threats.

When we introduced the gas scavenger, the system evaluated it on structural impact: would this require redesigning product lines? Would it shift market power? Would it expose existing inefficiencies? When Lansley attempted decentralisation, the system resisted because redistributing authority threatened established coordination mechanisms reinforced over decades. When Devi Shetty's model would challenge professional boundaries, resistance emerges from protective structures around licensing, professional identity, and quality assurance—structures that exist for good reasons but that also block beneficial innovation.

This pattern is so effective that it operates in plain sight without being recognised—or at least without being acknowledged. In March 2025, the Health Secretary told Parliament that Lansley's reforms were 'disastrous' and a 'calamity without international precedent,' before announcing yet another wholesale reorganisation: the abolition of NHS England itself [6]. He is not a stupid man. He is surrounded by capable colleagues and seasoned officials. Yet the entire Parliamentary debate proceeded as though the failure of the 2012 reforms was attributable to one minister's misjudgement, rather than to a management and governance infrastructure so deeply bunkered that it resists transformation from every direction—top-down, bottom-up, left, right, internal, external.

Either the pattern is genuinely invisible to people operating at the highest levels of government, which tells you how effective the camouflage is. Or they can see it but cannot say so, because no politician can stand at the dispatch box and admit that the system they are about to reorganise will quietly digest their reforms just as it digested their predecessor's. Both possibilities lead to the same conclusion: the immune response does not merely defeat reform. It erases the memory that resistance occurred at all, ensuring each new government arrives convinced that *this time* the problem was simply the last lot getting it wrong.

This is why replacing individuals does not change outcomes. New managers execute the same reversal patterns. Different manufacturers use the same blocking tactics. Fresh leadership faces identical resistance. The responses are structural, not personal.

Why the System Learns Dysfunction

All defensive systems face a fundamental tension: precise evaluation versus response speed. Properly assessing whether an innovation will improve patient outcomes requires evaluating multiple criteria, understanding contextual factors, predicting implementation challenges, and coordinating stakeholder perspectives. This takes time and cognitive resources.

Rigid rejection criteria—'does not fit strategic priorities,' 'insufficient evidence,' 'budgetary constraints'—can be applied universally without deep analysis. Fast, cheap, effective.

Organisations learn which defensive mechanisms work. Each time a rigid rejection criterion successfully prevents a politically dangerous innovation—one that threatens some stakeholder's interests—that criterion gets reinforced. Personnel learn that saying 'yes' to innovation is career-limiting. Risk-averse behaviour becomes cultural norm. Decision rules simplify: when in doubt, block.

The crudest, most efficient blocking mechanisms outcompete thorough evaluation through demonstrated success at protecting stakeholder interests. This is organisational path dependency meeting evolutionary selection [12, 13]. The system learns dysfunction because dysfunction is rewarded.

What This Changes

Understanding systematic responses rather than personal villainy changes your practice in three ways. You stop fighting ghosts—replacing 'bad actors' with 'good people' addresses nothing when the responses are structural. You start predicting resistance—because systematic responses follow patterns. Propose anything that redistributes decision-making authority and the managerial clustering reflex triggers. Threaten incumbent market position and standards become weaponised. Challenge professional boundaries and licensing concerns emerge. Require structural adaptation and the 'no appetite' reflex deploys. Knowing which reflex your innovation activates lets you prepare defences before the system responds, not after you are already under attack. And you sustain strategic energy over the years that transformation demands. Moral crusades against imagined villains are exhausting; managing predictable organisational responses is sustainable work. When you understand you are navigating system behaviour rather than fighting evil, you can maintain commitment across the full 18–24 month timeline your innovation needs to survive.

Recognition is the first step. Diagnosis is the second.

Diagnostic Framework: Recognising the Reflexes

The four campaigns reveal four distinct system reflexes. Each triggers under specific conditions and follows a predictable pattern. Recognising which reflex your innovation activates is the first step to surviving it.

Table 15.1 The Four Types of System Reflexes

Reflex Type	*You Are Triggering This Reflex If*
Reflex 1: Decentralisation	Your initiative distributes decision-making authority. Managers suddenly offer 'supportive' clustering or shared services. Implementation timeline keeps extending 'to ensure success.'
Reflex 2: Innovation Threat	Incumbents want extensive meetings before you have launched. Questions focus on scale and market impact, not clinical benefit. Standards suddenly require 'revision' for your product.
Reflex 3: Professional Boundaries	Your model involves task-shifting or role changes. Professional bodies request 'consultations.' Licensing 'concerns' emerge from regulators.
Reflex 4: Methodology Adoption	The system adopts your approach enthusiastically—too fast. Implementation funding secured easily. No structural changes required for adoption.

Reflex 4 is the most dangerous because it looks like success. When the system embraces your methodology without requiring structural change, it is absorbing and neutralising the threat. Lean received £1 billion precisely because accepting it was easier than implementing it. The methodology was adopted. The transformation was eliminated.

COUNTERINTUITIVE FINDING

When the System Says Yes, You Should Worry Most

The NHS invested approximately £1 billion in Lean methodology across 150 hospitals. By every conventional measure—funding secured, leadership buy-in achieved, rollout completed—this was a transformation success. Academic evaluation found no meaningful improvement in mortality, infections, satisfaction, or patient-reported outcomes. The methodology was adopted. The transformation was eliminated. Enthusiastic adoption without structural change is the system's most sophisticated defence. It neutralises the threat, consumes resources that might fund alternatives, and generates institutional memory ('we tried that') that blocks future attempts. Of the four reflexes, this is the only one indistinguishable from genuine success until it is too late. The diagnostic test: has your innovation required the organisation to change who makes decisions, how resources are allocated, or which outcomes are measured? If the answer is no, you have been absorbed, not adopted. Genuine transformation always creates structural friction. Frictionless adoption is the warning sign.

Resistance Levels

The resistance level framework introduced in Chapter 12 serves as your diagnostic compass. Level 1 innovations (drop-in replacements) face minimal resistance. Level 2 (process-dependent) requires workflow integration and moderate resistance management. Level 3 (disruptive pathway) triggers active defence that demands multi-year strategic commitment. Level 4 (governance-threatening) activates the full organisational defence—success at this level requires political and regulatory change beyond any single organisation's control.

Assess your innovation honestly. Most leaders overestimate their innovation's disruptive potential while underestimating the resistance level it triggers. A pink stethoscope is Level 1. An AI diagnostic that replaces specialist referrals is Level 3. A transparency tool that reveals cost variations across providers is Level 4. Each requires fundamentally different strategy, timeline, and resource commitment.

Critical Windows

Resistance follows a temporal pattern that is remarkably consistent across different types of transformation:

Month 6: Initial tolerance gives way to organised questioning. If you have not established your narrative and secured your coalition by this point, the system's counter-narrative gains dominance.

Month 12: Institutional memory forms. Your innovation is categorised as either 'part of how we work' or 'that project we are managing.' If you are still categorised as the latter, structural lock-in becomes exponentially harder.

Month 18: The reversion window opens. Budgets are reviewed. Champions move on or burn out. The system begins actively unwinding your progress through structural mechanisms—reorganisation, reprioritisation, leadership rotation.

Month 24: If reversion has not been completed, the system typically accepts the new reality. Your innovation is integrated rather than attacked. But reaching this point requires surviving the 18–24 month assault with sufficient structural commitments, economic independence, and narrative control intact.

Centralised Versus Fragmented Systems: Different Resistance, Same Outcome

The resistance patterns described above manifest differently depending on system architecture. Understanding which type you operate within determines your defensive strategy.

Centralised Systems—the NHS, Kaiser Permanente, large integrated health networks—deploy unified resistance quickly. When the NHS decided Lean had served its purpose, the abandonment was systematic across 150 Trusts. When the managerial class reversed Lansley's decentralisation, the clustering and recapture happened through coordinated mechanisms nationwide. Centralised systems have shorter decision chains, unified narrative control, and the ability to apply blocking criteria uniformly. The advantage: resistance is visible, identifiable, and follows clear institutional channels. The disadvantage: once the central system decides to block, there is no alternative pathway.

Fragmented Systems—US healthcare, many European multi-payer systems, developing healthcare systems—resist through uncoordinated but multiplicative barriers. No single entity blocks your innovation. Instead, you face separate resistance from each payer, each provider network, each regulatory body, each professional association, each procurement system. Each barrier is individually navigable. Collectively, they are lethal. A medical device startup in the US might secure FDA clearance, obtain reimbursement codes from Centers for Medicare & Medicaid Services (CMS), gain formulary inclusion at three hospital systems, achieve clinical champion endorsement—and still fail because the remaining twelve barriers consume all remaining capital and time.

Having experienced the NHS's unified blocking power through Innovations Factory—where a single governance structure could eliminate every innovation in our portfolio—and the US system's multiplicative barriers through OnKai—where FDA clearance, reimbursement coding, institutional adoption, federal policy and state-level variation each demanded separate navigation—the contrast is stark but the outcome identical.

The Diagnostic Implication: In centralised systems, identify the single decision pathway and concentrate your multi-domain defence on that pathway. In fragmented systems, identify the minimum viable set of barriers you must overcome for initial viability, establish a beachhead, and expand systematically. Both systems kill innovation through coordination failure—centralised systems coordinate resistance explicitly; fragmented systems coordinate it accidentally through independent actors applying the same blocking heuristics.

The resistance pattern is universal. The tactical response must be adapted to the system architecture you face.

Two Paths

Path 1: Excellence Without Defence

You design brilliant healthcare innovations using world-class methodology. You engage stakeholders beautifully. You develop compelling evidence. You present to leadership with passion and professionalism. The system deploys its reflexes.

Within 18–24 months, your innovation is quietly abandoned, defunded, or 'evolved' into something unrecognisable. You are demoralised. Your team is exhausted. Your champions are sceptical of the next initiative. You blame yourself for insufficient quality, inadequate stakeholder engagement, or poor communication.

But the innovation failed not because it lacked excellence. It failed because excellence without defence is vulnerability.

Path 2: Excellence with Defence

You design the same brilliant innovation using the same methodology. But before announcing, you build a coalition. You secure external funding. You establish narrative control. You create structural commitments. The system deploys the same reflexes.

But this time you are ready. Narrative attacks encounter pre-positioned countermeasures—your framing is already established, external voices are already amplifying, and stakeholders unconsciously adopt your language when discussing the innovation. Institutional resistance meets coordinated coalition pressure—your allies sit on the committees making decisions, your structural commitments make reversal costly, and your alternative pathways bypass the blockade. Economic strangulation fails because you have diversified funding across sources the system does not control. The reflexes still trigger. The resistance still emerges. The timeline still pressures you.

But you survive the critical 18–24 months. Your structural commitments make reversal politically and economically costly. Your coalition creates institutional momentum. Your external pressure makes blocking visible and accountable. By month 24, the system accepts the new reality. Your innovation is integrated rather than attacked. Patient benefit is being delivered rather than discussed.

You succeeded not because your design was better than Path 1. You succeeded because you defended the excellent design you created.

The Deeper Question

Why? Why do healthcare systems respond to transformation attempts with such predictable, coordinated resistance? Why across all three domains simultaneously? Why the 18–24 month reversion timeline? Why do advanced systems like the NHS resist more effectively than developing healthcare systems? Why do good people—people who genuinely care about patients—execute patterns that block beneficial innovation? The patterns we have observed in this chapter hint at something systematic. Five characteristics demand explanation:

Predictability. Systems follow consistent playbooks across different contexts—from political reform to technology innovation to methodology adoption. The campaigns differ. The strategy is identical.

Coordination. Resistance happens across multiple domains simultaneously without explicit conspiracy. No one convenes a meeting to plan the destruction of beneficial innovation. The coordination emerges from structural alignment of interests.

Evolution. More mature systems have more sophisticated resistance. The NHS blocks innovation more effectively than younger healthcare systems—its defensive mechanisms have had decades to develop and refine.

Independence from individuals. Replacing people does not change outcomes. New managers execute the same patterns. New leadership faces identical resistance. The behaviour belongs to the system, not the person.

Timeline consistency. The 18–24 month reversion window appears across different types of transformation, different healthcare systems, and different countries. Something structural drives that timeline.

These are not rhetorical questions. They have answers. Understanding why these patterns exist—the fundamental mechanisms that drive organisational responses to transformation—would change everything. It would let us design healthcare governance that welcomes rather than attacks beneficial change. That question is the subject of ongoing research that I will share in forthcoming work. But here is what matters for you as a healthcare leader: you do not need to understand why to succeed. You need to understand *that* and *how*.

Bridge to Part V

You now possess three complementary diagnostic frameworks: structural barriers (Chapter 13), political dynamics (Chapter 14), and resistance patterns (Chapter 15). You understand WHAT blocks innovation, WHO blocks it and why, and HOW systems fight back over time. Armed with these three diagnostic frameworks, you are ready for tactical implementation. Part V provides your implementation toolkit—the transformation control room that coordinates your response (Chapter 16) and the detailed tactical playbook for defending your innovation in every domain (Chapter 17).

Here is how to transform healthcare anyway.

References

1. Centers for Disease Control and Prevention (2025) *About Anesthetic Gases and Reproductive Health.* Reproductive Health and the Workplace. Available at: https://www.cdc.gov/niosh/reproductive-health/prevention/anesthetic-gases.html.
2. GOV.UK (2010) *Equity and Excellence: Liberating the NHS.* Available at: https://www.gov.uk/government/news/equity-and-excellence-liberating-the-nhs .

3. Kaffash, J. (2013) 'Revealed: Majority of GPs no more involved with commissioning under CCGs', *Pulse Today*. Available at: https://www.pulsetoday.co.uk/news/nhs-structures/revealed-majority-of-gps-no-more-involved-with-commissioning-under-ccgs/.
4. Majeed, A. (2015) 'Are CCGs a failed experiment?', *Pulse Today*. Available at: https://www.pulsetoday.co.uk/views/debate/are-ccgs-a-failed-experiment/.
5. Welikala, J. (2014) 'GPs hold only a quarter of accountable CCG roles', *Health Service Journal*. Available at: https://www.hsj.co.uk/integrated-care/gps-hold-only-a-quarter-of-accountable-ccg-roles/5075761.article.
6. UK Parliament (2025) 'NHS England update', *Hansard*, 13 March. Available at: https://hansard.parliament.uk/commons/2025-03-13/debates/25838956-1EFB-4AF7-BFB2-67CBCDA59DA9/NHSEnglandUpdate.
7. National Audit Office (2018) *A Review of the Role and Costs of Clinical Commissioning Groups*. Available at: https://www.nao.org.uk/reports/a-review-of-the-role-and-costs-of-clinical-commissioning-groups/.
8. Muralidhara, G.V. (2016) *Dr Devi Shetty of Narayana Hrudayalaya: Delivering Quality Cardiac Care to the Masses*. The Case Centre. Available at: https://www.thecasecentre.org/products/view?id=137186.
9. Jayakumar, D., et al. (2024) 'Dr. Devi Prasad Shetty: The visionary cardiothoracic surgeon who championed affordable healthcare', *Cureus*, 16. https://doi.org/10.7759/cureus.70683.
10. Radnor, Z.J., Holweg, M. and Waring, J. (2012) 'Lean in healthcare: The unfilled promise?', *Social Science & Medicine*, 74(3), pp. 364–371. https://doi.org/10.1016/j.socscimed.2011.02.011.
11. Pope, R. (2017) 'The NHS: Sticking fingers in its ears, humming loudly', *Journal of Business Ethics*, 145(3), pp. 577–598. https://doi.org/10.1007/s10551-015-2861-4.
12. North, D.C. (1990) *Institutions, Institutional Change and Economic Performance*. Cambridge: Cambridge University Press. https://doi.org/10.1017/CBO9780511808678.
13. Nelson, R.R. and Winter, S.G. (2004) *An Evolutionary Theory of Economic Change*. Digitally reprinted edition. Cambridge, MA: The Belknap Press of Harvard University Press.

IMPLEMENTATION TOOLKIT

V

Chapter 16

The Healthcare Transformation Control Room

TO DISRUPT OR NOT TO DISRUPT

In 2012 I was the Royal Academy of Engineering's Visiting Professor at Cranfield University and still Managing Director of the Innovations Factory based at a large NHS hospital. I had read Clayton Christensen's 'The Innovator's Prescription' [1] like one of the 'The Harry Potter' books—not putting it down until the end—as it provided the framework to fit my jigsaw pieces into place. One phrase I always remember is in his acknowledgement where the great man admitted about the healthcare sector: 'Wrapping my brain around the whole of it took 3.1416x more time, and 10x more intellectual energy than I imagined it could.' It was entirely predictable that so many of my endeavours failed: I had missed that several were potential disruptive innovations and had to be treated accordingly. Moreover, I chose to operate in the most complex sector—healthcare. If only Christensen had published his theory ten years earlier...

At Cranfield I had the opportunity to test and apply Christensen's theory. This was against the backdrop of the Lansley reforms to decentralise the NHS and give more power to primary care physicians—the General Practitioners (GPs)—and set up local Clinical Commissioning Groups (CCGs) [2].

In 2009, GE had introduced the Vscan—a pocket-sized ultrasound scanner that looked like a cross between an Apple iPod and a flip-top mobile phone [3]. They acquired a company that developed the device for cardiologists. GE saw a much wider application—their expectation was that it would become as ubiquitous as the stethoscope, that every clinician would carry one in their pocket or bag. A potential disruptive innovation, but adoption was disappointing.

In his book *Disrupting Class*, Christensen had already defined disruptive innovation as that which enables 'a larger population of less-skilled, less-wealthy people to do things in more convenient, lower-cost settings that historically could be done only by specialists in centralised, inconvenient locations' [4]. Unlike X-ray, ultrasound is a harmless technology

DOI: 10.4324/9781003752073-21

that requires no special protection or facilities. GPs doing diagnostic ultrasound in the comfort of the patient's home or community instead of them having to travel to a hospital, to be seen by a specialist sonographer or radiologist, completely met this description. Christensen also taught us that three conditions had to be in place for successful disruptive innovation: a simplifying technology, a business model innovation, and a value network. The GE Vscan certainly met the first criterion. So why the absence of adoption? Did GE omit the other two elements?

We managed to purchase a Vscan cheaply through one of the GE sales reps on condition we share our research findings. A couple of talented students dedicated several months to a textbook co-design process as part of their MSc projects. In the first diamond, we explored current diagnostic imaging practice in the NHS. After detailed pathway modelling and stakeholder mapping, we observed and interviewed GPs, commissioners, and followed patients on their pathway from referral to diagnostic imaging in hospitals. We interviewed radiologists, diagnostic sonographers, procurement managers [13].

We found that using an ultrasound device falls outside the medical curriculum and requires extensive additional training. The average clinician might interpret X-rays or even operate a simple X-ray machine; for ultrasound you need an excellent three-dimensional knowledge of normal anatomical and abnormal pathological structures. As soon as you put the probe on the patient's body you need to orientate yourself—where are you? What can you see? What is normal? What is suspect? What is definitely pathological? That takes years of training and supervision—not part of the GE Vscan package.

Across several regions and CCGs, we encountered a couple of GPs who could readily use Vscan because one had learned to use ultrasound as a doctor aboard cruise ships, the other because she had used ultrasound as a gynaecologist before becoming a GP. Other GPs lacked the skill. We also found that sonographers in NHS hospitals spent 80% of their time on patients who required no further imaging after the scan, suggesting that many referrals were of limited diagnostic value and highlighting the potential for better triage of ultrasound demand.

One of the students co-designed an app that helped GPs use the Vscan to explore the relatively straightforward diagnosis of gallstones—with guidance on probe positioning and movement, a library of reference pictures of normal and pathological conditions, and the ability to refer images to experienced radiologists or directly to surgeons. The other student developed an app for a GP practice to determine costs and benefits of different scenarios: whether they should train one of their physicians or a practice nurse, have a peripatetic sonographer visit once a week, or club together with neighbouring practices.

When we presented prototypes to a very experienced radiologist, close to retirement, he supported the idea and was prepared to accredit GPs who had completed a half-day 'gallstones' course. Another radiologist, who had just earned his consultant stripes, vehemently opposed the concept—'GPs could never correctly interpret such a sophisticated device and would pose a danger to patients.' Bypassing radiologists and directly sending pictures to surgeons was an absolute no-no. This confirmed the stakeholder interest dynamics mapped in Chapter 14.

The most telling outcome was the abject rejection by the NHS. Despite textbook co-design with stakeholders across the system—including directors of several CCGs—they should have bitten our hands off. The project was precisely aligned with what policy wanted: decentralisation, shifting power and activity into community care. We failed to get any appointment with decision-makers in CCGs or NHS headquarters. 'No time.' 'Too busy with re-organisation.' 'Not our current priority.'

The Vscan project taught me something the textbooks missed. Consider what we had in our favour. The timing was ideal: government policy was actively pushing decentralisation and shifting power to primary care through the new Clinical Commissioning Groups. We had institutional credibility: the Royal Academy of Engineering and Cranfield University. We followed textbook co-design methodology. The technology was proven, the business case was strong. A GP lead in a local CCG had bought into our solution. Individual stakeholders across the system—GPs, a senior radiologist, commissioners—could see the value.

None of it mattered. The system put the shutters up. We could not get a single appointment with any other decision-maker in CCGs or NHS headquarters. 'No time.' 'Too busy with re-organisation.' 'Not our current priority.' The very organisations created to decentralise healthcare refused to look at an innovation that would do exactly that. Christensen's three conditions for disruptive innovation require a fourth: a governance structure willing to listen.

COUNTERINTUITIVE FINDING

Perfect Strategic Alignment Cannot Overcome Governance Failure

A disruptive innovation that met every condition for adoption—policy alignment (Lansley decentralisation reforms), institutional credibility (Royal Academy of Engineering, Cranfield University), textbook co-design methodology, proven technology, strong business case, and individual stakeholder buy-in including a GP commissioning lead—was not merely rejected but ignored. The organisations specifically created to decentralise NHS care refused to even meet with innovators offering a decentralising innovation. This suggests that transformation failure is not primarily a problem of alignment, evidence, or methodology—it is a structural property of governance itself. Christensen's three conditions for disruptive innovation (simplifying technology, business model innovation, value network) require a fourth: a governance structure willing to listen.

This was more than a project failure. It was a trust failure—between innovators and institutions, between policy intent and operational reality, between communities and the systems that claimed to serve them. That erosion of trust, I would come to understand, ran far deeper than one rejected ultrasound project.

The Trust Deficit

There was a time, within living memory, that healthcare professionals were embedded in the communities they served. Midwives delivered babies across generations in the same family. Doctors knew what issues the community faced—poor harvests, unemployment, contamination, infectious diseases—and how it affected patients and families. Healthcare professionals were visible in and therefore accountable to the community. They built trust—the ingredient that binds communities together.

The COVID-19 pandemic revealed how completely this trust had broken down. Living in Bermondsey in London, I witnessed how quickly the local community rallied to support vulnerable people—informal networks, with the fishmonger on the local market square at the centre, that already knew who needed help. The healthcare system failed to match this community response. Hospitals discharged vulnerable people into communities and care homes to make room for critically ill patients. Political decision-makers proved illiterate about viral infections, setting up VIP lanes to fast-track their associates' PPE contracts. The very people elected to serve us ended up knee-jerking policies that were ineffective at best.

Experts—like myself and fellow members of the European Health Futures Forum (EHFF)—had warned for many years that healthcare was unsustainable. We had pointed out the danger of transposing just-in-time delivery from the automotive sector into healthcare. The scientific community had already warned a pandemic would occur. Exercise Cygnus in the UK had demonstrated that the NHS and public health would be woefully unprepared. Those warnings went unheeded [5]. When the pandemic struck, healthcare systems entered a rare state of plasticity. Rules were suspended, silos dissolved, innovation flourished at the edges. Scientists, regulators and pharma companies collaborated across disciplines. Digital health tools, trapped in pilot purgatory for years, were deployed at scale within weeks. For a moment, necessity achieved what decades of reform rhetoric had failed to deliver.

Then the system's defensive structures activated. As Chapter 15 documented, the same governance mechanisms that had long resisted change set about restoring the old equilibrium. Temporary freedoms were withdrawn. Emergency funding dried up. The rhetoric of transformation was replaced by the familiar language of recovery and backlog reduction. The pandemic was an extraordinary stressor: it triggered adaptive behaviour, but the underlying governance structures remained unchanged. Once the pressure eased, the system reverted—back into the same dysfunction, only with longer waiting times.

The tragedy was the failure to institutionalise the innovation. There was no mechanism to capture, encode, and stabilise adaptive learning within governance itself. Every act of ingenuity remained temporary: useful in crisis, disposable in normality.

The answer, as we shall see, is a coordination architecture I call the Healthcare Transformation Control Room.

A Precedent for Trustless Trust

We had seen this pattern before—in finance, not healthcare. The 2008 global financial crisis was caused by failed governance structures that allowed casino-bankers to gamble with public money with impunity. When the system crashed, they faced no accountability. Politicians and central banks bailed them out with taxpayers' money, then imposed austerity measures on those very citizens that deeply damaged trust in institutions. Cuts to education, healthcare, justice, and welfare were exploited by unscrupulous populists.

Almost immediately a counter-movement emerged, enabled by technology. The mysterious Satoshi Nakamoto timed the release of his white paper 'Bitcoin: A Peer-to-Peer Electronic Cash System' just weeks after the US government announced the $2 trillion Emergency Economic Stabilization Act [6]. Bitcoin gave rise to an alternative financial system based on 'trustless trust'—a distributed ledger where every transaction is cryptographically linked, verified by consensus across a decentralised network, and immutable once recorded. Consider a system where every safety incident report is immutably recorded, every response is tracked, and no report can be 'lost' in administrative processes. That's what blockchain governance enables. Chapter 9 introduced how this architecture applies to healthcare governance.

Building on blockchain's foundation, smart contracts—self-executing agreements coded directly into the ledger—remove ambiguity, delay, and discretionary control. From there emerged Decentralised Autonomous Organisations (DAOs): entities governed by collective decision rules rather than executives or boards, where every decision and transaction is visible on the public ledger. Governance becomes radically transparent.

Think of a DAO as a virtual board of trustees where every vote, every expenditure, and every decision is permanently recorded and publicly visible—no minutes that misrepresent what was agreed, no budgets that obscure where money went.

These characteristics directly address the structural pathologies documented throughout this book. Transparency counters the information asymmetry that allows inefficiency and vested interests to persist unchallenged. Distributed governance dismantles the bottlenecks that paralyse large institutions. Immutable record-keeping ensures that learning and accountability are preserved—unlike the pandemic, when system improvisations evaporated once the emergency receded. Programmable coordination through smart contracts allows incentives and feedback loops to be redesigned for collaboration and prevention, rather than throughput and control.

DAOs provide a fundamentally different governance substrate. They make it technically possible to deliver what healthcare reformers have long claimed to desire: genuine participation, continuous learning, and transparent accountability at scale.

Teal Organisations: The Diagnostic Lens

Architecture alone cannot transform healthcare. We also need to understand why existing organisations systematically reject innovation—and what the alternative looks like in practice.

Frederic Laloux's breakthrough book *Reinventing Organizations* provides a diagnostic framework already transforming companies across multiple industries [7]. Laloux identifies five organisational development stages, each colour-coded to represent fundamentally different operating logics:

Red organisations operate through power—a single leader commanding through fear. In healthcare: small autocratic private practices. Innovation capacity is whatever the boss decides.

Amber organisations operate through hierarchy and formal process—'this is how we've always done it.' In healthcare: traditional NHS Trusts and hierarchical hospitals. Innovation capacity is limited to incremental process improvement within rigid structures.

Orange organisations are achievement-oriented and mechanistic—'show me the ROI.' In healthcare: corporate hospital chains and efficiency-focused systems. Innovation proceeds only when it serves measurable profit or efficiency metrics.

Green organisations are values-driven and consensus-oriented—stakeholder inclusion, empowerment rhetoric. In healthcare: community health centres, some European systems. Innovation stalls through consensus paralysis.

Teal organisations are self-organising with evolutionary purpose—distributed authority, continuous adaptation. In healthcare: Buurtzorg in the Netherlands, and precious few others. Innovation emerges naturally from the frontline.

Most healthcare systems are Amber-Orange hybrids. Amber hierarchies (consultant clinicians above junior doctors above nurses above healthcare assistants) combine with Orange metrics obsession (waiting times, efficiency targets, cost per case) and Green aspiration (patient-centred care rhetoric, stakeholder engagement workshops). Zero Teal characteristics: centralised authority, standardised processes, metric-driven control.

This hybrid creates systematic innovation rejection. Amber says: 'That's not how we do things here.' Orange says: 'Show me the ROI before we pilot.' Green says: 'We need consensus from all stakeholders.' Result: innovation dies before implementation—precisely what happened with the GE Vscan.

Organisational colour matters for design thinking because that requires rapid prototyping (which fails in Amber: 'get approval first'), learning from failure (which fails in Orange: 'failure is not a KPI'), distributed decision-making (which fails in centralised structures), and user-centred iteration (which fails when process standardisation is the priority). Teal organisations enable design thinking naturally: authority at point of care, rapid local experimentation, learning through doing, evolutionary adaptation.

Healthcare systems cannot jump from Amber-Orange to Teal directly. But understanding organisational colour diagnoses why specific transformation initiatives fail, suggests appropriate transformation strategies, and reveals which innovations a system can absorb versus which it will reject. The 'teal-ising' tactics offer a practical pathway: create 'teal islands'—autonomous service lines or community clinics insulated from established rules; shift risk to capitated or value-based contracts where self-managing teams capture the upside; start with non-clinical functions to prove the model, then expand; use patient-journey design sprints to surface pain points clinicians already want solved, then let them own the solutions.

Buurtzorg demonstrates these principles at scale. As Chapter 9 detailed, 14,000 nurses in self-managing teams achieve superior outcomes at lower cost—higher patient satisfaction scores, better health outcomes, lower costs per patient, and higher nurse retention rates compared to traditional centralised home care [8]. The evidence is clear: Teal principles work in healthcare. The question is how to create the coordination infrastructure that enables more Buurtzorgs to emerge.

The InterAlign Transformation Framework

Understanding organisational colour reveals the diagnosis. Translating that diagnosis into action requires a holistic framework that maps the interdependencies between transformation elements.

The InterAlign Transformation Framework visualises the critical relationship between five key elements of healthcare transformation (Figure 16.1):

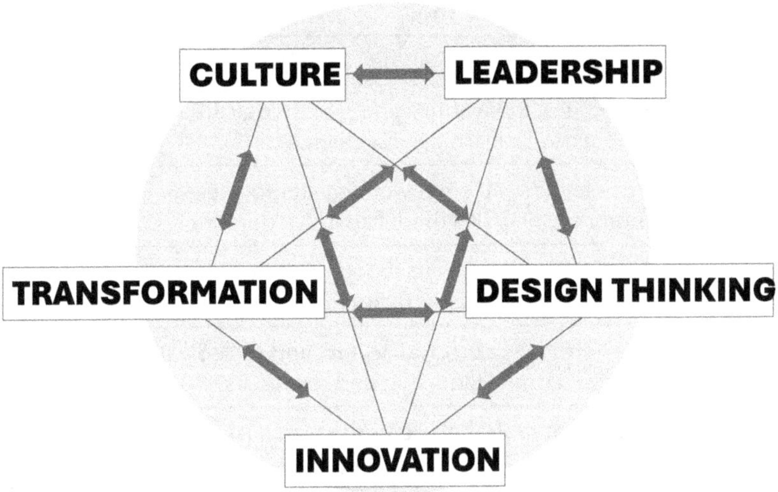

Figure 16.1 The InterAlign Transformation Framework.

> No transformation without innovation. No innovation without design thinking. No design without empowered leadership. No leadership without a culture that permits risk, purpose, and change. And no culture shift without the momentum of real transformation.

These five elements—Design Thinking, Innovation, Transformation, Leadership, and Culture—form a dynamic system where each element exists in continuous interaction with every other:

Design Thinking provides the structured approach and human-centred methods that make innovation possible and sustainable. **Innovation** creates the practical changes and novel solutions that enable transformation. **Transformation** represents the systemic evolution that reshapes healthcare delivery and experience. **Leadership** provides the vision, direction, and empowerment needed to initiate and sustain change. **Culture** creates the environment where innovation can flourish and transformation can take root.

This is not a menu from which organisations can choose. All five must be present. Remove any single element and the remaining four cannot compensate—the system does not degrade gracefully, it fails fundamentally. An organisation with strong leadership, innovation, culture, and transformation capacity but no design thinking methodology will build the wrong things brilliantly. One with everything except leadership will generate insights nobody acts on. Each element influences and is influenced by every other. Consider an ICU that invested in innovation and design methodology but ignored culture, finding that new protocols were technically superior but universally ignored by staff who hadn't been part of the process

When healthcare organisations align all five—treating them as a unified system rather than separate initiatives—transformation becomes achievable. Misalignment in any single element predicts failure.

The InterAlign assessment tool, based on the framework, provides a practical diagnostic (Table 16.1):

This assessment reveals where an organisation's transformation breaks down—and where intervention will yield the greatest return. Within the Control Room model described below, the

Table 16.1 The InterAlign Assessment Tool

Domain	*Guiding Question*	*Score (1–5)*
Culture	Are values, behaviours, and psychological safety aligned with learning and change?	
Leadership	Does leadership empower and support teams, embrace risk, and model adaptive thinking?	
Design Thinking	Are design methods used to understand needs, reframe problems, and co-create solutions?	
Innovation	Are new ideas nurtured, tested, and scaled with support from leadership and resources?	
Transformation	Has the organisation demonstrated sustained structural or behavioural change?	

InterAlign framework becomes one of the embedded diagnostic tools available to any participating community or organisation.

From Analysis to Action: The EHFF Journey

The European Health Futures Forum brought a distinctive lens to these challenges. As a network of networks, EHFF encompasses extraordinary diversity—from frontline healthcare providers to systems theorists, from patient advocates to policymakers [ehff.eu]. This diversity enabled pattern recognition that more specialised organisations would miss. EHFF had already abandoned the premise that existing healthcare systems could be incrementally improved into sustainability. Three foundational insights emerged. First, healthcare must shift from a damage-repair model to one centred on prevention and wellbeing. Second, care delivery must be redistributed from centralised institutions to communities. Third, transformation requires addressing the economic and social structures within which healthcare operates—healthcare cannot be fixed in isolation.

Against this backdrop, EHFF launched an ambitious foresight study in June 2020, supported by the Johnson & Johnson Foundation. We chose the Three Horizons framework, developed by Anthony Hodgson, Bill Sharpe, and colleagues, as our primary methodology [9]. Three Horizons visualises change as the interplay of three patterns: Horizon 1 represents the currently dominant system that increasingly fails to meet contemporary needs; Horizon 3 embodies the envisioned future aligned with emerging realities; Horizon 2 encompasses the transitional space where innovations emerge, some extending the life of the old system while others enable genuine transformation.

We distributed carefully crafted questions to thirty respondents representing the breadth of European healthcare expertise. Their responses—over 600 individual insights—were clustered, mapped, and analysed through iterative systems analysis. What emerged was stark: the current system is comprehensively failing across every dimension. Yet scattered throughout Europe, at the margins, genuine innovations are emerging—community-centred care models, preventive approaches, distributed decision-making (Figure 16.2). The challenge is not generating innovation; it is coordinating and scaling it against a governance structure designed to suppress rather than spread transformative change.

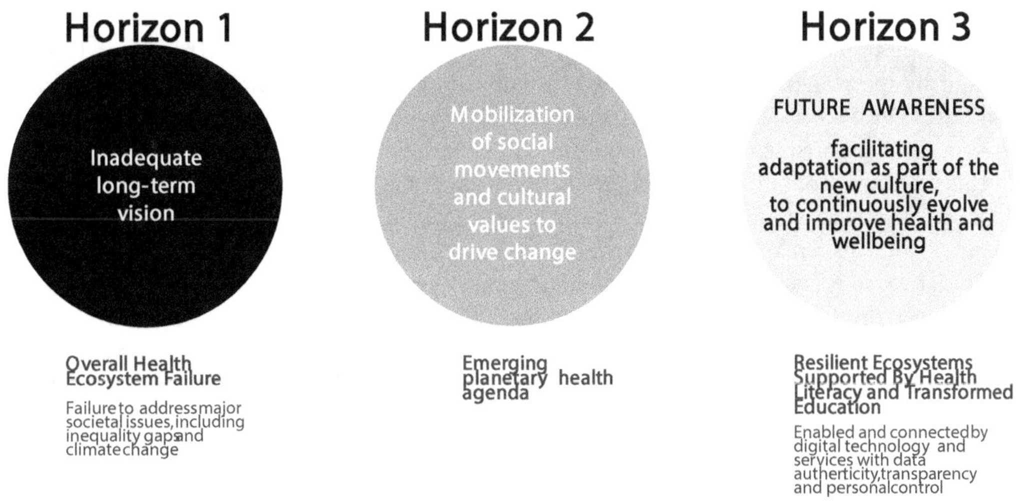

Figure 16.2 Overview of EHFF Three Horizons.

But a critical limitation emerged: while Three Horizons excels at shared vision-building, it provides limited guidance for practical implementation. We needed to move beyond diagnosis to treatment—not treatment of healthcare delivery, but treatment of healthcare governance itself. This recognition drove the development of 3H+, combining strategic foresight with design thinking principles for co-creation. Our stakeholder mapping identified over fifty organisations working on healthcare transformation, revealing both encouraging activity and critical gaps where essential work remained undone [12].

Three key insights emerged. First, evidence alone never creates change—successful transformation requires compelling evidence, emotional engagement, and practical pathways for action. Second, transformation demands ecosystem building rather than isolated initiatives. Third, transformation often begins where systems are weakest—underserved communities become spaces for innovation precisely because existing systems have failed them.

As EHFF contemplated how to maximise impact, a fundamental limitation emerged. Traditional organisational structures constrained our ability to provide continuous support. Dependence on voluntary contributions from busy experts, while producing extraordinary insights, limited continuous engagement. This recognition led to exploration of DAO structures—enabling EHFF to function as a true Transformational Catalyst, operating continuously rather than episodically. By 2023, we had developed something genuinely novel: a methodology combining Three Horizons foresight with design thinking co-creation, overlaid with a DAO governance structure that could coordinate transformation without recreating the centralised control that has failed so spectacularly. We are piloting this model—not as a theoretical exercise, but as an operational reality.

The Healthcare Transformation Control Room

For decentralised healthcare transformation to work, a swarm of local initiatives, however creative, must evolve into a coherent system. Without orchestration, the result becomes an ecosystem of disconnected pilots—each well-intentioned, each reinventing the wheel, and none achieving scale. The answer is coordinated intelligence, not central control.

I think of this as a Control Room function—analogous to air traffic control systems that keep thousands of aircraft moving safely and efficiently through shared airspace. The Control Room does not fly the planes; it ensures the overall pattern remains safe, efficient, and purposeful. A Healthcare DAO ecosystem requires a Control Room that observes, analyses, and facilitates learning across a distributed network of community initiatives.

This Control Room monitors what is emerging across the system—which problems are being addressed, which communities are innovating, where duplication or fragmentation occurs, and where critical gaps remain. It maps patterns of progress, identifies leverage points, and supports new initiatives to fill voids. Its function is situational awareness and intelligent coordination.

Crucially, this Control Room must operate with the same principles as the ecosystem it serves: transparency, decentralisation, and participation. Governance comes from representatives of community DAOs, professional networks, and knowledge partners, using open data and shared dashboards. Legitimacy derives from visibility and accountability, not authority.

Five Essential Functions

The transformation control room provides five essential functions:

Visibility. Comprehensive tracking across the transformation landscape—initiatives, patterns, opportunities, and obstacles in real-time. This panoramic view enables pattern recognition impossible from ground level. When multiple initiatives encounter similar obstacles, the Control Room identifies systemic barriers requiring a collective response. When innovations emerge in one context, it rapidly assesses transferability to others.

Coordination. Active management of relationships and interactions between stakeholders, identifying synergies, brokering connections, and facilitating collaborative action. Using stakeholder mapping and gap analysis, this function operates like a sophisticated switchboard—connecting the right people at the right time for maximum impact.

Navigation. Strategic guidance for transformation initiatives, helping them chart optimal paths based on accumulated wisdom and real-time conditions. Like GPS systems that provide route guidance while leaving drivers in control, navigation services offer strategic intelligence while respecting local autonomy and expertise.

Early Warning. Identification of emerging challenges before they derail transformation efforts. Every clinician understands triage—recognising which problems need immediate intervention and which can be safely monitored. The Early Warning function applies this principle at system level: tracking policy shifts that could block active initiatives, detecting funding cliffs before they arrive, and surfacing resistance patterns at the stage where they can still be addressed. When Chapter 15's immune response begins to activate, the Control Room spots it early enough to respond.

Resource Optimisation. Connecting initiatives with the support they need precisely when they need it—methodology guidance, tool provision, troubleshooting support, and connection to relevant expertise. This represents hands-on operational support, not distant consultation.

Three Operational Layers

The Control Room operates through three integrated layers. The *intelligence layer* continuously gathers and processes information about transformation initiatives, system conditions, and emerging opportunities. This goes beyond data collection to active sense-making—transforming raw information into actionable insight. The *coordination layer* manages relationships between stakeholders, using the mapping and analysis tools described above to identify synergies and broker connections. The *action support layer* provides direct assistance: methodology guidance, troubleshooting, and connection to expertise to those doing the difficult work of transformation.

The Control Room's power lies in its ability to maintain situational awareness across multiple transformation horizons simultaneously. While individual initiatives necessarily focus on their specific contexts and challenges, the Control Room maintains perspective across the entire system. When external conditions shift—whether through policy changes, technological developments, or social movements—the Control Room helps initiatives adapt their strategies accordingly.

This monitoring operates across multiple timescales. Real-time monitoring tracks immediate developments and urgent needs. Medium-term analysis identifies emerging trends and shifting patterns. Long-term assessment evaluates progress toward the transformation vision and adjusts strategies accordingly. Different stakeholders access the Control Room differently:

- Transformation initiatives receive strategic navigation that respects local autonomy while providing route intelligence based on system-wide pattern recognition.
- Funding organisations gain unprecedented visibility into transformation landscapes, enabling strategic investment rather than isolated project funding.
- Policymakers receive evidence-based insight into what is actually working, moving beyond traditional research to real-time feedback on policy impacts.
- Research institutions access a living laboratory for studying systemic transformation across multiple contexts simultaneously.

The technologies already exist to enable this architecture. Real-time dashboards can visualise activity across DAOs. AI-driven analytics can surface emerging themes, unmet needs, and successful prototypes ready for replication. Smart contracts can automatically trigger collaboration opportunities, funding flows, or peer support when specific conditions are met. The Control Room becomes the nervous system of a distributed healthcare organism—sensing, integrating, and coordinating, while leaving autonomy intact at the edges.

In design terms, the Control Room is a meta-level service: a continuous feedback loop transforming fragmented local learning into collective intelligence. It closes the loop between experimentation and strategy, ensuring that every local act of innovation contributes to the evolution of the whole. This is what differentiates transformation from disruption. Disruption shatters the old system; transformation reorganises it into a higher-order pattern. The Control Room makes that possible.

Bridging the Trust Gap: Networked Legitimacy

The question of who should coordinate healthcare transformation reveals a profound paradox. Logic suggests established institutions like the European Union or WHO should host such a control room—they possess formal authority, resources, and technical expertise. Yet these very institutions are part of the system that citizens increasingly distrust.

This paradox illuminates why decades of top-down reform efforts have failed. Institutions with the power to coordinate change lack the grassroots trust necessary to mobilise communities. Community movements that possess authentic trust lack the infrastructure for system-wide coordination. Traditional NGOs occupy a middle ground but remain constrained by funding dependencies.

The DAO model creates what we term 'networked legitimacy'—authority that emerges from transparent participation and demonstrated value. This transcends traditional dichotomies between institutional and community-based legitimacy. Blockchain technology ensures radical transparency: every decision is recorded immutably, resource flows are publicly traceable, and no single entity can capture or manipulate the system. Stakeholders verify all actions independently.

The DAO structure enables a unique dual legitimacy. Institutional credibility is preserved through established relationships with EU bodies, WHO collaborators, and national health systems—providing access to policy discussions, funding opportunities, and system-level insights. Simultaneously, grassroots legitimacy is built through participatory governance that gives a meaningful voice to communities traditionally excluded from health policy. Token-based voting ensures that those most affected by healthcare failures—patients, community health workers, local clinics—have direct input into transformation priorities.

Historical precedent suggests this approach can succeed. The Internet emerged from a similar dynamic—too important for governments to ignore, too decentralised for any government to control. Rather than choosing between institutional authority and grassroots innovation, the Internet created a parallel infrastructure that eventually became indispensable to official systems while maintaining fundamental independence. Similarly, a DAO-based control room creates complementary infrastructure that enables coordination and innovation at speeds impossible within traditional bureaucratic structures. Over time, healthcare institutions will recognise the DAO's value in achieving their own transformation goals.

This resolution of the trust paradox represents the greatest strategic advantage. Trusted enough by institutions to access resources and policy discussions, independent enough to maintain community credibility, and innovative enough to transcend traditional organisational limitations. The DAO model transforms the political challenge into an opportunity: coordination need not require centralised control, transformation need not wait for institutional permission, and trust can emerge from verifiable action rather than positional authority.

Toward a Healthcare DAO Ecosystem

A healthcare DAO ecosystem would function as a network of interconnected, purpose driven DAOs operating across different scales: community health cooperatives, disease-specific pathways, professional learning networks, and regional coordination hubs. Each DAO would function as a semi-autonomous organism—locally governed, transparently funded, and linked through shared protocols.

Within each DAO, design thinking frameworks, methods, tools, and techniques would be embedded as shared digital assets—co-developed and continuously improved by the community itself. These might range from foresight tools like Three Horizons for shared vision-building, through co-design frameworks for bringing together patients, clinicians, and local stakeholders, to learning systems that treat every intervention as an experiment with transparent data loops driving improvement.

The Decentralised Science (DeSci) movement demonstrates this is feasible.* Projects such as VitaDAO† and AthenaDAO‡ have shown that communities can collectively fund and govern

* https://www.desci.com/

† https://www.vitadao.com/

‡ https://www.athenadao.co/

biomedical research, own intellectual property, and make transparent decisions about priorities and investments.

More compelling still are operational deployments already demonstrating these principles at scale. Estonia became the first country to deploy blockchain for healthcare, using KSI Blockchain technology to secure all electronic health records nationwide [10]. Every Estonian citizen has an electronic health record accessible via their national digital ID. Ninety-nine per cent of health data generated by hospitals and doctors is digitised. Blockchain ensures data integrity—every access is recorded immutably, patients control who sees their records, and any tampering is immediately detectable. Estonia proves that blockchain-secured health data governance works at population scale, providing the technical precedent for the broader architecture this chapter proposes.

Outside healthcare, the Wellbeing Protocol in New Zealand demonstrates DAO governance for community wellbeing directly.* Founded on Elinor Ostrom's principles for governing commons [11], the project created a DAO that functions as a local economic operating system—with its own community currency, participatory grant-making, and transparent resource allocation. The government-funded Tane Ora trial tested community participatory grant-making, giving direct decision-making power to the people most affected by funding decisions. Larger trials are planned across New Zealand and the United Kingdom. The Wellbeing Protocol treats community wellbeing as a commons and embeds governance principles into decentralised technology—precisely the model this chapter advocates for healthcare.

Yet a critical gap remains. The current landscape is fragmented. Vita and Athena DAOs operate within research domains, disconnected from care delivery. Estonia's blockchain secures health records but does not extend to governance transformation. The Wellbeing Protocol demonstrates community DAO governance but applies to social welfare rather than healthcare delivery. Design thinking, where it appears at all, is treated as external facilitation rather than embedded community capability.

The synthesis—Healthcare DAO ecosystems that embed design frameworks as co-owned digital assets—has not yet been done. That is both the challenge and the opportunity.

Healthcare transformation ceases to be the exclusive domain of policymakers, funders, or professional elites. It becomes a civic function, exercised collectively through transparent, rule-based mechanisms that reward contribution, trust, and value creation. DAOs provide the architecture for distributed governance; design thinking provides the methodology for distributed innovation. Together, they form the foundation of a truly community-centric healthcare ecosystem.

Practical Steps for Healthcare Leaders

Transformation at this scale requires phased implementation. Healthcare leaders ready to act can follow a structured pathway that progressively builds toward full Control Room capability:

Phase 1: Foundation Building (0–6 months). Establish the intelligence layer. Audit current governance structures for transparency gaps and stakeholder exclusion. Apply the InterAlign assessment to identify which of the five transformation elements—culture, leadership, design thinking, innovation, or transformation capacity—represents the greatest constraint. Begin stakeholder mapping using 3H+ methodology principles. Identify one transformation

* https://www.thewellbeingprotocol.org/

initiative suitable for enhanced stakeholder participation. This phase creates the visibility function: you cannot coordinate what you cannot see.

Phase 2: Pilot Implementation (6–18 months). Activate coordination and navigation. Launch transparent decision-making processes for selected initiatives. Implement token-based feedback mechanisms for affected communities. Create 'teal islands'—autonomous teams insulated from established hierarchical rules—to demonstrate distributed decision-making. Connect pilot initiatives through shared dashboards, enabling the early warning function to detect resistance patterns before the 18-month reversion window identified in Chapter 15. Measure coordination efficiency gains and stakeholder satisfaction improvements against baseline.

Phase 3: Scaling (18+ months). Build the full Control Room. Expand successful approaches to additional transformation initiatives. Activate resource optimisation by connecting initiatives with expertise, methodology, and funding across the network. Consider formal DAO structure for multi-stakeholder coordination. Build network effects with other forward-thinking healthcare organisations and connect to broader DAO ecosystems for shared learning.

Each phase builds on previous achievements while maintaining operational continuity. The evolutionary approach provides immediate value while building toward full capability. Start with non-clinical functions to prove the model. Use patient-journey design sprints to surface pain points clinicians already want solved—then let them own the solutions. Small but telling wins—self-scheduling nursing units, patient-run councils—build momentum and substitute permission with expectation.

The control room model transforms how we think about systemic change. Rather than hoping that multiple isolated initiatives somehow aggregate into transformation, it provides the coordination mechanism enabling genuine systemic evolution. For individual initiatives, it reduces isolation, accelerates learning, and enhances the probability of success. For the transformation ecosystem, it creates network effects that amplify collective impact beyond the sum of individual efforts.

Bridge Insight: Governance Innovation Enables Design Thinking

The intersection of design thinking and healthcare governance represents an emerging frontier. While this book has focused on practical implementation of design thinking methodology, deeper questions remain about why healthcare systems systematically resist innovation—even when evidence supports change. Ongoing research suggests that organisational resistance patterns may operate with the sophistication and coordination of biological immune systems, inadvertently blocking beneficial innovations through mechanisms that evolved to protect organisational stability. A pilot programme in Uganda's healthcare system is exploring these dynamics, examining how governance structures can be redesigned to enable rather than resist transformation. This theoretical framework—connecting governance structures to innovation capacity—will be explored in depth in forthcoming work.

For practitioners implementing design thinking, the key insight is this: sustainable change requires attention to the organisational ecosystems in which the methodology operates, not just the methodology itself. Design thinking's emphasis on stakeholder collaboration and rapid prototyping naturally creates governance conditions more receptive to innovation. By implementing the approaches outlined in this book, you are beginning to shift governance culture itself.

If we want truly transformative healthcare systems, design must be more than a toolkit. It must become a way of being. We must obsess over user experience and build teams that self-replicate excellence. We must question the status quo and take bold action—with deep social responsibility. We must treat healthcare institutions as living systems capable of growth, healing, and purpose. The Control Room provides the infrastructure to make this possible.

Chapter 17 provides your complete implementation roadmap—tailored pathways by role, tactical countermeasures for every domain of resistance, and a detailed 90-day plan for getting started. The diagnostic frameworks from Part IV, combined with the coordination architecture from this chapter, equip you for effective action. The methodology exists. The technology exists. The precedents exist. What remains is leadership willing to act.

References

1. Christensen, C.M., Grossman, J.H. and Hwang, J. (2009) *The Innovator's Prescription: A Disruptive Solution for Health Care*. New York: McGraw-Hill.
2. Wikipedia contributors (2026) 'Health and social care act 2012', *Wikipedia*.
3. GE HealthCare (2009) *Latest Innovations*. Available at: https://www.gehealthcare.com/about/latest-innovations (Accessed: 28 February 2026).
4. Christensen, C.M., Johnson, C.W. and Horn, M.B. (2008) *Disrupting Class: How Disruptive Innovation Will Change the Way the World Learns*. 1st edn. New York: McGraw-Hill.
5. GOV.UK (2020) *Annex B: Exercise Cygnus Report (accessible)*. Available at: https://www.gov.uk/government/publications/uk-pandemic-preparedness/exercise-cygnus-report-accessible-report.
6. Nakamoto, S. (2008) *Bitcoin: A Peer-to-Peer Electronic Cash System*. https://bitcoin.org/bitcoin.pdf.
7. Laloux, F. (2014) *Reinventing Organizations*. Brussels: Nelson Parker.
8. Gray, B., Sarnak, D. and Burgers, J. (2015) *Home Care by Self-Governing Nursing Teams: The Netherlands' Buurtzorg Model*. Available at. https://doi.org/10.26099/6CES-Q139.
9. Sharpe, B., Hodgson, A., Leicester, G., Lyon, A. and Fazey, I. (2016) 'Three horizons: A pathways practice for transformation', *Ecology and Society*, 21(2), Art. 47. https://doi.org/10.5751/ES-08388-210247.
10. Järv, K. and Institute for Digital Society (2025) 'Estonia's blockchain-based e-government and citizen security: Balancing data integrity and privacy in the digital state', in *Congress Proceedings of the 1st International Congress on Law and the Future of Global Justice*. Gostivar, North Macedonia: International Vision University, pp. 170–185. https://doi.org/10.55843/ICL2025cong170j.
11. Ostrom, E. (2015) *Governing the Commons: The Evolution of Institutions for Collective Action*. Canto Classics edn. Cambridge: Cambridge University Press.
12. Sørensen, K., Kendrick, I., Münter, L., Conlâin, S.Ó., Steenstra, D., Harrington, N., Somekh, D., (2026). A long-term vision for a sustainable European health eco-system grounded in social mobilization, health literacy, planetary health and economy of well-being. *Nordic Journal of Wellbeing and Sustainable Welfare Development* 5, 6–12. https://doi.org/10.18261/njwel.5.1.2.
13. Erkoyuncu, J.A., Bolshchikov, S., Steenstra, D., Rajkumar, R., Dori, D., 2013. Constructing and evaluating "as-is" and "to-be" OPM models for the healthcare sector for adoption of Vscan.

Chapter 17

Your Design Thinking Journey Begins Here

This chapter is in two parts: Part I gives you your strategic orientation—where to focus given your role, your organisation's current state, and the specific challenges you face; Part II gives you your tactical arsenal—how to defend what you build once the system deploys its resistance.

Part I: Your Personalised Roadmap

You've reached this chapter through one of three paths.

Perhaps you've followed this book from the beginning, working through each chapter as it built on the last. You've wrestled with the Double Diamond, questioned your assumptions about improvement approaches, and begun to see your healthcare challenges through a design lens.

Or maybe you arrived here seeking answers to a specific problem—declining clinical trial enrolment, stalled digital transformation, workforce burnout that resists every intervention. You're looking for practical guidance, not academic theory. Or possibly someone handed you this book with a simple message: 'Read this. It explains what we need to do differently.'

Whichever path brought you here, you've arrived at the right place. What follows isn't just a summary of what came before. It's your personalised roadmap for what comes next.

For Hospital Executives: The Patient-Centred Imperative

Your immediate challenge likely centres on operational transformation—improving patient experience while managing costs, reducing wait times while maintaining quality, deploying technology while keeping clinicians engaged.

Start here:

- **Chapter 8**: 'From Hospital-Centred to Patient-Centred: A Systems Approach' gives you the strategic framework for fundamental reorientation.

 DOI: 10.4324/9781003752073-22

- **Chapter 16**: 'The Healthcare Transformation Control Room' provides the coordination mechanism you need to orchestrate change across departments.
- **Chapter 5**: 'The Hidden Truth: Why Every Clinician Is Already a Design Thinker' helps you unlock the design capability already present in your workforce.

Why this sequence?

You can't transform operations without first understanding the shift from institutional to patient-centred thinking. The control room concept then gives you a practical structure for coordinating multiple transformation initiatives simultaneously. Finally, recognising that your clinicians already think the same way as designers—they just don't call it that—accelerates cultural adoption.

Your first 90-day action:

Conduct the InterAlign Transformation Readiness Assessment (below) with your executive team. Identify which of the five domains in the InterAlign Transformation Framework (Chapter 16)—Culture, Leadership, Design Thinking, Innovation, Transformation—shows the weakest score. That's where system resistance will be strongest. Address it first.

For Pharmaceutical Leaders: The Clinical Trials Revolution

Your industry faces an existential challenge: the current model for developing and testing new therapies is unsustainable. Trials are too slow, too expensive, too centralised, and systematically exclude the diverse populations who need these therapies most.

Start here:

- **Chapters 6 and 4**: 'Redesigning Clinical Trials' and 'Design Thinking Principles and Methods' provide the foundational methodology.
- **Chapters 9, 13, and 14**: 'Decentralised Healthcare,' 'The Structural Trap,' and 'The Political Reality' explain the governance patterns that will attack your transformation efforts.
- **Chapter 7**: 'AI and Healthcare Equity' shows how AI amplifies rather than replaces design thinking approaches.

Why this sequence?

You need both the 'how' (methodology) and the 'why transformation fails' (governance understanding) to succeed. Most pharma innovations die not from regulatory barriers but from internal governance dysfunction. Understanding resistance patterns lets you defend against them.

Your first 90-day action:

Select one upcoming Phase III trial. Apply the Double Diamond framework—Discover, Define, Develop, Deliver—starting with the Problem diamond. Who are the underserved populations experiencing this condition? Where do they actually receive care? What barriers prevent their participation? Build your protocol from those insights rather than from institutional convenience.

For Policymakers: Beyond Regulation to System Design

You occupy a unique position: the ability to create conditions that enable transformation across entire healthcare systems. But traditional policy tools—regulation, funding mechanisms, quality metrics—often generate unintended consequences that undermine the changes you seek to create.

Start here:

- **Chapter 10**: 'Policymaking as Design' gives you the framework specifically adapted for policy design.
- **Chapters 11, 9, and 13**: The Lean, Decentralisation, and Structural Trap chapters explain why well-intentioned policy interventions predictably fail.
- **Chapters 2 and 3**: 'Learning from Other Industries' and 'The Hidden Costs of Bad Healthcare Design' provide case studies of system design successes and failures.

Why this sequence?

Most policy failures stem from trying to regulate problems that require governance redesign. Going through chapters in this order will provide you with a firm grounding to start policy design.

Your first 90-day action:

Choose one significant policy initiative currently under development. Apply stakeholder mapping to identify whose interests, incentives, and power dynamics your policy will affect. Then use the Double Diamond to discover whether the problem you're solving is actually the problem stakeholders experience. Policy rarely fails for lack of good intentions—it fails from misalignment with lived reality.

For Innovation Leaders: The Complete Transformation Journey

You're the ones trying to change healthcare from within—launching new care models, implementing digital health platforms, redesigning patient pathways. You face the full spectrum of challenges: from initial concept through governance approval to sustainable implementation.

Start here:

- **Read the complete book in order.** Your role requires understanding the full landscape.
- **Pay particular attention to Chapters 11–15** on why innovations die and governance resistance patterns. This is your field manual for survival.
- **Use Chapter 16** as your coordination framework for managing multiple simultaneous initiatives.

Why the complete book?

Innovation leadership is the role that requires the fullest systems view—the one place where clinical insight, design methodology, governance awareness, and economic strategy must operate together. That's why the complete book is your toolkit, not just the implementation chapters.

If you're innovating in medical devices specifically, Pitfall 2's analysis of tight coupling is your primary threat intelligence—healthcare's regulatory and reimbursement architecture means that device innovations face dependency cascades that software and service innovations don't. Add Chapter 3's hidden costs analysis to your reading sequence.

Your first 90-day action:

Map your current innovation portfolio using the Transformation Assessment Tool. Identify which initiatives score lowest in Culture, Leadership, Design Thinking, Innovation, or Transformation domains. Those scores predict where each initiative will face greatest resistance. Develop domain-specific strategies before launching.

For Specialist Clinicians: Using Your Diagnostic Skills Differently

If you're a consultant, a specialist, or a senior clinical practitioner, you've spent years training to diagnose complex systems under uncertainty—gathering incomplete information, generating hypotheses, testing them against evidence, and revising your working diagnosis in real time. That's design thinking. You've been doing it at the bedside for your entire career.

The challenge isn't learning a new methodology. It's applying a familiar one to a different domain: the systems you work within, rather than the patients you care for.

Start here:

- **Chapter 5**: 'The Hidden Truth: Why Every Clinician is Already a Design Thinker' validates what you already know.
- **Chapters 8 and 4**: The patient-centred systems and methodology chapters translate your clinical reasoning skills into organisational design capability.
- **Chapters 13, 14, and 15**: Understanding structural, political, and behavioural resistance is essential if you want your clinical insights to survive governance.

Why this sequence?

Clinical wisdom about what patients actually need is the most powerful input to healthcare transformation—and the most systematically ignored. Chapter 5 explains why. Chapters 13–15 explain the mechanisms by which clinical insight gets filtered out of decision-making. Understanding those mechanisms is the first step to circumventing them.

Your first 90-day action:

Identify one clinical problem that you encounter repeatedly and that no administrative process has successfully addressed. Apply the first diamond—Discover—through direct observation and conversation. What do patients actually experience? What do frontline colleagues actually face? Start there.

The InterAlign Transformation Readiness Assessment

The InterAlign Transformation Framework introduced in Chapter 16 provides the diagnostic structure for this assessment. Before deciding where to focus your transformation efforts, understand your current state. This assessment helps you diagnose organisational readiness across the five interdependent domains that determine transformation success.

Instructions

For each domain, honestly assess your organisation's current state on a 1–5 scale:

- **1** = **Absent**: This capability doesn't exist in any meaningful way
- **2** = **Emerging**: Early signs but inconsistent and unsupported
- **3** = **Developing**: Present in pockets but not systematic
- **4** = **Established**: Systematic across most areas with leadership support
- **5** = **Transformative**: Fully integrated, self-reinforcing, driving continuous evolution

Domain 1: Culture

Guiding question: Are values, behaviours, and psychological safety aligned with learning and change?

Assessment criteria:

- Do people feel safe raising concerns about current processes?
- Is failure treated as a learning opportunity rather than a cause for blame?
- Do teams actively seek diverse perspectives rather than defaulting to hierarchical consensus?
- Can frontline staff challenge leadership decisions without career risk?
- Are patients and families treated as genuine partners rather than passive recipients?

Score: ____ / 5

What this reveals: Culture provides the soil where design thinking either flourishes or withers. Scores below 3 indicate that even technically excellent design interventions will struggle—not because the methodology doesn't work, but because organisational culture actively resists the inquiry, experimentation, and adaptation that design thinking requires.

Domain 2: Leadership

Guiding question: Does leadership empower and support teams, embrace risk, and model adaptive thinking?

Assessment criteria:

- Do leaders actively demonstrate curiosity about problems before rushing to solutions?
- Is leadership willing to pause initiatives that aren't working rather than defending sunk costs?
- Do leaders create space for teams to experiment without demanding guaranteed outcomes?
- Are resources allocated based on learning potential as well as expected returns?
- Does leadership model the vulnerability of saying 'I don't know' and seeking input?

Score: ____ / 5

What this reveals: Leadership behaviour cascades throughout organisations. Leaders who claim to value innovation while punishing failure create environments where design thinking becomes performative rather than transformative. Scores below 3 suggest that transformation initiatives will remain isolated experiments rather than systematic practice.

Domain 3: Design Thinking Methods

Guiding question: Are design methods used to understand needs, reframe problems, and co-create solutions?

Assessment criteria:

- Do teams routinely engage in ethnographic research to understand user experiences?
- Is the Double Diamond—Discover, Define, Develop, Deliver—familiar and actively used?
- Are stakeholders involved in co-design rather than just consulted?
- Do teams prototype and test solutions iteratively rather than pursuing big-bang implementations?
- Is patient journey mapping used to identify pain points and opportunities?

Score: ____ / 5

What this reveals: Methods provide the systematic approach that distinguishes design thinking from simple creativity. Scores below 3 indicate that while your organisation may value 'innovation,' it lacks the structured methodology to consistently generate and implement improvements. This is usually the easiest domain to develop—design methods can be taught and practised—but only if culture and leadership provide supportive conditions.

Domain 4: Innovation

Guiding question: Are new ideas nurtured, tested, and scaled with support from leadership and resources?

Assessment criteria:

- Does a clear process exist for moving from idea to pilot to implementation?
- Are resources—time, budget, expertise—allocated to support promising innovations?
- Can innovations progress based on evidence rather than requiring political champions?
- Does the organisation actively scan for external innovations worth adapting?
- Are innovation failures analysed for learning rather than for determining culpability?

Score: ____ / 5

What this reveals: Innovation as organisational capability differs from occasional innovative projects. Scores below 3 suggest that innovations depend on heroic individuals rather than systematic support. Even when design thinking generates excellent solutions, they struggle to progress through implementation.

Domain 5: Transformation

Guiding question: Has the organisation demonstrated sustained structural or behavioural change?

Assessment criteria:

- Can you point to fundamental shifts in how work gets done, not just incremental improvements?

- Have changes persisted beyond the tenure of their original champions?
- Do transformation efforts build on each other rather than starting from scratch?
- Has organisational structure evolved to support new ways of working?
- Are metrics and incentives aligned with transformation goals?

Score: ____ / 5

What this reveals: Transformation represents the ultimate test—whether design thinking has moved from methodology to organisational practice. Scores below 3 indicate that while your organisation may be busy with change initiatives, they haven't yet achieved genuine transformation. This isn't failure—transformation is the longest-term outcome. But it clarifies where to focus: building the foundational capabilities that enable sustained change.

Interpreting Your Assessment

Total your scores across all five domains: ____ / 25

0–10—Pre-design thinking state. Your organisation operates primarily in command-and-control mode with limited systematic innovation capability. This isn't a criticism—most healthcare organisations score here. Start small with a single pilot initiative that can demonstrate design thinking value while building organisational capability.

11–15—Early adoption. You have pockets of design thinking practice but they're not yet systematic or consistently supported. Strengthen the weakest-scoring domain first. If Culture or Leadership scored lowest, address those before expanding design thinking methodology. Cultural resistance will undermine even excellent design work.

16–20—Developing capability. Design thinking is becoming part of how your organisation works, though not yet fully integrated. Create connections between initiatives. Establish communities of practice, share learnings systematically, and begin documenting your emerging methodology.

21–25—Transformation momentum. You're approaching InterAlign Transformation Readiness with systematic capability across domains. Focus on scaling and sustainability. How do you ensure these capabilities persist beyond current leaders? How do you accelerate the pace of transformation while maintaining quality?

Critical Pattern: The Cascade Effect

Notice which domains scored lowest. These predict where your transformation efforts will encounter greatest resistance.

If Culture Scored Lowest: Even technically excellent design work will struggle to gain traction. People won't engage honestly in discovery processes if they fear blame. Address psychological safety and blame-free learning before expanding design thinking adoption.

If Leadership Scored Lowest: Design thinking initiatives will remain isolated experiments rather than systematic practice. Develop capabilities in adaptive leadership, systems thinking, and embracing uncertainty.

If Design Thinking Scored Lowest: You have the cultural conditions for transformation but lack systematic methodology. This is the easiest domain to develop—invest in training, bring in external design expertise, and create opportunities for practice.
If Innovation Scored Lowest: Ideas generate but struggle to progress to implementation. Create clear pathways from idea to pilot to scale, with defined resources and decision criteria.
If Transformation Scored Lowest: You're active but not yet achieving lasting change. This often indicates that individual initiatives show promise but aren't yet connected into a coherent transformation strategy. Apply the Control Room concept from Chapter 16 to coordinate initiatives systematically.

Reading Guide: Navigating the Book by Challenge

Beyond role-based pathways, you may have arrived here seeking answers to specific challenges. Here's how to navigate the book based on the problem you're trying to solve.

'Our digital health initiatives keep failing'

Read: Chapters 4, 2, 9, 13, and 14
Why: Digital health failures rarely stem from technology problems. They fail because they're designed from technology capabilities rather than user needs, because healthcare systems actively resist beneficial innovations, or because governance structures systematically attack them.
Action: Before your next digital health initiative, spend the first diamond—Discover and Define—understanding the problem from clinical and patient perspectives. What actual workflow challenges do clinicians face? What barriers prevent patients from engaging with existing digital tools? Build your solution from those insights rather than from technology features.

'We can't recruit diverse participants for clinical trials'

Read: Chapters 6, 4, 7, and 9
Why: Trial diversity failures stem from centralised design that optimises for institutional convenience rather than participant needs. Communities don't lack interest in research—they lack trust, access, and culturally appropriate engagement.
Action: Apply ethnographic research to understand barriers from community perspectives. Where do underserved populations actually receive care? What historical factors shape their trust or distrust of clinical research? Build trial infrastructure in community settings rather than requiring communities to come to academic medical centres.

'Our Lean implementation didn't deliver promised results'

Read: Chapters 11, 10, 9, 2, and 3
Why: Lean healthcare failures aren't accidents—they're predictable consequences of applying manufacturing optimisation principles to complex adaptive systems. Healthcare isn't a factory producing standardised widgets. It's a dynamic system responding to infinite clinical variation.

Action: Stop thinking about healthcare transformation as process optimisation. Start thinking systemically about how the interconnected elements—culture, leadership, innovation, governance—must evolve together.

'Our staff is burned out and change-resistant'

Read: Chapters 5, 8, 11, and 2

Why: Clinician burnout stems largely from being forced into systems designed without their input, where professional judgement is overridden by algorithmic protocols. The resistance you're seeing isn't opposition to change—it's exhaustion from poorly designed change initiatives.

Action: Your clinicians already think like designers—they just aren't given opportunities to apply that thinking to system design. Create co-design processes where clinicians redesign the workflows, technologies, and protocols they work within. Shift from 'change management' to 'co-design for change.'

'I'm a clinician who's been given organisational authority for the first time'

Read: Chapters 5, 13, 14, 15, and 4

Why: The transition from clinical authority to organisational power is the most underestimated challenge in healthcare leadership. Your diagnostic methodology is sophisticated—more sophisticated than the MBA frameworks currently running the systems you're about to lead. The obstacle isn't capability. It's translation: learning to apply bedside reasoning to boardroom problems, and understanding why the governance structures around you will resist clinical insight even when it's demonstrably correct.

Action: Before your first week in the new role, read Chapter 5 to recognise what you already know. Then read Chapters 13–15 in sequence—not for motivation, but for intelligence threats. The structural, political, and behavioural resistance mechanisms documented there aren't abstract theory. They are the specific forces that will attack your first initiative, probably around Month 6, in ways that will feel personal but aren't. Understanding the pattern before you encounter it is the difference between interpreting resistance as a signal that you're wrong and recognising it as evidence that you're right.

'I'm developing a medical device for the NHS market'

Read: Chapters 13, 4, 3, 14, and 15

Why: Medical device innovation fails at a higher rate than almost any other healthcare intervention—not because devices don't work, but because the NHS procurement and regulatory environment is among the most tightly coupled systems in the world. A device that performs flawlessly in clinical testing can be simultaneously blocked by MDR compliance requirements, NICE evaluation timelines, NHS Supply Chain procurement rules, reimbursement classification disputes, and trust-level adoption decisions—each governed by a different body, on a different timeline, with different success criteria. Chapter 13's analysis of tight coupling was written with this world in mind. The dependency cascade isn't a metaphor here. It's your product roadmap.

Action: Before your next development sprint, map your regulatory, reimbursement, and procurement pathways as a dependency chain, not a sequential checklist. Identify which single dependency, if delayed, blocks all others—that's your critical path risk, and it almost certainly isn't the one your engineering team is currently managing. Then read Chapter 15's multi-domain defence framework and ask which of your current investors, clinical champions, and institutional allies would still be standing at Month 18 if NHS procurement stalled. If the answer is fewer than three, your Naval domain is already under-resourced.

'Our transformation initiatives show early promise but don't sustain'

Read: Chapters 16, 13, 14, 15, and 11

Why: Most transformation initiatives die not from poor initial design but from systematic governance resistance that emerges 18–24 months after launch. The system's defensive response attacks beneficial innovations because they threaten existing stakeholder interests.

Action: Use the Transformation Control Room framework from Chapter 16 to coordinate and protect multiple transformation initiatives simultaneously. Early in implementation, establish the multi-domain defence—narrative, institutional, economic—that innovations require to survive governance resistance.

'We need to redesign our policy or regulatory frameworks'

Read: Chapters 10, 13, 14, 11, and 9

Why: Traditional policy design focuses on regulation—ensuring safety—while ignoring governance, which shapes behaviour. Well-intentioned policies fail because they do not account for the complex incentives and power dynamics they disrupt.

Action: Apply the Double Diamond to policy design. Spend the first diamond understanding the system you're trying to influence—not as described in official documents but as actually experienced by stakeholders.

Seven Transformation Pitfalls—and How to Avoid Them

Across 16 chapters, certain failure modes appear so consistently that they deserve their own inventory. These aren't random misfortunes. They're predictable patterns that reveal themselves at specific stages of transformation, in specific organisations, triggered by specific decisions. Recognising them before they claim your initiative is the point.

Pitfall 1: Optimising when you need to transform.

The most common failure in healthcare improvement is applying the right tool to the wrong problem. Lean, Six Sigma, and continuous improvement methodologies are powerful instruments for refining existing processes. They are not instruments for changing what a system fundamentally does or how power and resources flow through it. When a hospital invests in Lean to address a patient flow problem rooted in governance structure, or applies process mapping to a problem caused by misaligned incentives, the effort produces data without change. As Chapter 11 demonstrates, the NHS invested approximately £1 billion in Lean across 150 hospitals with no measurable improvement in mortality, infection rates, or patient satisfaction. The methodology worked. The problem was that optimisation cannot substitute for redesign.

Warning Sign: Your improvement data shows local gains that don't aggregate into system-level change.

Course Correction: Before selecting your methodology, diagnose whether you're facing an efficiency problem (appropriate for improvement tools) or a design problem (requiring redesign from first principles).

Pitfall 2: Designing without understanding tight coupling.

Chapter 13's pink stethoscope vignette illustrates a trap that claims every ambitious innovator eventually: adding Bluetooth connectivity to a stethoscope appears simple until it triggers data protection obligations, professional accreditation reviews, reimbursement reclassification, medical records integration requirements, liability implications, and workflow redesign—simultaneously. Healthcare is a tightly coupled system where changes in one component necessarily propagate through interconnected layers of clinical practice, financial structure, regulatory compliance, and organisational culture. Most initiatives underestimate this. Founders and leaders who succeeded in less coupled industries are particularly susceptible because their previous experience taught them that simple changes stay simple.

Warning Sign: Your implementation timeline keeps extending due to 'unexpected dependencies.'

Course Correction: Before any implementation, map at least three dependency layers: what must change upstream for your innovation to function, and what will be forced to change downstream once it does.

Pitfall 3: Underestimating coordination complexity.

Eight stakeholders create 28 unique bilateral relationships requiring management. Twelve stakeholders create 66. The mathematics of stakeholder proliferation—$N(N-1)/2$—means that coordination complexity grows quadratically as you add parties. Most transformation initiatives plan for six to eight core stakeholders and discover, at the point of implementation, that they've entered a system with twelve to fifteen active parties, each with distinct interests, each requiring a distinct management approach. The initiative doesn't fail because of any single stakeholder. It fails because the aggregate coordination load exceeds the available capacity.

Warning Sign: You're spending more time in stakeholder management than in implementation.

Course Correction: Complete your stakeholder map before announcing any initiative. Categorise stakeholders by power and alignment—not by title or seniority. Build your coordination infrastructure to match the actual complexity you will face, not the complexity you would prefer to face.

Pitfall 4: Misreading the political landscape.

Chapter 14 describes a fundamental asymmetry that governs healthcare leadership behaviour: innovation failure is career-ending, while innovation success yields only modest credit. This asymmetry means that saying 'yes' to transformation is personally dangerous while saying 'no' carries almost no consequence. The senior leader who appears supportive in meetings but never allocates budget, never removes barriers, and never publicly champions your initiative isn't a coward. They're a rational actor responding to a system that punishes support for beneficial change. Until you understand whose interests the status quo serves—and the personal risk calculus those stakeholders face—you'll keep misidentifying resistance as ignorance or obstruction rather than as self-preservation.

Warning Sign: You've briefed all the right people, received positive signals, and still can't get a decision.

Course Correction: For each key decision-maker, ask explicitly: what do they personally risk if this succeeds? What do they risk if it fails? Whose support do they need that depends on the status quo? Build your political strategy from those answers.

Pitfall 5: Launching without multi-domain defence.

The gap between designing an excellent solution and successfully implementing it is defended by three simultaneous attack vectors: narrative control (the system frames your innovation as risky or premature before you establish patient benefit), institutional resistance (committees, procurement processes, and standards bodies create procedural barriers), and economic strangulation (budgets freeze, resources redirect, and alternative funding is blocked). Chapter 15 maps these mechanisms in detail. What it reveals is that most innovations die not because they were poorly designed but because their creators assumed that evidence of clinical benefit would be sufficient protection. It isn't. You can win the design battle and lose the implementation war entirely.

Warning Sign: You're defending your methodology repeatedly in forums where the decision should already have been made on evidence.

Course Correction: Part II of this chapter is your field manual. Build your narrative, institutional, and economic defenses before you announce your initiative, not after it comes under attack.

Pitfall 6: Missing the critical temporal windows.

Chapter 15 documents a pattern that is consistent across different types of transformation: at Month 6, initial tolerance gives way to organised questioning; at Month 12, institutional memory forms; at Month 18, the reversion window opens and the system begins actively unwinding apparent progress; at Month 24, if reversion hasn't succeeded, the system typically accepts the new reality. Each of these windows requires a different response—and the responses must be prepared before the window arrives, not after. Transformation leaders who understand the methodology but not the timeline repeatedly arrive at Month 12 unprepared for the institutional lock-in they need to have already created.

Warning Sign: Your initiative has survived its first year but has no structural commitments that would make reversal costly.

Course Correction: Build backwards from Month 18. What structural commitments—contracts, regulatory approvals, capital investments, staffing—must be in place by Month 12 to raise the political and financial cost of reversal? Start creating those commitments in the first 90 days.

Pitfall 7: Mistaking enthusiastic adoption for transformation.

This is the most dangerous pitfall precisely because it looks like success. When an organisation adopts your methodology without requiring any structural change—new language, new meeting formats, new job titles, perhaps even a dedicated team—what you're witnessing is absorption, not transformation. The system has learned that enthusiastic adoption is cheaper than genuine change. It consumes the resources that might otherwise fund alternatives, generates institutional memory ('we tried that'), and ensures that future attempts face the response: 'we already did design thinking.' Chapter 15's analysis of Lean in the NHS is the clearest documented example.

The methodology received £1 billion and complete institutional acceptance. The transformation was eliminated. Frictionless adoption is not a success marker. It's a warning sign.

Warning Sign: Your initiative is progressing smoothly through governance approval with no significant structural friction.
Course Correction: Apply the diagnostic test from Chapter 15. Has your innovation required the organisation to change who makes decisions, how resources are allocated, or which outcomes are measured? If the answer is no, you haven't been adopted. You've been absorbed. Reintroduce the structural friction that genuine transformation requires.

These seven pitfalls are not academic concerns. They appear in virtually every transformation attempt described across the preceding chapters—from Lean to CCG decentralisation, from pharma clinical trial design to digital health implementation. Recognising them in your own context is the difference between a well-designed initiative that succeeds and an equally well-designed initiative that doesn't.

From Strategy to Survival: Part II

The role-based roadmaps, readiness assessment, and reading guide in Part I answer a strategic question: where should you focus? The seven pitfalls answer a diagnostic question: what will predictably go wrong?

Part II answers a different question entirely: when the system deploys its defences—as it will—how do you survive long enough to deliver the transformation you've designed?

In Chapter 15, we mapped how healthcare systems use narrative, institutional, and economic mechanisms to attack innovations that threaten established interests. We called these the Air, Land, and Sea of coordinated system resistance. Here, we reverse that map. What follows isn't theory. It's your counter-move for each domain the system will attack.

Part II: The Tactical Arsenal

Why Multi-Domain Defence Determines Implementation Survival

If the system attacks by air, land, and sea, your countermeasures must operate across all three domains simultaneously. This is your field manual.

What follows are specific tactics, tested through both painful defeats and successful defenses. Each domain includes resource requirements, deployment timelines, success indicators, and—critically—the warning signs that tell you a domain is failing before it's too late to recover.

Domain 1: Air Superiority—Narrative Warfare

Why this domain matters most:

The narrative battle happens first and fastest. Once the system frames your innovation as 'risky,' 'untested,' or 'disruptive to patient care,' you're defending rather than advancing.

The system owns the institutional airspace. It controls official communications, board presentations, policy documents, and internal messaging. Your only advantages are speed and external pressure.

Critical Timeline: You have 60–90 days from announcement before the system's counter-narrative becomes dominant. After that, you're fighting uphill.
Core Principle: The governing principle is pre-emption: your framing must be established before the system finds its counter-narrative.
Your Goal: Establish your framing so thoroughly that stakeholders unconsciously adopt it when discussing your innovation—even stakeholders who might resist it.
Their Goal: Reframe your innovation using institutional risk language before you can establish a patient benefit narrative.

Tactic 1: Pre-Emptive Framing (Weeks 1–4)

Before announcing your initiative, craft your core narrative around three unassailable values:

- Patient safety and benefit (primary frame)
- Regulatory compliance and enhancement (defensive frame)
- Professional standards (legitimacy frame)

Why this works: You've framed innovation as solving a compliance problem, not creating a commercial disruption. The system finds it harder to block 'safety compliance' than 'better product.'

Resources needed: Half-day workshop with 3–5 clinical champions to test messaging; professional communications advisor (£2–5K); draft narrative tested with friendly stakeholders before wide release.

Success indicator: When you mention the project, stakeholders respond using your framing, not the system's.

Failure warning: Stakeholders use different terms when discussing it among themselves.

Tactic 2: External Pressure Creation (Weeks 2–8)

Build pressure that makes blocking politically costly. Identify external amplifiers: healthcare journalists, patient advocacy groups, respected external clinicians, professional associations. Brief journalists on background, provide patient advocacy groups with impact data, secure clinical champion endorsements, submit to relevant professional conferences.

Why This Works: The system can block an internal project meeting. It cannot easily block a clinical champion quoted in the *Health Service Journal*, a patient advocacy group citing your impact data, and a submitted conference abstract. External presence changes the political calculation.
Resources Needed: £5–10K for professional content development; 20–30 hours for relationship building; travel budget for conference presentation; open-access publication budget if pursuing academic route.
Success Indicator: Senior stakeholders mention 'external interest' when discussing your innovation.
Failure Warning: No external parties reference your innovation within 60 days.

Tactic 3: Metrics Lock-In (Weeks 1–6)

Define success metrics before the system can redefine them. Document and gain agreement on 3–5 success metrics that directly measure patient or clinical benefit, are objective and measurable, have established baseline data, and cannot be easily gamed or reinterpreted.

Critical Step: Get these metrics formally documented in the project charter, board presentation, or funding approval. Make them part of the official record.
Success Indicator: Metrics appear in official documentation and stakeholders reference them consistently.
Failure Warning: Stakeholders introduce new or different success criteria after Month 3.

Tactic 4: Rapid Response Protocol (Ongoing)

Counter negative narratives within 48 hours. Establish daily monitoring of key stakeholder communications, internal discussion channels, external media, and professional network discussions. When negative framing appears:

- Hours 1–6: Assess scope and source
- Hours 6–24: Prepare counter-narrative with evidence
- Hours 24–48: Deploy response through appropriate channels

Air Domain Investment Summary

Minimum Viable: £10–15K external; 60 hours internal; 8–12 weeks to establish air superiority.
Premium: £25–40K* external (professional PR, multiple publications, conference circuit); 120–150 hours internal coordination.†

Domain 2: Ground Forces—Coalition Warfare

Why this domain determines survival:
You can win the narrative battle and lose the ground war.
Institutional structures determine what actually happens. Standards boards, professional hierarchies, licensing requirements, procurement processes—this is where innovations live or die.

Your Goal: Build coalitions that make blocking institutionally costly, and create structural commitments that can't be easily reversed.
Critical Timeline: You must occupy institutional territory in the first 12 months. After that, institutional memory forms against you and recapture becomes exponentially harder.

---

* Cost ratios are practitioner estimates based on observed implementation outcomes; they are indicative, not derived from published research.

† In our experience, narrative control investments typically prevent implementation delays that dwarf the original outlay—often by an order of magnitude.

Tactic 1: Power Mapping (Weeks 1–3)

Before any announcement, map the institutional terrain. Create a stakeholder power matrix identifying:

- **Category 1: Essential Allies**—Who has veto power? Who controls critical resources? Who has undismissable credibility?
- **Category 2: Valuable Allies**—Who controls patient or data access? Who influences Essential Allies? Who has external credibility?
- **Category 3: Potential Blockers**—Who benefits from the status quo? Whose authority is threatened? Who has blocking power through committees?
- **Category 4: Fence-Sitters**—Who lacks a strong position but has relevant authority?

For Each Potential Blocker: What specific threat do they perceive? What would make blocking costly for them? Can they be neutralised if not converted?

Success Indicator: You can predict how each key stakeholder will respond before they take a position.

Failure Warning: You're surprised by who blocks or supports.

Tactic 2: Sequential Coalition Building (Weeks 2–8)

Build from strongest allies outwards, creating momentum.

Phase 1: Secure Essential Allies individually before group settings. Present the problem, not the solution—let them see the need first. Ask for their input on the solution approach to create co-ownership. Secure private commitment before public announcement.

Phase 2: Expand to Valuable Allies. Leverage the first coalition: 'Dr. [Essential Ally] is supportive and suggested I speak with you.'

Phase 3: Neutralise Potential Blockers. Don't try to convert everyone. Offer compromises that address their concerns. Make blocking costly: 'Given support from [Essential Allies list], we're moving forward. We'd prefer to have your input shaping this rather than opposing it.'

Tactic 3: Structural Lock-In (Months 3–12)

Create institutional commitments that can't be easily reversed.

Hard Commitments (Very Difficult to Reverse): Multi-year contracts with external parties; capital investments in equipment or facilities; staff roles specifically created for the initiative; regulatory approvals requiring continued implementation; published commitments to patients or external stakeholders.

Soft Commitments (Easily Reversed): Pilot programmes with sunset clauses; 'innovation projects' separate from core operations; initiatives dependent on a single executive sponsor.

Strategic Principle: Front-load hard commitments. Back-load soft pilots.

By Month 12, reversal requires breaking regulatory commitments, terminating external contracts, making staff redundant, and unwinding integrated systems. The system's 18–24 month reversion reflex encounters structural barriers it cannot easily overcome.

Tactic 4: Committee Infiltration (Months 1–6)

Get your allies onto decision-making bodies. Identify key committees with authority over your innovation: standards and quality, technology and innovation, safety and risk, professional practice, procurement. For each committee, determine appointment processes and get an Essential or Valuable Ally appointed. Frame it as: 'We need clinical expertise on this committee.' Once appointed, they represent 'institutional voice,' not your project.

Ground Domain Investment Summary

Minimum Viable: 100–150 hours coalition building; 40–60 hours from allies; £5–10K for structural commitments (legal, contracts); 6–12 months to occupy institutional territory.[1]

Domain 3: Naval Strategy—Economic Independence

Why this domain is your lifeline:

You can win narrative and institutional battles but still die from resource starvation. Economic control is the system's ultimate weapon. Procurement 'has no appetite.' Budgets 'are frozen.' Funding 'must go through standard channels.' These phrases are the naval blockade that starves innovations of the resources they need to survive.

Your Goal: Secure resource flows that the system doesn't fully control.
Critical Timeline: You need economic independence secured before Month 6. After that, you're fighting for survival rather than building momentum.

Tactic 1: External Funding First (Weeks 1–12)

Never depend entirely on internal funding. Before announcement, secure 50–75% of year-one funding from sources outside system control: government innovation grants (ARPA-H in the US, Innovate UK, NIHR), charitable foundations, patient advocacy organisations, international funding bodies (EU Horizon, WHO).

Why This Works: External funding comes with external accountability—harder for the system to block. It creates economic pressure ('We have £200K from [external funder] contingent on implementation'), demonstrates external validation, and makes blocking financially costly.
Success Indicator: 50%+ of year-one budget secured externally before Month 6.
Failure Warning: 100% dependent on internal budget allocation.

Tactic 2: Economic Benefit Documentation (Weeks 1–8)

Make blocking economically painful. Build a rigorous economic case with three components:

- **Current-State Cost**—What does the problem cost in staff absence, litigation, regulatory non-compliance, missed opportunities, patient harm?
- **Innovation ROI**—Implementation cost, year-one operational impact, three-year projected savings, break-even timeline.

- **Opportunity Cost of Inaction**—What happens if we don't implement? Regulatory exposure grows. Competitive disadvantage widens. Reputation risk accumulates.

Finance teams might feel touched by 'this is the right thing to do'—they are paid to move by 'This saves £X per year starting Month 3'—a different language entirely, spoken by the only people in the room with budget authority.

Tactic 3: Alternative Market Access (Months 3–12)

If the primary procurement path is blocked, build alternative routes:

- **Academic or Research Route**: Position as a research project; access research budgets; build evidence base that forces future procurement consideration.
- **Partnership Model**: Joint venture with an external organisation that handles commercialisation.
- **Direct-to-Department Model**: Individual departments purchase directly, bypassing central procurement. Start where you have strong allies.
- **Charity or Donation Model**: External charity purchases and donates; the system cannot easily refuse donations. Once installed, it becomes the standard of care.

Central procurement blockade only works if there's one path to market. Create multiple paths.

Tactic 4: Economic Coalition Building (Months 1–6)

Build a coalition of stakeholders with economic interest in your success.

Internally: departments that bear current costs, units measured on metrics that your innovation improves, quality and safety teams with regulatory risk exposure.
Externally: payers interested in cost reduction, insurers with liability exposure, commissioners looking for innovation.

Naval Domain Investment Summary

Minimum Viable: £10–20K external funding applications; £5–10K economic analysis[1]; 80–120 hours developing alternative pathways; 6–12 months to secure economic position.

In our experience, economic blockade kills over 80% of innovations that succeed clinically and institutionally; other estimates are even higher [1]. Naval domain investment has the highest return on investment in failure prevention.

Coordination Across All Three Domains

Single-domain excellence fails. Multi-domain coordination wins.

Your air superiority makes ground coalition building easier—external validation becomes a recruitment tool. Your ground coalitions make economic arguments more credible—clinical champions carry weight with finance. Your economic independence gives you negotiating power in institutional battles—'we have external funding' changes the conversation.

The coordination principle:

- Air superiority without ground forces = narrative without implementation
- Ground coalition without air cover – vulnerable to negative framing
- Economic security without institutional buy-in = resources with nowhere to deploy

Victory requires superior coordination across all three domains, simultaneously.

Weekly domain assessment (every Monday):

Air Domain: Are stakeholders using our framing or the system's? Have any negative narratives appeared this week? Are external voices still amplifying our message?

Land Domain: Coalition solid or showing cracks? Any unexpected institutional resistance? On track for structural commitments timeline?

Sea Domain: Funding secure for next 90 days? Any budget or procurement blockers emerging? Are alternative pathways still viable?

If any domain shows warning signs, deploy immediate countermeasures before the problem spreads.

Your 90-Day Deployment Timeline

Days 1–30: Preparation and Coalition Building

Week 1: Intelligence and Planning

- Complete power mapping (land)
- Draft core narrative (air)
- Research external funding sources (sea)
- Identify clinical champions
- Secure executive sponsor

Weeks 2–3: Coalition Building Begins

- One-to-one meetings with Essential Allies (land)
- Develop economic model (sea)
- Test messaging with friendly stakeholders (air)
- Submit first grant applications (sea)

Week 4: Pre-Launch Coordination

- Confirm Essential Ally support (land)
- Finalise narrative and communication plan (air)
- Identify alternative market pathways (sea)
- Prepare for public announcement

Days 31–60: Launch and Defence

Week 5: Public Launch

- Announce with Essential Allies visibly supporting (land)
- Deploy pre-prepared narrative through multiple channels (air)
- Announce external funding commitments if secured (sea)
- Begin media outreach (air)

Weeks 6–7: Rapid Expansion

- Expand to Valuable Allies (land)
- Monitor and counter any negative narratives (air)
- Continue external funding applications (sea)
- Begin committee infiltration (land)

Week 8: Consolidation

- Assess which potential blockers can be neutralised (land)
- Ensure external voices are amplifying your message (air)
- Secure first external funding commitments (sea)

Days 61–90: Securing Territory

Weeks 9–10: Structural Lock-In Begins

- Initiate first hard commitments (land)
- Maintain narrative momentum (air)
- Execute alternative market access if the primary path is blocked (sea)
- Formalise coalition structure (land)

Weeks 11–12: Defensive Preparation

- Prepare long-term structural defences for Month 18 reversion pressure (land)
- Build sustained external pressure (air)
- Diversify funding streams (sea)
- Document and communicate early wins across all three domains

Week 13: 90-Day Assessment

- Traffic light review of all three domains
- Adjust resource allocation based on domain status
- Plan Months 4–12 structural commitments
- Identify and brief your three most effective coalition members for the Month 4–12 phase.

Success Indicators and Red Flags

When You're Losing

Air Domain Failure Signals:

- Week 4: Stakeholders aren't using your framing
- Week 8: Negative narrative appearing in official communications
- Week 12: External voices silent or contradicting your message
- Month 6: You're still explaining and defending rather than advancing

Land Domain Failure Signals:

- Week 4: Essential Allies non-committal or hedging
- Week 8: Coalition not expanding beyond initial supporters
- Month 3: Unexpected institutional resistance from 'friendly' stakeholders
- Month 12: Initiative still categorised as a 'pilot' or 'innovation project'

Sea Domain Failure Signals:

- Week 4: No external funding applications submitted
- Month 3: 100% dependent on internal budget
- Month 6: Budget 'frozen' or 'under review'
- Month 9: Only one market access path, and it's blocked

Multi-Domain Cascade Warning: If you see failure signals in two or more domains simultaneously, you're in cascade failure. Emergency protocol:

- Stop offensive operations—no new announcements, no expansion
- Assess which domain is salvageable
- Consolidate all resources to that domain
- Rebuild from a position of strength

When You're Winning

Month 3 Success Markers:

- Air: Stakeholders consistently use your framing; minimal counter-narrative
- Land: Essential Allies committed; Valuable Allies expanding
- Sea: 30%+ external funding secured or committed

Month 6 Success Markers:

- Air: External voices actively amplifying; negative narratives contained within 48 hours
- Land: Coalition includes members from all key stakeholder groups; first hard commitment executed
- Sea: 50%+ funding diversified; at least one alternative market path viable

Month 12 Success Markers:

- Air: Narrative so established that new stakeholders adopt your framing without prompting
- Land: Multiple hard structural commitments in place—reversal would require board-level decision
- Sea: Economically self-sustaining or clear path to sustainability

If you hit all Month 12 markers, you've successfully defended through the first critical year. The system's 18–24 month reversion reflex will encounter significant structural barriers. Your innovation has achieved institutional beachhead.

RESOURCE SUMMARY

What Multi-Domain Defence Actually Costs

Minimum Viable Defence (£25–45K total, 300–400 hours internal)

- Air: £10–15K, 80 hours / Land: £5–10K, 150 hours / Sea: £10–20K, 120 hours[1]
- Timeline: 12 months / Success rate: 60–70%

Premium Defence (£60–120K total, 600–800 hours internal)

- Air: £25–40K, 150 hours / Land: £15–30K, 300 hours / Sea: £30–50K, 200 hours[1]
- Timeline: 12 months with acceleration in months 3–6 / Success rate: 80–90%

(For clinician-led initiatives, clinical champions are your most powerful air domain asset: they provide credibility that no external communications budget can buy).

What failure costs by comparison: A typical major innovation failure runs £200K–2M in sunk costs, 18–36 months wasted, reputational damage, and a demoralised team. The ROI of multi-domain defence: 4:1 to 17:1 in prevented failure costs—plus the innovation succeeds and delivers patient benefit.

PRE-LAUNCH CHECKLIST

Before launching your next transformation initiative, verify:

Air Domain Ready:

☐ Core narrative tested and refined
☐ Clinical champions prepared to speak publicly
☐ 2–3 external amplifiers identified and briefed
☐ Success metrics documented and agreed
☐ £10–15K allocated for external communications

Land Domain Ready:

☐ Power mapping completed
☐ Essential Allies individually recruited and committed

☐ Coalition expansion plan developed
☐ Committee infiltration opportunities identified
☐ £5–10K allocated for coalition support

Sea Domain Ready:

☐ External funding applications submitted (3–5 sources)
☐ Economic ROI model built and validated
☐ Alternative market access pathways identified
☐ £10–20K allocated for economic independence

Coordination Ready:

☐ Weekly domain assessment protocol established
☐ Monthly strategic review scheduled
☐ Traffic light warning system understood by team
☐ Emergency response protocols defined
☐ 90-day timeline shared with coalition

If you cannot check 80%+ of these boxes, you are not ready to launch. Better to delay 30–60 days and launch with proper defences than to launch unprepared.

Your Journey Begins Here

We've travelled together through sixteen chapters, building from foundations to applications, from theory to practice, from diagnosis to action. If you've read them all, you've invested substantial time in developing new capabilities. Thank you for that commitment.

But reading creates knowledge, not transformation. Knowledge becomes transformation through application. The gap between where healthcare is and where it needs to be isn't primarily a knowledge gap. We know what patient-centred care looks like. We know that diverse clinical trials produce better therapies. We know that centralised, hospital-centric models are unsustainable. We know that current governance structures resist beneficial change.

The gap is an application gap—the distance between knowing and doing.

Design thinking provides the bridge. Not because it's magic, but because it's systematic. It gives you structured methods for moving from insight to action, from prototype to implementation, from pilot to scale. If you've spent your career watching clinical insight get filtered out of system design, that changes now.

So here's my final question, and it's not rhetorical: What's the one transformation you'll commit to starting in the next 30 days?

Not the comprehensive reorganisation. Not the five-year strategic plan. The single, tangible intervention where you'll apply design thinking methods to a real problem.

Maybe it's conducting ethnographic research, e.g., using direct observation and structured conversation, with patients experiencing a particular pain point in your care pathway. Maybe it's facilitating a co-design session with clinicians to redesign a frustrating workflow. Maybe it's applying stakeholder mapping to understand why your last innovation initiative failed. Maybe it's running a rapid-cycle test of a new approach to patient engagement.

Whatever it is, make it specific. Make it achievable in 30–90 days. Make it something you can learn from whether it succeeds or fails.

Your first week: Before anything else, complete the InterAlign Transformation Readiness Assessment and share the results with one colleague whose judgement you trust. That conversation—what your scores mean, which domain to address first, what the first concrete step looks like—is where your design thinking practice begins.

Then apply the Double Diamond:

- **Discover**: What do we really understand about this problem from users' perspectives?
- **Define**: What's the real problem we're solving—not the symptoms but the underlying challenge?
- **Develop**: What range of potential solutions should we test?
- **Deliver**: How do we implement, measure, learn, and iterate?

Whatever you discover—about the problem, the methodology, or the resistance you encounter—write it down. The next person in your organisation who faces this challenge will need it. Because transformation doesn't happen through grand strategy. It happens through accumulated small changes that, over time, shift the entire system.

Your journey begins with a single step. What will yours be?

Reference

1. Eidlisz, J., von Simson, I. and Gold-von Simson, G. (2024) 'Exploring the current state of technology transfer in the United States: Perspectives and improvement strategies from the experts', *Frontiers in Research Metrics and Analytics*, 9, 1376185. https://doi.org/10.3389/frma.2024.1376185

Conclusion: The Path Forward

'Some men see things as they are and say why.

I dream things that never were and say why not.'

George Bernard Shaw

(Carried forward by Robert F. Kennedy, and by his brother's grief)

Claudia Marchetti pauses at the end of the ward round. It is a Tuesday morning at Massachusetts General Hospital, three years from now. The intensive care unit is not, on this particular morning, a place of crisis. That is itself a small miracle, though no one on the unit would use that word. They would use the word they have been learning to use: design.

A junior resident—six months out of medical school, all anxious competence and barely concealed exhaustion—stops Claudia near the nurses' station. She has a question, but not a clinical one. She has been reading the discharge summaries from the new patient transition pathway. She has noticed that readmission rates for heart failure patients have dropped by 31% since the pathway was redesigned last year, and she wants to understand how.

'We redesigned it with the patients,' Claudia says. 'Sat with them. Asked what actually happened when they got home. What confused them. What frightened them. What the instructions assumed they had that they didn't have. Then we changed the pathway to match their reality, not our convenience.'

The resident nods slowly. Then she asks: 'Is that design thinking?'

'It's clinical reasoning applied to the system instead of the patient,' Claudia says. 'Which is something you've been doing since your first day of medical school. You just hadn't applied it here.'

She moves on. The corridor is the same corridor it has always been—linoleum, fluorescent light, the particular institutional smell of every hospital in the world. But something in how it is navigated has changed. There are fewer workarounds. Fewer small acts of

 DOI: 10.4324/9781003752073-23

compensatory heroism to make up for what the system got wrong. The improvements are not large, each one. But they have accumulated. And Claudia knows—as she has known for some time now—that healthcare systems do not transform in a single moment. They transform in ten thousand small corrections, each one made by someone who decided to ask why not instead of simply why.

That is where this book began. That is where healthcare transformation begins. And that is where you, the reader, are standing now.

What We've Built Together

Seventeen chapters ago, we started with a provocation: that healthcare's transformation crisis is not primarily a knowledge problem, a funding problem, or even a political problem. It is a design problem. We do not lack evidence about what good care looks like. We lack the structured methodology to build systems that reliably deliver it.

The journey since that opening claim has been neither simple nor comfortable. We have examined why the healthcare workforce already possesses the cognitive capabilities of design thinking—only to ask why those capabilities so rarely survive contact with governance. We have learned from the automotive and technology industries that user-centred design produces better outcomes—and then examined exactly why those lessons have been so difficult to transplant. We have seen how clinical trials might be redesigned to serve the patients who need them most, how AI can amplify rather than entrench inequality, and how the shift from hospital-centred to patient-centred systems requires not just new thinking but new architecture.

In Part III, we moved from principles to domains: the redesign of clinical trials, the responsibilities of AI, the transition to community-based and decentralised care, the specific challenges facing policymakers who must design systems rather than regulate symptoms. Each of these applications tested the same central thesis: that empathy, iteration, prototyping, and co-design—the pillars of design thinking—produce fundamentally different outcomes from the top-down approach that has dominated healthcare management for half a century.

Part IV was the hardest material in the book, and deliberately so. Understanding why innovations fail—the structural traps, the political realities, the immune responses that healthcare systems deploy against beneficial change—is not pessimism. It is diagnostic intelligence. You cannot treat a condition you have not named. The five chapters of Part IV gave you a complete diagnostic vocabulary for the resistance your transformation efforts will face. Lean's limits, venture capital's consistent misreading of healthcare, the architectural barriers built into most healthcare governance, the political dynamics of stakeholder interests, and the behavioural patterns by which institutions fight back over time: these are not obstacles unique to your situation. They are the terrain.

Part V equipped you for that terrain. The InterAlign Transformation Framework and the Control Room model of Chapter 16 provided the coordination architecture. Chapter 17 gave you personalised roadmaps, readiness diagnostics, and the multi-domain defence strategies—narrative, coalition, economic—that distinguish transformations that survive from those that are quietly extinguished.

Together, these 17 chapters constitute something this book has tried, with care, not to overstate: a practical methodology for doing the hardest thing in contemporary healthcare. Transforming at the root. The question is no longer whether design thinking works in healthcare. The question is whether you will use it.

The System Has Not Changed. You Have.

While you have been reading this book, the context it describes has not improved. Emergency departments in health systems across Europe and North America continue to operate at or beyond capacity. Clinical trial enrolment continues to systematically exclude the patients most likely to benefit from new therapies. Digital health implementations continue to promise transformation and deliver technical debt. The workforce—nurses, junior doctors, allied health professionals—continues to experience levels of burnout that would be treated as a crisis in any industry with a smaller tolerance for its own dysfunction. These are not new problems. They are the same problems that opened Chapter 1. The system has not been waiting.

What has changed is your relationship to it.

You arrived at this book—most readers do—with some version of a familiar frustration: that despite good intentions, rigorous effort, and genuine clinical or leadership capability, the system resists change in ways that feel disproportionate, irrational, and exhausting. Part IV gave that frustration a name and a mechanism. The resistance is real, it is structural, and it is not a reflection of your inadequacy. It is the terrain. But you are no longer in that terrain without a map.

There is a particular irony that runs through healthcare leadership: the diagnostic rigour that clinicians apply at the bedside—gathering incomplete information, generating hypotheses, testing them against evidence, revising the working diagnosis in real time—is precisely the intellectual method that design thinking formalises. Clinicians already possess it. The question is why that rigour so rarely survives the transition from the bedside to the committee room; why the same consultant who will challenge a diagnosis on incomplete evidence will accept a governance decision made on even less. The answer, as Chapter 5 explores, is structural rather than personal. The system provides no reliable channel for clinical reasoning to reach system design. Design thinking is one such channel. Not the only one, and not sufficient on its own. But a methodology that brings patient experience, clinical wisdom, and frontline insight into the design process rather than treating them as problems to be managed once decisions have already been made.

The imperative—to transform healthcare systems that harm people they should help, waste resources they should direct to patients, and burn out professionals who entered the field to heal—has not diminished. But the reader who reaches this page is not the same person who opened Chapter 1. That shift is the point. And it is where the work begins.

Your Next Steps

What you do with this book in the next thirty days matters more than what you have understood from it in the past several hours. Knowledge does not transform healthcare. Application does. The 17 chapters you have read are not an endpoint. They are a preparation. Whatever your role in the system, the principle is the same: start with the smallest intervention you can actually complete in thirty days. Not the comprehensive transformation. The single step you can complete and learn from. Transformation is not a grand event. It is an accumulation of small corrections, each building on the last, each shifting the culture a degree or two toward the healthcare system patients actually need.

Finding that first step is its own kind of work, and it differs for every reader and every system. A companion resource in development at interqbit.com is one place to think it through. The InterQB-it™ assistant is built on the approach this book sets out, and is intended to help you reason about your own context rather than hand you a general answer. It is early and evolving — treat it as a workbench, not a verdict. interqbit.com is where to find it.

The Deeper Question

I want to be honest with you about something this book does not fully answer. The 17 chapters you have read address the what and the how of healthcare transformation. They explain why existing approaches fall short, equip you with a rigorous alternative methodology, map the terrain of resistance you will face, and give you practical tools to navigate it. In that sense, the book delivers what it promised.

But there is a question that kept surfacing during the research and writing: not why individual transformations fail—Part IV addresses that in detail—but why even the most sophisticated, most evidence-based, most expertly executed transformations still encounter what appears to be a systemic pattern of rejection. As if healthcare governance itself were equipped with something analogous to an immune response: a capacity to recognise 'foreign' patterns of change and neutralise them, not through deliberate opposition, but through the accumulated weight of institutional reflex. The underlying mechanism—why governance systems are architecturally predisposed to resist transformation rather than enable it—is a question this book can identify but not fully resolve.

That question is the starting point for the work that follows this book. That work—exploring what I am calling governance immunity engineering, the mechanisms by which institutional governance systems inadvertently block beneficial change—is ongoing, including a pilot programme examining these dynamics in Uganda's healthcare system. The theoretical framework that emerges from that work, connecting governance architecture to innovation capacity, will be the subject of a companion volume.

For now, the practical implication is this: if your transformation encounters resistance that seems disproportionate to the evidence, out of scale with the opposition you can identify, and persistent despite political skill and stakeholder support—you are probably experiencing something architectural rather than personal. The system is not rejecting you. It is responding to change in the way it has been structured to respond. Understanding that distinction changes how you respond to it.

The methodology in this book is not the last word. It is the current best practice, grounded in evidence across industries, tested against healthcare's specific constraints, and honest about its own limits. The field will develop, and so will your practice. The questions that remain open are not a failure of the methodology—they are its invitation.

Things That Never Were

I want to return, for a moment, to Claudia Marchetti. She reflects a shift that is already occurring, in pockets. Claudia's ward—the ICU with its 31% reduction in readmissions—exists in prototype, in pieces, in the work of the clinicians and executives and innovators who have already started applying these methods without waiting for institutional permission. The brighter future she inhabits is not a distant speculation. It is a few design iterations away from the systems that exist today.

That is the nature of transformation when it is approached with the right methodology: the destination is not as far as the obstacles make it appear. The obstacles are real. The resistance documented in Part IV is real. The governance challenges are real. But so is the capability you already possess. And so is the methodology this book has placed in your hands.

George Bernard Shaw wrote: You see things; and you say, 'Why?' But I dream things that never were; and I say, 'Why not?' Robert Kennedy carried those words into the most contested spaces of his time. His brother quoted them back at his funeral, in a voice broken by grief, as a charge to everyone left behind to keep going.

I reach for that lineage carefully, because healthcare transformation is not politics and this book is not a eulogy. But the design thinker's fundamental posture—the refusal to accept that things as they are represents the limit of what is possible—is exactly what Shaw's question captures. It is also exactly what clinical reasoning, at its best, has always embodied: the refusal to accept a diagnosis as a sentence, the insistence on asking whether there is another explanation, another intervention, another way.

You have spent your career asking that question about patients. You have, most likely, felt the particular exhaustion of caring deeply about a system that does not yet care enough about the people it serves. But you have also—if you have read this far, in this book, with this degree of commitment—already decided that things as they are do not represent the limit of what is possible. That decision is where design thinking begins. And it is where transformation begins.

Claudia Marchetti is on a Tuesday morning ward round, three years from now, in a corridor that smells of every hospital that has ever existed, answering a resident's question about readmissions. She is a consultant physician who learned to apply clinical reasoning to systems as well as patients, and who taught others to do the same, and who is now watching those others teach the same thing again.

That is how transformation propagates. Not through grand strategy. Through accumulated small corrections. Through the patient work of people who dreamed things that never were and kept asking why not.

Your journey begins here.

Daniel Steenstra
Blijham, The Netherlands
March 2026

Index

For Product Safety Concerns and Information please contact our EU
representative GPSR@taylorandfrancis.com
Taylor & Francis Verlag GmbH, Kaufingerstraße 24, 80331 München, Germany

www.ingramcontent.com/pod-product-compliance
Lightning Source LLC
LaVergne TN
LVHW061030130926
847902LV00029B/437
* 9 7 8 1 0 4 1 2 6 9 3 3 5 *